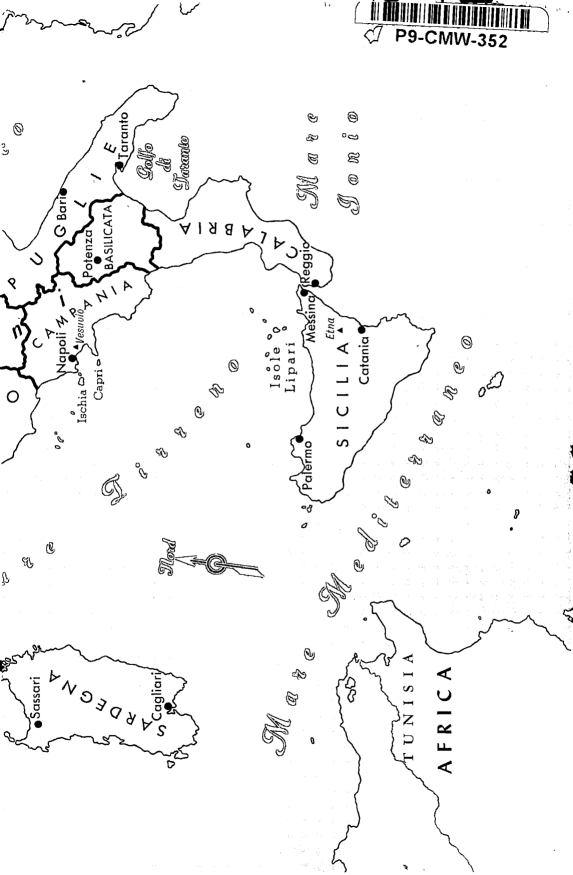

P9-CMW-352

The Italian Heritage

The Italian Heritage

Michele Cantarella

Smith College

HOLT, RINEHART AND WINSTON   NEW YORK

MAY, 1968
3150554

TO

H. P. C.

Preface

It is the consensus today that the teaching of a foreign language should aim primarily at enabling the student to come in direct contact with the people and the civilization of a country other than his own. To fulfill the first part of this objective greater stress is being laid in elementary courses on the teaching of the spoken language. In the field of Italian, however, it has been difficult to achieve the cultural part of the second objective because the majority of students cannot afford to devote more than two years to college Italian or three years to high school Italian, and only comparatively few college students can continue long enough to study Italian literature and civilization.

In view of this situation, it has become necessary to introduce the study of Italian civilization earlier; either at the end of the first or at the start of the second year of college Italian, or at the third-year level of high school Italian. THE ITALIAN HERITAGE is an attempt to fill this need and demand for an anthological reader of Italian civilization which combines a historical and literary survey in English with illustrative annotated excerpts in Italian.

The book may be said to fall into two parts. In the introductory chapter of the first part (Chapter I), Carducci presents a poetic vision of Italy and its people as they emerge from the Middle Ages; Chapters II–IX deal with the development of Italy's civilization from its early origins to the dawn of humanism. The second part (Chapters X–XXXIII) offers highlights of Italian civilization from the Renaissance to the present. In view of its complexity, the second part has been subdivided into centuries. Six special introductory sections in English—one for each century—are dedicated to the history of Italy and to the contributions she has made to the various fields of human knowledge.

The reading passages contained in the thirty-three chapters have been carefully selected from the writings of Italian saints, artists, poets, novelists, dramatists, discoverers, patriots, political thinkers, composers, scientists, philosophers and penologists, ranging from St. Francis of Assisi to Benedetto Croce.

This mature reading material should fire the student with a genuine interest in the study of Italian by making him realize that grammar is not dull, futile drudgery but a precious key which can quickly open the doors of the vast storehouse of Italy's rich cultural life.

In order to enable the beginner to concentrate on and enjoy the thought-provoking ideas of each author, and in an effort to protect him from the serious danger inherent in studying and possibly retaining archaic forms while still in the process of mastering modern Italian, we have on occasion modernized the vocabulary, the spelling and certain involved constructions, especially in the earlier prose selections. A number of passages have also been abridged and some phrases have been deleted when absolutely necessary, but only when the author's ideas were in no way affected by the changes. Thus, every selection is still the author's in thought, feeling and color. Non-recurring words and idioms have been translated or annotated marginally on the page where they occur.

The poetry passages have been left untouched except in the *Laude* of St. Francis and the *Lamento della Madonna* of Jacopone da Todi where archaic forms have been modernized, whenever possible. Poetical forms and difficult constructions are translated and explained in the marginal notes.

Each Italian selection is preceded by an introduction in English which provides information about the author, his works and his times, and places him in the proper historico-literary perspective.

Sets of questions in both English and Italian, based on the English introductory passages and the Italian excerpts, will be found at the end of the text. They will furnish the instructor and the student with topics for composition, conversation or discussion.

A complete end vocabulary has been provided for all recurring, un-annotated words and phrases contained in both prose and poetry selections.

The student should prepare himself by first studying the English introductions and then reading aloud each Italian selection, trying to understand as much of it as possible by himself, relying as far as he can on the marginal notes. The end vocabulary should be consulted only as a last resort. Later, in the classroom, after the instructor has explained to the students whatever difficulties they may have encountered, the Italian excerpts should be read aloud by the students in turn or by the instructor and the students together. It is highly desirable, especially for poetry, to translate as little as possible. The student should form the habit of understanding what he reads directly from the Italian without depending on the English translation.

We advise the following procedure for the best use of the reading material: Chapters I to IX should serve for the last weeks of first-year Italian, and Chapters X to XXXIII should be used during the first semester of second-year Italian in college. At the high school level, THE ITALIAN HERITAGE is best adapted for use in the third year.

It is our hope that this book will offer our students an integrated cultural experience, a direct acquaintance with the writings of world-famous Italians, and supplementary help in the study of the fine arts, drama, music, history and English literature. It is also hoped that it can serve as a refresher for former students of Italian and as a guide for those Americans of Italian origin, who wish to learn something about their cultural heritage.

I wish to express my gratitude to my wife for her unfailing assistance. I am also indebted to Nicola Zanichelli Editore, Valentino Bompiani e C., the Amministrazione degli eredi di Luigi Pirandello, the Accademia Nazionale dei Lincei, and Giuseppe Laterza e Figli for having granted me permission to use some of the reading material included in this text, and to Professer Bruno Zevi for allowing me to reproduce the photos on pages 307 and 308.

M. C.

Contents

L'ANNO MILLE

I

Giosuè Carducci

(1835-1907)

Giosuè Carducci is considered the poet of the Third Italy which was unified in 1870. A Tuscan of profound culture, he was for many years Professor of Italian literature at the University of Bologna. His poetry, which seeks its inspiration in the classics and in the greatness of Rome, exalts the major events of Italian history and expresses his intense love of justice, liberty and humanity. Originally a pagan and a republican, he became reconciled toward the end of his life to Christianity and monarchy. In 1906, he was awarded the Nobel Prize for Literature.

COMINCIA LA STORIA DEL POPOLO ITALIANO

[In the passage which follows Carducci gives a poetic vision of Italy and the Italians as they emerge from the Middle Ages, "the dark age", while the new sun, heralding the dawn of humanism and the revival of learning, looms on the horizon.]

V'immaginate il levar del sole nel primo giorno dell'anno mille? Ricordate che questo fatto di tutte le mattine fu quasi miracolo, fu promessa di vita nuova, per le generazioni uscenti dal secolo decimo?
5 Il termine assegnato dalle profezie etrusche all'esistenza di Roma; la venuta del Signore a rapire seco i morti e i vivi nell'aere, annunziata già imminente da San Paolo ai primi cristiani; i pochi secoli di vita che fin dal tempo di Lattanzio si credeva
10 rimanere al mondo; il presentimento del giudizio finale prossimo attinto da Gregorio Magno nelle disperate rovine degli anni suoi; tutti insieme questi terrori, come nubi diverse che aggroppandosi fanno un temporale, confluirono sul finire del millennio
15 cristiano, in una sola e immane paura.—Mille, e non più mille—aveva detto Gesù secondo la tradizione. Dopo mille anni, leggevasi nell'Apocalissi, Satana sarà disciolto. Infatti nelle nefandezze del secolo decimo, in quello sfracellarsi della
20 monarchia e della società dei conquistatori nelle infinite unità feudali, in quell'abiettarsi ineffabile del pontificato cristiano, in quelle scorrerie procellose di barbari nuovi e orribili, non era lecito riconoscere i segni descritti dal veggente di Patmo?
25 E già tra la gente correvano voci di nascite mostruose, di grandi battaglie combattute nel cielo da guerrieri ignoti a cavalcioni di draghi. Per tutto ciò nessun altro secolo fu torpido, sciagurato, codardo come il decimo. Che doveva importare della patria
30 e della società umana ai morituri, aspettanti d'ora in ora la presenza di Cristo giudicatore? . . . Non era meglio dormire tutti insieme sepolti sotto le rovine delle Alpi e degli Appennini? Battezzarsi e

levar *rising*

fatto di tutte le mattine *everyday occurrence*

termine *end*

del Signore *of our Lord*
rapire seco *take away with Him*
aere *Heaven*

Lattanzio *Lactantius* (*Christian writer of the 4th century*)

attinto *drawn*
Gregorio Magno *Gregory the Great* (*during his papacy* [590–604] *Italy was invaded by the Lombards and Greeks*)
rovine *calamities*
anni suoi *his day*
aggroppandosi *massing*
confluirono *merged*
non più *no more than a*
nefandezze *wickedness*

sfracellarsi *breakdown*

unità *units (factions)*
abiettarsi *abjection*
scorrerie procellose *turbulent incursions*

veggente di Patmo *seer of Patmos* (*St. John the Evangelist, author of "Revelations"*)
voci *rumors*

a cavalcioni di *astride*

sciagurato *base*

Che doveva importare della *Of what importance was the*
morituri *those about to die*
giudicatore *the Judge*
era tutta la vita *was their sole concern in life*

5

prepararsi alla morte era tutta la vita. Alcuni, a dir vero, si movevano: cercavano, come pellegrini, la valle di Giòsafat, per aspettare lì più da vicino il primo squillo della tromba suprema.

Fu questo l'ultimo grado della fievolezza e dell'avvilimento a cui le idee degli ascetici e la violenza dei barbari avevano condotto l'Italia romana. E che stupore di gioia e che grido salì al cielo dalle turbe raccolte in gruppi silenziosi intorno ai manieri feudali, accasciate e singhiozzanti nelle chiese tenebrose e nei chiostri, sparse con pallidi volti e sommessi mormorii per le piazze e nelle campagne, quando il sole, eterna fonte di luce e di vita, si levò trionfante la mattina dell'anno mille! Folgoravano ancora sotto i suoi raggi le nevi delle Alpi, ancora tremolavano commosse le onde del Tirreno e dell'Adriatico, superbi, correvano dalle rocce alpestri per le pingui pianure i fiumi patrii, si tingevano di rosa al raggio mattutino i ruderi neri del Campidoglio e del Foro come le cupole azzurre delle basiliche di Maria. Il sole! Il sole! V'è dunque ancora una patria? v'è il mondo? E l'Italia distendeva le membra raggricciate dal gelo della notte, e si toglieva d'intorno al capo il velo dell'ascetismo per guardare all'oriente.

Infatti sin dai primi anni del secolo undecimo si sente come un brulicare di vita ancor timida e occulta, che poi scoppierà in lampi e tuoni di pensieri e di opere; di qui veramente comincia la storia del popolo italiano.

From: *Scritti: Dello svolgimento della letteratura nazionale*. Zanichelli, Bologna, 1924.

DALLE ORIGINI

ALL'UMANESIMO

II

San Francesco d'Assisi

(1182-1226)

The general political and religious breakdown with the ensuing widespread violence and corruption so deplored by Carducci did not end with the 10th century, but rather increased. This state of affairs prompted many men to leave their homes and renounce their fortunes to go about the world trying to rekindle by eloquent word and exemplary deeds faith in Christ and in the brotherhood of man.

The most noted was Francesco Bernardone, son of a wealthy merchant of the lovely Umbrian town of Assisi. Revolted by the degeneration of society which he had seen at close range during his own dissolute youth and a year spent in Perugia as a prisoner of war, he decided to forswear the empty pleasures of life in order to espouse poverty and dedicate his life to the mystic love of God and of his fellow creatures.

St. Francis set forth on foot to preach humility, peace, love and the brotherhood of man, and carried his message as far as Morocco, Egypt and the Holy Land. His influence was great and his followers grew in such numbers that he organized them in a religious order called the "Frati Minori." His life and good works inspired such poets and painters as Dante, Giotto, Ghirlandaio and Rubens who celebrated the deeds of the saint which had been narrated by some of his followers in a book called *I Fioretti*.

LAUDE DELLE CREATURE A DIO

[St. Francis himself has left only the *Laude delle Creature a Dio* (also called *Il Cantico del Sole* and *Il Cantico delle Creature*), a canticle which he composed for the most part in 1224, during a period of illness and of mystical ecstasy.

This *laude* is one of the most valued documents of early Italian literature. It is couched in the new Italian idiom, the vulgar tongue, as it was emerging from Latin and as it was spoken by the unlettered masses of Umbria. Its style is original, spontaneous, direct, heartfelt and completely devoid of artificiality; it is, in short, the very embodiment of the Franciscan style which influenced much of the painting, architecture and writing of the period.

The saint, suffused with the love of all things created and of all mankind for their creator, sings to the Lord the praises, glory, honor and blessing of them all: the sun, the moon, the stars, the four elements (air, water, fire, earth), and even death, which, in his all-embracing love, he affectionately calls sisters and brothers.]

Altissimo, onnipotente bon Signore,

<table>
<tr><td>tue . . . laudi   Thine be the praise</td><td>tue son le laudi, la gloria e l'onore e ogni benedizione.</td></tr>
<tr><td>si confanno   they belong
e . . . enne   and no man is
te mentovare   to name Thee</td><td>A te solo, Altissimo, si confanno
e nullo omo enne degno te mentovare.   5</td></tr>
<tr><td>Laudato sii   Praised be Thou</td><td>Laudato sii, mio Signore, con tutte le tue creature,</td></tr>
<tr><td>messer . . . Sole   our lord and brother, the Sun</td><td>specialmente messer lo frate Sole,
il quale, il giorno, allumini per noi.</td></tr>
<tr><td>ello   it (the Sun)</td><td>Ed ello è bello e radiante con grande splendore;</td></tr>
<tr><td>di te, . . . significazione   it is the symbol of Thee, Most High</td><td>di te, Altissimo, porta significazione.   10</td></tr>
<tr><td>sora   our sister</td><td>Laudato sii, mio Signore, per sora Luna e le Stelle,</td></tr>
<tr><td>chiarite   clear</td><td>in cielo l'hai formate, chiarite, preziose e belle.</td></tr>
</table>

Laudato sii, mio Signore, per frate Vento
  e per Aere e Nuvolo e Sereno e ogni tempo,
  per il quale alle tue creature dai sustentamento.

e per . . . tempo **for air and clouds and sunshine and every kind of weather**
per il quale **by means of which**
sustentamento **sustenance**

Laudato sii, mio Signore, per sora Acqua,
5 la quale è molto utile, e umile, e preziosa e casta.

casta **pure**

Laudato sii, mio Signore, per frate Fuoco,
  per il quale ci allumini la notte;
  ed è bello e giocondo e forte.

giocondo **gay**

Laudato sii, mio Signore, per sora nostra madre
10   Terra,
  la quale ci sostiene e governa
  e produce diversi frutti, con coloriti fiori ed erba.

per . . . madre **for our sister and mother**
ci . . . governa **sustains and feeds us**
coloriti **many-colored**

Laudato sii, mio Signore, per quelli che perdonano
  per il tuo amore
15 e sostengono infirmitate e tribolazione;
  beati quelli che le sosterranno in pace,
  chè da te, Altissimo, saranno incoronati.

e . . . infirmitate **and bear illness**

Laudato sii, mio Signore, per sora nostra Morte corporale,

> dalla quale nullo omo vivente può scampare;

guai a quelli che morranno nei peccati mortali!

Beati quelli che si troveranno nelle tue santissime 5

> voluntati,

ché la morte seconda non farà loro male.

Laudate e benedicite mio Signore,

> e ringraziate e servitelo con grande umiltade.

guai . . . morranno *woe unto . . . will die*

si troveranno . . . voluntati *will have conformed with Thy most Holy Will*

ché (*perchè*) *because*

la morte seconda (*the damnation of the soul*)

benedicite *bless*

umiltade *humility*

III

Jacopone da Todi

(1230?-1306)

In addition to its importance as the earliest document of Italian literature, St. Francis' *Laude delle Creature a Dio* is notable as the first milestone
in the development of the modern drama. Originally composed as a mono-
logue in lyrical form for only one person or character who sang the praises
of God, the Virgin and the saints, the *Laude* soon evolved into a dialogue to
be chanted by two voices or two groups of voices.

As time went on, other characters were introduced as well as scenery,
costumes, music and a chorus. Under this form it became known as *Laude
drammatica* or *Laude spirituale*. Produced on solemn occasions in the churches
and cloisters of Umbria, the new *laude* dramatized legends stemming from
the lives of the saints and the passion of Christ. In form it is somewhat
primitive but it has the warmth, sincerity and spontaneity which characterize
the Negro spiritual.

The *Laude spirituale* later spread beyond Umbria and assumed real
literary and artistic form particularly in Florence where, in 1449, *Abramo e
Isacco* by Feo Belcari was performed in the church of Cestello as a *Sacra
rappresentazione*, a type of play from which, as will subsequently be seen,
sprang the Italian national theater, and from the latter the modern European
theater.

The most celebrated composer of *Laudi spirituali* was Jacopone da Todi, a lawyer, poet and profligate who, after the accidental death of his wife, abandoned the world, joined the Franciscan order and subjected his body to the most extravagant and painful tests in order to mortify his flesh and exalt his spirit for the greater glory of God. Jacopone wrote over two hundred poems, satires and *laudi* which are a profoundly moving expression of his impetuous, tender and ascetic nature. To him is attributed the *Stabat Mater*, one of the most renowned of Christian hymns.

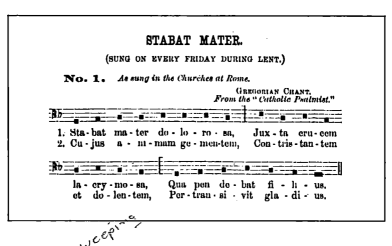

IL PIANTO DELLA MADONNA

(Laude drammatica)

[Perhaps the most poignant *Laude spirituale* is Jacopone's *Il pianto della Madonna* in which lyrical poetry and drama are admirably fused and germinal elements of the secular theater can easily be detected. In swiftly-moving scenes Jacopone gives a gripping, realistic picture of the anguish of the Virgin during the *via crucis* of Christ. In the excerpts which follow, a messenger frantically announces to Mary that Jesus has been betrayed, arrested, lashed and handed over to Pilate. Mary, undaunted by her sorrow, pleads with Pilate and with the crowd on behalf of her Son while the infuriated mob shouts: "Crucify Him! Crucify Him!" The messenger describes the horrifying act of the crucifixion, whereupon Mary, in despair, rushes to the foot of the cross. The last heart-rending words between Mary and Jesus are followed by a final lamentation of the mother over her dead Son.]

15

Personaggi: Il Nunzio, la Madonna, Maddalena, Pilato, la Folla, Cristo, Giovanni.

Nunzio   *Messenger*
Donna   *Lady*
priso   *being taken away*

Accorri   *hasten*
vide   *behold*
l'allide   *strike him*

flagellato   *lashed*

esser porrìa   *could it be possible*
ché (*poichè*) *since*
non fe' mai follia   *he has never done wrong*
speme   *hope*
omo l'avesse pigliato   *that they should have laid hands on him*
traduto   *betrayed*

denari   *pieces of silver*
n'ha avuto   *he has gotten for him*
gran mercato   *shameful transaction*
Soccorri   *Hasten*
giunta m'è addosso pena   *I have been struck by sorrow*
se mena   *is being lashed*

ch' (*ché, perchè*) *because*
si sputa   *they are spitting upon*
lo muta   *they are carrying him away*
hanlo dato   *they have handed him over*

a torto   *wrongly*

Crucifige   *Crucify him*
rege   *king*
lege   *law*
contraddice   *disobeys*

Nunzio (alla Madonna)
> Donna del paradiso,
> il tuo figlio è priso,
> Gesù Cristo beato.
> Accorri, donna, e vide   5
> che la gente l'allide!
> Credo che lo s'uccide
> tanto l'han flagellato.

Madonna
> Come esser porrìa
> ché non fe' mai follia   10
> Cristo, la speme mia,
> omo l'avesse pigliato?

Nunzio
> Madonna, egli è traduto
> Giuda se l'ha venduto;
> trenta denari n'ha avuto,   15
> fatto n'ha gran mercato!

Madonna (a Maddalena)
> Soccorri, Maddalena;
> giunta m'è addosso pena!
> Cristo figlio se mena
> come m'è annunziato!   20

Nunzio
> Soccorri, Madonna, aiuta!
> ch'al tuo figlio si sputa,
> e la gente lo muta
> hanlo dato a Pilato!

Madonna (a Pilato)
> O Pilato, non fare   25
> il figlio mio tormentare,
> ch'io ti posso mostrare
> come a torto è accusato!

Folla
> Crucifige! Crucifige!
> Uomo che si fa rege   30
> secondo nostra lege
> contraddice al Senato.

16

Madonna (alla folla) *listen*
      Prego *pe* che m'intendiate,
      al mio dolor pensate,
      forse ora vi mutate   vi mutate da *you will recon-*
      da quel ch'avete pensato.   *sider*

Nunzio   *drag forth the thieves*
5   Traggon fuori li ladroni   li (*i*)
      ché sian suoi compagnoni!   ché (*affinchè*) *so that*
                                compagnoni *companions*

Folla

      Di spine si coroni   Di spine . . . s'è chiamato!
      chi rege s'è chiamato!   *Let him be crowned with thorns*
                             who has called himself king.

Madonna (a Cristo)
      O figlio, figlio, figlio!
10   Figlio, amoroso giglio!
      Figlio, chi dà consiglio
      al cor mio angustiato?   angustiato *distressed*

      O figlio, occhi giocondi,   occhi giocondi *smiling eyes*
      figlio, che non rispondi?
15   Figlio, perchè t'ascondi   t'ascondi dal . . . lattato *do*
      dal petto ove se' lattato? . . .   *you shun* (*hide from*) *your own*
                                mother's breast

[The Nunzio describes the crucifixion of Christ. The Madonna rushes to her Son who, upon seeing her, exclaims:]

Cristo (alla Madonna)
      Mamma, dove sei venuta?
      Mortal mi dai feruta,   feruta *wound*
      ché'l tuo pianger me stuta   me stuta *overwhelms me*
20   ché'l véggio sì afferrato.   véggio sì afferrato *I see how*
                               bitter it is

Madonna (a Cristo)

m'agio anvito *I have reason to*

> Piango ché m'agio anvito,
> figlio, padre e marito;
> figlio, chi t'ha ferito?
> figlio, chi t'ha spogliato?

Cristo (alla Madonna)

lagni *mourn*

remagni *remain alive*

ché serva *in order to serve*
a li compagni *my followers*
al mondo agio acquistato *I have acquired for the world*

> Mamma, perchè ti lagni?   5
> Voglio che tu remagni
> ché serva a li compagni
> ch'al mondo agio acquistato.

Madonna (a Cristo)

> Figlio, questo non dire,
> voglio teco morire,   10
> non me voglio partire

finchè mo m'esce 'l fiato *while I still breathe*

> finchè mo m'esce 'l fiato;

agiam *may we have*

scura *sorrowful*

Trovarsi . . . affogato *Let the Mother and her dead Son remain united in their anguish*

> ch'una agiam sepoltura
> figlio di mamma scura!
> Trovarsi in affrantura   15
> madre e figlio affogato!

Cristo (alla Madonna)

core (*cuore*)

> Mamma, col core afflitto,
> dentro a le man ti metto

mio eletto *my chosen companion*
sia il tuo figlio appellato *let him be called your son*

> di Giovanni mio eletto;
> sia il tuo figlio appellato.   20

> (a Giovanni)

esta mia mate *behold my Mother*
tollela in caritate *accept her mercifully*
abbine pietate *pity her (as a mother)*
ché ha il core forato *for her heart is pierced (lit. for she has her heart pierced)*

> Giovanni, esta mia mate,
> tollela in caritate,
> abbine pietate
> ché ha il core forato.

[The Madonna, seeing that her Son is dying, throws herself at the foot of the cross.]

18

Madonna (a Cristo)

Figlio, l'alma t'è uscita!
Figlio de la smarrita!
Figlio de la sparita!
Figlio mio attossicato!

5   Figlio bianco e vermiglio!
Figlio senza simiglio!
Figlio, a chi m'appiglio?
Figlio, pur m'hai lasciato!

alma	*soul*
uscita	*flown*
smarrita	*bewildered Mother*
sparita	*lifeless Mother*
attossicato	*poisoned*
vermiglio	*blood-stained*
senza simiglio	*unlike any other*
m'appiglio	*shall I lean*
pur	*alone*

19

giocondo *smiling*

disprezzato *scorned*

dolente *sorrowing one*
atti *(ti ha)*

novello *newly acquired*
lo *(il)*
sentito aggio il coltello *I have felt the point of the sword*

Percosso ha figlio e mate *It has struck Son and Mother*
e in un colpo atterrate *and felled them with one blow*
Trovarsi *Thus shall be found*
a un cruciato *on the same cross*

O figlio bianco e biondo,
figlio, volto giocondo!
Figlio, perchè t'ha il mondo,
figlio, così disprezzato?

Figlio dolce e piacente,   5
figlio de la dolente!
Figlio, atti la gente
malamente trattato.

(a Giovanni)

Giovanni, figlio novello,
mort'è lo tuo fratello,   10
sentito aggio il coltello
che fu profetizzato:

Percosso ha figlio e mate
e in un colpo atterrate.
Trovarsi abbracciate   15
madre e figlio a un cruciato!

IV

Marco Polo

(1254-1325?)

The first three centuries following the millenium were marked not only by the appearance of the Italian language and the resurgence of religious fervor (which found its highest form of expression in St. Francis, St. Thomas Aquinas (1225-1274), Fra Bonaventura (1221-1274), the Crusades and the founding of the Franciscan and Benedictine orders), but also by a general literary and artistic reawakening which began to manifest itself in many fields. Thus we witness the emergence of Italian lyrical poetry with the Sicilian school at the court of Frederick II in Palermo; the affirmation of the "dolce stil novo" school of poetry in Bologna and Florence; and the consti-tution of the first universities in Bologna (1158), Padua (1222) and Naples

(1224), which soon became centers of European learning. The rebirth of faith in God and life found concrete expression in the erection of such great Romanesque and Arabo-Norman cathedrals as the Duomo of Modena, Sant' Ambrogio in Milan, San Zeno in Verona, the Duomo of Monreale, the cathedral of Pisa with its leaning tower, and in the building of cloisters and *palazzi comunali* (city halls).

As a result of this new and feverish interest in architecture, sculpture and painting also began to flourish; the former, through the consummate artistry of Nicola Pisano (1205-1278), whose breathtakingly beautiful carved pulpits in the Baptistry of Pisa and the Duomo of Siena established the first link with the sculpture of classical antiquity; the latter, through the creative genius of Cimabue (1240-1302) and Giotto (1267?-1337) who broke away from the hieratic and bloodless Byzantine style, introduced form and realism into their works and infused them with life, beauty and movement.

Even music, whose traditions had been lost, began to give signs of new life after a system of notation and the solmization of syllables had been introduced by Guido d'Arezzo (990?-1050), a Benedictine monk, called "inventor musicae". It gradually started to emancipate itself from its wholly liturgical character by the introduction of such secular motifs as the stanza, the ballad and the madrigal, and the development of new rhythms and melodies. There followed the addition of a new lower voice which, with the use of a viol, a harp and a bass instrument, formed the accompaniment. This new type of music, with its center in Florence, became known as the "nova ars florentina" and soon spread beyond Italy.

Another event of capital importance which favored the new love of arts and letters was the establishment of the communes or city-states, fountain-heads of the modern democratic state. The Italian people, seizing upon the collapse of feudalism and the wars between emperors and popes, organized into professional and trade guilds (*Arti maggiori, mediane e minori*), as in Florence, drafted their own constitutions, elected their councils and officers, and provided for their own defense. A number of city-states later became republics or principalities.

The participation of a large segment of the population in the administration of the state resulted in increased productivity and in the expansion of commerce. Thanks to its geographic position and to the contacts established with the East during the Crusades, Italy soon became the center of a thriving export and import trade between Europe and the Orient. Venice, Genoa and Florence grew into prosperous and powerful states. The merchant marine of

24

Venice and Genoa, laden with goods, plowed the seas from England to India. Besides specializing in the silk and wool industries, Florence established and introduced everywhere the banking system and the letter of credit and before very long her banks and merchants had agencies in all the important cities of the world. Thus the three cities were to the world of that era what Wall Street is today.

Furthermore, their widely-traveled merchants were not only financiers but penetrating observers of the history, life and customs of the peoples with whom they had dealings. Their prototype is Marco Polo, son of a Venetian banker, and a trader by profession, who spent some twenty-five years traveling and exploring the continent of Asia and its islands, as far as Japan, and served the Emperor Kublai Khan for seventeen years as governor and ambassador. Endowed with a prodigious memory and a keen sense of observation, he mastered languages and stored up facts. He returned to Venice in 1295, and in 1298, during a naval battle between Venice and Genoa, was taken prisoner by the Genoese. While in prison he dictated in dialect the story of his travels to a fellow-prisoner who transcribed it in French. The

book, in Italian, was entitled *Il milione* to suggest incredible and inconceivable adventures. It contains a detailed description of the countries of Asia, their laws, customs, legends, outstanding personalities, products and fabulous wealth. In opening these new horizons, Marco Polo contributed to the knowledge of the earth's surface and of the populations with whom no other European before him had had direct contact. He did for the Asian continent what Columbus was to do two centuries later for the American continent.

IL MILIONE

1. Un deserto

[The first of the two following chapters which describe northeastern Persia (Iran), reveals Marco Polo as a keen observer of nature and life, and as a graphic reporter of his travels. The vast immensity, the loneliness and aridity of the desert are communicated with the greatest economy, in no more than a few suggestive phrases. The reader feels relieved when Marco perceives on the far horizon cities, castles and lush plane-trees which he soon leaves behind him, however, to push forward through hundreds of miles of more desert, his mind still filled with the memory of people and things just seen and heard.]

Quando si parte da Cobinan per ben otto giornate si traversa un deserto, nel quale c'è grande siccità e non vi sono frutti nè acqua se non amara. Chi lo traversa deve portare da bere e da mangiare.
5 E dopo otto giornate c'è una provincia chiamata Tonocaìn con molti castelli e molte città. Essa confina con la Persia verso tramontana. E qui c'è una grandissima provincia tutta piana dove cresce l'albero "solo" che i cristiani chiamano l' "albero
10 sécco". Vi dirò com'esso è fatto. È grande e grosso. Ha le foglie verdi da una parte e bianche dall'altra. Fa frutti come quelli delle castagne, ma dentro non c'è nulla. Il legno è forte e giallo. Non vi sono altri alberi per circa cento miglia, salvo da una parte
15 distante dieci miglia. Gli abitanti dicono che qui ci fu la battaglia tra Alessandro e Dario. I paesi e i castelli hanno grande abbondanza di ogni cosa. Il clima è temperato. Vi si adora Maometto. Qui la gente è bella e le donne sono oltremodo belle. Ora
20 partiamo di qui, e vi dirò di una contrada che si chiama Mulehet, ove il Veglio della montagna soleva dimorare.

Il milione: Cap. XXX.

ben otto *eight full*

se non *except*

da *something to*

confina con la Persia *marks the Persian border*

l'albero "solo" *a species of plane tree*
grosso *with a large trunk*

la battaglia *(of Gaugamela, in 331 B.C.)*

contrada *province*
Veglio *Old Man*

2. Il Veglio della Montagna

[Coming as he did from a cultured city, Marco's interests during his travels were not merely materialistic. He had an eye and an ear for all that might appeal to the spirit. Genuinely interested in the cultural life of the native populations, he learned and related with charm, gusto and skill some of their stories and legends, such as the one about the mythical Old Man of the Mountains, which follows.]

anticamente *in ancient times*

Messer *Mister*

tutti dipinti ad oro *painted in gold*
a bestie e a uccelli *with designs of animals and birds*
condutture *pipes*
donzelli e donzelle *young men and women*

non entrava se non *nobody entered except*
voleva far diventare assassino *had chosen to be a murderer*

Mulehet è una regione dove anticamente dimorava il Veglio della montagna. Ora vi conteremo la sua storia così come Messer Marco Polo l'apprese da diverse persone. Il Veglio nella lingua del luogo è chiamato Alaodìn. Egli aveva fatto fare 5 in una valle tra due montagne il più bello e il più grande giardino del mondo. Lì c'erano tutti i frutti e i più bei palazzi del mondo, tutti dipinti ad oro, a bestie e a uccelli. Lì c'erano condutture in cui scorreva acqua, miele e vino. Lì c'erano donzelli e 10 donzelle i più belli del mondo che sapevano cantare, suonare e ballare meravigliosamente. Il Veglio faceva creder loro che quello era il paradiso. Egli diceva questo perchè così Maometto aveva descritto il paradiso. E i Saraceni di quella regione 15 credevano veramente che quello era il paradiso. E in questo giardino non entrava se non colui che egli voleva far diventare assassino. Alla sola entrata del giardino c'era un castello sì forte che non temeva nessun uomo del mondo. Il Veglio teneva nella sua 20 corte tutti i giovani dai dodici ai venti anni i quali,

30

PLVZ OVLTRE

✠

℃Libzo del famoso Marco
polo veneciano delas cosas maraui
llosas q̃ vido enlas partes orien-
tales: conuiene saber enlas
Jndias/Armenia/Ara
bia/persia/τ Tarta-
ria. E del poderio
del gran Can y
otros reyes.
Con otro
tratado
de mi
cer
pogio Flozentino τ trata
delas mesmas tie-
rras τ islas.

✠

a quattro . . . alla volta *four,*
ten, twenty at a time
faceva dar *had administered to*
per ben tre dì *for three whole*
days

secondo lui, potessero diventare uomini valorosi.
Quando il Veglio li faceva mettere nel giardino, a
quattro, a dieci, a venti alla volta, prima faceva dar
loro dell'oppio, ed essi dormivano per ben tre dì.
Poi li faceva portare nel giardino e al momento 5
opportuno li faceva svegliare.

Quando i giovani si svegliavano, e si trovavano
là dentro e vedevano tutte queste cose, veramente
si credevano essere in paradiso . . . e mai sarebbero

per volontà loro *of their own*
free will

andati via da quel giardino per volontà loro. 10
Quando il Veglio vuol mandare alcuni di quei

bevanda *potion*

giovani in qualche luogo, fa dare loro una bevanda
che li addormenta e quindi dal giardino li fa
portare nel suo palazzo. Quando loro si svegliano
e si trovano lì, si meravigliano molto e sono molto 15

32

tristi perchè si trovano fuori del paradiso. Allora se
ne vanno subito dal Veglio, credendo che sia un
gran profeta, e s'inginocchiano davanti a lui. Egli
domanda loro:—Da dove venite? —Rispondono:
5 —Dal paradiso; —e gli contano quello che vi hanno
veduto, e hanno gran voglia di tornarvi. E quando
il Veglio vuol fare uccidere qualche persona, egli
fa prendere il giovane che gli sembra più forte e gli
fa uccidere chi egli vuole. Loro lo fanno volentieri
10 perchè vogliono tornare in paradiso. Se scampano,   scampano *survive*
ritornano al Veglio; se son presi, vogliono morire,   presi *taken prisoner*
credendo di ritornare nel paradiso. E quando il
Veglio vuole che un giovane si uccida, egli lo
chiama e gli dice:—Va, suicidati; e ti faccio fare
15 questo perchè ti voglio fare ritornare al paradiso.—
Così gli assassini si suicidano molto volentieri.

E in questa maniera nessun uomo è salvo   è salvo *feels safe*
innanzi al Veglio della montagna. Per questo,
molti re, per paura che egli li faccia uccidere, gli
20 fanno tanti onori. È vero però che nell'anno 1277,
Alau, signore dei Tartari del levante, che sapeva   levante *East*
tutte queste malvagità, pensò tra se medesimo di   malvagità *crimes*
distruggerlo; e mandò alcuni suoi baroni a con-
quistare il palazzo del Veglio. Tre anni durò
25 l'assedio del castello e lo conquistarono solo a   a causa della *because of*
causa della fame. Così per fame il Veglio fu preso e
poi ucciso con tutta la sua gente.

E d'allora in poi non ci fu più nessun Veglio.
Con lui finì tutta la signoria. Ora lasciamo qui e   tutta la signoria *all his power*
30 andiamo più innanzi.   più innanzi *further on*

Il milione: Cap. XXXI.

33

DANTES DI ALEGIERS FLORETINI

V

Dante Alighieri

(*1265-1321*)

The Italian language was still in its embryonic stage when St. Francis composed the *Laude delle creature a Dio*, yet, within the lapse of a century Dante Alighieri, the greatest of all Italian poets, had lived and died and in the interim had raised the vulgar tongue to the level of the classics and had used it to write the *Divina Commedia*, one of the world's most enduring literary masterpieces.

Dante was born in Florence of an ancient and noble family. As was customary with boys of his rank, he very likely received his training from the Franciscan monks of Santa Croce. At first he dedicated himself to poetry, but as he grew older he turned to the study of philosophy and politics. He married and had to our knowledge three, or four children. Between 1295 and 1301, he served the Republic of Florence as soldier, magistrate and ambassador. It was his political activity that determined the course of his life.

Italy was in Dante's time divided into two major political camps: the Ghibellines, who sustained the authority of the Emperor; and the Guelphs, who upheld that of the Pope. Florence was controlled by the Guelphs who, in turn, were split into two factions: the *Neri* ("The Blacks"), subservient to the Pope and inexorable toward the Ghibellines; and the *Bianchi* ("The Whites"), who favored a policy of independence from the Pope and were tolerant toward the Ghibellines. Dante belonged to the latter group. In the summer of 1300 the *Bianchi* had been elected to the government of the city and Dante was one of the six magistrates called to office. The following year, the *Neri*, in an effort to overthrow the *Bianchi*, turned for help to Pope Bonifazio VIII (1217-1303), a crafty and politically ambitious man, who dispatched to Florence Charles de Valois, brother of the French King, Philip the Fair, ostensibly as a peacemaker, but actually to overthrow the *Bianchi*, which he did after several days of murdering, sacking and burning, followed by the imposition of heavy sentences upon the remaining leaders of the opposition. Among them was Dante who, fortunately, happened to be in, or on his way back from Rome where he had been sent by the *Bianchi* to negotiate a compromise with the Pope.

The *Neri* accused Dante of "graft" and of having plotted against the Pope, Charles de Valois and the Guelphs. He was ordered to appear for trial and to pay, within three days, a fine of five thousand florins under pain of having his property confiscated, of being banished for two years from the territory of the Republic and prohibited from holding office for the rest of his life. The accusation was false. Dante, knowing with whom he had to deal, refused to appear, whereupon he was sentenced on March 10, 1302 to perpetual banishment from Florence and to the stake, if ever caught alive. From that day on, abandoning country, family and friends, Dante was forced to wander—as he was to write in *Convivio*—". . . per quasi tutte le parti, nelle quali questa lingua si stende, peregrino, quasi mendicando, . . . come legno senza vela e senza governo, portato a diversi foci e lidi dal vento secco che vapora la dolorosa povertà . . ." Thirteen years later the government of Florence offered Dante an amnesty on condition that he publicly confess to his "guilt". To a Florentine friend who informed him of the offer, Dante replied: ". . . Questo è il premio dell'innocenza manifesta a chiunque? dei lunghi faticosi studi? . . . Pagare tributo ad offensori come a benefattori, no, non sia mai in uomo che si fa banditore di giustizia e che l'offesa patì . . . Non è questa la via del rimpatrio." As a result of his refusal, Dante, and this time also his children who had joined their father in exile, were condemned to death in absentia. The new threats proved useless. Dante stood steadfast. Comforted only by his conscience, he never yielded and never returned to his beloved Florence. On the night between September 13th and 14th, 1321, he

36

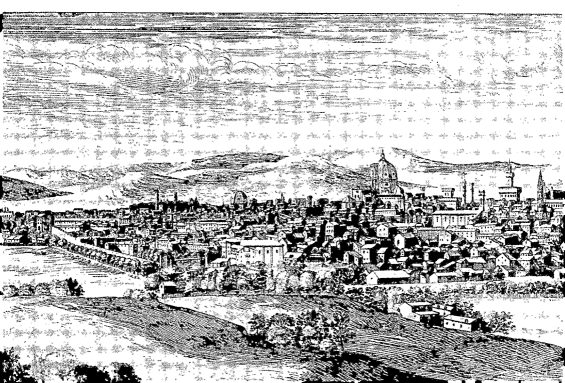

died in Ravenna where he still lies buried. Florence has several times claimed his remains. Ravenna has always refused to give them up.

Thus, through the centuries, Dante has come close to symbolize the moral conscience of the Italians who, in times of political crisis, turn for inspiration to his life and works. He is both an ancient and a modern. Solitary, he stands like a mighty peak between the Middle Ages and the Renaissance.

Dante's singularly systematic mind and prodigious knowledge are both reflected in his Latin and Italian works: *Convivio*, an unfinished philosophical treatise, intended as a kind of encyclopaedia of human knowledge; *De Vulgari Eloquentia*, a philological treatise, also uncompleted, which lays the foundation of the new Italian language; and *De Monarchia*, which demonstrates the need for a world government headed by a single monarch and a single pope under God's guidance, in order to achieve peace and the preservation and progress of mankind. Dante's eternal fame, however, rests with his poetry.

Until the end of the 12th century the Provençal poetry of courtly love was the dominating literary form in Italy. It was only toward the end of the 13th century, and most particularly in Palermo, at the Court of Frederick II (1194-1250), that Italian poetry appears. Though still an imitation of Provençal models and studded with vernacular expressions, it begins to show 1st school of signs of originality and genuine inspiration. Known as the "Scuola Siciliana", literature it soon penetrated into central Italy. However, toward the end of the century it was superseded by the "Scuola del dolce stil novo", as it was called by

Dante. The initiator of the new school was Guido Guinizelli (1240?-1272?)
of Bologna, who considered love as emanating from and elevating to God,
and dwelling in every "gentle heart". Woman was, for Guinizelli, an angelic
being descended from Heaven to lead man to eternal salvation. This philosophical concept of love found two of its most outstanding exponents in the
poet Guido Cavalcanti (1260?-1300), one of Dante's Florentine friends, and,
above all, in Dante himself who glorified it in the *Vita Nova*.

Dante's first work, the *Vita Nova*, is an introduction to the *Divina
Commedia*. It is a collection of poems, linked by explanatory passages, about
Beatrice, a beautiful and virtuous Florentine girl whom he had first seen and
loved when both were but nine years of age. Although she later married
someone else and died soon thereafter, the poet continued to love her throughout his life. In the *Vita Nova* Dante sings of his physical and, later, his
spiritual love for Beatrice, her death, his attentions to other women, and
finally, the return of his allegiance to Beatrice. There follows a wondrous
vision which inspires him to dedicate himself entirely to study so that he can
say of her things never before said about any other woman.

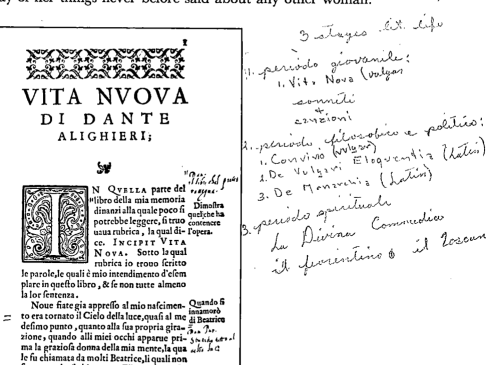

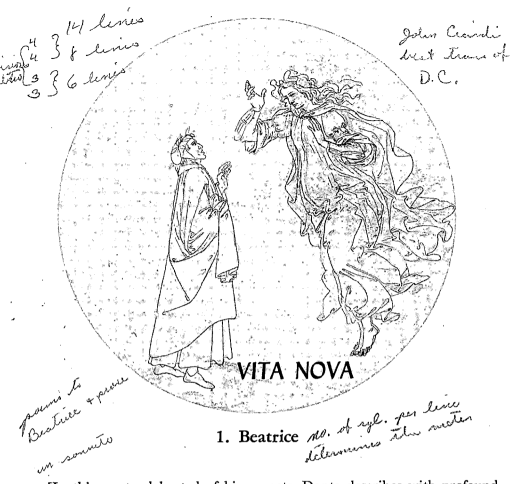

VITA NOVA

1. Beatrice

[In this most celebrated of his sonnets, Dante describes with profound psychological insight the effects of Beatrice's mere greeting upon those who meet her; he shows how unaffected she is by the admiration and happiness she inspires, as if she were indeed a heavenly beauty descended on earth. At about the time this was written Dante began to surmise that Beatrice must really have been an angelic woman dispatched to earth by God on some mysterious mission.]

Tanto gentile e tanto onesta pare
la donna mia quand'ella altrui saluta,
ch'ogni lingua deven tremando muta
e li occhi no l'ardiscon di guardare.
Ella si va, sentendosi laudare,
benignamente d'umiltà vestuta;
e par che sia una cosa venuta
da cielo in terra a miracol mostrare.

gentile *noble*
onesta *modest*
pare *appears*
donna *lady*
deven (*diviene*)
li (*gli*)
no l'ardiscon di guardare
 (*non ardiscon di guardarla*)
si va *passes by*
laudare *praised*
vestuta *clothed in*

39

Mostrasi (sì) piacente a chi la mira
che dà per li occhi una dolcezza al core,
(che 'ntender no la può chi non la prova;)
e par che da la sua labbia si mova
un spirito soave pien d'amore,   5
che va dicendo a l'anima: "Sospira".

Cap. XXVI.

labbia *countenance*
si mova *emanates*
va , *keeps*

2. Visione della prossima morte di Beatrice

[Dante often had visions of Beatrice, the symbolic significance of which he was to discover later. Once, while lying abed seriously ill, he pondered on the frailty of human life and on the fact that some day both he and Beatrice would die. Thus his thoughts began to wander and, as in delirium, he saw dishevelled women going about a street, weeping and sighing; suddenly the sun grew dark and, together with the planet Venus, began to shed tears. At this point a friend came to him and announced the death of Beatrice. He then saw angels ascending to Heaven preceded by a small cloud (Beatrice's soul). Finally Love led Dante to see Beatrice lying dead with a serene expression on her face as though she were saying: "I rest in peace!"]

dubitose *fearful*
nel vano imaginare *in the unreal vision*
parea (*pareva*)
loco (*luogo*) *place*
andar per via disciolte *pass by with dishevelled hair*
qual *some*
traendo guai che di *uttering laments which*
tristizia saettavan foco *pierced (your heart) with grief*
turbar *darken*
lo (*il*)
stella (*Venus*)
elli ed ella *both (the Sun and Venus)*
augelli *birds*
are (*aria*)
omo *a man*
scolorito e fioco *pale and hoarse*
novella *the news*

. . . vidi cose dubitose molte
nel vano imaginare ov'io entrai;
ed esser mi parea non so in qual loco,
e veder donne andar per via disciolte,   10
qual lagrimando, e qual traendo guai
che di tristizia saettavan foco.
Poi mi parve vedere a poco a poco
turbar lo sole e apparir la stella,
e pianger elli ed ella;   15
cader li augelli volando per l'are,
e la terra tremare;
ed omo apparve scolorito e fioco,
dicendomi:—Che fai? non sai novella?
morta è la donna tua, ch'era sì bella.—   20

40

Levava li occhi miei bagnati in pianti,
e vedea, che parean pioggia di manna,
li angeli che tornavan suso in cielo,
ed una nuvoletta avean davanti,
5 dopo la qual gridavan tutti: Osanna;
. . . .
Allor diceva Amor:—Più nol ti celo;
vieni a veder nostra donna che giace.—
Lo mio imaginar fallace
mi condusse a veder madonna morta;
10 e quand'io l'avea scorta,
vedea che donne la covrian d'un velo
ed ella avea seco umiltà verace
che parea che dicesse:—Io sono in pace.—

Cap. XXIII.

levava — I raised
pianti — tears
vedea (vedevo)
parean (parevano)
suso in cielo — up to heaven
avean (avevano)
dopo — behind

nol ti (non te lo)

giace — lies dead

imaginar fallace — fallacious vision
madonna — my lady
l'avea scorta — had looked upon her
covrian (coprivano)
avea seco — had
umiltà verace — a humility so true

3. La mirabile visione

[This is the concluding prose passage of the *Vita Nova* which pre-announces the *Divina Commedia*.]

Appresso . . . apparve a me una mirabile
15 visione, ne la quale io vidi cose, che mi fecero
proporre di non dire più di questa benedetta infino a
tanto che io potessi più degnamente trattare di lei.
E di venire a ciò io studio, quanto posso, sì com'ella
sae veracemente. Sì che, se piacere sarà di colui a
20 cui tutte le cose vivono, che la mia vita duri per
alquanti anni, io spero di dicer di lei quello che
mai non fue detto d'alcuna. E poi piaccia a colui
che è sire de la cortesia, che la mia anima se ne
possa gire a vedere la gloria de la sua donna: cioè
25 di quella benedetta Beatrice, la quale gloriosamente
mira ne la faccia di colui *qui est per omnia secula
benedictus.*

proporre di — resolve
infino a tanto che — until

di venire a ciò — to this end

sae veracemente — truly knows
colui a cui tutte le cose vivono (God)
dicer (dire)
fue (fu)
colui che è sire de la cortesia (God)
gire (andare)

colui "qui est per omnia secula benedictus" — He who is blessed throughout the ages (God)

Cap. XLII.

41

VI

Dante Alighieri

DIVINA COMMEDIA

Dante absorbed during his lifetime all the knowledge of his era and embodied it in the *Divina Commedia*. Like St. Francis before him, he tried through the example of his life and works to lead mankind back to the path of peace, love, reason, order, justice and progress, which is the way to God. In his poem he describes in the form of a mystic vision the journey which, from Good Friday, April 8, 1300, to the following Thursday, April 14, he imagines he made into the beyond. According to him, the *Commedia* has four meanings: literally, it is the account of his journey; allegorically, it relates the vicissitudes of his life and the travail of his soul; morally, it shows how man, of his own free will, by becoming a slave to his passions, may fall into sin and incur eternal damnation, or contrariwise, by living a life of virtue, may gain everlasting peace; anagogically, it portrays the depths to which contemporary humanity had sunk and points the way to its redemption.

The structure of the poem and the architecture of the three realms of the beyond are carried out with flawless symmetry, based on the symbolical numbers: 3 (for the Holy Trinity); 9 (a sacred symbol and square of 3); 10 (considered during the Middle Ages a symbol of perfection); and 100 (square of 10). Thus the whole poem is composed of 3 *cantiche: Inferno*, *Purgatorio* and *Paradiso* and each *cantica* of 33 cantos, making a total of 99 cantos, or 100 with the addition of the first introductory canto. Each canto is made up of tercets (3 lines) each interlaced in rhyme with the successive one. Architecturally, the *Inferno* has 9 circles, the *Purgatorio* 9 terraces, and the ___ .

La struttura: diversa in tre parti; L' 9 Inferno — una cantica
prima cantica è d'introduzione   Il Purgatorio
Inferno diviso in cerchi nove   Il Paradiso
Purgatorio . , . terrazza (e) nove

Paradiso 9 heavenly spheres. Moreover, the word *stelle* is used 3 times as the final word of each *cantica* to indicate the destination of Dante's journey; the pronoun *Io* (Dante, Man) is the subject of the opening sentence of the poem, while *Amor* (God) is the subject of the concluding one.

Because the *Divina Commedia* is concerned not with a single man or nation, but with the whole of mankind, it has universal literary, moral, social and political appeal which, far from dying out, continues to increase with the passing of time. It has been translated into all languages and new translations continue to appear almost every year. In English alone there are more than thirty different ones, half a dozen of which have appeared within the last decade. Today, outside of Italy, England and the United States are among the major contributors to Dante studies. Dante societies have been established in various nations in order to cultivate the study of the life and works of the Italian poet. The oldest of them is that of Cambridge, Mass., started informally in 1865, and organized officially in 1881 by Henry Wadsworth Longfellow, James Russell Lowell and Eliot Norton. In 1954 it was incorporated as the Dante Society of America.

1. La selva oscura

[In the opening lines of the *Divina Commedia*, Dante, having strayed from the rightful path (virtue), imagines himself, at the age of thirty-five ("Nel mezzo del cammin di nostra vita"), lost in a life of sin ("una selva oscura").

He tries to find his way out of the dark forest, but cannot do so alone. Virgil (Reason) comes to his aid and leads him through the Inferno (Sin) and Purgatory (Expiation), whereupon Beatrice (Revelation) leads him through Paradise (Salvation) into the presence of God (Eternal Truth).]

cammin *journey*

ché (*perché*)
via *path*
Ah quanto a dir qual era è cosa dura esta selva selvaggia e aspra e forte *Alas, what a difficult thing it is to say how wild and rough and thick this forest was*
poco è più *scarcely more is*
v' (*vi*)

Nel mezzo del cammin di nostra vita
  mi ritrovai per una selva oscura
  ché la diritta via era smarrita.
Ah quanto a dir qual era è cosa dura
  esta selva selvaggia e aspra e forte   5
  che nel pensier rinova la paura!
Tant'è amara che poco è più morte;
  ma per trattar del ben ch'io vi trovai,
  dirò dell'altre cose ch'io v'ho scorte.

Inferno I, 1–9.

CANTO PRIMO DELLA PRIMA CANTICA O VERO COMEDIA DEL DIVINO POETA FIORENTINO DANTHE ALEGHIERI : CAPITOLO PRIMO :

NEL
ME
ZO
DEL
CA
MI
NO
DI
NO
S T
RA
VI
TA

Mi ritrouai peruna selua obscura
che la diricta uia era smarrita
Et quanto adire quale era e/cosa dura
esta selua seluaggia et aspra et forte
che nel pensier rinuoua lapaura
Tanto era amara che pocho e piu morte
ma per tractar del ben chro ui trouai
diro dellaltre cose chio uho scorte
I non so ben ridire chomio uentrai
tantera pien disonno insu quel puncto
che lauerace uia abbandonai
Ma pot chio fui appie dun colle giunto
la oue terminaua quella ualle
che mhauea dipaur el cor compuncto
Guardai inalto et uidi lesue spalle
coperte gia deraggi delpianeta
che mena dricto altrui per ogni calle
Allhor fu lapaura un pocho queta
che nellago del chuor mera durata
lanotte chio passai con tanta pieta

h   abbiamo narrato non solamente lauita del
poeta et elutelo dellibro et che cosa sia po
eta Ma etiam quito sia uetusta et anticha quito
nobile et uaria quanto utile et iecenda tal doc
trina. Quanto sia efficace a mucuere lhumane
meti; et quito dilecti ogni liberale igegno. Ne
giudicammo da tacere quanto in si diuina disci
plina sia stata la excellentia dello ingegno del
nostro poeta. Inche sisono stato piu breue che
forse non si conuerrebbe; consideri chi legge che
lanumerosa et quasi infinita copia dellecose del
le quali e necessario tractare misforza non uole
do chel uolume cresca sopra modo; a inculcare
et inuiluppare piutosto che explicare: et disse
dere moltecose et maxime quelle lequali quido
ben caeessi non pero ne restera obscura la expo
sitione del testo. Verremo adunque aquella.
Ma perche stimo non esser lectore alcuno ne di
si basso ingegno; ne di si pocho giudicio; che ha
uendo inteso; quanto sia et laprofondita et ua
rieta della doctrina; et la excellentia et diuinita
dello ingegno delnostro toscano; et fiorentino
poeta; non si persuada che questo principio
delprimo canto debba per sublimita et grande
za esser pari alla stupenda doctrina delecchose
che seguitano; pero con ogni industria in uesti
ghercmo che allegoricho senso archi seco que
sto mezo delcamino; et che cosa sia selua Diche
ueggio non piccola differentia essere stata tra
glinterpreti et expolitori diquesta cantica. Im
pero che alchuni dicene; che il mezo della uita
humana, e el sonno mossi; credo dalla sentetia
datistotele dicendo lui nellethica nessuna diffe
rentia essere tra felici; et miseri nella meca della
uita per che lenioti che sono lameta del tempo
cinducono sonno; et daquello nasce che ne bene
nemale sentir possiamo. Ilperche uoglieno que
sti; che el poeta pengha el mezo della uita per la
nocte; et lanocte pelsonno; ad ne care che questo
poema non sia altro che una uisione che gliap
parue dormeo pel laquale hebbe cognitce del
le cose dalliu descripte i queste tre comedie. Di
cono adunque che lui imita Ioanni euangelista el
quale dormeo sopra elpecto di christo redemptore hebbe uisione delle chose celeste; cueramete
ponghi lanocte dimostrando lui hauere cominciato elsuo poema dinocte nella quale raccogliedosi
lanimo insemedesimo et absoluendosi et liberandosi da ogni cura meglo intenda. Ma benche tale
sententia quadri al poeta: nientedimeno leparole non la dimostrono senon cō tanto obscura ambi
guita: che non pare degna della eleganza dirauto poeta Prima perche nonseguita che benche nelle
reuolutioni deltempo tanto spatio occupin lenocti quanto e di: perquesto dicendo io scripsi dincc
te sintenda io scripsi nel mezo della mia eta: perche et nel principio et alfine della eta humana so
no lenocti chome nel mezo et similmente et di. Il perche per lamedesima ragione si potrebbe fare
tale interpretatione pel di chome per lanocte. Altridicono che uolle pelmezo del camino intende
re che nelmezo dellera dette principio alsuo poema. Ma non e unamedesima opinione deltermine
della nostra eta: per che diuersi scriptori diuersamente sentono. Aristotile nel suo de republica

2. Paolo e Francesca

[As he wends his way through the Inferno, Dante encounters the souls
of the great men and women of antiquity and those of some of his contemporaries who were to owe their lasting fame to inclusion in the *Divina
Commedia*. Combining to an unparalleled degree the skills of dramatist,
painter, sculptor and composer, Dante fires the imagination of the reader
and leaves upon his mind an indelible impression of personages and episodes.

The story of Paolo and Francesca, perhaps the best known of the *Divina
Commedia*, has inspired poets, playwrights, artists and composers of many
countries. According to history and legend, Francesca, daughter of Guido da
Polenta, Lord of Ravenna, was promised in marriage by her father to
Gianciotto Malatesta, the ugly, deformed and bloodthirsty Lord of Rimini.
She had meanwhile been led to believe that she was betrothed to Paolo, the
handsome, young and cultivated brother of Gianciotto, with whom she was
in love. In 1296, she was married to Gianciotto who, as Francesca relates to
Dante, surprised her and Paolo in a kiss one day and instantly killed them
both. Dante finds Paolo and Francesca still bound together in the second
circle of the Inferno among the Lustful who, eternally driven by a powerful
and never ceasing wind, symbol of their passion, are granted neither rest
nor respite.]

46

I' cominciai: "Poeta, volentieri
    parlerei a quei due ch'insieme vanno,
    e paion sì al vento esser leggeri.
    Ed elli a me: "Vedrai quando saranno
5   più presso a noi; e tu allor li priega
    per quello amor che i mena, ed ei verranno."
    Sì tosto come il vento a noi li piega
    mossi la voce: "O anime affannate,
    venite a noi parlar, s'altri nol niega!"
10 Quali colombe, dal disio chiamate,
    con l'ali alzate e ferme al dolce nido
    vegnon per l'àere dal voler portate;
    cotali uscir della schiera ov'è Dido,
    a noi venendo per l'àere maligno,
15   sì forte fu l'affettüoso grido.
    "O animal grazïoso e benigno
    che visitando vai per l'àere perso
    noi che tignemmo il mondo di sanguigno,
    se fosse amico il re dell'universo,
20   noi pregheremmo lui della tua pace,
    poi c'hai pietà del nostro mal perverso.

I'   (Io: Dante)
Poeta   (Virgil)

elli   (egli)
più presso   nearer
priega   (preghi)
i   (li) . . . ei   (loro)
Sì tosto . . . piega   As soon as
    the wind blew them toward us
affannate   wearied
s'altri nol niega   if no one
    (God) forbids it
Quali   As
disio   (desiderio)
àere   (aria)
cotali . . . Dido   so left they
    the group wherein is Dido
    (Queen of Carthage, beloved of
    Aeneas)
maligno   dark
grido   call
animal   living creature
perso   dark
di sanguigno   with blood

della   for
poi c'   (poichè)
mal perverso   evil plight

vui (voi)

come fa, si tace *quiets down as it is doing*

terra *city (Ravenna)*

marina *sea coast*

co' seguaci sui *with its followers (affluents)*

al cor gentil ratto s'apprende *quickly seizes the gentle heart*

prese costui della bella persona *possessed this man with desire for my beautiful body*

Amor, ch'a nullo amato amar perdona *Love, which exempts no one who is loved, from loving (in return)*

del costui piacer *for his manly beauty*

una *a common*

Caìna *(Section of Hell reserved for traitors to their kin)*

chi a vita ci spense *the one who took our lives*

fur porte *were addressed*

offense *(offese)*

tanto *so long* ... il *(lo)*

fin che *till* ... pense *(pensi)*

Oh lasso *Alas*

costoro *these souls*

martiri *torments*

a lacrimar mi fanno triste e pio *fill me with grief and pity*

a che *by what means*

concedette amore che conosceste i dubbiosi disiri? *did love grant you to know your hidden desires?*

quella *she*

dottore *teacher (Virgil)*

s' *(se)*

prima radice *origin*

cotanto affetto *such a great desire*

Lancialotto *Lancelot*

strinse *seized*

sospetto *suspicion (of our love)*

Per più fïate *Often*

sospinse *drew together*

scolorocci *(ci scolorò)*

disïato riso *the desired lips (Guinevere's)*

cotanto amante *such a lover (Lancelot)*

questi, che ... fia diviso *this person (Paolo) who will never be separated from me*

Di quel ch'udire e, che parlar vi piace,

noi udiremo e parleremo a vui,

mentre che 'l vento, come fa, si tace.

Siede la terra dove nata fui

su la marina dove 'l Po discende   5

per aver pace co' seguaci sui.

Amor, ch'al cor gentil ratto s'apprende,

prese costui della bella persona

che mi fu tolta; e 'l modo ancor m'offende.

Amor, ch'a nullo amato amar perdona,   10

mi prese del costui piacer sì forte

che, come vedi, ancor non m'abbandona.

Amor condusse noi ad una morte:

Caìna attende chi a vita ci spense."

Queste parole da lor ci fur porte.   15

Quand'io intesi quell'anime offense,

chinai il viso, e tanto il tenni basso,

fin che il poeta mi disse: "Che pense?"

Quando risposi cominciai: "Oh lasso,

quanti dolci pensier, quanto disio   20

menò costoro al doloroso passo!"

Poi mi rivolsi a loro e parlai io,

e cominciai: "Francesca, i tuoi martiri

a lacrimar mi fanno tristo e pio.

Ma dimmi: al tempo de' dolci sospiri,   25

a che e come concedette amore

che conosceste i dubbiosi disiri?"

E quella a me: "Nessun maggior dolore

che ricordarsi del tempo felice

nella miseria; e ciò sa il tuo dottore.   30

Ma s'a conoscer la prima radice

del nostro amor tu hai cotanto affetto,

dirò come colui che piange e dice.

Noi leggevamo un giorno per diletto

di Lancialotto come amor lo strinse: 35

soli eravamo e senza alcun sospetto.

Per più fïate li occhi ci sospinse

quella lettura, e scolorocci il viso;

ma solo un punto fu quel che ci vinse.

Quando leggemmo il disïato riso   40

esser baciato da cotanto amante,

questi, che mai da me non fia diviso,

48

all Trembling; kissed my mouth

la bocca mi baciò tutto tremante. _that wrote it_

  Galeotto fu il libro e chi lo scrisse:

  quel giorno più non vi leggemmo avante."

Mentre che l'uno spirto questo disse,

5 l'altro piangea, sì che di pietate

  io venni men, così com'io morisse;

e caddi come corpo morto cade.

Galeotto *Galehout (the go-between in the romance of Lancelot)*

più non vi leggemmo avante *we read no further*

spirto *soul*

l'altro *(Paolo)*

di pietate *for compassion*

io venni ... morisse *I fainted just as if I were dying*

Inferno V, 73–142.

Notice:

1. Francesca's expressions, all in symmetrical opposition to the nature of her punishment (p. 48 l. 4-6): Siede la terra (she and Paolo never sit); la marina (as against the darkness of Hell); discende (while they are constantly hurled about); per aver pace (they will never have peace); coi seguaci sui (Paolo, who follows her).

2. The conciseness of the story told in three tercets (l. 7-15), one for each episode, as in a three-act tragedy, with Amor—having here the power of Fate—set at the beginning of each act, dominating the action of the two lovers and suggesting their helplessness before the irresistible power of Love.

3. In the antepenultimate line of the canto the reader is made aware ·for the first time of the active presence of Paolo who has been weeping while Francesca relates their sad story. Thus the whole episode suggests an aria sung by a soprano in the foreground of a stage to the accompaniment of a viola obbligato played softly in the background.

4. The rhythm of the last closing line conveying the sound produced by the fall of a dead body.

49

VII

Dante Alighieri

DIVINA COMMEDIA

ULISSE

[The legendary figure of Ulysses, the mythological Greek hero who for ten years sailed the seas in search of new places, must have had an extraordinary appeal for Dante who had undertaken the account of his own imaginary voyage in the beyond. Drawing either from some ancient legend or from his own imagination, Dante visualized Ulysses as an old man who has come to the end of his travels. But, instead of dreaming of returning to his home and family, he is consumed by an ardent desire to acquire greater knowledge of the world. He harangues his faithful companions, reminds them that they have not been created to live out their lives as brutes, but rather to pursue virtue and knowledge, and bids them to accompany him to explore the "uninhabited world" lying beyond the forbidden Pillars of Hercules. Spurred on by Ulysses, they follow him into this new adventure. But just as they sight their long-desired goal, a tempest rises and, as God would have it, the ocean engulfs Ulysses and his shipmates.

There can be no doubt that Dante made Ulysses symbolize the unflinching efforts of man who, even at the risk of life, challenges the mysteries of nature in his unceasing search for truth and knowledge. Some Dante scholars have seen in Ulysses the symbol of that latent new spirit of research which was later to become manifest under the names of humanism and Renaissance, particularly through the inventions, discoveries and investigations of such men as Leonardo da Vinci, Columbus, Vespucci and Galileo; others, being more specific, have sustained that Ulysses' voyage, "always gaining on the left side (south-west)", in search of the "uninhabited world" is a concrete Dantean prophecy of Christopher Columbus' voyage and the discovery of America. There are still others who claim that the "uninhabited world" Ulysses sought and the "mountain" he saw are nothing else than the mountain of Purgatory.

50

Dante meets Ulysses in the eighth pit of the eighth circle of Hell to which are condemned the souls of false counselors, each enveloped in a long flame floating upon the air. The shrewdest of all Greek leaders is punished by being imprisoned together with his companion Diomed within a two-pronged flame for having advised acts of fraud, not the least among them being that of the Wooden Horse which brought about the fall of Troy. At the request of Virgil, the larger of the tongues of fire, containing the soul of Ulysses, wavers, flickers, then sends forth a voice which tells the following story.]

51

corno   horn (tongue)

crollarsi   to undulate

pur . . . affatica   just like one
  (i.e., flame) blown by the wind

indi   then

menando   flickering

gittò   threw

mi diparti' . . . me   I left

Circe, who had detained me

Gaeta   (city north of Naples)

sì   (così)

nomasse   (chiamasse)

Lo maggior corno della fiamma antica

cominciò a crollarsi mormorando

pur come quella cui vento affatica;

indi la cima qua e là menando,

come fosse la lingua che parlasse,

gittò voce di fuori, e disse: "Quando

mi diparti' da Circe, che sottrasse

me più d'un anno là presso a Gaeta,

prima che sì Enea la nomasse,

5

52

nè dolcezza di figlio, nè la pièta
  del vecchio padre, nè ’l debito amore
  lo qual dovea Penèlope far lieta,
  vincer poter dentro di me l’ardore
5 ch’i’ ebbi a divenir del mondo esperto,
  e delli vizi umani e del valore;
  ma misi me per l’alto mare aperto
  sol con un legno e con quella compagna
  picciola dalla qual non fui diserto.
10 L’un lito e l’altro vidi infin la Spagna
  fin nel Marocco, e l’isola de’ Sardi
  e l’altre che quel mare intorno bagna.
  Io e i compagni eravam vecchi e tardi
  quando venimmo a quella foce stretta,
15 dov’ Ercole segnò li suoi riguardi,
  acciò che l’uom più oltre non si metta:
  dalla man destra mi lasciai Sibìlia,
  dall’altra già m’avea lasciata Setta.
  ‘O frati,’ dissi, ‘che per cento milia
20 perigli siete giunti all’occidente,
  a questa tanto picciola vigilia
  de’ nostri sensi ch’ è del rimanente,
  non vogliate negar l’esperienza,
  di retro al sol, del mondo senza gente.
25 Considerate la vostra semenza:
  fatti non foste a viver come bruti,
  ma per seguir virtute e conoscenza.’
  Li miei compagni fec’ io sì aguti,
  con questa orazion picciola, al cammino,
30 che a pena poscia li avrei ritenuti;
  e volta nostra poppa nel mattino,
  dei remi facemmo ali al folle volo,
  sempre acquistando dal lato mancino.
  Tutte le stelle già dell’altro polo
35 vedea la notte, e il nostro tanto basso,
  che non surgea fuor del marin suolo.
  Cinque volte racceso e tante casso
  lo lume era di sotto dalla luna,
  poi che ’ntrati eravam nell’alto passo,
40 quando n’apparve una montagna, bruna
  per la distanza, e parvemi alta tanto
  quanto veduta non avea alcuna.

nè dolcezza di *neither fondness for my*
pietà del *compassion for my*
’l debito *the rightful*
dovea *(doveva)*
Penèlope *(Ulysses’ wife)*
poter *(poterono)*
l’ardore . . . valore *the burning desire I had to learn from experience about the world and the vices and virtues of men*
misi me *I set out*
un legno . . . diserto *a ship and those few companions by whom I was not deserted*
L’un lito e l’altro *both shores*
infin *as far as*
fin nel *as far as*
de’ Sardi *of Sardinia*
mare *(the Mediterranean Sea)*
tardi *slow (weak)*
foce stretta *narrow mouth (the Straits of Gibraltar)*
segnò *set up*
riguardi *limits (his Pillars)*
acciò che l’uom più oltre non si metta *in order that no man should venture beyond them*
Sibìlia *Seville*
Setta *Ceuta (in Morocco)*
frati *(fratelli)*
milia *(mila)*
perigli *(pericoli)*
all’occidente *the West*
a questa . . . rimanente *to the few years left of our lives*
di retro *(dietro)*
semenza *origin*
virtute *(virtù)*
Li *(I)*
aguti *eager*
picciola *brief*
al cammino *for the voyage*
a pena poscia li avrei ritenuti *hardly then could I have held them back*
poppa *stern*
nel mattino *eastward*
remi *oars*
al *in the*
acquistando dal lato mancino *gaining southward*
altro *(Southern)*
vedea la notte *at night we could see*
non surgea fuor del marin suolo *did not rise above the surface of the ocean*
Cinque . . . passo *five times rekindled and as many times extinguished had been the light beneath the moon since we had set out on our arduous voyage*
n’ *(ci)*
bruna *dim*
avea *(avevo)*

in pianto *to grief*
della *(dalla)*
un turbo nacque *a whirlwind rose*
primo canto *forepart*
il fe' *(lo fece) it made it*
levar la poppa in suso *(it made) the stern rise*
e la prora ire in giù, com' altrui piacque *and the prow go down, as pleased another (God)*

We were filled with gladness + soon it turned to ...
Noi ci allegrammo, e tosto tornò in pianto;
for from the new found a alarm rose
che della nova terra un turbo nacque,
+ struck the forepart of the ship
e percosse del legno il primo canto.
3 times it whirled her round with all the H₂0
Tre volte il fe' girar con tutte l'acque:
the 4th time lifted the poop about
alla quarta levar la poppa in suso   5
+ plunged the prow below, as One willed
e la prora ire in giù, com' altrui piacque,
until the sea closed over us again
infin che 'l mar fu sopra noi rinchiuso."

Inferno, XXVI, 85-142.

Notice:

1. The long, slow cadence of lines 1-5 (p. 52), and the two gerunds (mormorando, menando) which describe the prolonged efforts of the voice to find an outlet through the flame, in contrast with its sudden gushing forth, expressed with two short, sharp past absolute forms (gittò, disse) in line 6.

2. The still slow movement of lines 7-9, describing the captivity of Ulysses, soon followed by three short, persistent and gradually lengthening negative phrases (nè. . . nè. . . nè. . .) of lines 1-3 (p. 53), devised to hold in check both the narration and the ardor of Ulysses which finally erupts in his resolute decision (lines 7-9, page 53).

3. The contrast between "l'alto mare aperto" and the "sol con un legno" with "quella compagna picciola" (lines 7-9), revealing by implication the audacity, the grandeur of the adventure and the daring of a few old men in one small vessel.

4. Again, the slow rhythm of lines 10-27, describing the length of the voyage, and the lands left behind.

5. The noble, stirring and impressive appeal contained in the oratorical lines 19-27.

6. The rapid crescendo of the rhythm in lines 31-32, describing the second leg of their journey, followed by a largo movement rendered with the past descriptive form of the verbs to convey the lapse of time, the distances covered and the immensity of the ocean (lines 34-39).

7. The sudden appearance of the mountain made more dramatic by the use of the two past absolute forms: m'apparve, párvemi (lines 40-41).

8. Sudden joy and sudden sorrow—victory and defeat, crime and punishment, life and death—all expressed within the compass of a single brief line, 1, (page 54).

9. The cadenza of the closing line (7), imitating the movement of the waves closing in over the vessel and its intrepid navigators to whom Dante could not have given a worthier or nobler resting place than the abyss and the immense solitude of the Atlantic Ocean.

VIII

Francesco Petrarca
(1304–1374)

The political and spiritual life of the *Trecento* was characterized by the decline and then the general collapse of both imperial and papal authority. After the death of Henry VII (1313), all hope for the reconstitution of the empire vanished. The Papal See, undermined by corruption and dissensions, was transferred to Avignon where it was kept in "Babylonian captivity" (1308–1378). The breakdown of religious and secular authority had its effects on the communes which exhausted their vitality in internecine warfare, giving rise to the *Signorie* under which a single powerful and influential individual either seized or was given full power to govern. The only state to retain its democratic institutions was the republic of Florence and to it flocked artists and scholars from all parts of Italy. Under its enlightened government Florence soon became the center of Italian life and the fountain-head of a new civilization.

During the long, slow process of disintegration, St. Francis and Jacopone da Todi had sought, as we have seen, the regeneration of mankind through a return to the teachings and the example of Christ, while Dante hoped

that the same ends might be achieved through a world government. Later, Caterina da Siena (1347–1380), a mystic who combined a rare gift for diplomacy with selfless activities as a saintly nun, advocated in her letters to the most important personalities of her age, a federation of Italian states under papal rule as the best means of bringing peace and happiness to the Italian people.

Francesco Petrarca, while aware of man's divine origin and mission, believed, on the other hand, that the salvation of mankind had to be sought in and through man alone, by the scientific and systematic scrutiny of his inner self, as a prelude to the study of history and nature.

The son of an exiled Florentine notary, Petrarch was born in Arezzo. As a child his father brought him to the papal court, then at Avignon. After receiving his early education in Montpellier, he went to Bologna to study law but he soon turned definitively to literature. Upon his return to Avignon, he took the minor orders and was made a canon. Later he traveled through Europe as the personal envoy of Italian rulers, popes, and cardinals. During the intervals between his diplomatic missions and frequent trips to Italy, he used to withdraw in Vaucluse, near Avignon, to write and study. His love

poems, written in Italian, brought him such fame that in 1340, the University of Paris vied with the Senate of Rome in offering him the crown of poet. He accepted Rome's offer and the crown of laurel was bestowed upon him the following year.

In 1368, Petrarch retired to Arquà where he died on July 9, 1374. His small villa, surrounded by the tranquil Euganean hills, has been for centuries a literary shrine visited by scholars and admirers of the poet from all over the world.

Petrarch believed that the degradation of humanity during the Middle Ages was mainly due to man's loss of contact with his own great past. This being so, it was imperative to weld anew the broken chain of knowledge linking the present with antiquity. Since the beliefs, doctrines and philosophies of the age were rooted mostly in legends, traditions and ignorance, they had to be discarded. A return to primary sources, through the study of the ancient texts, was essential in order to recapture and reinterpret with an unbiased mind the life, thought and real spirit of the ancient writers. Spurred on by a boundless thirst for knowledge, he read, copied, corrected and annotated as many ancient manuscripts as he could lay hands on during his

European travels. He deduced that the literature, virtues and glories of the Romans could serve as inspiration and model to his own and to future generations. Man's speculations and theories directed to the understanding of God, His nature and His mind were futile; it was sufficient to believe in God and to love Him. The teaching and practice of poverty, humility, resignation, penitence and mortification could not solve the problems of life. Humanity could not be saved unless it first obtained knowledge about its major component: man. Had not "Nosce te ipsum" (Know thyself) been the guiding principle of the ancient philosophers? Had not St. Augustine lamented in his *Confessions* that human beings admire the mountains, rivers, oceans and the stars but neglect to look within themselves ("et relinquunt se ipsos")? It was evident that the salvation of mankind had to be sought in man by man himself. It was imperative for man to know and understand himself, to uphold the freedom and dignity of his mind, to train himself to life in a world shaped, not by fate and chance, but by the reason, will and genius of the individual. From the knowledge of man would be derived the knowledge of mankind. Only through this progression would man come to the knowledge of nature, to the solution of the problems of life and to a spiritual regeneration of humanity.

This radical new approach to an understanding of man and nature, clearly enunciated by Dante in the episode of Ulysses,

> Fatti non foste a viver come bruti,
> ma per seguir virtute e conoscenza

and the idea of returning to the classics for a re-evaluation of their content, as reiterated by Petrarch in his voluminous erudite Latin works and correspondence, became the touchstone of Italian thought, a kind of new religion. The classics were read, studied, annotated, venerated and imitated. The movement, assuming the name of humanism, spread everywhere and affected all aspects of human life. In a period of religious, political and moral decline it provided a new faith, a new hope, a new mission. It united in a sort of "republic of letters" all the intellectuals of Europe. Considered the first great secular movement since the advent of Christianity, it was accepted as a new manifestation of the Christian spirit. Had it not been stated in the Genesis: ". . . poi Dio disse: 'Facciamo l'uomo a nostra immagine, e abbia dominio sui pesci del mare e sugli uccelli del cielo e sulle bestie e su tutta la terra. . .'"? In point of fact, during the first part of the next century, the papal court, under Julius II, Leo X, Clement VII and Paul III, welcomed the humanists.

Rome became a center of the new culture and the triumph of humanism was celebrated by Raphael in *La Scuola d'Atene*, a great fresco which faces another glorifying *Il Trionfo della Cristianità* in one of the halls of the Vatican Palace.

While humanism still constitutes both the basis and driving power of Western civilization, Petrarch's Latin works dealing with, or inspired by, his humanistic faith have been forgotten, and he owes his lasting fame to his *Canzoniere*, the collection of exquisite love poems written in praise of Laura, a beautiful and virtuous young woman he first saw in a church at Avignon and whom he loved all his life, even after her death. Into the *Canzoniere* Petrarch poured all the feelings of his heart, the joys and sorrows of his love, the ever-present conflict between faith and reason and, above all, he portrayed with unsurpassed skill and delicacy the beauty of Laura.

CANZONIERE

Chiare fresche e dolci acque . . .

[In this song, the most famous of the *Canzoniere*, Petrarch has depicted and fused with supreme felicity the comeliness of Laura and the beauties of nature. In so doing, his torments lose their sting, and even death seems less cruel. It is difficult to determine in the poetic counterpoint whether nature is a reflection of Laura's loveliness or the contrary. But so great is the intensity of the harmonious vision of human and natural beauty which fires the poet's imagination that he believes himself in heaven.

After reading the poem one cannot help noting the differences between Beatrice and Laura for they reveal the evolution in the concept of woman from the Middle Ages to humanism and epitomize the main characteristics of the two epochs. Beatrice is a symbol of philosophy, theology, of divine virtues and beauty. Dante never describes her physical attributes but only the effects of her presence upon those about her. Laura, on the other hand, is a tangible human being whom Petrarch admires, loves, praises and describes. Beatrice is all spirit, a heavenly creature, whereas Laura is of flesh and blood, a terrestrial woman. The first leads man to the divine peace of Heaven, the latter takes him through the maze of joys and sorrows of earthly life.

The *Canzone* is divided into five stanzas:

I Consumed by his ardent passion for Laura, Petrarch addresses himself to nature that has witnessed his love and anguish.

II Foreseeing that his unrequited love will lead him to death, he expresses the wish to be buried in the very spot where he first saw Laura.

III He then imagines that Laura may some day return to that spot and, upon discovering his grave, will at last be moved by love and beseech God to grant peace to his soul.

IV This sad vision evokes in his memory, by contrast, the happy moments during which Laura first appeared to him there under a shower of flowers and captured his heart, an episode which suggests Botticelli's *Primavera*.

V Finally, the poet describes his ecstasy in the contemplation of Laura's beauty, and tells the reasons why he can find no peace away from this enchanted place.]

SÌ DOLCE · FIAMMA · NON M'ARSE · DVE · IN · CO REI

NON · V'SALTRO · DA · TE · CH'IL SOL · DEGLI OCCHI

POI CH'EN · A · L · COR · A MEGLI OCCHI RI · GO

SONETTI
CANZONI E TRIOMPHI DI
M. FRANCESCO PETRARCA,
CON LA SPOSITIONE DI
Bernardino Daniello da Lucca.

Con priuilegio Del Illuſtriſſimo
Senato Vinitiano.

IN VINEGIA
M. D. X L I X.

61

acque (*of the Sorgue River, in Vaucluse, near Avignon*)	Chiare, fresche, e dolci acque,
ove . . . donna [*Construct: where bathed her lovely limbs the only one (Laura) who is to me the epitome of womanhood*]	ove le belle membra pose colei che sola a me par donna;
ramo, ove *tree against which*	gentil ramo, ove piacque
mi rimembra *I recall*	(con sospir mi rimembra) 5
a lei di fare al bel fianco	a lei di fare al bel fianco colonna;
colonna *to lean her fair body*	erba e fior che la gonna
leggiadra *graceful*	leggiadra ricoverse
ricoverse *covered*	con l'angelico seno;
con *together with*	àer sacro, sereno, 10
seno *bosom*	ove Amor co' begli occhi il cor m'aperse;
àer *air*	date udienza insieme
co' *by means of her*	a le dolenti mie parole estreme.
aperse *opened*	
date udienza insieme *give heed all together*	
estreme *last*	S'egli è pur mio destino
	(e il cielo in ciò s'adopra), 15
S'egli . . . s'adopra *If it is really my destiny (and heaven so contrives it)*	ch'Amor quest'occhi lagrimanti chiuda;
lagrimanti *still weeping*	qualche grazia il meschino
qualche grazia . . . ricopra *may some benign fate bury my wretched body in your midst*	corpo fra voi ricopra,
l'alma . . . ignuda *my naked soul to its own abode*	e torni l'alma al proprio albergo ignuda.
fia *shall be*	La morte fia men cruda, 20
dubbioso passo *doubtful passage (from life to death)*	se questa speme porto
ché . . . porto *for the tired spirit could never in a calmer haven*	a quel dubbioso passo;
	ché lo spirito lasso
la carne . . . l'ossa *my tortured flesh and bones*	non poria mai 'n più riposato porto, né in più tranquilla fossa 25 fuggir la carne travagliata e l'ossa.
verrà ancor forse *may yet come*	Tempo verrà ancor forse
usato soggiorno *habitual place*	ch'a l'usato soggiorno
fera bella e mansueta *wild and graceful creature (Laura)*	torni la fera bella e'mansueta,
'v' ella mi scorse *where she first saw me*	e là, 'v' ella mi scorse 30
volga la vista disiosa e lieta *may she turn her longing and benign eyes*	nel benedetto giorno, volga la vista disiosa e lieta,
già terra in fra le pietre vedendo *upon seeing me already returned to dust amid the stones*	cercandomi: ed, o pietà! già terra in fra le pietre
guisa *such a way*	vedendo, Amor l'inspiri 35
mercè m'impetre *she will obtain mercy for me*	in guisa che sospiri
e faccia forza al Cielo *obliging Heaven to yield*	così dolcemente che mercè m'impetre
co'l (*con il*)	e faccia forza al Cielo asciugandosi gli occhi co'l bel velo.

Da' bei rami scendea

(dolce ne la memoria)

una pioggia di fior sopra 'l suo grembo;

ed ella si sedea

5 umile in tanta gloria,

coperta già de l'amoroso nembo.

Qual fior cadea su 'l lembo,

qual su le treccie bionde,

ch'oro forbito e perle

10 eran quel dì a vederle;

qual si posava in terra, e qual su l'onde;

qual con un vago errore

girando parea dir: —Qui regna Amore.—

Quante volte diss'io

15 allor pièn di spavento:

—Costei per fermo nacque in paradiso.—

Così carco d'oblio

il divin portamento

e 'l volto e le parole e 'l dolce riso

20 m'aveano, e sì diviso

da l'imagine vera,

ch'i' dicea sospirando:

—Qui come venn'io, e quando?—

credendo esser in ciel, non là dov'era.

25 Da indi in qua mi piace

quest'erba sì, ch'altrove non ho pace. . . .

Canzoniere: CXXVI.

scendea *fell*

grembo *lap*

si sedea *sat*

de l'amoroso nembo *by the
halo of love (flowers)*

Qual *some*

lembo *hem (of her gown)*

qual *others*

forbito *burnished*

a vederle *to my sight*

onde *water*

qual con . . . dir *some turning
with a graceful flutter seemed to
say*

spavento *reverent wonder*

Costei per fermo *this creature
most assuredly*

Così carco d'oblio *Into such
oblivion*

portamento *bearing*

m'aveano, e sì diviso *had
swept me, and so estranged me*

i'dicea *(io dicevo)*

era *I was*

Da indi . . . sì *from that time
forward this grassy bank pleases
me so much*

IX

Giovanni Boccaccio

(*1313–1375*)

Boccaccio, the son of an Italian merchant, was probably born in Paris, and died in Certaldo, near Florence the year following Petrarch's death. While still a child, his father took him to Florence and later to Naples where he studied and came in contact with eminent scholars at the royal court. It was in a Neapolitan church that he first saw and loved Fiammetta, natural daughter of King Robert, who inspired some of his idyllic novels and poems, written in Italian (*Rime, Filòloco, Filòstrato, Fiammetta*).

During his lifetime he served republics and principalities as ambassador to kings and popes, a position which enabled him not only to earn his living and travel but also to devote a great deal of his time to studying and writing.

A great admirer of Dante, he wrote his biography as well as a commentary on the first seventeen *Cantos* of the Inferno. He was, besides, a devoted friend of Petrarch with whom he shared a love for the Latin and Greek classics. Although for Boccaccio's contemporaries his most significant works, due to the display of erudition, were those of a biographical and historical nature, including his *Epistolae*, all in Latin, he owes his immortality to the *Decamerone*, the first great collection of short stories ever written.

Boccaccio imagines that in 1348, while Florence was ridden by a deadly plague, three young noblemen and seven young noblewomen flee the city, first to a lovely villa and then to a magnificent palace in the Tuscan hills where they spend their time feasting, dancing, playing music and games. Each morning, one member of the group is appointed king or queen and directs the day's program. Gathered in a cool spot near the water, under shady trees or among flowers, they while away the hottest hours of the day telling stories. The days dedicated to story-telling are ten, whence the title of *Decamerone*. Since each member of the group tells a story every day, the *Decamerone* is made up of a hundred stories.

Boccaccio's tales offer a vast and vivid panorama of 14th century life with all its vices and some of its virtues. They express the gamut of human passion and depict all social strata. The *Decamerone* is the human comedy, and in a certain sense, it can be called the reverse of the *Divina Commedia*. While Dante, imbued with the mysticism of the Middle Ages, observed with his imagination and reported vividly on the condition of man's soul in the beyond, Boccaccio, a product of humanism, observed and reported on the condition of man on earth. It is interesting to note that the contemplative poem of Dante and the introspective lyrics of the *Canzoniere* are followed by the pulsating, earthy life of the *Decamerone*. Heaven is definitively replaced by nature and life in all their manifestations. Poetry yields to prose, contemplation to action. The realism of the *Decamerone* pre-announces the advent of the Renaissance.

Just as Dante and Petrarch provided both solid bases and loftiness to Italian poetry, so did Boccaccio endow Italian prose with form, elegance, dignity and stability. All three made Italy supreme in European literature. The *Decamerone* enjoyed enormous success throughout Europe. Translated into the most important foreign languages of the times, it had many imitators and served as a fertile source for Chaucer, Shakespeare, Molière, La Fontaine and others.

VMANA COSA ELHAVER COMPASSIONE
A GLI AFFLITTI. e come che a ciaschuna psona stia
bene a choloro massimamête e richiesto liquali gia hã
no di cõsorto hauuto misteri: & hánolo trouato in al
cuno fra liquali se alcuno mai nebbe:ogli fu caro o gia
né riceuete piacere :Io sono uno di quelli p cio che dal
la mia ptima giouenezza insino a questo tempo :oltra
modo essendo stato acceso da altissimo & nobile amo
re forse piu assai chella mia bassa conditione non pare
be narrandolo io si richiedesse : quantunque doppo
coloro che discreti erano: & alla cui noticia puéne:o ne fussi lodato & da mol
to piu reputato. Non dimeno mi fu egli di grãdissima fatica a soffrire:certo
non per crudelta della donna amata:ma per souecchio amore nella mente con
cepto da pocho regolato appetito .ilquale percio a niuno rególato cõueneuo
le termine milascia contento stare piu di noia che di bisogno nõ era spesse uól
te sentire mi faceua. Nella qual noia tanto refrigerio mi porsero li piaccuoli
ragionamenti dalcuno amico & le deletteuole sue cõsolatiõe che io porto fer

DECAMERONE

Chichìbio e la gru

[*Chichìbio e la gru*, one of the stories told on the sixth day, which was devoted to the exploits of quick-witted and nimble-tongued individuals who succeed in squirming out of embarrassing situations, gives a graphic picture of the carefree life of the period and shows the importance attached to such amenities as hunting, feasting and gastronomy.

Boccaccio sketches his characters in swift, masterful penstrokes. Gianfigliazzi, "cittadino nobile, liberale e magnifico," suspecting that Chichìbio, his cook, has stolen the drumstick of his delicious roast crane and is lying about it, nonetheless curbs his mounting anger and gives him more and more rope, curious to see whether the fear of a beating will sharpen the cook's wits. His wrath is soon turned to laughter at Chichìbio's implausible but astute retort. We get a measure of Boccaccio's good-natured wit and admiration for human ingenuity in the characterization of the gullible Chichìbio who, not to displease and lose his petulant girl, exposes himself to the fury and punishment of his master, and in the guile with which Chichìbio invents an obvious lie and sustains it until a preposterous alibi jumps to his mind and provokes such general merriment that peace is finally reestablished between master and servant.

The story of Chichìbio opens as Lauretta, one of the seven noble damsels, finishes her story about Nonna, a Florentine lady whose quick repartee silences a bishop who had mocked her. Neifile is then called upon by the Queen of the Day to tell her story.]

La Lauretta già faceva e la Nonna era stata da tutti molto lodata, quando la Regina impose a Neifile che continuasse; la quale disse:

Amorose donne, quantunque il pronto ingegno, secondo le circostanze, presti spesso parole belle e 5 utili ai dicitori, —anche la fortuna, quando aiuta i paurosi, pone subito sopra la lor lingua parole tali che colui il quale sa parlare non avrebbe mai sapute trovare: il che io intendo di dimostrarvi con la mia novella. 10

donne *ladies*
presti *inspires*
dicitori *speakers*

68

Corrado Gianfigliazzi, come ciascuna di voi
può aver udito e veduto, è stato sempre un cittadino
nobile, liberale e magnifico della nostra città, il   liberale *generous*
quale s'è sempre dilettato in cani e in uccelli. Un   città *(Florence)*
5 giorno, avendo egli con un suo falcone ammazzata
una gru e trovandola grassa e giovane, la mandò   gru *crane*
ad un suo buon cuoco, che era chiamato Chichìbio
ed era veneziano, mandandogli a dire che l'ar-   mandandogli a dire *asking*
rostisse e la cucinasse bene per la cena. Chichìbio,   *him*
10 preparata la gru, cominciò a cuocerla con grande
cura. Quando essa era quasi cotta ed emanava un
graditissimo odore, avvenne che una femminetta   femminetta della contrada
della contrada, la quale era chiamata Brunetta, e   *girl from the neighborhood*
di cui Chichìbio era molto innamorato, entrò nella
15 cucina; e, sentendo l'odor della gru e vedendola,
pregò caramente Chichìbio che gliene desse una   caramente *winningly*
coscia. Chichìbio le rispose cantando e disse: coscia *drumstick*

Voi non l'avrì da mi, donna Brunetta,   non l'avrì da mi *won't get it*
      voi non l'avrì da mi.   *from me*
                                                       donna *Milady*

20   Turbata, Brunetta gli disse: Turbata *Angered*
    —In fè di Dio, se tu non me la dai, tu non   In fè di Dio *God be my witness*
avrai mai da me cosa che ti piaccia.
    In breve, le parole furono molte. Alla fine
Chichìbio, per non crucciare la sua donna, spiccata   crucciare *displease*
25 una coscia della gru, gliela diede.   donna *girl*
                                                       spiccata *having pulled off*
    Più tardi, quando la gru senza coscia fu messa
davanti a Corrado e ai suoi ospiti, questi meravi-   questi *(Corrado)*
gliandosene, fece chiamare Chichìbio e gli domandò
che fosse avvenuto dell'altra coscia della gru. Il
30 veneziano bugiardo subito rispose:
    —Signor mio, le gru non hanno che una coscia
e una gamba.
    Allora Corrado turbato disse:
    —Come diavolo è che hanno solo una coscia e
35 una gamba? È forse questa la prima gru che io
abbia vista?
    Chichìbio seguitò:
    —Messere, è proprio così com'io vi dico, e   Messere *Sir*
quando vi piace, ve lo farò vedere nelle gru vive.

69

amor   *the sake*

Corrado, per amor degli ospiti che aveva seco,
non volle continuare la discussione, ma disse:
   — Poiché tu dici di farmelo vedere nelle gru
vive, cosa che io mai vidi nè udii, io voglio che tu
ciò mi faccia vedere domani mattina, e sarò 5
contento, ma ti giuro che se tu non me lo farai

ti farò conciare   *I will have*
 you beaten up

vedere, ti farò conciare in maniera che ti ricorderai
sempre del nome mio finchè vivrai.

   La mattina seguente, come il giorno apparve,
Corrado, a cui il dormire non aveva fatto cessare 10
l'ira, si levò ancora arrabbiato, e comandò che i
cavalli gli fosser menati. Fatto montare Chichìbio

ronzino   *nag*

sopra un ronzino, lo menò verso un fiume lungo la

sul far del dì   *at daybreak*

cui riva sul far del dì si vedevano spesso delle gru,
dicendo: 15

70

—Presto vedremo chi avrà ieri sera mentito,
o tu o io.

Chichìbio, vedendo che l'ira di Corrado durava
ancora e che gli toccava dar prove della sua bugia,
non sapendo come fare, cavalcava dietro a Corrado   come   *what*
con la maggior paura del mondo, e volentieri, se
avesse potuto, sarebbe fuggito; ma non potendo, si
riguardava ora davanti e ora di dietro e ora di   di fianco   *to one side*
fianco, e ciò che vedeva credeva che fossero gru che
stessero su due piedi. Ma arrivati vicino al fiume,   piedi   *legs*
vide per il primo sulla riva ben dodici gru, le quali   vide per il primo   *he was the first to see*
stavano tutte su un piede, così come sogliono fare   ben   *no less than*
quando dormono. Perciò, mostratele subito a   così come sogliono fare   *as is their custom*
Corrado, disse:

—Assai bene potete vedere, messere, che ieri
sera vi dissi il vero, che le gru non hanno che una

coscia e un piede. Guardate a quelle che stanno colà.

Corrado, vedendole, disse:

—Aspetta, che io ti mostrerò che ne hanno due. E avvicinandosi un pò alle gru, gridò: —Ho! 5 Ho! A quel grido le gru, messo l'altro piede giù e fatti alcuni passi, se ne fuggirono tutte. Allora Corrado, rivolto a Chichìbio, disse:

—Che te ne pare, ghiottone? Ti pare che ne abbiano due? 10

Chichìbio, quasi sbigottito, non sapendo egli da dove gli venisse l'idea, rispose:

—Messer sì, ma voi non gridaste Ho! Ho! a quella di ieri sera; perchè se voi aveste gridato Ho! Ho! essa avrebbe mandato fuori l'altra coscia e 15 l'altro piede, come hanno fatto queste.

A Corrado piacque tanto questa risposta, che tutta la sua ira si convertì in festa e riso, e disse:

—Chichìbio, tu hai ragione; ben lo dovevo fare. 20

Così dunque con la sua pronta e divertente risposta Chichìbio evitò la bastonatura e si pacificò con il suo signore.

Decamerone: Giornata VI, Novella IV.

72

IL QUATTROCENTO

Characteristics of the Century

15 century

The Italian *Quattrocento* presents two contradictory facets: one positive, the other negative. It is the age of the great schism, spiritual deterioration, moral turpitude and political corruption, of the captains of fortune and their mercenary soldiers, of wars, plagues and famine, of simony, nepotism and the Borgias, along with assassinations by poison and dagger. And yet, if one considers its positive side, it is one of the most resplendent periods in the history of mankind, during which the bases of civilization, as we know it today, were laid down. It is, besides, the age that produced Brunelleschi, Verrocchio, Donatello, Masaccio, Beato Angelico, Botticelli and Luca Signorelli; that fired the indomitable courage of Christopher Columbus and Amerigo Vespucci to discover a new world, and that found its culmination in the universal man, Leonardo da Vinci.

The achievements of the *Quattrocento* proceeded from the diffusion, consolidation and triumph of humanism through the broadened study of the humanities—*studia humanitatis*—which instilled in man a sense of his personality and potentialities. It induced him to investigate the physical world, to

admire and enjoy life and the beauty of nature. It trained him to free himself from the authority of scholasticism, to think with his own mind, to experiment and to develop his critical abilities. It inspired him to extend his knowledge to all fields of human thought and activity. Thereafter, the ideal humanist came to be represented as a man whose mind was a synthesis of all knowledge.

The centers of humanistic activity were the courts of the great city-states like that of the Medici in Florence, the Visconti and Sforzas in Milan, the Gonzagas in Mantua and the Montefeltros in Urbino, the newly established libraries, the literary academies, the artists' workshops and the universities. The most effective medium for the diffusion of the new culture was provided by the discovery of the printing press.

In politics, the ideals of a universal government were forgotten and the *Principati*, new autocratic regional dynasties, which opened their courts to the humanists, were either accepted or tolerated.

Religion among the masses was not affected by humanism. The religious orders and schools remained faithful to scholasticism. The intellectuals and the upper classes, however, substituted the earth for Heaven, rationalism for mysticism, science for faith, while professing their attachment for the formalities of the cult. The popes, although weakened by the great schism, fought as best they could against the corrupting influence of certain aspects of neo-paganism upon the customs of the times, until even Nicolò V and Pio II fell under the spell of humanism and promoted the revival of arts and letters.

The new creative fervor reached its highest expression in architecture. Breaking away from medieval forms, Leon Battista Alberti, Filippo Brunelleschi, Bramante and Michelozzi recreated the classical style, introduced the rounded arch and stamped their constructions with a characteristic combination of severity and elegance, simplicity and harmony. This is the period which produced the magnificent cupola of Santa Maria del Fiore, the Rucellai, Pitti, Strozzi and Riccardi palaces of Florence, the Palazzo Ducale of Urbino, the Certosa of Pavia, and brought forth from the waters of the Grand Canal of Venice the airy elegance of its stupendous palaces designed with the exquisite craftsmanship usually reserved for glass and lace.

Sculpture, under the stimulus given by the Pisanos during the previous century, assimilated the ideals of classicism and gave them back in modern form vibrant with new life, poetic emotion and Christian faith. Both Jacopo della Quercia (1374?–1438) and Lorenzo Ghiberti (1378–1455) carved in tormented and heroic style widely admired bronze church and baptistry doors, marble altar-pieces, baptismal fonts, tabernacles, monumental tombs and public fountains. The most original, realistic and vigorous sculptor of the century, however, is Donatello (1382–1466), who expressed the deepest human feelings in such diverse media as bronze, marble, terra cotta, sandstone and wood. The supreme achievements of his art and of his period include the *Davide vittorioso*, the bust of Nicolò da Uzzano, both in the National Museum of Florence, and the equestrian statue of the condottiere Gattamelata in Padua, the first of its kind since antiquity. Verrocchio (1436?–1488), silversmith, sculptor, painter and engineer, whose *bottega* turned out such masters as Botticelli, Il Perugino, Lorenzo di Credi and Leonardo da Vinci, manifested the astonishing range of his skill in such diverse works as his exquisitely chiselled religious bas-reliefs, the graceful but swaggering figure of David, modeled after a Florentine street urchin, and the gigantic equestrian statue of Colleoni in Venice.

In striking contrast to the style of Ghiberti, Donatello and Verrocchio are the joyful, angelic works of Luca della Robbia (1400–1482), who applied the techniques of painting and sculpture to that most humble of all materials, the earth, and while using no more than two colors—white on pale blue—achieved works of such originality and beauty that he resurrected the art of glazed terra cotta.

Painting, which had started to develop before and independently of the humanistic revival, should be considered not so much as a reborn, but as a new-born art. The reasons behind this phenomenon are simple. To begin with, no ancient works had been found to serve as models; moreover, in contrast to architecture and sculpture, painting required no profound erudition, no great outlay of capital and needed little space; and lastly, being of a religious character and easily accessible to the masses, it had soon become a popular art. In the 15th century, however, under the influence of the classical revival, it came to express the feelings and aspirations of humanism.

Here again, Florence and Tuscany provided the main stimulus. The painter's school was the *bottega* or workshop where he began to work at an

ALINARI

early age as an apprentice. Here the masters, through new uses of perspective, color and movement, sought to break away from the symbolism and conventionalism of past styles in order to give expression to the new philosophic and aesthetic trends of their times. Their aim was to arrive at a synthesis of heaven and earth, of paganism and Christianity, of divinity and humanity, of soul and body, of the sacred and the profane, and to convey divine mysteries through human realities, sacred history through the history of man. By this process, the divine becomes human and the human divine, with the result that Heaven and earth, God and man are brought closer together.

The painters of the Florentine school were both stylists and realists. In investigating and seeking solutions to problems of color, space, relief, anatomy and perspective, they used the visible world around them as background for the religious scenes which they depicted. Their madonnas are beautiful Florentine girls drawn from life. The saints are richly garbed churchmen, friars, bishops, nuns and nobles who could be seen in the various churches or convents of Florence or of neighboring hill towns. The religious episodes are set in the streets, squares, porticos, gardens or palaces of Florence. Thus, the birth of the Virgin is usually depicted as having taken place in a typical Florentine interior of the period, with nurses and relatives bustling in characteristic fashion around St. Anne's bed (Lippi); or again, a young patrician lady, escorted by four handmaidens, makes her first call on the Virgin in an elegant hall of that era, while a servant girl prepares the bath (Ghirlandaio); the drunkenness of Noah is laid in the garden of a charming Tuscan villa, where peasants are gathering and treading grapes; Salome performs her

78

ritual dance in a typically Florentine banquet hall, and paradise is transferred to a garden of Florence.

These characteristics first appear in Fra Angelico (1387–1455) whose saints and angels of supernatural beauty are an expression of his deeply mystical and ascetic soul. They were most fully displayed, however, in the works of the iron-willed Masaccio (1401–1428) who, notwithstanding frail health and premature death at the age of 27, left his stamp on the history of painting through the striking simplicity and powerful, plastic austerity of his frescos which express the essential and the eternal. Aware of all technical problems, he excelled in the anatomy of his nudes. His style, called the "maniera nuova," was to serve as an object of study and inspiration for future generations of artists.

Close in time and spirit to Masaccio was Andrea del Castagno (1423–1457), an aggressive, unadorned painter whose works recall the techniques of sculpture. Paolo Uccello (1397–1475) mastered perspective and chiaroscuro.

79

His concern with volume and geometry and the illusionistic effects of his battle-pieces make him seem a forerunner of modern cubism. By blending mysticism and naturalism, idealism and realism, Filippo Lippi (1406–1469) humanized the divine. Piero della Francesca (1416–1492), speculative and imaginative, statuesque and tumultuous, solved the problems of light and atmosphere, and brought the Florentine style of painting to most of central Italy. Luca Signorelli (1441?–1523), a titanic genius, a realist of violent and dramatic powers, spiritualized the human body, while Il Perugino (1446–1523), through a fascinating poetic and musical style, imparted incomparable beauty to his saints and madonnas.

Many other great artists profusely illustrated contemporary manners and customs, and immortalized local notables in their mythological, biblical and idyllic paintings. They include the inexhaustibly imaginative Benozzo Gozzoli (1420–1497), whose joyous and fascinating works give us a spirited insight into the naturalistic and scientific trends of his generation; Pinturicchio (1454–1513), gay, youthful, exuberant, fond of colors and crowds; and Domenico Ghirlandaio (1449–1494) who, in the virtuosity, balance and grace of his altarpieces and frescos, embodies all the technical achievements of his century. It was in his *bottega* that the tormented genius of Michelangelo was shaped.

ANDERSON

A unique place is occupied by Sandro Botticelli (1444–1510), the most individualistic yet representative painter and illustrator of humanistic culture. In the presentation of his mythological subjects he was inspired by the classics, particularly by Lucretius, as well as by Dante and Petrarch. In the rhythmical refinement and sensitivity of his lines and their lyrical and harmonious quality, he was influenced both by Poliziano's stanzas and the songs of Lorenzo il Magnifico. Through his discordances, or *deformazione ideale*, he attempted to explain the inexplicable, to give body to the mysteriousness of his poetic vision. His admiration for Dante is expressed in the eighty-eight remarkable silverpoint and pen drawings he made to illustrate the *Divina Commedia*.

81

A number of other painters evolved quite independently of the various schools and nonetheless enjoyed wide influence. We need but mention Andrea Mantegna of Vicenza (1431–1506), a perfectionist in perspective, closer to antiquity than to his contemporaries, who imbued his statuesque forms with intense composure and dramatic life; and Antonello da Messina (1430?–1479), a Sicilian master, who excelled in the laws of foreshortening, introduced painting with oil, and displayed stupendous objective vitality in his soul-searching portraits.

Literature, particularly during the first half of the century, manifests an almost fanatical veneration of Latin and Greek writers whose languages, especially Latin, became the official medium of expression and communication of humanists, poets, historians, philosophers and scientists. Italian was scorned and Dante, Petrarch and Boccaccio were pitied for having written in the vernacular. However, some of the greatest humanists—Leon Battista Alberti, man of letters, architect, sculptor, painter and scientist, Matteo Palmieri, Poliziano and Sannazzaro—wrote in both languages. The short story was cultivated by Masuccio Salernitano and Gentile Sermini, while Gerolamo Savonarola and Bernardino da Siena reached new heights in religious literature. Toward the end of the century, the Italian language began to reassert its influence with the poetry of Poliziano, Lorenzo dei Medici, Pulci and Boiardo, and in Leonardo da Vinci found the creator of the scientific style.

82

X

Leonardo da Vinci

(1452–1519)

Leonardo da Vinci, painter, sculptor, scientist, engineer, architect, writer and musician, epitomizes the ideal of the universal mind. Giant-like, he stands between two centuries, embodying the multiform knowledge and the boundless ardor of discovery of both humanism and the Renaissance.

The natural son of a Florentine notary and a peasant girl, he was born in the Tuscan town of Vinci. While still in his early teens, he entered the *bottega* of Verrocchio in Florence where he developed his extraordinary talents in art and science, talents which were never separated in his work. Strikingly handsome, strong and eloquent—to use the words of one of his contemporaries—he absorbed, assimilated and developed to the highest degree all the knowledge of his predecessors. Possessed of a speculative yet practical mind and mistrustful of bookish knowledge, he investigated the phenomena of the physical world and the essence of living things on earth, in the air and in the sea. He struggled to solve the insoluble and to excel over the excellent. He recorded the results of his countless investigations, experiments and discoveries in his *Trattati e Appunti* in mirror-writing, as was his custom, that is to say, backwards from right to left, and illustrated them with drawings. Most have been preserved, collected and published in the *Codice Atlantico* and in the National Edition of his writings. Of particular importance are those dealing with scientific subjects which disclose how accurately he anticipated the achievements of modern science.

Leonardo worked in Florence, Milan, Rome and other Italian cities. He traveled twice to France and spent the last years of his life in the castle of Cloux, near Amboise, where he died at the age of sixty-seven.

His paintings stand high among the world's absolute masterpieces. Those which escaped destruction—*L'Adorazione dei Magi*, *La Vergine delle Rocce*, *Il Cenacolo*, *Sant' Anna*, and *San Giovannino*—reveal perfect integration of dramatic movement, intense insight into the human soul, inexhaustible invention and sublimity of spiritual content. The power and secret of Leonardo's art are perhaps best synthetized in the face of *La Giconda*, suggesting mankind's ideals of beauty, with her enigmatic smile, symbol of the mysteries of the universe.

La Gioconda- Mona Lisa

ANDERSON

1. Leonardo, "uomo senza lettere"

[Since Leonardo considered himself primarily a scientist and an artist, the study and imitation of the classic poets and writers, so fashionable in his times, did not interest him as such. He believed in acquiring knowledge directly from nature and experimentation rather than from books. In like manner, he acquired the art of writing not through imitation but through rigorous training in self-expression. In this respect Leonardo is considered the creator of scientific prose writing which was to reach its peak with Galileo Galilei.]

So bene che, per non essere io letterato, qualche presuntuoso crederà di potermi ragione-volmente biasimare allegando che io sono uomo senza lettere. Gente stolta! Non sanno che io potrei
5 rispondere come Mario rispose ai patrizi romani dicendo che coloro i quali adornano sè medesimi con le fatiche altrui, non vogliono concedere a me di adornarmi con le mie.

Loro diranno che, non conoscendo io le lettere,
10 non posso dire bene quello di cui voglio trattare. Ora non sanno questi che le mie cose devono essere trattate più con l'esperienza che con le parole, e che l'esperienza fu maestra di chi scrisse bene. E così, come maestra, la citerò in tutti i casi.

Libro di pittura: Proemio.

per . . . letterato *since I am not a man of letters*
Crederà di . . . biasimare *will think he can with reason blame me*
allegando *alleging*
senza lettere *without bookish knowledge*
stolta *foolish*
Mario *Roman consul (156–86 B. C.)*
fatiche altrui *labors of others*
lettere *literature*

le mie cose . . . le parole *the subjects I am concerned with must be approached through experience rather than through words*
citerò *shall quote*

85

2. Il pittore è signore e dio

[During the 15th and 16th centuries there were frequent polemics among such artists and writers as Michelangelo and Castiglione as to the superiority of one art over the other. In the passage which follows Leonardo claims the supremacy of painting and compares the painter to a god.]

lo innamorino . . . generarle *will enchant him, he is master of creating them*
buffonesche *ludicrous*
risibili *comic*
egli . . . dio *he is the lord and creator of them*
siti *towns*
tempi *seasons*
figura *he paints*
così *likewise*
scoprire gran campagna *survey a great plain*
dopo quelle *beyond them*
e *likewise*
spiagge *seashores*
E infatti *Indeed*
ciò che . . . immaginazione *whatever is in essence, in appearance or in fancy present in the universe*
queste *(la mente e le mani)*
in pari tempo *simultaneously*
qual fanno le cose *just as things (in nature) do*

Se il pittore vuol vedere bellezze che lo innamorino, egli è signore di generarle; e se vuol vedere cose mostruose, che spaventino, o che siano buffonesche e risibili, o veramente compassionevoli, egli ne è signore e dio. E se vuol generare siti e 5 deserti, boschi ombrosi o freschi nei tempi caldi egli li figura; e così luoghi caldi nei tempi freddi. Se vuole valli, se vuole dalle alte cime dei monti scoprire gran campagna, e se vuole dopo quelle vedere l'orizzonte del mare, egli ne è signore; e se 10 dalle basse valli vuol vedere gli alti monti, o dagli alti monti basse valli e spiagge. E infatti ciò che è nell'universo per essenza, presenza o immaginazione, egli lo ha prima nella mente, e poi nelle mani; e queste sono di tanta eccellenza, che in pari tempo 15 generano in uno sguardo solo una proporzionata armonia, qual fanno le cose.

Paragone: Trattato 13.

86

3. Regola ai giovani pittori

[One of the basic principles of Leonardo's method for the discovery and study of nature's secrets was *saper vedere*, to know how to see things. In this passage he instructs a hypothetical young man in a straightforward and convincing manner on how to apply this principle to the art of painting.]

vista *sight*

nondimeno *nevertheless*
non comprende se non *it takes in only*
Poniamo caso *Let's suppose*
guarderai in un'occhiata *will glance at*
in *during*

onde *therefore*

verso per *line by*

Ancora *Moreover*

a grado a grado *step by step*

volge *inclines*
arte *(painting)*

altro *otherwise*

prestezza *speed*

Noi conosciamo chiaramente che la vista è una delle più veloci operazioni che ci siano, e in un istante vede infinite forme; nondimeno non comprende se non una cosa per volta. Poniamo caso che tu, lettore, guarderai in un'occhiata tutta 5 questa carta scritta, subito giudicherai questa esser piena di varie lettere, ma non conoscerai in questo tempo quel che le lettere siano, nè quel che vogliano dire, onde ti bisogna vedere parola per parola, verso per verso affinchè tu possa capire queste 10 lettere. Ancora, se vorrai montare in cima a un edifizio, dovrai salire a grado a grado, altrimenti ti sarà impossibile pervenire in cima. Così dico a te, il quale la natura volge a quest'arte, se vuoi veramente conoscere le forme delle cose, comincia 15 con i particolari di esse e non andare al secondo, se prima non hai bene nella memoria e nella pratica il primo. E se altro farai, getterai via il tempo o certamente allungherai assai lo studio. E ricordati di acquistare prima la diligenza e poi la prestezza. 20

From: *Libro di Pittura*.

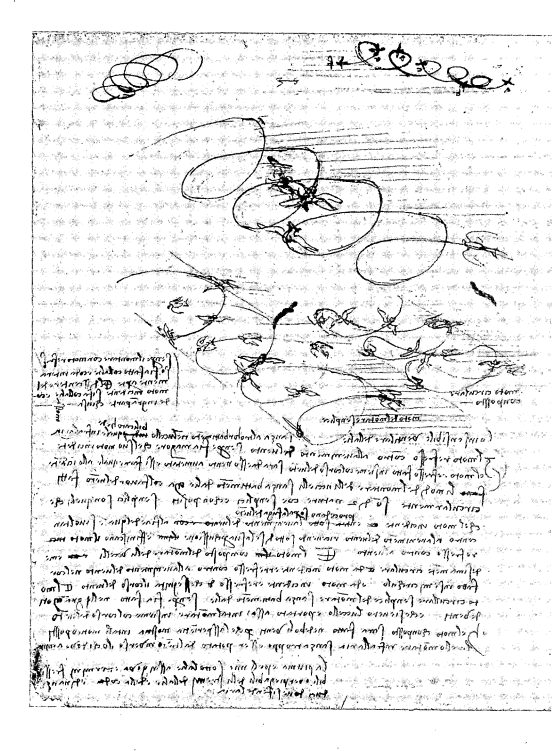

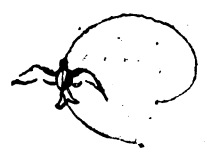

Leonardo spent many years studying the flight of birds in order to build a machine for man to fly. His numerous investigations and drawings mark the beginning of scientific studies on flight. He also conceived an extraordinary number of peace and war machines which he never realized for lack of time and also because he feared that man might become a slave to the machine.

Among Leonardo's *Appunti* (Notes) and *Profezie* we find illuminating information on the following topics:

4. Principio del più pesante dell'aria

[How he derived the principle, now called the law of aerodynamics, according to which a body can remain afloat in the air.]

L'aria che è percossa con maggior velocità da
un corpo mobile, si condensa con maggior somma
di sè medesima. Questo si prova perchè un corpo
fluido meno denso non sosterrà mai sopra di sè un
5 altro corpo fluido più denso come, per esperienza,
si vede l'incudine nuotare sopra il bronzo fuso, e
l'oro e l'argento liquefatti stare sotto il piombo fuso.
Perciò, essendo l'aria un corpo atto a condensarsi
in sè medesimo, quando essa è percossa da un moto
10 di maggior velocità della sua fuga, essa si condensa
in sè medesima e si fa, fra l'altra aria, simile al
nuvolo, cioè della medesima intensità.

Ma quando l'uccello si trova fra il vento, esso
può sostenersi sopra di quello senza batter le ali,
15 perchè quell'ufficio che fa l'ala contro l'aria,
quando questa è senza moto, lo fa l'aria mossa
contro le ali, essendo esse senza moto.

si ... medesima *is compressed
to the highest degree in itself*
si prova *comes about*

incudine *anvil*
bronzo fuso *melted bronze*
piombo *lead*

un moto di *a body moving at*
fuga *flight*
fra l'altra aria *within the rest
of the air*

fra *within*
di quello *it*
ufficio che fa *function performed by*
lo fa *is performed by*

From: *Codice atlantico.*

5. L'aliante

[How he planned the construction of a great glider (*grande uccello*) with movable wings to be catapulted from the summit of Monte Céceri (*sopra del dosso del suo magno Cécero*), near Florence.]

will take back *flight* *astonishment* *filling*

e *and bringing*

Piglierà il primo volo il grande uccello sopra del dosso del suo magno Cécero, empiendo l'universo di stupore, empiendo di sua fama tutte le scritture e gloria eterna al luogo dove nacque.

From: *Codice sul volo degli uccelli.*

6. L'aviazione nelle guerre mondiali

[His prophetic fear that man would some day use airplanes (*gli alberi delle grandi selve*) in world wars for the destruction of mankind.]

Tàuro *Taurus (in SE Asia Minor)*
Sìnai *(in NE Egypt)*
Appennino *Apennine Mountains (Italy)*
Atlante *Atlas Mountain (in NW Africa)*
voti *vows*

Si vedranno gli alberi delle grandi selve del 5
Monte Tàuro, del Monte Sìnai, dell'Appennino e dell'Atlante correre per l'aria da oriente a occidente, da settentrione a meridione e portare per l'aria gran moltitudine di uomini. Oh quanti voti! Oh quanti morti! Oh quanti saranno quelli che 10 non rivedranno più le loro provincie nè le loro patrie, e che moriranno senza sepoltura con le loro ossa sparse in diversi siti del mondo!

to run *West* *North* *South* *bring* *bones strewn*

From: *Profezie.*

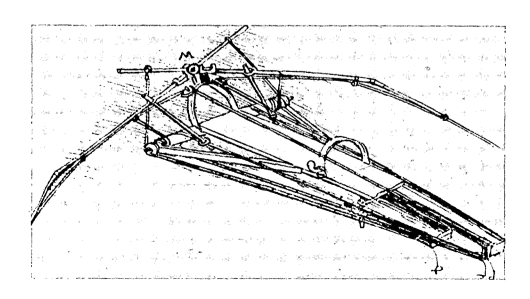

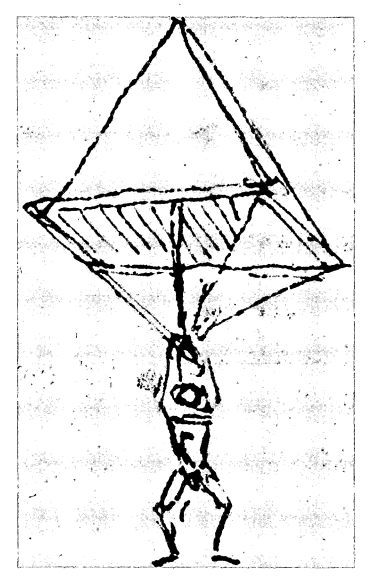

7. Il paracadute

[His concept of the parachute.]

Se un uomo ha un padiglione di pannolini intassato, che sia di 12 braccia per faccia e alto 12, potrà gittarsi da ogni grande altezza senza danno di sè.

padiglione di pannolini intassato   *tent of linen impervious to the air*
12 braccia per faccia e alto 12   *twelve arm's length square*

From: *Codice atlantico.*

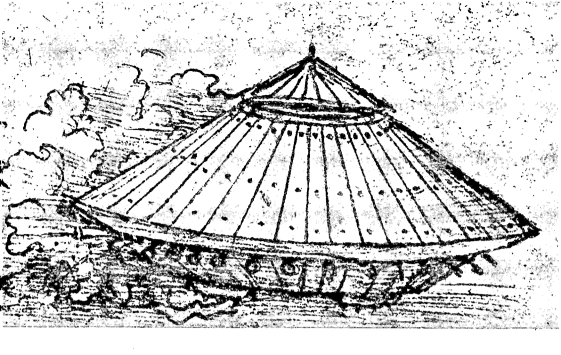

8. Carri armati

[The armored car or tank.]

Farò carri coperti, sicuri e inoffensibili, i quali, entrando con le proprie artiglierie tra i nemici, non c'è moltitudine di gente d'arme che non possano rompere. E dietro ad essi potranno seguire le fanterie assai illese e senza alcuno impedimento.　　5

> From a letter by Leonardo to Lodovico il Moro, Duke of Milan, offering his services.

sicuri *safe*
inoffensibili *invulnerable*

gente d'arme *troops*

rompere *break up*

illese *safely*

9. La radiotelefonia

[The advent of radiotelephony.]

Gli uomini si parleranno e si risponderanno l'uno all'altro da remotissimi paesi.

> From: *Profezie.*

These last three passages testify to the profound humanity of Leonardo's genius, intent on the peaceful advancement of mankind rather than on its violent destruction, and to his religious love and respect for human life.

10. Il sommergibile

Come molti con uno strumento stiano alquanto sotto l'acqua; come e perchè io non descrivo il mio metodo di stare sotto l'acqua tanto quanto io possa stare senza mangiare. Questo metodo io non lo
5 pubblico, o divulgo per la mala natura degli uomini, i quali lo userebbero per assassinamenti nel fondo dei mari col rompere i navigli in fondo sommergendoli insieme con gli uomini che vi sono dentro, benchè io insegni altri metodi, i quali non
10 sono di pericolo, perchè sopra l'acqua apparisca la bocca di una canna, onde alitano, posta sopra otri o sughero.

strumento *device* (*evidently:* il sommergibile *the submarine*)
alquanto *for some time*
tanto quanto *for as long a time as*

per *on account of*
assassinamenti *killings*
col rompere . . . sommergendoli *by torpedoing the keels of vessels, sinking them*

la bocca . . . sughero *the end of a tube through which men may breathe, placed on (floating on) goatskins or cork*

From Leonardo's personal annotations in his introduction to the *Libro di pittura*.

11. L'uomo è modello del mondo

Ora, vedi che la speranza e il desiderio del rimpatriare e ritornare nel primo caos fa a simili-
15 tudine della farfalla al lume. E l'uomo che con continui desideri aspetta sempre con festa la nuova primavera, sempre la nuova estate, sempre i nuovi mesi e i nuovi anni—parendogli che le desiderate cose, venendo, siano troppo tarde—non s'avvede
20 che desidera la sua distruzione. Ma questo desiderio è la quintessenza dello spirito degli elementi, la quale, trovandosi rinchiusa con l'anima, dall'umano corpo desidera sempre ritornare al suo mandatario. E vo' che tu sappia che questo medesimo desiderio
25 è quella quintessenza, compagna della natura, e che l'uomo è modello del mondo.

primo *original*
fa a similitudine della farfalla *is like the night-moth*

mandatario *sender (creator)*
vo' *(voglio)*
compagna della *inseparable from*
modello *the image*

From: *Massime morali.*

93

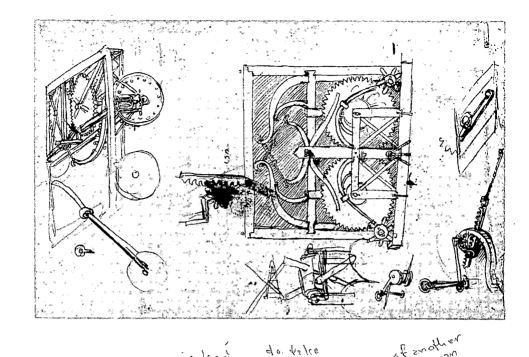

12. È cosa nefandissima il togliere la vita all'uomo

mia fatica *work of mine*

opere mirabili *marvels*

il distruggerla *to destroy it (my work)*

la sua composizione *his physical structure*

architettura *edifice*

quale essa sia *be it what it may*

nella . . . volere che *in its own structure, at its own good will, and let not*

distrugga una tanta *destroy such a*

stima *value*

E tu, uomo, che consideri in questa mia fatica l'opere mirabili della natura, se giudicherai essere cosa nefanda il distruggerla, ora pensa essere cosa nefandissima il togliere la vita all'uomo. E se la sua composizione ti pare una meravigliosa opera d'arte, 5 pensa che essa è nulla rispetto all'anima che in tale architettura abita. E veramente, quale essa sia, ella è cosa divina. Sicchè lasciala abitare nella sua opera a suo beneplacito, e non volere che la tua ira o malignità distrugga una tanta vita, chè veramente, 10 chi non la stima non la merita.

From: *Massime filosofiche.*

94

XI

Cristoforo Colombo

(1451–1506)

The stimulus given by Leonardo to the study of the universe, the visions of fabulous riches in the Grand Khan's vast empire as described by Marco Polo, the experience and skill accumulated by Venetian, Genoese and Portuguese navigators in their voyages along the eastern part of the Atlantic, and the new threats to sea trade arising from the expansion of the Turkish empire, kindled the imagination of many men. They wondered: Why should it not be possible to reach Japan, China and India by sailing westward? It was King Alphonse V (1438–1481) of Portugal who helped give substance to the idea.

There was at that time in Florence a learned mathematician and astronomer named Paolo del Pozzo Toscanelli (1397–1482), whose scientific studies had brought him to the conclusion that it was possible to reach the East through the West. King Alphonse asked Toscanelli to elucidate his views, which he did in a letter dated from Florence, June 25, 1474, accompanied by a chart describing in detail the whole course to be followed from Lisbon to China, with an alternate route to Japan.

The idea had been conceived, the course to effectuate it mapped out, yet no king, no man did anything about it until eighteen years later when

Christopher Columbus, one among the many who believed in the existence of islands lying beyond the Atlantic, succeeded after countless supplications, humiliations and disappointments, in overcoming the traditionalism, timidity and ignorance of the powerful and convinced Ferdinand and Isabella, King and Queen of Spain, to support his enterprise. He finally sailed from Palos on August 3, 1492, with three caravels, taking along with him a copy of Toscanelli's chart, to gain "l'esperienza di retro al sol, del mondo senza gente." He crossed the Atlantic in thirty-three days and, on October 12, set foot on new land. Thus the thought and aspirations of many were courageously translated into fact through the plan that Columbus had clearly conceived, stubbornly defended and carefully prepared, and the history of a new world began, a history of faith, hope, courage and incredible accomplishments.

Columbus was born in Genoa in 1451. As a youth he worked for his father, a wool weaver, but soon, following his own inclination and the custom of the Genoese, he sailed to the east and west, and as far north, it would appear, as Iceland.

Although the power of the rich and glorious republic of Genoa had begun to wane after the naval defeat received at the hands of the Venetians at Chioggia in 1381, Genoa nonetheless still kept alive her long tradition of shipbuilding and of training pilots, navigators, discoverers and chart makers. Columbus grew up in this environment and learned the art of navigation which—as he wrote to the Spanish sovereigns about 1501—"inclines him who follows it to want to know the secrets of this world," a phrase which echoes the urge of Ulysses "a divenir del mondo esperto."

When Columbus was about twenty-seven years old, he established himself in Lisbon, at that time the most active and enterprising of Atlantic ports, where he had been preceded by one of his brothers, Bartolomeo, an expert chart maker. During this period he became an experienced seaman, made voyages along the Atlantic, gained geographical knowledge through the reading of ancient and medieval authors, corresponded with Toscanelli and continued to cherish his ambition "to know the secrets of this world." A Venetian, who had known him in Spain, describes him as follows: "Christopher Columbus, Genoese, a tall, well-built man of great creative ability, with a long, ruddy face." Columbus never returned to his native city, but always remembered it, even in the midst of his triumphs and sorrows. In an entail, made out on Thursday, February 22, 1498, before sailing on his third voyage, he enjoins his son, Diego, "to do always everything he can for the honor, the good and the aggrandizement of the city of Genoa," and also "to support any of their relatives so that they may live honorably as befits persons of their lineage who have foot and root in the above-mentioned city . . . since from it I came and in it I was born."

LETTERA

La scoperta delle "Indie"

[The following passages, which describe the West Indies, and particularly Cuba, Santo Domingo and Haiti, are taken from what is now known as the Christopher Columbus Letter of the First Voyage. It is the first report written by Columbus during his return trip and it announces to his Majesties, Ferdinand and Isabella, the discovery of what he called "The Indies", but was in reality America. The letter, originally written in Spanish, is addressed to Luis de Santangel, treasurer of the king, who was his friend and had been influential in convincing the sovereigns to support Columbus' expedition.]

Signore,

poichè so che avrete piacere della gran vittoria
che il Signore Iddio mi ha dato nel viaggio, vi
scrivo la presente, per la quale apprenderete come
in trentatrè giorni io sono passato dalle Isole
Canarie alle Indie con l'Armata che gli illustrissimi 5
Re e Regina, nostri Signori, mi affidarono, e dove
ho scoperto moltissime Isole popolate di gente
infinita, di tutte le quali ho preso possesso per le
Loro Altezze con bando e bandiera reale spiegata,
senza che nessuno si opponesse . . . 10

Alla prima isola che io incontrai posi il nome
di San Salvatore, per commemorazione della Sua
Alta Maestà, la quale tutto questo ha miracolosa-
mente donato, e gli Indiani la chiamano Guana-
hani; la seconda denominai l'Isola di Santa Maria 15
della Concezione; la terza Fernandina; la quarta
Isabella; la quinta Isola Giovanna, e così a ciascuna
diedi un nuovo nome . . .

Tanto questa [la Giovanna] quanto le altre
Isole sono fertilissime in modo straordinario, ma 20
questa lo è in maniera superlativa. Sulla costa si
aprono molti porti senza paragone migliori di
quanti io ne conosca in Europa, e molti fiumi buoni
e grandi che è una meraviglia. Le sue terre sono
elevate, ed essa contiene molte catene di montagne 25
con monti altissimi . . . e tutte sono bellissime, di
mille forme e tutte praticabili e piene di alberi di
mille specie e di tale altezza che pare tocchino il
cielo. Io sono certo, per quanto mi è dato di capire,
che questi alberi non perdono mai le foglie, e li 30
vidi così verdeggianti e belli come si vedono di
maggio in Ispagna. Di essi alcuni erano in fiore,
altri con i frutti pendenti e altri in un diverso
stadio secondo la loro qualità. E l'usignolo cantava,
e cantavano altri uccellini di mille specie in quel 35
mese di novembre in cui io mi trovavo colà. Vi
sono palme di sei od otto specie, che per la bella
diversità che le distingue destano stupore in vederle.
E così sono gli altri alberi, e piante ed erbe. Vi sono
pini in numero straordinario, grandissime cam- 40

Signore Iddio *Our Lord*

la presente *this letter*

Indie (*West Indies*)
Armata *fleet*
Signori *Highnesses*

Loro Altezze *Their High-
nesses*
bando e bandiera reale spie-
gata *proclamation and Royal
flag displayed*
San Salvatore (*San Salvador,
also Watlings Island*)
Sua Alta Maestà *Our Lord,
the Saviour*
Santa Maria della Concezione
(*Rum Cay*)
Fernandina (*Long Island*)
Isabella (*Crooked Island*)
Isola Giovanna (*Cuba*)

Tanto questa [la Giovanna]
quanto *This one as well as*

di quanti *than any*

per quanto *as far as*

così verdeggianti *growing as
green*

stadio *condition*
usignolo *nightingale*

destano stupore in vederle
are a wonder to behold

campagne *fields*

98

Haiti

pagne coltivate, miele, molte specie di uccelli e
frutti diversissimi. Nell'interno vi sono molte
miniere di metalli e abitanti in numero con-
siderevole . . .

5   Le popolazioni di questa Isola [la Spagnola],
come quelle delle altre Isole che ho scoperto e delle
quali ho avuto notizia, vanno nude, uomini e
donne, come vengono generate, per quanto alcune
donne si coprano una sola parte del corpo con una
10 foglia o una pezzuola di cotone che preparano per
tale scopo. Non hanno ferro, nè acciaio, nè armi,
al cui uso non sono adatti, non perchè non siano
gente ben disposta e di buona statura, ma perchè
sono straordinariamente paurosi . . . Vero è che,
15 quando si sentono rassicurati e perdono un pò
della loro paura, si dimostrano tanto onesti e
liberali di quanto possiedono che non lo crederebbe

[la Spagnola] (Spanish "Es-
pañola", formerly "Hispa-
niola," now the island of
Haiti, on which are the Republic of Haiti and the
Dominican Republic)
come vengono generate *as
they are born*
per quanto *although*
pezzuola di cotone *piece of
cloth*
ben disposta e di buona
statura *well built and well
formed*
paurosi *timorous*

onesti *artless*
di quanto *with whatever*

99

chi non lo constatasse. Qualunque cosa si domandi loro di quello che hanno, mai rispondono negativamente, anzi la offrono e mostrano tanto affetto che par vogliano dare il cuore. Si tratti di cosa di valore oppure di poco prezzo, ugualmente la danno 5 in cambio di qualsiasi bagattella, dichiarandosene contenti . . .

Essi non professano nè setta nè idolatria veruna, ma tutti credono che la potenza e il bene siano nel cielo, e credevano fermamente che io con 10 le mie navi e la mia gente fossi sceso dal cielo, e con questa persuasione mi ricevevano ovunque, dopo che avevano smesso le loro paure. E questo non avviene perchè siano ignoranti, ma al contrario sono di ingegno molto acuto e navigano per tutti i 15 mari ed è incredibile come sappiano dare buone informazioni su tutto, eccetto che non hanno mai visto gente vestita nè navi simili alle nostre.

Non appena giunsi nelle Indie, nella prima
Isola che scoprii presi con la forza alcuni di quegli
abitanti affinchè apprendessero la nostra lingua e
mi dessero notizie di quanto vi era in quelle parti,
5 e così avvenne che ben presto ci intendemmo, un
po' con le parole e un po' coi gesti. Ciò fu di molta
utilità . . .

    Questa terra è da desiderare e, quando uno
l'ha vista, da non mai abbandonare . . . Nel luogo
10 più conveniente della Spagnola e nella regione
migliore per lo sfruttamento delle miniere d'oro e
per l'attivamento di ogni traffico, tanto della
Terraferma di qui quanto della Terraferma del
Gran Can, dove si avrà gran commercio e guadagno,
15 ho preso possesso di un gran villaggio al quale ho
dato il nome di Villa del Natale, e in essa ho
costruito fortificazioni e una fortezza, che a questa
ora spero sarà interamente finita.

    In conclusione, a tener conto solo di quanto è
20 stato fatto in questo viaggio che fu compiuto tanto
rapidamente, le Loro Altezze possono vedere che
io darò loro quanto oro vorranno, con un poco di
aiuto che le Loro Altezze mi daranno, e inoltre io
darò loro spezie e cotone quanto ne ordineranno,
25 gomma e àloe e schiavi quanto vorranno cari-
carne . . .

    . . . l'eterno Dio Signor Nostro concede a tutti
quelli che seguono il suo cammino la vittoria in
cose che sembrano impossibili; e questa segnata-
30 mente fu una di esse perchè, sebbene alcuni abbiano
parlato e scritto di queste terre, lo hanno fatto solo
per congiuntura, ma nessuno ha potuto affermare
di averle viste, per cui i più non solo davano poca
importanza a quanto io affermavo, ma lo giudi-
35 cavano una fiaba.

    Cosicchè, poichè il nostro Redentore ha dato
questa vittoria ai nostri illustrissimi Re e Regina e
ai loro Regni, che saranno famosi per tanto alto
fatto, tutta la Cristianità deve rallegrarsi e celebrare
40 grandi feste e ringraziare solennemente e con molte
orazioni la Santa Trinità per l'esaltamento che

Non appena *As soon as*

quelle parti *that area*

ben *very*

da desiderare *desirable*

da non mai abbandonare
never to be abandoned

traffico *trade*

tanto della Terraferma di qui
quanto della Terraferma del
Gran Can *both with this
Continent and with that of the
Great Khan*

Villa del Natale (*Nativity
City, in Haiti*)

a tener conto solo di *taking
into consideration only*

spezie *spices*

gomma e àloe *gum mastic and
aloe*

cammino *path*

segnatamente *particularly*

per cui *therefore*

i più *the majority*

Redentore *Redeemer*

tanto alto fatto *such a great
event*

beni *benefits*

sollievo *relief*

Fatto *written*
sopra *off*

avrà con la conversione di tanti popoli alla nostra
santa fede e inoltre per i beni materiali che ne
deriveranno, perchè non solo la Spagna, ma tutti
i Cristiani troveranno qui sollievo e guadagno.

Questo, come rapidamente fu compiuto, simil- 5
mente in breve viene narrato.

Fatto sulla caravella sopra le Isole Canarie il
15 febbraio dell'anno 1493.

Farà quello che comanderete

L'Ammiraglio. 10

From: *Giornale di Bordo di Cristoforo Colombo,*
a cura di Rinaldo Caddeo.
Bompiani, Milano, 1939.

102

XII

Amerigo Vespucci

(1454–1512)

Columbus died without knowing that he had discovered a new continent. It fell to another Italian, Amerigo Vespucci, to finally impress the world with the magnitude of Columbus' discovery by proving that the so-called "Indies" were not Asia, but a vast new world.

Vespucci was born in Florence of a distinguished family that pursued, true to the custom of the times, both trade and learning. The classical education which he had received imbued him with a consuming interest in the physical sciences, particularly cosmography, astronomy and geography. Although a born scholar, family reasons forced him into the import-export trade and he became manager of a firm owned by the younger branch of the Medici, then represented by Lorenzo di Pier Francesco de' Medici. After a number of business trips to Spain he settled in Seville in 1492. There he combined business with navigation, observation with study.

During those years the news of Columbus' discoveries attracted his attention and soon absorbed all his activities. From his studies in cosmography and astronomy he deduced that the water route to the "Indies" must be not the one followed by Columbus, but another, passing south of the equator. Determined to be the first man to reach the mainland of India, the practical scholar within him awoke and joined forces with the business man. By pooling his financial resources and exploiting his political connections, he succeeded in setting sail from Cadiz on May 18, 1499, in search of a passage to India and in June discovered the coast of Brazil. He spent a year exploring more than three thousand miles of coast line and making there invaluable astronomical observations. In June, 1500, he returned to Seville. He sailed on his second voyage from Lisbon on May 13, 1501, and explored the coast of Brazil 50 degrees south of the equator. In June of the following year, having returned to Lisbon, he disclosed one of the most astonishing feats ever accomplished by man: the discovery of a new "continent," the western hemisphere, unknown to anyone, even to any geographer. Ten years later, in Seville, he died of malaria contracted during his voyages.

Vespucci revealed himself to be a daring and original thinker. His inestimable discoveries revolutionized cosmography and geography. He was the first to apply astronomy for the determination of longitude. He explored scientifically the coasts of Brazil, Colombia, Uruguay and Argentina; discovered three of the world's greatest rivers: the Amazon, the Parà and the Plata. By being the first man to navigate the western coast of the Atlantic, fifty degrees south of the equator, he dispelled the legend that the southern hemisphere was uninhabited. By proving that the way to India was blocked, he revealed the existence of a new continent. He furthered and completed the mission that Columbus had been first to undertake. Columbus extended the ocean, Vespucci extended the earth. Both extended the world for mankind and died without being aware of the incalculable and undreamable benefits which their discoveries would bring to future generations.

Toward 1505, Martin Waldseemüller, a German cartographer, published an *Introduction to Cosmography* which contained a map that reported the new "region" discovered by Vespucci and incorporated the following suggestion: "I believe it just that it should be called Amerige after its discoverer, Americus, a man of keen and perspicacious mind, or America, since both Europa and Asia bear feminine names." Thus, the New World was named with a newly-coined word and has since been known under that name.

LETTERA

La scoperta dell'America

[It was Vespucci's habit to report his activities to his patron, Lorenzo di Pier Francesco de' Medici. The excerpts which follow are taken from a letter written to Lorenzo at the end of his first voyage, but which was published for the first time in *Vita e Lettere di Amerigo Vespucci* by Angelo Maria Bandini in Florence, in 1745.]

Magnifico Signor mio Signore,

È da molto tempo che non scrivo a Vostra Magnificenza, e ciò non lo ha causato altra cosa salvo non essermi accaduto nulla degno di memoria. E la presente serve per darvi nuova che, circa un
5 mese fa, tornai salvo e con la grazia di Dio dalle parti dell'India per la via del Mare Oceano, in questa città di Siviglia. Credo che Vostra Magnificenza avrà piacere di apprendere tutto il successo del viaggio e quelle cose che io vidi. E se io sono
10 alquanto prolisso, legga la presente quando avrà tempo, o come frutta alla fine del pasto. Vostra Magnificenza saprà come, per commissione dell'Altezza dei Re di Spagna, il 18 maggio del 1499 partii con due caravelle per andare a scoprire nella
15 parte del Sud-ovest per la via del Mare Oceano.

Magnifico Signor mio Signore
 My most excellent Lord
Vostra Magnificenza *Your Excellency*
ciò ... memoria *that has been due only to the fact that nothing worthy of note has happened to me*
nuova *news*
salvo *safely*
parti dell'India *Indies*
Mare Oceano *(Atlantic)*

alquanto *somewhat*
come frutta *as dessert*
per commissione dell'Altezza dei Re *commissioned by their Highnesses, the King and Queen*
nella parte *in the direction*

105

V I T A
D I   A M E R I G O
V E S P V C C I
SCRITTA DALL' ABATE
ANGELO MARIA BANDINI.

C A P I T O L O I.

Dell' origine della Famiglia Vespvcci, *e degli Vomini illuftri della medefima.*

Uella infinita provvidenza, ed arte, che ordinò le cofe tutte, affinchè da effe ne rifultaffe l' alto potere dell' ineffabile Creatore, fece da picciolì luoghi, e agli occhi noftri i meno confiderati, forgere maravigliofa virtù, o nel terreno, o nelle piante da effo prodotte, o fivvero negl' ingegni degl' uomini, che in detti umili luoghi traffero i natali. E tralafciando molte volte la magnificenza delle

b

Andai lungo la costa dell'Africa fino alle Isole Fortunate, che oggi si chiamano le Isole Canarie. Dopo di essermi provvisto di tutte le cose necessarie, e fatte le nostre orazioni, facemmo vela verso l'Isola di Gomera e mettemmo la vela per il Sud-ovest. Navigammo 24 giorni, con vento fresco, senza vedere nessuna terra. Alla fine del ventiquattresimo giorno vedemmo terra e trovammo aver navigato circa mille e trecento leghe dalla città di Cadice per il Sud-ovest. Vista la terra, demmo grazie a Dio e calammo le barche con 16 uomini e andammo verso terra. La trovammo tanto piena di alberi che era una cosa meravigliosa, non solamente per la loro grandezza, ma per il fogliame, perchè mai perdono le foglie, e per il soave odore

fatte *said*
facemmo vela *we sailed*
Gomera (*one of the Canaries*)
mettemmo la vela *we pointed our prows*

terra (*the northern coast of Brazil*)
mille e trecento leghe (*5,200 miles*)
Cadice *Cadiz*
demmo grazie *thanked*
calammo *put out*

5

10

15

106

che da essi veniva. Essi sono tutti aromatici e
davano tanto piacere che ci sentivamo molto
rinvigoriti.

Andammo con le barche lungo la terra per
5 vedere se trovassimo un posto per saltare a terra.   a terra   *ashore*
Remammo tutto il dì e mai trovammo un approdo
perchè la terra era bassa e gli alberi molto spessi;   la terra era bassa   *it was shallow*
di maniera che decidemmo di tornare alle caravelle   di maniera che   *therefore*
e di tentare la terra in un'altra parte . . .
10   Navigammo verso il Sud e lungo la costa
vedemmo uscire dalla terra due grandissimi fiumi.   uscire   *flowing*
Uno veniva dall'Ovest, scorreva verso l'Est e aveva   fiumi   *(the Amazon and the Parà)*
quattro leghe di larghezza, che sono sedici miglia;
l'altro scorreva dal Sud al Nord ed era largo tre
15 leghe . . .
E tanto navigammo per la Zona Torrida verso
il Sud, che ci trovammo sotto l'Equatore con l'un
polo e l'altro alla fine del nostro orizzonte. Là   alla fine   *at the edge*
passammo sei gradi sotto l'Equatore e perdemmo
20 completamente la Stella del Nord . . . Desiderando
essere il primo a scoprire la stella polare dell'altro
emisfero, perdei molte volte il sonno per contemplare il movimento delle stelle del Polo Sud . . .
E facendo questo, mi ricordai di alcuni versi del
25 nostro Poeta Dante il quale, nel primo Canto del
Purgatorio, quando finge di salire da questo
emisfero e di trovarsi nell'altro, volendo descrivere
il Polo Sud, dice:

"Io mi volsi a man destra, e posi mente   posi mente   *gazed upon*
30   all'altro polo, e vidi quattro stelle
non viste mai, fuor che alla prima gente.   fuor che alla prima gente   *save by Adam and Eve*
Goder pareva il Ciel di lor fiammelle: fiammelle   *rays*
oh settentrional vedovo sito,   vedovo sito   *bereft region*
poichè privato sei di mirar quelle!"   quelle   *(the four stars)*

35   Mi pare che il Poeta in questi versi, per mezzo
delle quattro stelle, voglia descrivere il Polo Sud.
Non ho ragione di credere che quello che egli dice   Non ho ragione di   *I have no reason to*
non sia la verità, perchè io notai quattro stelle a
forma di mandòla che si movevano poco. Se Dio   mandòla   *cithern*
40 mi dà vita e salute, io spero di tornare presto in

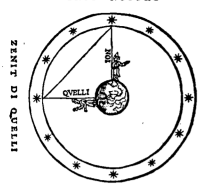

questo emisfero e di non ritornarne senza avere
identificato il Polo Sud . . .

Mi pare, Magnifico Lorenzo, che l'opinione
della maggior parte dei filosofi, i quali dicono che
dentro la Zona Torrida non si può abitare a causa 5
del gran calore, sia errata. Io ho trovato in questo
mio viaggio essere il contrario. L'aria è più fresca e
temperata in quella regione, ed è tanta la gente
che vi abita che il loro numero è maggiore di
quello della gente che abita fuori di essa. È un 10
fatto certo, diciamolo sotto voce, che vale più la
pratica che la teoria.

Fino a qui ho dichiarato quanto navigai alla
parte del Sud, e alla parte dell'Ovest, ora mi resta
di dirvi della caratteristica della terra che tro- 15
vammo, della natura degli abitanti, dei loro
costumi, e degli animali che vedemmo e di molte
altre cose degne di memorie. Dopo di esserci
diretti verso il Nord, la prima terra abitata che
trovammo fu un'isola distante 10 gradi dall'Equa- 20
tore. Quando vi fummo vicini, vedemmo sulla
spiaggia molta gente che ci guardava con grande
meraviglia . . . Noi armammo le barche e andammo
a terra con 22 uomini bene armati. La gente, come
ci vide saltare a terra e conobbe che eravamo gente 25
di natura differente dalla loro—perchè essi non
portano barba, nè abiti, così gli uomini come le
donne . . . ,—e anche a causa della differenza di

maggior parte *majority*

Io . . . contrario *in this trip of
mine I have found the contrary
to be true*

Fino a qui *Up to now*

isola *(Trinidad)*

armammo *manned*

a terra *ashore*

così gli uomini come *the men
as well as*

colore—chè loro sono di colore grigiastro e leonino, leonino *fawn-colored*
e noi bianchi—avendo essi paura di noi, fuggirono
nel bosco. Con grande fatica, per mezzo di segni, li
rassicurammo e ci avvicinammo a loro. Trovammo
5 che erano di una razza chiamata Cannibali. Quasi
la maggior parte di essi, o tutti, vivonò di carne
umana. E questo Vostra Magnificenza lo tenga per E questo . . . loro *and rest*
certo, non si mangiano fra di loro, ma navigano su *assured on this point, Your*
certe barche, che si chiamano "canoè", e vanno a *Excellency, they do not eat one*
                                                    another
                                                    "canoè" *canoes*
10 far preda nelle isole, o nelle terre vicine. Non a far preda *to prey*
mangiano nessuna femmina, a meno che essa non
sia loro schiava . . . Sono gente di gentile disposizione e di bella statura . . . Le loro armi sono
l'arco e la freccia. Sono ottimi balestrieri e hanno balestrieri *cross-bowmen*
15 grande coraggio. In conclusione, facemmo amicizia
con loro e ci portarono in un loro villaggio che era
a due leghe dal mare. Ci diedero colazione e
qualsiasi cosa che domandassimo la davano,
credo, più per paura che per amore. Dopo di aver
20 passato un'intera giornata con loro, ritornammo
alle nostre caravelle, restando buoni amici . . .
   Siamo al dì 18 di luglio del 1500, e non c'è
altro da menzionare. Guardi Nostro Signore, e Guardi Nostro Signore *May*
accresca come desidera, il magnifico Stato della *God watch over*
25 vostra signorile Magnificenza.
   Di vostra Magnificenza

Servitore
Amerigo Vespucci

109

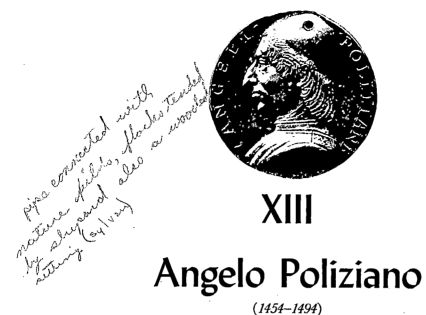

XIII

Angelo Poliziano

(*1454–1494*)

Poliziano is the most representative poet of his century. Born in Monte-pulciano, near Siena, he was sent to Florence at the age of ten after the death of his father, a notary. There he studied and came in contact with the illustrious humanists of the day. His Latin translation of Homer, when he was but sixteen, and his numerous poems in Greek and Latin brought him to the attention of Lorenzo il Magnifico, statesman, banker, patron of the arts as well as distinguished poet and humanist, who admitted him to his court and entrusted him with the education of his sons, including Giovanni, who became Pope Leo X. Poliziano served the republic of Florence as ambassador on several occasions. He was made a canon and also professor of Greek and Latin eloquence (the Humanities) at the University of Florence.

In Italian he wrote ballads, *canzoni* and *rispetti* on rustic themes in classic style, some nostalgic, others exuberant with the joy of life, all suffused with elegance and melody. He became famous for his *Stanze*, a long, unfinished poem describing a tournament won by Giuliano de' Medici. In it Poliziano transposed contemporary personalities and events to the realm of mythical heroes and legends and achieved a perfect, harmonious fusion of present and past, of classic and modern spirit, a style which also found favor with Botticelli, Gozzoli and Raphael. Poliziano's poetry is almost pictorial with its high relief of lights and shades, its weaving lines of melodious sounds that suggest the movements of a dance. His portraits and pastoral scenes are etched with such passionate simplicity as to make them seem evanescent, ethereal.

The work, however, which established Poliziano's reputation as a poet of great originality is *La favola di Orfeo*, a pastoral drama written in two days, when he was twenty-six, to be performed at a feast given in 1480 at the court of the Gonzagas at Mantua.

The *Orfeo* marks, so to speak, the birth of modern drama. Up to that time plays had been mainly of a religious character. The *Orfeo* is the first and most outstanding profane play written in the vernacular. For the Angel or Messenger who, in the *Rappresentazione sacra*, announced the subject of the play, Poliziano substitutes Mercurio, for the Virgin Proserpina, for Christ Pluto, for the Devils the Maenads, for the Madonna's lamentations over the death of Jesus Orfeo's lamentations on the death of Euridice, for the Christian Hell the pagan Hades.

The *Orfeo* is composed of lyrics, music, songs, choruses and dances. As such it may be considered the precursor of the melodrama and modern opera. It is also worth pointing out that, while religious plays were still being staged indoors, under the porticos or on church squares, a real theater was built for the performance of the *Orfeo*, the first private theater, in the modern sense of the word, ever erected in Italy.

Poliziano's version of the ancient myth runs as follows: Aristeo, a young shepherd, comes upon Euridice, the young and beautiful wife of Orfeo, in the woods and immediately falls in love with her. Upon hearing his entreaties, she flees and is pursued by him. During the chase she is bitten by a poisonous snake, dies and descends into Hades. Orfeo, learning of his wife's death, appeals in his despair to Pluto, ruler of the kingdom of darkness. Touched by Orfeo's sweet singing and melodious music, Pluto is induced to let him have Euridice back but on condition that Orfeo will not turn to look upon his wife until they have both emerged from Hades. Orfeo, who has tamed wild beasts, controlled rivers and moved even Pluto's heart, can not resist temptation and turns to gaze at Euridice who, then, must be brought back to Hades. Orfeo, enraged, swears to hate all women, whereupon the Maenads, in revenge, tear him to pieces.

In the character of Orfeo, the classical hero whose music had the power to soothe wild beasts and to move mountains and stones, one may see the symbol of the power of poetry, music and the arts (humanism) which had civilized Europe. Or, again, it may be interpreted as a prophecy of the approaching tragedy of Italy (the country which had awakened the peoples of Europe from the lethargy of the Middle Ages; which had given Europe a new civilization through her learning, her poetry, her arts and her love of man, nature and beauty; and, with Columbus and Vespucci, had opened up a new world for the old), soon to fall prey to the armed hordes which, Maenads-like, would swoop down upon her from France, Germany and Spain and tear her to pieces.

ANDERSON

LA FAVOLA DI ORFEO

Aristeo, giovane pastore, a Mopso, vecchio
pastore.

speco *grotto*	Ieri vidi sotto quell' ombroso speco
	una Ninfa più bella che Dïana,
amadore *suitor*	ch'un giovane amadore aveva seco.
vista *fair sight*	Com'io vidi sua vista più che umana,
mi si scosse *leapt*	subito mi si scosse il cor nel petto
	e mia mente d'amor divenne insana,
tal *so*	tal ch'io non sento, Mopso, più diletto;
	ma sempre piango, e 'l cibo non mi piace,
	e senza mai dormir son stato in letto . . .

5

Lamento di Aristeo perchè Euridice non corrisponde al suo amore.

Canzone

	Udite, selve, mie dolci parole,
	poichè la Ninfa mia udir non vuole.
	La bella Ninfa è sorda al mio lamento,
fìstula *reed-pipe*	e 'l suon di nostra fìstula non cura,
cura *heeds*	di ciò si lagna il mio cornuto armento
cornuto armento *hornèd herd*	

10

nè vuol bagnare il grifo in acqua pura,
nè vuol toccar la tenera verdura,
tanto del suo pastor gl'incresce e dole.
  Udite, selve, mie dolci parole.
5 Ben si cura l'armento del pastore,
 la Ninfa non si cura dello amante,
 la bella Ninfa, che di sasso ha il cuore,
 anzi di ferro, anzi di diamante.
 Ella fugge da me sempre davante,
10 come agnella dal lupo fuggir suole.
  Udite, selve, mie dolci parole.
Digli, zampogna mia, come via fugge
 con gli anni insieme la bellezza snella:
 e digli come il tempo ne distrugge,
15 nè l'età persa mai si rinnovella:
 digli che sappi usar sua forma bella,
 che sempre mai non son rose e vïole.
  Udite, selve, mie dolci parole.
Portate, venti, questi dolci versi
20 dentro all'orecchie della Ninfa mia:
 dite quant'io per lei lacrime versi,
 e lei pregate che crudel non sia:
 dite che la mia vita fugge via,
 e si consuma come brina al sole.
25   Udite, selve, mie dolci parole,
 poichè la Ninfa mia udir non vuole . . .

bagnare *to dip*
grifo *snout*
verdura *grass*
tanto . . . dole *so much does it (the herd) grieve and sorrow for its shepherd*

si cura *cares for*
amante *suitor*

anzi *nay, rather*
da me . . . davante *before me*
fuggir suole *is wont to flee*

Digli, zampogna mia *Tell her, my pipe*
snella *tender*
ne *us*
l'età persa *the lost years*
digli che sappi (dille che sappia) *tell her to learn how to*
forma *body*
sempre mai non son *do not last forever*

versi *shed*

brina *dew*

La Jftozia ⁊ fauola di Ozfeo: il quale per la mozte di Euridice volfe andare nel Jnferno.

Jn Siena.

Un pastore annuncia ad Orfeo la morte di Euridice.

Crudel novella ti rapporto, Orfeo,
    che la tua Ninfa bellissima è defunta.
    Ella fuggiva l'amante Aristeo:
    ma quando fu sopra la riva giunta,
    da un serpente velenoso e reo,   5
    ch'era fra l'erbe e' fior, nel piè fu punta,
    e fu tanto potente e crudo il morso,
    che ad un tratto finì la vita e 'l corso.

Orfeo si lamenta per la morte di Euridice.

Dunque piangiamo, o sconsolata lira,
    che più non si convien l'usato canto;   10
    piangiam, mentre che 'l ciel ne' poli aggira,
    e Filomena ceda al nostro pianto.

riva riverside
reo deadly
e' (e i)
nel piè fu punta her foot was bitten
corso flight

più non si convien is no longer suitable
aggira revolves
Filomena ceda let Philomela (the nightingale) yield

114

O cielo, o terra, o mare, o sorte dira!
Come potrò mai soffrir dolor tanto?
Euridice mia bella, o vita mia,
senza te non convien che in vita stia.
5 Andar convienmi alle Tartaree porte;
e provar se là giù mercè s'impetra.
Forse che svolgerem la dura sorte
con lacrimosi versi, o dolce cetra.
Forse che diverrà pietosa Morte;
10 chè già cantando abbiam mosso una pietra.
La cèrvia, e 'l tigre insieme abbiamo accolti,
e tirate le selve, e' fiumi svolti . . .

Orfeo inginocchiato dinanzi a Plutone dice così:

O Regnator di tutte quelle genti
che hanno perduto la superna luce
15 al qual discende ciò che gli elementi,
ciò che natura sotto il ciel produce;
udite la cagion de' miei lamenti.
Pietoso Amor di nostri passi è duce,
non per Cerber legar fo questa via,
20 ma solamente per la Donna mia.
Una serpe tra' fior nascosa e l'erba
mi tolse la mia Donna, anz'il mio core;
ond' io meno la vita in pena acerba,
nè posso più resistere al dolore.
25 Ma se memoria alcuna in voi si serba
del vostro celebrato antico amore,
se la vecchia rapina a mente avete,
Euridice mia bella mi rendete . . .

Proserpina a Plutone dice così:

Io non credetti, o dolce mio consorte,
30 che pietà mai venisse in questo regno.
Or la vèggio regnare in nostra corte,
e io sento di lei tutto il cor pregno.
Nè solo i tormentati, ma la Morte
vèggio che piange del suo caso indegno.
35 Dunque tua dura legge a lui si pieghi,
pel canto, per l'amor, pe' giusti prieghi.

Right-margin glossary:

dira *bitter*

Tartaree porte *gates of Tartarus*
mercè s'impetra *my entreaty may win mercy*
che svolgerem *we may change*
cetra *lyre*

La cèrvia . . . svolti [Construct: *We have made . . . herd together, . . . follow us and . . . flow backward*]

superna *heavenly*

duce *the guide*

non per Cerber legar fo *not to chain Cerberus have I taken*

nascosa *hidden*

anz' *nay, rather*

ond' io . . . acerba *wherefore I live a life of bitter anguish*

si serba *remains*

celebrato *famous*

vecchia rapina *ancient abduction (of Proserpine by Pluto)*

vèggio *see*

pregno *filled*

caso indegno *undeserved woes*
Dunque . . . si pieghi *therefore let your harsh law be modified in his favor*
prieghi *entreaties*

115

Plutone risponde a Orfeo, e dice così:

leggi *conditions*

Io te la rendo; ma con queste leggi:
  ch'ella ti segua per la cieca via,

véggi *gaze upon*

e che tu mai la sua faccia non véggi
  finché tra' vivi pervenuta sia.

disir *desire*
correggi *restrain*
se non . . . ti sia *otherwise she*
  will be taken from you at once
plettro *prayer*

Dunque il tuo gran disir, Orfeo, correggi;   5
se non che tolta subito ti sia.
Io son contento che a sì dolce plettro
s'inchini la potenza del mio scettro.

[Orfeo takes leave of Pluto and, leading Euridice away, sings some joyful verses from Ovid, adapted for the occasion. Suddenly, he turns back to look at Euridice.]

       Euridice si lamenta con Orfeo per essergli
         tolta violentemente:

Oimè, che 'l troppo amore

ci ha disfatti ambedua *has*
 separated us
furore *violence*

  ci ha disfatti ambedua.   10
Ecco ch'io ti son tolta a gran furore,
  nè sono ormai più tua.

Ben tendo . . . ma non vale
 I keep stretching my arms out to
 you; but to no avail.
vale! *farewell!*

Ben tendo a te le braccia; ma non vale,
  chè indietro son tirata. Orfeo mio, vale!

    Orfeo, seguendo Euridice, dice così:

semmi tu tolta *have you been*
 taken away from me
furore *madness*

Oimè, semmi tu tolta,   15
  Euridice mia bella? oh che furore,
  oh duro Fato, oh Ciel nemico, oh Morte!
  oh troppo sventurato è il nostro amore! . . .

From: *La favola di Orfeo.*

116

ANDERSON

IL CINQUECENTO

ALINARI

Characteristics of the Century

The period which runs from the last decade of the 15th century to the death of Tasso (1595), embraces the Italian Renaissance. It is the age during which the seeds sown by humanism came to fullest fruition, and Italian arts and letters reached unparalleled heights. It is the century of Machiavelli, Ariosto, Castiglione, Bandello, Aretino and Tasso; of Correggio, Titian, Giorgione, Raphael, the Sansovinos, del Sarto, Veronese, Cellini, Palladio, Tintoretto and Palestrina. Above them soars the all-embracing genius of Michelangelo, painter, sculptor, architect and poet, who sums up the Renaissance as Leonardo summed up humanism.

Like all other great eras, this one too had its ugly side. It is also the century when far-reaching events changed the course of Italian civilization and held it in check for a long time. The splendor of its artistic achievements was followed by an extravagant and widespread tendency to substitute aesthetic for moral standards which blinded the eye to such a degree that Italian political and moral life hit its lowest ebb.

The beginning of the change may be set in the year 1492, which was marked by the death of Lorenzo il Magnifico whose policy, anchored in the balance of power and the status quo, had succeeded in maintaining peace among the Italian states; and by Columbus' discovery of America, which, while opening a new world to trade and industry, shifted the commercial center of Europe from Italy and the Mediterranean to the countries facing the Atlantic. Italy, consisting of some fifteen rival states of varying sizes in discord among themselves and jealous of each other, was confronted with the growing economic, political and military power of such countries as France and Spain which had already constituted themselves into strong unitary monarchical states.

The main contemporary events that affected the course of the history of Italy at this time may be briefly summarized as follows: In 1494, Charles VIII of France invaded Italy; in 1495, the Holy League began to shape Italian policies; in 1498, Gerolamo Savonarola, who had raised his eloquent voice against the power and luxury of the clergy, was burned as a heretic in Florence; in 1517, Luther initiated the Protestant Reformation; in 1527, Rome was sacked by Spanish, German and Swiss armies; and, in 1530, Charles V of Spain, instigator of the sack, was crowned King of Italy by Pope Clement VII who asked, in return, the capture of Florence and the restoration of his family, the Medici, as hereditary rulers of the city. Thus, within less than forty years from the death of Il Magnifico, the republic of

Florence, representing the last free Italian state, was suppressed and the political servitude of Italy to foreign rulers became complete.

Threatened by the rapid spread of the Protestant Reformation, the Papacy meanwhile called the Council of Trent from which issued the Counter-Reformation. Catholicism on the one hand was being regenerated and was regaining its lost spiritual power; on the other hand, the rigidity, orthodoxy and intolerance of the Counter-Reformation, which was manifested especially through the Inquisition and the *Index of Prohibited Books*, dealt the last blow to the free and creative spirit of the Renaissance.

By the end of the 16th century, Italy had also lost the position of pre-dominance which she had held in European culture for three hundred years and the veiled prophecy of Poliziano implicit in the merciless fate of Orfeo, was revealed in its full significance. What a contrast between now and that day when, to use Carducci's words, "il sole, eterna fonte di luce e di vita, si levò trionfante la mattina dell'anno mille . . . e l'Italia distendeva le membra raggricciate dal gelo della notte, e si toglieva il velo dell'ascetismo per guardare all'oriente!" That triumphant sun had set. Italy was once more devastated and enslaved by "scorrerie procellose di barbari nuovi e orribili" and this time, the cowl of the Inquisition was thrown over her head. Her bitter tragedy was dramatically symbolized in Michelangelo's statute of *La Notte*, reclining over the tomb of Giuliano dei Medici in Florence, and the

awareness of her ruin and shame were expressed in the celebrated lines that Michelangelo put on her lips:

> Caro m'è il sonno e più l'esser di sasso
> mentre che 'l danno e la vergogna dura.
> Non vedere, non sentir m'è gran ventura;
> però non mi destar, deh! parla basso!

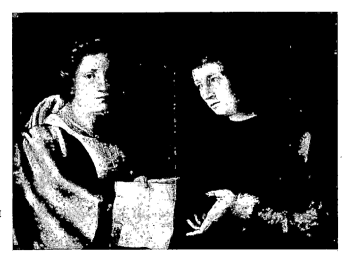

The swan song of the Renaissance was sung by Torquato Tasso (1544–1595), a great and unhappy poet, in *Aminta*, a lyrical drama of pastoral life and love, considered one of the most precious gems of Italian literature; and in *Gerusalemme Liberata*, an epic poem which celebrates the daring exploits of the first Crusade and the romantic love of the Knight Rinaldo for the beautiful and perfidious Armida, niece of the King of Damascus.

ALINARI

XIV

Niccolò Machiavelli

(*1469–1527*)

The wars between the Italian states and the loss of Italian independence induced statesmen and diplomats to take stock of and analyze the events which had led to these catastrophes. They also studied the history of the human race in order to uncover the causes which determine historical events and thus be able to draw from the past a remedy for the political ills of the present.

The most prominent figure in this field of endeavor was unquestionably Niccolò Machiavelli who may be considered the founder of modern political science and international relations. Nothing is known of his youth or his studies. The son of a Florentine notary, he was born poor and, to quote him, he had to learn first how to struggle and later how to enjoy. Poor he was when he died. He is portrayed as a slight man, with a small head, a pale face, black hair, piercing jet eyes, a sharp nose, subtle lips, and an enigmatic smile. His name first appears when, at the age of 25, he became secretary of the Second Chancellery of the republic of Florence the year that Charles VIII of France invaded Italy. He was subsequently sent on momentous diplomatic missions to other Italian states and to foreign countries where he met the most powerful rulers of the time and learned the intricacies of diplomacy. The reports which he sent home give a measure of his extraordinary political insight and precise evaluation of diplomatic realities. In 1512, when the exiled Medici were restored to power, he was dismissed from his post and under the unjust charge of conspiracy was imprisoned, tortured and banished to a small farm near Florence. He was forty-three years old. He never regained his position and died embittered and disappointed in 1527, the year of the sack of Rome.

Machiavelli spent part of his enforced leisure in contact with the humble life of his small town. During the day he could be found in the village tavern playing cards, listening to and quarreling with the peasants and shopkeepers. But above all, he read, wrote and pondered on the ways and means of saving his country. "When evening falls," he wrote a friend in 1513, "I return home and enter my study. On the threshold, I remove my country suit, filthy with mud and dirt, and put on my royal and courtly attire. When I am worthily dressed, I enter into the courts of the ancients who receive me with love, and there I feed on that food which is mine alone and for which I was born. I am not ashamed to speak to them and ask them the reasons for their actions, and they reply with kindness. For four hours I feel no boredom. I forget all my troubles. Poverty does not frighten me nor death terrify me . . ."

It was during this period that he wrote his major works. The best and least known, in which his real general theory of politics is clearly expressed, is *Discorsi sopra la prima Deca di Tito Livio*, a thorough discussion of the administration, expansion and defense of a modern state, which he envisaged as a democratic republic upheld by the consent of the masses, protected by a national army, ready to resort to ruthless measures, whenever necessary, to ensure its survival, and morally cemented by a state religion which teaches not meekness, resignation and humility but extols man's strongest virtues.

Convinced that one of the main causes of Italy's political enslavement sprang from the use of mercenary armies, Machiavelli advocated the institution of a citizens' army to be made up of the fittest members of all classes, trained during stated intervals while allowed the exercise of their civilian duties, and ready to either win or die in the defense of their country. He elaborated these principles in the *Arte della guerra*, the first treatise on military science and modern warfare. Besides purely historical works such as *Istorie*

TVTTE LE OPERE
DI NICOLO MACHIAVELLI
CITTADINO ET SECRETARIO
FIORENTINO,
DIVISE IN V. PARTI,
ET DI NVOVO CON SOMMA ACCVRATEZZA
RISTAMPATE.

M. D. L.

fiorentine, he wrote poetry, biographical sketches, stories and two plays, the most celebrated of which is the *Mandragola.* A realistic and cynical portrait of the society of that day, it is the first modern play and the best of the century.

It is quite likely, however, that Machiavelli's name might have remained obscure had he not written *Il Principe,* a brief political treatise, offshoot of the *Discorsi,* composed for the express and noble purpose of unifying and liberating Italy from foreign domination, this to be achieved during a period when intrigue, corruption, deceit and ruthlessness prevailed and only might was right. In his handbook, Machiavelli instructs his Prince in the science of establishing, maintaining and defending a strong state. Unfortunately, the rules of conduct he advocated for a particular situation, at a particular time and place, were either deliberately or ingenuously interpreted at home and abroad as a doctrine to be applied, not in time of war, but to any and all situations, at all times and everywhere. They were consequently denounced and condemned by his contemporaries. It was thus that Machiavelli's whole

125

political philosophy became crystallized in that familiar and opprobrious phrase: "The end justifies the means." And the irony of fate is that whereas some of the bitterest denunciators of this "doctrine"—such as Frederick the Great of Prussia and Prince Metternich of Austria—were to gain power and fame by putting it scrupulously into practice, the man who supposedly formulated it died as obscure and as poor as he was born, and his name passed to posterity as the synonym of "political immorality."

In reality, Machiavelli's reasoning in *Il Principe* may be summed up as follows: Italy is divided and invaded by barbarians. She must be united and liberated. This can be accomplished by a "new-risen man," by a new Italian prince "appointed by God for her redemption." There exists a state of war. This war must be won. The foreign oppressors are immoral. War in itself is immoral. The Prince cannot win this war by moral means. He is therefore obliged to become immoral. But this is not enough. The Prince must become more immoral than his enemies, otherwise he cannot defeat them. Evil must be fought with greater evil. All the devices and means employed by the Prince in order to defeat evil will be justified. They will be justified by the end for which they are used. Since this end is the unification and liberation of Italy from foreign oppressors, it is clear why this end justifies the means. Any Italian prince who achieves the liberation and unification of Italy by any means at his disposal, will be admired by everyone including, tacitly, the defeated enemy.

Machiavelli's purpose in teaching this doctrine to the Prince is explained clearly, dramatically and poetically in the last chapter of the book which has too often remained unread and ignored by his critics. Machiavelli's ideas are neither new nor original. They are deductions from his studies of history, from his observations of reality. They had and have been practiced, more or less intelligently, in all ages by rulers and generals engaged in the business of winning wars. Actually, if they failed to use them, public opinion would consider them not leaders but fools. The greatness of Machiavelli and *Il Principe* lies in the fact that for the first time these ideas were gathered, analyzed, organized in rational form, presented with sincerity, objectivity and detached realism, and couched in a concise and crystal-clear style. Writing in 1513 a treatise for the liberation of Italy, Machiavelli unwittingly spelled out the theory of power politics. That is why his treatise has had a phenomenal impact on modern thought and has been used, rightly or wrongly, to shape the destinies of the world.

IL PRINCIPE

1. In che modo i prìncipi abbiano a mantenere la fede

Ciascuno intende quanto sia lodevole in un
principe mantenere la fede e vivere con integrità e
non con astuzia. Nondimeno nei nostri tempi si
vede per esperienza che grandi cose sono state fatte
5 da quei prìncipi i quali hanno tenuto poco conto
della fede e hanno saputo raggirare con l'astuzia
i cervelli degli uomini superando alla fine quei
prìncipi che si sono fondati sulla lealtà.

Dovete dunque sapere che ci sono due modi di
10 combattere: uno con le leggi, l'altro con la forza.
Il primo è proprio dell'uomo, il secondo delle
bestie. Ma perchè il primo molte volte non basta,
conviene ricorrere al secondo. Perciò è necessario
che un principe sappia usare bene la bestia e l'uomo.
15 Questa parte è stata insegnata ai prìncipi
copertamente dagli antichi scrittori, i quali scrivono
come Achille e molti altri prìncipi antichi furono
dati ad allevare al centauro Chirone affinchè li
educasse sotto la sua disciplina. Ciò non vuol dire
20 altro che un principe deve avere per maestro uno
che sia mezzo bestia e mezzo uomo, e che deve
sapere usare l'una e l'altra natura poichè l'una non
è durabile senza l'altra.

Essendo dunque necessario che un principe
25 sappia bene usare la bestia, egli deve pigliare la
volpe e il leone; perchè il leone non si difende dai
lacci, la volpe non si difende dai lupi. Coloro che
desiderano essere semplicemente leoni, non se ne
intendono. Non può perciò un signore prudente, nè
30 deve, osservare la fede quando tale osservanza sia
contro i propri interessi e le ragioni che gliela
fecero promettere non esistono più. Se gli uomini
fossero tutti buoni questo precetto non sarebbe
buono, ma perchè sono cattivi, e non la osser-
35 verebbero a te, tu non l'hai a osservare a loro. . .

intende *knows*

astuzia *astuteness*

hanno tenuto poco conto della
 fede *had little esteem for good*
 faith
raggirare *deceive*
superando *overcoming*
si sono fondati *relied*

Il primo . . . uomo *the first is*
 peculiar to man

ricorrere *have recourse*

usare *to act as*
parte *role*
copertamente *covertly*

ad allevare *to be brought up*

l'una e l'altra *both*

pigliare *imitate*

lacci *traps*
non se ne intendono *know*
 nothing about it
signore *ruler*
osservare *keep*

la (*faith*)

127

IL PRENCIPE

DI NICOLO MA=
CHIAVELLI,

Al Magnifico Lorenzo di Piero
de Medici.

*Con alcune altre operette, i titoli delle quali trouerai nella
seguente facciata:*

IN PALERMO
Appresso gli heredi d'Antoniello dagli Antonielli
a xxviij. di Gennaiò, 1 5 8 4.

A un principe dunque non è necessario avere
tutte le soprascritte qualità, ma è molto necessario
parere di averle. Anzi ardirò di dire questo, che
avendole e osservandole sempre, sono dannose, e
5 parendo di averle, sono utili; come parere pietoso,
fedele, umano, integro, religioso, ed essere; ma deve
tenersi preparato in modo che, bisognando non
essere, egli possa e sappia fare il contrario . . .
Deve dunque avere un principe gran cura che
10 non gli esca mai di bocca una cosa che non sia
piena delle soprascritte cinque qualità, e paia, a
vederlo e udirlo, tutto pietà, tutto fede, tutto
integrità, tutto religione. E non è cosa più necessaria
a parere di avere che questa ultima qualità; e gli
15 uomini in generale giudicano più con gli occhi che
con le mani, perchè ognuno può vedere e pochi
possono sentire. Ognuno vede quello che tu pari,
pochi sentono quello che tu sei; e quei pochi non
ardiscono opporsi alla opinione dei molti che
20 abbiano la maestà dello Stato che li difenda; e nelle
azioni di tutti gli uomini, e specialmente dei
prìncipi, dove non c'è tribunale a cui appellarsi, si
guarda al fine. Agisca quindi un principe in modo
da vincere e da mantenere lo Stato; i mezzi sempre
25 saranno giudicati onorevoli e da ciascuno lodati . . .

soprascritte *above-mentioned*

ardire – to dare

dannose *harmful*

come *likewise (it is useful)*

integro *upright*

che non gli esca mai di bocca *never to utter*

paia *he must seem*

a parere di avere che *than to seem to have*

sentire *feel*

fine *goal (end)*

da vincere *to seize*

Capitolo XVIII.

2. Esortazione a pigliare l'Italia e liberarla dalle mani dei barbari

Avendo dunque considerato tutte le cose
descritte nei precedenti capitoli, e pensando se al
presente in Italia i tempi erano propizi affinchè un
nuovo principe potesse farsi onore, e se c'era
30 l'occasione per uno prudente e virtuoso di introdurvi una forma di governo che facesse onore a lui
e bene a tutti i cittadini, mi pare che tante cose
concorrano a benefizio d'un principe nuovo, infatti
non so che altri tempi fossero più propizi di questo.

farsi onore *distinguish himself*

uno prudente e virtuoso *a cunning and powerful man*
facesse onore *bring honor*
bene *well being*
a benefizio *to favor*
che altri tempi fossero *of any other times*

129

virtù *power*
fosse *should be*

si riducesse *should be reduced*
spogliata *stripped*
lacera *lacerated*
corsa *overrun*
avesse sopportato *should have suffered*

taglie *retaliatory levies*

infistolite *festering*
Vedasi *Behold*

pigli *to raise it*
Casa Vostra (*that of Lorenzo di Piero dei Medici, duke of Urbino, to whom "Il Principe" is dedicated*)
quale *what*

esterne *foreign*
ostinata *steadfast*
pietà *love*
si serrerebbero *would be closed against*

ossequio *allegiance*

puzza *is abhorrent*
dominio *rule*
Pigli *May . . . undertake*
assunto *task*
animo *courage*
insegna *flag*
si verifichi *will prove true*
detto *saying*

Virtù *Valor*
furore *wrath*
fia *will . . . be*
valore *courage*
cor *hearts*

E se era necessario, per vedere la virtù di Mosè, che il popolo d'Israele fosse schiavo in Egitto; . . . così al presente, per conoscere la virtù d'uno spirito italiano, era necessario che l'Italia si riducesse nelle condizioni in cui è ora; . . . senza 5 capo, senza ordine, battuta, spogliata, lacera, corsa; e avesse sopportato rovine di ogni sorta . . . In modo che, rimasta senza vita, aspetta, chi sani le sue ferite, e ponga fine ai saccheggi di Lombardia, alle taglie del Reame di Napoli e di Toscana, e la 10 guarisca di quelle sue piaghe già per lungo tempo infistolite. Vedasi come prega Dio che le mandi qualcuno che la redima da queste crudeltà e barbare insolenze. Vedasi ancora tutta pronta e disposta a seguire una bandiera, purchè ci sia uno 15 che la pigli. Nè si vede al presente in chi lei possa più sperare che nella illustre Casa Vostra . . .

Non si deve, dunque, lasciar passare questa occasione, affinchè l'Italia veda dopo tanto tempo un suo redentore. Nè posso esprimere con quale 20 amore egli sarebbe ricevuto in tutte quelle provincie, che hanno patito per queste invasioni esterne; con che sete di vendetta, con che ostinata fede, con che pietà, con che lagrime. Quali porte gli si serrerebbero? Quali popoli gli negherebbero 25 l'obbedienza? Quale invidia gli si opporrebbe? Quale Italiano gli negherebbe l'ossequio? A ognuno puzza questo barbaro dominio! Pigli, dunque, la illustre Casa Vostra questo assunto con quell'animo e con quella speranza, con cui si pigliano l'imprese 30 giuste; affinchè sotto la sua insegna questa patria sia nobilitata, e sotto i suoi auspici si verifichi quel detto di Petrarca:

"Virtù contro a furore
Prenderà l'arme; e fia il combatter corto; 35
Chè l'antico valore
Negli italici cor non è ancor morto."

Capitolo XXVI.

XV

Ludovico Ariosto

(1474–1533)

No prince, no "new man" arose to give heed to Machiavelli's dramatic appeal and Italy had to wait more than three centuries for unification and liberation. While she was being subjugated by foreign armies, her men of genius, impelled by their love of beauty, continued to think, write, compose, build, carve and paint with unflagging ardor. Art had become their religion, their fatherland, their *raison d'être*. And they built for Italy, not the strong temporal state excogitated by Machiavelli, but a new imperishable spiritual empire which was to humanize the barbarian invaders and become the common heritage of modern civilization.

In striking contrast to Machiavelli, the analytical, rational and realistic political scientist, stands his contemporary, the poet Ludovico Ariosto, the embodiment of unfettered and olympic imagination and creator of a fantastic dream world.

Ariosto was born in Reggio Emilia. His father, an army captain in the service of the Este family, wanted his son to study law, which he did in Ferrara. However, his humanistic training aroused in him an irresistible vocation for letters which he was allowed to follow and to which he intended to devote his life. But when he was twenty-six years old his father died, leaving ten children. To support them, since he was the eldest, he entered against his inclination the service of the Este court in Ferrara where he served first as courtier then as secretary, administrator, military governor and ambassador. During his spare time he wrote poetry in Latin and Italian and composed satires, five plays, and an epic poem of chivalry, *Orlando Furioso*.

The legends of Charlemagne and those of King Arthur had become popular in Italy as early as the 13th century and had thereafter been treated in prose and verse and sung in public squares by storytellers. It was not until the Renaissance, however, when they penetrated into the Italian courts, that they achieved literary stature. In 1483, Luigi Pulci, a witty Florentine poet, published the *Morgante*, a burlesque heroic poem in twenty-eight cantos which narrates with gusto the adventures of Orlando, one of Charlemagne's knights, of his squire Morgante, a gentle giant the size of a mountain who could devour a whole elephant at one meal, and of Margutte, a half-giant, past-master of fraud and trickery, who dies from laughing too much while

Morgante is killed by the bite of a tiny crab. In 1506, there appeared *Orlando Innamorato*, by Count Matteo Maria Boiardo of Reggio Emilia, a distinguished classicist poet who lived at the court of the Estes. The *Innamorato* consists of sixty-nine cantos celebrating the loves, jealousies, hatreds and heroic deeds of Orlando and his cousin Rinaldo, both enamored of Angelica, the beautiful daughter of the King of Cathay, who has been sent by her father to Paris so that the Christian knights might fall under her spell and lose their reason. This is exactly what comes to pass. Orlando and Rinaldo desert Charlemagne's army to pursue the unresponsive and recalcitrant Angelica through endless adventures. The poem ends with the two cousins fighting a duel over the bewitching Angelica outside Paris while the city, besieged by the Saracens, badly needs their help.

In 1494 Boiardo had to interrupt his poem at this point because Charles VIII and his invading armies had reached Reggio Emilia. He records this not without irony in the last stanza of the poem which is addressed to the readers:

> Mentre che io canto, o Iddio redentore,
> vedo la Italia tutta a fiamma e a fuoco
> per questi Galli, che con gran valore
> vengon per disertar non so che loco;
> perciò vi lascio . . .

Boiardo planned to complete his poem once the invasion was over but he died that same year.

The *Innamorato* is important because for the first time the Carolingian and Arthurian cycles are fused; for the first time they are treated by a great poet; for the first time a great literary work is produced by a non-Tuscan poet, thus proving that the vernacular was asserting itself over Latin and had become the national literary language of Italy. It is also important because the final episode contains what may be interpreted as an allegorical symbol of the Italian states (the cousins) fighting against each other while Italy (Paris) is threatened by invaders (the Saracens); or, again, it may be construed as representing the attitude of the Italian artists who, dazzled by an ideal and blind to reality, are intent on the pursuit of absolute beauty (Angelica) while Italy loses her independence.

Ariosto's poem begins at the point where Boiardo's *Innamorato* was interrupted. It takes up the same main characters but the plot is developed along quite independent lines. The Saracens have now inflicted a military defeat upon the Christians and have captured Namo, the duke to whom Charlemagne had entrusted Angelica. In the ensuing confusion, Angelica

Chivalric Tradition

jumps on a horse and runs away, pursued through the most fantastic adventures by Orlando and a number of other knights who are all in love with her. In a forest she comes upon a humble Saracen soldier named Medoro who has been wounded in battle and lies bleeding to death on the ground. The haughty, frigid heart of the royal Angelica is moved for the first time. She nurses Medoro, saves his life, falls in love with him, marries him and both go to her faraway native land of Cathay, of which Medoro will become king.

When Orlando discovers this, he becomes mad, runs amok and, armed only with a club, spreads death and ruin through France, Spain and Africa until another knight, Astolfo, inspired by God, flies to the moon on a winged horse and brings back to Orlando his lost senses in a phial. Thus Orlando, restored to reason, resumes his fight against the Saracens, kills their leaders, ends the war and saves Christendom.

First published in 1516, the *Orlando Furioso* appeared in its revised and final edition in 1532, the year before Ariosto's death. Its success was immediate and phenomenal. During the 16th century it had several imitators, was widely translated, and had about one hundred and eighty printings in Italy. It inspired Cervantes, Spencer, Voltaire, Byron and many artists; it has been for centuries an object of study and admiration for scholars, a source of endless enjoyment for the masses, and has taken its place among the masterpieces of world poetry.

Leonardo, in extolling the power of the brush, compared the painter to a god; Michelangelo, in one of his sonnets, praised the power of the hand which serves the brain; Ariosto demonstrated what the power of the word can accomplish when it is fired by an imagination unfettered by time, space, nature and logic. He had the magic gift of making the unreal appear real, the incoherent coherent, and of unleashing the human mind in boundless freedom. With the genius of a master painter, he depicted with words on a vast canvas the dream-world of his fantasy, populating it with knights-errant, fair ladies, saints, angels and giants; monsters and flying horses, mountains, forests, rivers and fairy gardens; enchanted islands, castles and palaces, magic words, rings, horns and fountains; duels, battles, raids into Hell, flights to the Garden of Eden and to the moon. His limpid images emerge from his cantos accompanied by exquisite, fluid, musical sound. He fused together, with the skill of an alchemist, not only the legends of the Carolingian and Arthurian cycles, but also elements of the *Iliad*, the *Odyssey*, the *Aeneid*, the *Divina Commedia*, the *Decamerone*, Petrarch's poetry, and the *Thousand and One Nights*, mythology and Christianity, classicism and medievalism, producing an eclectic literary monument of harmonious beauty which immortalizes the spirit of the dying Renaissance suspended between the ideal and the real, the goodness of a beautiful free world and the meanness of a corrupt and enslaved society.

Orlando

Furioſo di Ludouico Ario
ſto nobile Ferrareſe ri-
ſtampato & con molta diligentia da lui
corretto & quaſi tutto formato
di nuouo & ampliato.

Se vendano alla botecha di Legnano
al ſegno de Langelo.

ORLANDO FURIOSO

1. Pròtasi

Le donne, i cavalier, l'arme, gli amori,
le cortesie, l'audàci imprese io canto,
che furo al tempo che passaro i Mòri
d'Africa il mare, e in Francia nocquer tanto,
5 seguendo l'ire e i giovanil furòri
d'Agramante lor re, che si diè vanto
di vendicar la morte di Traiano
sopra re Carlo imperator romano.

Dirò d'Orlando in un medesmo tratto,
10 cosa non detta in prosa mai, nè in rima;
che per amor venne in furore e matto,
d'uom che sì saggio era stimato prima . . .

Canto I, stanzas 1-2.

arme	*combats*
furo (furono)	*happened*
passaro (passarono)	*crossed*
nocquer tanto	*did such great harm*
si diè (diede) vanto	*boasted*
Traiano	*Trajan (his father, killed by Orlando)*
in un medesmo tratto	*at the same time*
venne in furore e matto	*was driven to fury and madness*
d'	*(da)*

135

PRIMO

Giuseppe Moli in.

2. Angelica e Medoro

[Medoro is discovered by Angelica, bleeding to death.]

Giacque gran pezzo il giovine Medoro,
spicciando il sangue da sì larga vena,
che di sua vita al fin saria venuto,
se non sopravvenìa chi gli diè aiuto.
5   Gli sopravvenne a caso una donzella,
avvolta in pastorale ed umil veste,
ma di real presenza, e in viso bella,
d'alte maniere e accortamente oneste.
Tanto è ch'io non ne dissi più novella,
10 ch'appena riconoscer la dovreste:
questa, se non sapete, Angelica era,
del Gran Can del Catai la figlia altiera.

Canto XIX, stanzas 16–17.

gran pezzo *a long time*
spicciando il sangue *bleeding profusely*
sarìa *would have*
se non sopravvenìa *had there not arrived*

pastorale ed umil *humble shepherd's*
real *royal*
d'alte . . . oneste *of lofty (noble) and artfully modest manners*
io non ne dissi più novella *I have made no more mention of her to you (the reader)*
Gran Can del Catai (*Kublai Khan, 1216?–1294, emperor of China*)

[Angelica falls in love with Medoro while she nurses him back to health.]

Nè finchè nol tornasse in sanitate
volea partir: così di lui fe' stima;
15 tanto s'intenerì della pietate
che n'ebbe, come in terra il vide prima.
Poi, vistone i costumi e la beltate,
roder si sentì il cor d'ascosa lima;
roder si sentì il core, e a poco a poco
20 tutto infiammato d'amoroso fuoco.

Ibid, stanza 26.

nol tornasse in sanitate *he was fully recovered*
di lui fe' stima *she cared for him*
tanto . . . prima *so moved to pity did she become when she first saw him (lying) on the ground*
beltate *beauty*
roder *being corroded*
d'ascosa lima *by a hidden file*
amoroso *of love*

[Angelica's fresh wound grows, her health begins to fail, her beauty fades, whereas Medoro's wounds heal, his health returns, his manly beauty is restored. In order not to die of lovesickness, the proud Angelica, daughter of the Emperor Kublai Khan, who has spurned royal wooers, is now compelled to declare her love to Medoro, a humble foot soldier!]

La sua piaga s'apre e più incrudisce,
quanto più l'altra si ristringe e salda.
Il giovine si sana; ella languisce
di nuova febbre, or agghiacciata or calda.
25 Di giorno in giorno in lui beltà fiorisce;
la misera si strugge, come falda
strugger di neve intempestiva suole,
ch'in loco aprico abbia scoperta il Sole.

più incrudisce *gets worse*
salda *closes up*
nuova *strange*
or *at times*
beltà *beauty*
come falda strugger di neve intempestiva suole *as an untimely snowflake is accustomed to do*
aprìco *exposed*

137

aìti *help*	Se di disio non vuol morir, bisogna
	che senza indugio ella sè stessa aìti:
agogna *longs for*	e ben le par che di quel ch'essa agogna,
la' nviti *make the first move*	non sia tempo aspettar ch'altri la' nviti.
freno *restraint*	Dunque, rotto ogni freno di vergogna, 5
arditi *bold*	la lingua ebbe non men che gli occhi arditi;
colpo *wound*	e di quel colpo domandò mercede,
mercede *mercy*	che, forse non sapendo, esso le diede . . .
diede *caused*	

Ibid, stanzas 29–30.

[Angelica and Medoro are wed in the hut of the shepherds who have sheltered them. Inseparable, they spend a month's honeymoon of complete bliss.]

adombrar *protect*	Per adombrar, per onestar la cosa,
onestar la cosa *legalize their love*	si celebrò con cerimonie sante 10
àuspice *as its sponsor*	il matrimonio, ch'àuspice ebbe Amore,
prònuba *as bridesmaid*	e prònuba la moglie del pastore.
Fersi (si fecero) *were celebrated*	Fersi le nozze, sotto all'umil tetto
	le più solenni che vi pòtean farsi;
stero (stettero) a diletto *remained at their will*	e più d'un mese poi stero a diletto 15
tranquilli *undisturbed*	i due tranquilli amanti a ricrearsi.
ricrearsi *enjoy themselves*	Se stava all'ombra, o se del tetto usciva,
a lato *at her side*	avea dì e notte il bel giovine a lato;
riva *river bank*	mattino o sera, or questa or quella riva
	cercando andava, o qualche verde prato: 20
antro *grotto*	nel mezzogiorno un antro li copriva . . .
arbor dritto *straight tree*	Fra piacer tanti, ovunque un arbor dritto
ombrare *offering shade*	vedesse ombrare o fonte o rivo puro,
rivo *brook*	v'aveva spillo o coltel subito fitto:
v'aveva spillo o coltel subito fitto *she would at once carve it with a pin or a knife*	così se v'era alcun sasso men duro. 25
così *likewise*	Ed era fuori in mille luoghi scritto,
in casa in altri tanti il muro *in as many other places on the walls inside the house*	e così in casa in altri tanti il muro,
	Angelica e Medoro, in vàri modi
	legati insieme di diversi nodi.
quivi *there*	Poichè le parve aver fatto soggiorno 30
fe' disegno *she made plans*	quivi più che abbastanza, fe' disegno
in India del Catai *(to China in Asia)*	di fare in India del Catai ritorno,
	e Medoro coronar del suo bel regno . . .

Ibid, stanzas 33–37.

138

3. La Gelosia di Orlando

[Orlando, still in desperate pursuit of Angelica, has gone through incredible adventures. He has now come to the bank of a limpid river running amidst tender meadows covered with bright flowers and majestic trees. His eyes are drinking in this beauty when they are suddenly attracted by writing on the bark of the trees. Upon looking carefully, Orlando recognizes Angelica's handwriting. Her name, entwined with Medoro's, is carved on the trunk of every tree. Each inscription is like a nail driven into Orlando's heart. He would like to believe that Medoro's name stands for his own, but to no avail. Driven by suspicion he searches until he comes to a grotto on the stone entrance of which Medoro had engraved the story of his and Angelica's love.]

Tre volte e quattro e sei lesse lo scritto
quello infelice, e pur cercando invano
che non vi fosse quel che v'era scritto;
e sempre lo vedea più chiaro e piano:
5 ed ogni volta in mezzo il petto afflitto
stringersi il cor sentia con fredda mano.
Rimase al fin con gli occhi e con la mente
fissi nel sasso, al sasso indifferente.
Fu allora per uscir del sentimento;
10 sì tutto in preda del dolor si lassa.
Credete á chi n'ha fatto esperimento,
che questo è 'l duol che tutti gli altri passa.
Caduto gli era sopra il petto il mento,
la fronte priva di baldanza, e bassa;
15 nè potè aver (che 'l duol l'occupò tanto)
alle querele voce, o umore al pianto.

quello infelice *(Orlando)*
e pur cercando *still hoping*

in mezzo il petto afflitto
within his tormented bosom
sentia *(sentiva)*

al sasso indifferente *no different from the stone (petrified)*

sì tutto in preda del dolor si
lassa *so overcome was he by grief*
duol *grief*
la fronte priva di baldanza
his brow devoid of its wonted boldness
nè potè . . . pianto *nor could he (so overcome was he by grief) give voice to his complaints or fluid to his tears*

Canto *XXIII*, stanzas 111–112.

4. La Pazzia di Orlando

[A shepherd has related to Orlando how Angelica had fallen in love with Medoro, and has described their marriage, happiness and departure. The news drives Orlando mad.]

Conte (*Orlando*)

allo spuntar della diurna fiamma *at daybreak*
lo tornò *led him back*
inculse l'epigramma *had carved the inscription*
l'ingiuria sua *the affront to him*
dramma *the slightest particle*

nè più ... fuore *and he delayed no more but drew his sword*

a volo alzar fe' *scattered*
schegge *splinters*
stelo *tree*

Così restar (restarono) ... ch'ombra nè gielo (gelo) *In such a state were they left that day that neither shade nor coolness*
gregge *herd*
cotanta *such great*
poco sicura *not very safe*
ceppi *stumps*
zolle *clods*
onde *waters*
sommo *top*
imo *bottom*
turbolle (le turbò) *muddled them*
non furo mai più *never more were they*
nè monde *or clean*
molle *soaking*
lena *strength*
grave *deep*
ficca *fixes*
si serba *remains*
commosso *driven*
e magli, e piastre si stracciò di dosso *tore off the coat of mail and breastplate he wore*
scudo *shield*
lontan ... l'usbergo *his body armor far off, and his hauberk still farther*
insomma vi concludo *in short, to conclude*
albergo *resting place*
E poi ... 'l tergo *and then he tore his clothes to shreds, and naked revealed his bristling paunch, all his chest and back*
follia *madness*
della più non sarà mai ch'intenda *never will anyone hear of a more horrible one*

Pel bosco errò tutta la notte il Conte;
e, allo spuntar della diurna fiamma,
lo tornò il suo destin sopra la fonte
dove Medoro inculse l'epigramma.
Veder l'ingiuria sua scritta nel monte 5
l'accese sì, ch'in lui non restò dramma
che non fosse odio, rabbia, ira e furore;
nè più indugiò, che trasse il brando fuore.
Tagliò lo scritto e 'l sasso, e sino al cielo
a volo alzar fe' le minute schegge. 10
Infelice quell'antro, ed ogni stelo
in cui Medoro e Angelica si legge!
Così restar quel dì ch'ombra nè gielo
a pastor mai non daran più, nè a gregge:
e quella fonte, già sì chiara e pura, 15
da cotanta ira fu poco sicura.
Ché rami e ceppi e tronchi e sassi e zolle
non cessò di gittarne le bell'onde,
finchè da sommo ad imo sì turbolle
che non furo mai più chiare nè monde; 20
e stanco alfin, e alfin di sudor molle,
poi che la lena vinta non risponde
allo sdegno, al grave odio, all'ardente ira,
cade sul prato, e verso il ciel sospira.
Afflitto e stanco alfin cade nell'erba, 25
e ficca gli occhi al cielo, e non fa motto,
senza cibo e dormir così si serba,
che 'l Sole esce tre volte, e torna sotto.
Di crescer non cessò la pena acerba,
che fuor del senno alfin l'ebbe condotto. 30
Il quarto dì, da gran furor commosso,
e magli, e piastre si stracciò di dosso.
Qui riman l'elmo, e là riman lo scudo;
lontan gli arnesi, e più lontan l'usbergo:
l'arme sue tutte, insomma vi concludo, 35
avean pel bosco differente albergo.
E poi si squarciò i panni e mostrò ignudo
l'ìspido ventre, e tutto 'l petto e 'l tergo;
e cominciò la gran follia, sì orrenda,
che della più non sarà mai ch'intenda. 40

Ibid, stanzas 129–133.

ANDERSON

XVI

Michelangelo Buonarroti

(1475–1564)

Italian art reached its zenith in the 16th century, with Bramante, Raphael and Michelangelo as its greatest masters. Of this triumvirate Michelangelo is unquestionably the figure that casts the brightest light over the century. A sublime and tormented Titan, he incarnates and upholds, with Dantesque majesty, the highest traditions of the Renaissance.

He was born in Caprese, near Arezzo, where his father was mayor. Shortly after his birth, his family had to return to Florence and Michelangelo was entrusted to a nurse who was descended from and married into a family of stone cutters of Settignano. Hence the origin of Michelangelo's quip that he had absorbed his love for chisel, mallet and stone with his nurse's milk.

141

At the age of thirteen he was admitted to Ghirlandaio's *bottega* as an apprentice. Two years later he began to study on his own in the San Marco gardens where Lorenzo dei Medici kept his collection of antiquities. The work done even at this tender age bore such an unmistakable stamp of genius that Lorenzo decided to take him into his court. There the fifteen-year-old lad came in contact with Poliziano and fell under the influence of two of the most cultivated humanists of the era, Pico della Mirandola and Marsilio Ficino, who introduced him to poetry and to Greek philosophy. At the same time he studied the paintings of Giotto and Masaccio and the sculpture of Donatello which, together with the sermons of Savonarola and the *Divina Commedia* of Dante, were to exercise a profound influence on his life and art. The subject matter and treatment of his first work, a bas-relief of the Battle of Hercules and the Centaurs, already bear the imprint of what was later to become known both as the "michelangelesque style" and the "terrible manner."

At the age of twenty-four, and again when twenty-seven, he achieved supremacy in his style by making death beautiful and life sublime in two great masterpieces: the Pietà of St. Peter's in Rome and the David in Florence.

142

From then on, popes, kings and emperors contended for his services. He was no courtier and he hated tyrants; but, like all the artists of his time, he was completely dependent on the favor of great, powerful and rich patrons for his work and this was the tragedy of his life. Of the thirteen popes elevated to the throne of St. Peter during his life-time, he served seven. He spent most of his life working at various intervals in Rome on the Mausoleum of Pope Julius II, the painting of the Sistine Chapel and the building of the dome of St. Peter's, or in Florence on the Church of San Lorenzo and the Medici Chapel.

The Mausoleum of Pope Julius II was a source of rivalries, disputes and humiliations which so embittered Michelangelo for almost forty years that it became known as "la tragedia del sepolcro." Because of it the artist was continuously torn between the heirs of Julius who wanted him to complete the mausoleum and the Medici who insisted that he work solely on their tomb in Florence.

Michelangelo has been described as a well-proportioned man of medium weight and height, somewhat large-boned though lean, with a round, sad face, black hair, a wide square forehead, small grey eyes, a broken nose, thin

lips, jutting brows and ears, and a black parted beard of medium length. His appearance suggested pride and dignity. He had a forthright and unyielding temper, and harbored no tolerance for stupidity, arrogance or tyranny. On the other hand, he was patient with the humble and extravagantly generous with the poor. Parsimonious for himself, he sent home whatever money he made in order to help his parents and those among his relatives who happened to be in distress.

His memory was nothing short of prodigious and he used to claim that he remembered every line he had ever drawn. He lived and worked propelled always by vehement passions. His mind, teeming with herculean concepts, was in perpetual rebellion against the human limitations which kept him from achieving the sublime, the divine, the eternal. He often destroyed or left unfinished works which he came to believe he might never bring to the degree of perfection he had envisaged. During his whole life he remained a slave to art and beauty, but they had to be superhuman in scale. Like Dante and Petrarch, he felt and expressed the conflicts and the tragedy inherent in human life, but while Dante and Petrarch found solace toward the end of their lives in the realization that a harmonious universal unity governed every phase of creation, Michelangelo found no such appeasement. He could neither accept nor resign himself to limitations. He was never at peace with God, the universe or himself. The eternal conflict between body and spirit, first manifested in Petrarch, becomes in Michelangelo a titanic struggle between the human and the divine which he transmuted into the dimensions and convulsive energy of his figures and in the tragic sense of life which permeates all his works. This never-ending aspiration toward the infinite is most poignantly expressed in his unfinished *Prigioni* (The Captives) struggling to free themselves from the block of marble in which they are imprisoned. In their vain but unyielding effort there is implicit the fervent prayer of man to God to free him from the bonds of matter and from the limitations of the finite.

ANDERSON

145

SONETTI

[Sculpture, painting and architecture did not suffice to give full expression to what lay in the depth of Michelangelo's soul. He therefore often resorted to poetry as an outlet for his innermost feelings on life and death, doubt and faith, love and sin. His *Rime* were first collected, edited and rewritten by one of his nephews. It was not until 1865 that they appeared in their original form.

Michelangelo claimed to be a sculptor who had been forced into painting by Pope Julius at the instigation of Raphael who, prompted by envy, had wanted to humiliate him. Be that as it may, Michelangelo's predilection for sculpture over other art forms is apparent in the way he applies the technique of the plastic arts to both colors and words. In writing a poem he hammers and chisels his lines, which are as hard as stone, in a strenuous effort to infuse into them the thoughts that lie buried within his mind. His style is unadorned, taut, severe. In common with all his works, his poetry has that cogency of expression which suggests a wealth of veiled allusions. He wrote the first of the two sonnets which follow, when he was almost seventy. One will recognize in the simile on love a personal reference to his technique in sculpture. The concept of the sonnet is as follows: Any figure which a sculptor conceives lies hidden within a block of marble; he can hew it out and set it free provided his hand obeys his intellect. Love, like death, lies hidden in much the same way within the heart of the poet's lady, but he can extract only death. The fault lies with his art which works against his desired purpose.

The second sonnet, written at the age of eighty, shows a Michelangelo grown wise with age and who, now that he is drawing near the end of the stormy journey of his life, looks back and realizes how vain and fallacious had been his worship of earthly art. From now on—he laments—neither painting nor sculpture can soothe his soul which, troubled by the impenetrable mystery of its ultimate destiny, turns to divine love for solace.]

1. Non ha l'ottimo artista . . .

(1544?)

concetto *thought (figure)*	Non ha l'ottimo artista alcun concetto,
circonscriva *include*	ch'un marmo solo in sè non circonscriva
col suo soverchio *within its*	col suo soverchio, e solo a quello arriva
outer part	la man, che ubbidisce all'intelletto.
quello *(figure)*	
arriva *reaches*	

146

Il mal ch'io fuggo, e 'l ben, ch'io mi prometto

in te, Donna leggiadra, altera e diva,

tal si nasconde; e perch'io non viva,

contraria ho l'arte al disiato effetto.

5   Amor dunque non ha, nè tua beltate,

o durezza, o fortuna, o gran disdegno,

del mio mal colpa, o mio destino, o sorte;

se dentro del tuo cor morte e pietate

porti in un tempo, e che 'l mio basso ingegno

10 non sappia, ardendo, trarne altro che morte.

Lettere e Rime

147

io mi prometto	*I seek*
diva	*divine*
tal	*likewise*
perch'io non viva	*to my grief*
disiato effetto	*desired purpose*
Amor . . . colpa	[Construct: *Therefore neither love, nor your beauty, nor . . . are the cause of my misfortune . . .*]
in un tempo	*together*
che 'l mio basso ingegno	*my inadequate skill*

2. Giunto è ormai ’l corso della vita mia . . .

(1555)

Giunto è ormai ’l corso della vita mia
con tempestoso mar, per fragil barca,
al comun porto, ov’a render si varca
conto e ragion d’ogni opra trista e pia.

Onde l’affettuosa fantasia,   5
che l’arte mi fece idol e monarca,
conosco or ben, com’era d’error carca,
e quel c’a mal suo grado ogn’uom desia.

Gli amorosi pensier, già vani e lieti,
che fien or, s’a due morti m’avvicino?   10
D’una so ’l certo, e l’altra mi minaccia.

Nè pinger nè scolpir fie più che quieti
l’anima volta a quell’Amor divino
c’aperse a prender noi ’n croce le braccia.

Ibid.

comun porto   (*verge of death*)
ov’a . . . ragion *where all
enter to give a full account*
opra *deed*
Onde . . . carca [Construct:
*Onde conosco or ben, com’era
d’error carca l’affettuosa fantasia
che mi fece idol e monarca l’arte
e quel c’a mal suo grado
ogn’uomo desia.] Wherefore I
well know how full of sin was
the self-deluding imagination
that made art and love of woman
(i.e., what every man desires
despite himself) my idol and
master.*
che fien or *what can they be
now*
due morti *i.e., death of the
body and the soul*
D’una so ’l certo *Of one
(death) I know for certain*
Nè pinger nè scolpir fie più
che quieti *Neither painting
nor sculpture can any longer
soothe*
c’ (*che*)

148

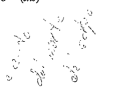

LETTERE

1. A Giovan Simone di Lodovico Buonarroti
in Firenze

[Michelangelo never married. He was wedded to art. He was, however, deeply attached to all the members of his family whom he supported and protected until he died. Inordinately proud of his family name, he was merciless with whoever dishonored it. One of his four brothers, who became something of a black sheep, went so far one day as to threaten his own father. Hearing of this incident in Rome, Michelangelo wrote him a fiery letter the postscript to which we reproduce below since it provides a rare insight into Michelangelo's personal life, his sense of family pride and temper.]

Roma (luglio 1508)

Giovan Simone,

. . . Io non posso fare che io non ti scriva ancora due righe. E questo è, che io sono andato
5 da dodici anni tapinando per tutta l'Italia; ho sopportato ogni vergogna; patito ogni stento; lacerato il corpo mio in ogni fatica; esposto la mia vita a mille pericoli, solo per aiutar la casa mia; e ora che io ho cominciato a sollevarla un poco, tu
10 solo voglia essere che scompigli e rovini in un'ora quel che io ho fatto in tanti anni e con tante fatiche. Al corpo di Cristo che non sarà vero! ché io sono capace di scompigliare diecimila tuoi pari, se sarà necessario. Ora sii savio, e non tentare chi ha altra
15 passione.

Io non posso fare che io non ti scriva *I can't help writing you*
sono . . . tapinando *I have led a wretched life*
patito *endured*
stento *hardship*
lacerato *racked*
casa *family*

scompigli *upset*

Al corpo . . . vero! *I swear this will never come to pass!*
tuoi pari *like you*
sii savio *behave yourself*
passione *woes*

Michelangelo in Roma
Ibid.

2. Il Mausoleo di Giulio II

[Thirty years after the death of Julius II, his heir, the Duke of Urbino, had it bruited about that Michelangelo had misappropriated the initial sum given him by Julius for the erection of his tomb. In a letter written to a

149

church dignitary, probably Bishop Marco Vegerio, Michelangelo, in refuting the charge, relates the story of the monument and lists the reasons which had induced him to leave Rome and sever relations with the Pope. Commenting on his abrupt departure from Rome, Michelangelo said: "If I had stayed on any longer, I would have had to prepare my own tomb before finishing the Pope's." The dispute lasted forty years. The mausoleum was never completed. We have of it the imposing statues of Moses and of the six Captives, four of them unfinished.

The letter brings out vividly Michelangelo's upright and unwavering character, an uncommon trait in a period of cowering servility and flattery.]

Roma (ottobre 1542)

Monsignore,

. . . Seguitando ancora circa la sepoltura di Papa Giulio, dico che dopo che egli si mutò di fantasia, cioè del farla in vita sua, essendo arrivate certe barche di marmi a Ripa, che da molto tempo avevo ordinato a Carrara, non potendo io avere 5 denari dal Papa, per essersi pentito di tale opera; mi bisognò per pagare i noli, cento cinquanta o duecento ducati, che me li prestò Baldassare Balducci, per pagare i noli dei sopradetti marmi. Ed essendo anche venuti in questo tempo gli 10 scalpellini da Firenze, i quali io avevo ordinati per detta sepoltura . . . mi pareva, senza denari, di essere molto impacciato, quindi cercavo quanto più potevo di convincere il Papa a continuarla. Una mattina che io ero andato per parlargli per tal 15 conto, mi fece mandare fuori da un palafreniere. Un vescovo lucchese che vide questo atto, disse al palafreniere: "Voi non conoscete costui?" E il palafreniere mi disse: "Perdonatemi, gentiluomo, io ho commissione di fare così." Io me ne andai a 20 casa, e scrissi questo al Papa: —"Beatissimo Padre: io sono stato stamani cacciato di Palazzo da parte della vostra Santità; onde io le fo intendere che da ora innanzi, se mi vorrà, mi cercherà altrove che a Roma." . . . E io andai, e montai in su le poste e me 25 ne andai verso Firenze. Il Papa, avendo ricevuto la mia lettera, mi mandò dietro cinque cavallari, i quali mi raggiunsero a Poggibonsi alle ore tre di

Glossary (margin):

sepoltura *mausoleum*
si mutò di fantasia *changed his mind*
del farla *to build it*
barche di marmi *boatloads of marble blocks*
Ripa *(a landing on the Tiber)*
per . . . opera *since he had changed his mind about said enterprise*
noli *freight*
ducati *ducats (once $2.25 each)*

scalpellini *stone-cutters*

impacciato *embarrassed*
continuarla *(its construction)*
tal conto *said matter*
mi fece mandare fuori *had me driven out*
palafreniere *guard*
lucchese *from Lucca*

ho commissione *have been ordered*
cacciato di Palazzo *driven out from the (Vatican) Palace*
da parte della *by order of*
onde io le fo intendere *I therefore inform you*
altrove che *elsewhere than*
montai in su le poste *took the stagecoach*
cavallari *mounted couriers*
Poggibonsi *(between Siena and Florence)*

150

notte circa, e mi consegnarono una lettera del Papa, la quale diceva: "Subito vista la presente, sotto pena della nostra disgrazia, ritorna a Roma." I detti cavallari vollero che io rispondessi. Risposi al
5 Papa, che ogni volta che egli osservasse i suoi obblighi, io tornerei; altrimenti non sperasse di avermi mai. Poi, mentre io stavo a Firenze, Giulio mandò tre Brevi alla Signoria. All'ultimo, la Signoria mi mandò a chiamare e mi disse: —"Noi
10 non vogliamo fare una guerra pèr te contro Papa Giulio. Bisogna che tu te ne vada. E se tu vuoi ritornare da lui, noi ti daremo delle lettere di tanta autorità, che se egli facesse offesa a te, la farebbe a questa Signoria."—E così feci: ritornai dal Papa, e
15 quel che seguì sarebbe lungo a dire. Basta, che questa cosa mi fece perdere più di mille ducati, perchè partito che io fui da Roma, ne fu gran rumore con vergogna del Papa; e quasi tutti i marmi che io avevo sulla Piazza di San Pietro
20 furono saccheggiati; onde io li ebbi a rifare una altra volta. Di modo che io dico e affermo che io resto avere, o di danni o di interessi, dagli eredi di papa Giulio, cinquemila ducati; e chi m'ha tolta tutta la mia giovinezza e l'onore e la roba mi
25 chiama ladro! . . . In queste cose che scrivo, posso errare solo in tempi, ogni altra cosa è vera.

Prego Vostra Signoria, per l'amor di Dio e della verità, quando ha tempo, di leggere queste cose, affinchè, avendone l'occasione, mi possa
30 difendere col Papa da questi che dicono male di me, senza nulla sapere, e che, con false informazioni, mi hanno messo nel cervello del Duca per un gran ribaldo. Tutte le discordie che nacquero tra Papa Giulio e me, furono causate dall'invidia di Bra-
35 mante e di Raffaello da Urbino. E questa fu la causa perchè non continuò la sua sepoltura in vita sua, per rovinarmi: e ne aveva bene cagione Raffaello, ché ciò che aveva dell'arte, l'aveva da me.

Michelangelo Buonarroti
40 *Ibid.*

151

---

sotto pena della nostra disgrazia *unless you wish to incur my disfavor*
ogni volta *any time*

Brevi *(papal) letters*
Signoria *Government (of Florence)*

da lui *to him*

Basta *Let it suffice to say*

partito . . . rumore *as soon as I had left Rome, many rumors went around*

saccheggiati *stolen*
io resto avere *I am entitled to*

tempi *chronology*
Signoria *Excellency*

col *before*
da *against*

mi hanno messo nel cervello del Duca per un gran ribaldo *have put it into the Duke's mind that I am a great rascal*

ne aveva bene cagione *had good motives (for acting thus)*
aveva *knew*
aveva *learned*

3. A Cornelia, vedova d'Urbino

[Michelangelo lived a solitary life. If he did not frequent society and made but few friends it was not because he disliked people but rather because he was always harassed by work and preoccupied with his own thoughts. However, his friendship, once granted, was sincere and everlasting. The two persons whom he loved best were undoubtedly the distinguished poetess, Vittoria Colonna, Marchioness of Ferrara, and Francesco d'Amadora, nicknamed Urbino for his home town, who was his faithful servant for twenty-five years. Michelangelo assisted Urbino day and night during the last days of the latter's life and when he died, the artist was so grieved that he was unable to work for months. The letter that follows, addressed to Urbino's widow, reveals one of the lesser known aspects of Michelangelo's character: his simplicity, his warmheartedness, his affection and concern for the humble for whom he could always find time and a kind word. When he wrote this letter, he was eighty-two years old, still busy with the raising of the dome of St. Peter, and still sought after by princes.

His dream of retiring to Florence to spend the last few years of his life was never realized because he was forced to remain in Rome to work on a number of projects, most especially on the dome. Seven years later, when he closed his eyes for the last time, it was to be the last thing he would see silhouetted against the Roman sky outside his bedroom window.]

Io m'ero accorto che tu t'eri sdegnata meco,
ma non trovavo la cagione. Ora per l'ultima tua
mi pare avere inteso il perchè. Quando tu mi
mandasti i caci, mi scrivesti che mi volevi mandare
5 altre cose, ma che i fazzoletti non erano ancora
finiti; e io perchè tu non spendessi denaro per me,
ti scrissi che tu non mi mandassi più niente, ma che
chiedessi a me qualche cosa, che mi faresti grandis-
simo piacere, sapendo, anzi dovendo esser certa
10 dell'amore ch'io porto ancora a Urbino, benchè
morto, e alle cose sue. Circa al venire costà a vedere
i putti, o mandar qui Michelagnolo, bisogna che
io ti scriva in che condizioni mi trovo. Il mandar
qua Michelagnolo non è opportuno, perchè sto
15 senza donne e senza servi, e il putto è ancora troppo
tenero, e gli potrebbe accadere qualche cosa che
mi darebbe molto dispiacere; poi c'è anche che il
duca di Firenze da un mese in qua fa del tutto
affinchè io torni a Firenze con grandissime offerte.
20 Io gli ho chiesto tempo, tanto che io acconci qua
le cose mie, e che io lasci in buon termine la fabbrica
di San Pietro; in modo che io stimo star qua tutta
questa estate; e acconciate le cose mie e le vostre,
questo inverno andarmene a Firenze per sempre,
25 perchè son vecchio, e non ho più tempo di ritornare
a Roma; e passerò di costà; e se mi vuoi dar
Michelagnolo, lo terrò in Firenze con più amore
che i figliuoli di Leonardo, mio nipote, insegnan-
dogli quello che io so che il padre desiderava
30 ch'egli imparasse. Ieri a dì ventisette marzo ebbi
l'ultima tua lettera.

Michelangelo Buonarroti
Ibid.

Roma, 28 marzo 1557

sdegnata meco   *annoyed with me*
cagione   *cause*
ultima   *(letter)*
caci   *cheeses*

sapendo, . . . certa   *since you know, in fact, you must be certain*
Circa al   *As for*
putti   *children*
Michelagnolo   *(Urbino's son and Michelangelo's godchild)*
donne   *maids*

duca di Firenze   *(Cosimo dei Medici)*
da un mese in qua   *for the last month*
tanto che io acconci qua le cose mie   *until I settle my affairs here*
termine   *shape*
fabbrica   *Dome*

passerò di costà   *will stop by*

a dì   *on the . . . day of*

ALINARI

XVII

Baldassare Castiglione

(1478–1529)

While Renaissance artists were striving to achieve the perfect work of art through stone and color, a number of writers were working to produce imaginary models of the perfect man, the perfect woman and the ideal of perfect beauty through the media of pedagogical dialogues, ethical essays and aesthetic treatises. Matteo Palmieri (1406–1475) had already described during the previous century the type of the ideal citizen (*Della vita civile*) and the eclectic Leon Battista Alberti (1404–1472) had drawn up his rules for the establishment of the ideal family and for its perpetuation (*Trattato della famiglia*). Now, Agnolo Firenzuola (1493–1543) defines and analyzes the archetype of feminine beauty (*Delle bellezze delle donne, Della perfetta bellezza della donna*); and Pietro Bembo (1470–1547) expounds on the nature of the various forms of love, with particular praise for the Platonic concept (*Gli Asolani*).

At about the same time, Giovanni della Casa (1503–1556) wrote *Il Galateo*, an entertaining manual on good breeding and good conduct for gentlemen in society. Since it was the most comprehensive treatise of its kind on the subject, it soon enjoyed wide popularity throughout Europe. The first English translation appeared in 1576. Its title, under which the author concealed his identity, made its entrée into the Italian vocabulary in such expressions as "sapere il galateo" and "non sapere il galateo" which still today are equivalent to "being well-bred" and "being ill-bred."

The standard work on social perfection, however, was *Il Cortegiano* by Baldassare Castiglione, a poet and diplomat who established the norms of behavior for the perfect courtier, furnished 16th century Europe with the model of the perfect gentleman, and in providing a panoramic picture of the culture, taste, standards and customs of the Renaissance, gave expression to its highest aspirations.

Castiglione, who was born of noble parents near Mantua, was trained in the humanities in Milan. He served at the courts of Lodovico il Moro in the same city, of Francesco Gonzaga in Mantua and, from 1504 to 1508, in that of Guidobaldo da Montefeltro, Duke of Urbino. During these four years he was sent on various diplomatic missions, including one to Henry VII in England, composed poems in Latin and Italian and began to write *Il Cortegiano* which he was unable to publish before 1528, beset as he was by diplomatic activities. He spent the last years of his life as ambassador of Pope Clement VII to the court of Charles V in Toledo, where he died in 1529, one year after the publication of his book, and two years after the sack of Rome. It is related that upon the announcement of his death, Charles V had exclaimed: "One of the world's greatest gentlemen has died."

The purpose of Castiglione's treatise is "to form with words the perfect courtier." To this end he describes all the qualifications and rules of behavior required to deserve such a title.

The action takes place sometime in March 1507, in the cultivated and scintillating court of Urbino of which Castiglione intended to paint "a portrait, not by the hand of Raphael and Michelangelo, but [by that] of a humble painter who only knows how to draw lines." We enter the ducal palace through its frescoed halls and meet Duke Guidobaldo, his Duchess Elisabetta Gonzaga, and all the celebrities attached to their court: statesmen, soldiers, prelates, scholars, poets, artists and ladies who devote the long evenings to music, dancing and to "giuochi," which are learned and amusing discussions on a serious theme.

The assembled ladies and gentlemen decide that the game for that particular evening should consist of a description of the perfect courtier. In view of the importance and timeliness of the subject, the game takes up four evenings, to each of which one of the four parts of the book is devoted. The discussions that Castiglione supposedly reports from memory in dialogue form are exhaustive, lively and interwoven with humorous stories and piquant anecdotes from which emerges a composite picture of the perfect courtier in mind, soul and body.

He must be, preferably, of noble lineage, well-built, manly yet graceful, a man of thought and action, a soldier and scholar, effective both on the battlefield and in the council chamber. He must keep his body fit with exercises in horsemanship, fencing, hunting, swimming, jumping, racing, tennis or soccer, and dancing. His mind must be adorned with noble virtues; he must know classic and modern literatures, at least two foreign languages, be a writer, a poet and an orator. He must also know how to draw and paint and is advised to be able to sing and play two stringed instruments. He must use tact, caution, grace and shun affectation. In doing the things he knows best he should act with studied carelessness since true art always appears artless.

These qualities are required of him in order that he may derive full enjoyment from life, inspire others, and above all, enlighten the prince so that he, in his turn, may govern wisely and become the ideal prince of the ideal state.

Having completed the portrait of the courtier and the prince, and outlined the organization of the State, the company devotes the third evening to defining the virtues and perfections of the lady of the court. Then there arises the question as to whether the courtier should love, and if he should, in what manner. A discussion on love and beauty occupies the fourth and last evening which is climaxed by a disquisition on the part of Pietro Bembo who glorifies

ALINARI

IL LIBRO DEL CORTEGIANO
DEL CONTE BALDESAR
CASTIGLIONE.

Haffi nel priuilegio, & nella gratia ottenuta dalla Illuftriffima
Signoria che in quefta, ne in niun'altra Citta del fuo
dominio fi poffa imprimere, ne altroue
impreffo uendere quefto libro
del Cortegiano per x. anni
fotto le pene in effo
contenute.

the rational contemplation of beauty which, by elevating love, leads it first to the enjoyment of abstract universal beauty and later, through the contemplation of the soul and angelic beauty, to the contemplation of perfect divine beauty.

Thus Castiglione, in enunciating the direct relation which exists between morality and politics, heaven and earth, man and God, summed up and defined the motives and purposes which impelled the man of the Renaissance to achieve perfection in all aspects of human life.

The significance of *Il Cortegiano* and the vast influence it exerted upon European thought and life may be gauged by the fact that during the 16th century alone there appeared over a hundred editions in Italian, sixteen in Spanish, fourteen in French, eight in Latin, three in English and two in German. There is also considerable evidence that Shakespeare used *Il Cortegiano* as a model for Hamlet.

In the court of Urbino, as it is described by Castiglione, we may perceive the forerunner of the modern cabinet; in its social life an anticipation of the academies and the French salon; and in the Courtier the prototype of the modern gentleman and diplomat. Just as Machiavelli, the realist, founded the science of politics, so did Castiglione, the idealist, establish the art of diplomacy and in codifying a moral and universal way of life, set a standard for all people, everywhere and always.

Il primo libro del Cortegiano, del Coute Baldaſſar Caſtiglioni, a meſſer Alfonſo Arioſto.

Le premier Liure du Courtiſan par le Comte Baltaſar Caſtillon, au ſieur Alfonſe Arioſte.

The firſt booke of the Courtier of Counte Baldeſſer Caſtilio, vnto Maiſter Alfonſus Arioſto.

FRA ME ſteſſo lungamēte ho dubitato, meſſer Alfonſo cariſſimo, qual di due coſe più difficil mi fuſſe, o il negarui quel, che con tanta inſtanza più volte ni hauete richieſto, o il farlo, perche da vn canto mi pareua duriſſimo negár alcuna coſa, & maſſimamente laudeuole, a perſona, che io amo ſommamente, & da cui ſommamente mi ſento eſſer amato: dall'altro ancor pigliar impreſa, la qual'io non conoſceſſi poter condur a fine, pareami diſconuenirſi a chi eſtimaſſe le giuſte riprenſioni, quanto eſtimar ſi debbono.

In vltimo dopo molti penſieri ho deliberato eſperimentare in queſto, quanto aiuto pòrger poſſa all.t diligenza mia, quella affettione, & deſiderio intenſo di compiacer, che nelle altre coſe tanto

MONSIEVR, i'ay lōg tēps debatu en moy-meſme laquelle de ces deux choſes me ſeroit la plus difficile, ou de vous refuſer, ce que pluſieurs fois m'auez demandé, auec ſi grande inſtance, ou bien de le faire: pource que d'vn coſté me ſembloit rude & choſe fort eſtrange de refuſer aucune choſe, principallement louable, à celuy que i'ayme grandemēt, & duquel ieme ſens eſtre grādemēt aymé: d'autre coſte, d'entreprendre choſe que ie cognoiſſe n'eſtre en moy, de pouuoir conduire à bonne fin, me ſembloit n'eſtre conuenable à celuy qui eſtime les iuſtes reprenſions autant qu'elle ſe doiuent eſtimer.

En fin, apres auoir pēſé & repenſé lōguement ſur ceſte affaire, i'ay propoſé d'experimēter en cecy de combien peut aider ma diligēce, celle mienne affection & deſir extreme que i'ay de vous com-

HAVE long time douted with my ſelfe (moſte louing M. Alphonſus) whiche of the two were harder for me, either to denie you the thing that you haue with ſuch inſtance many times required of me, or to take it in hand: becauſe on the one ſide mee thought it a verie hard matter to denie any thing, eſpecially the requeſt being honeſt, to the perſon whom I loue dearely, and of whom I perceiue my ſelfe dearly beloued. Againe, on the other ſide, to vndertake an enterpriſe which I doe not know my ſelfe able to bring to an ende, I iudged it vncomly for him that weyeth due reproofes ſo much as they ought to bee weyed.

At length, after much debating, I haue determined to prooue in this behalfe, what ayde that affection and great deſire to pleaſe can bring vnto my diligence, which in other things

IL CORTEGIANO

1. Il fine del perfetto Cortegiano

Il fine del perfetto Cortegiano io credo che sia
il guadagnarsi talmente la benevolenza e l'animo
di quel principe che egli serve, che possa dirgli e
sempre gli dica la verità d'ogni cosa che al principe
5 convenga sapere senza timore e pericolo di dis-
piacergli; e, conoscendo egli che la mente del
principe è inclinata a far cosa non conveniente,
ardisca di contraddirlo, e con modo gentile valersi
della grazia acquistata con le sue buone qualità per
10 dissuaderlo da ogni intenzione viziosa, e indurlo al
cammino della virtù. E così il Cortegiano, avendo
in sè la bontà accompagnata con la prontezza
d'ingegno e piacevolezza, con la prudenza e
conoscenza di lettere e di tante altre cose: saprà in
15 ogni occasione far vedere destramente al suo
principe quanto onore e utile provengono a lui e
ai suoi dalla giustizia, dalla liberalità, dalla magnanimità, dalla mansuetudine e dalle altre virtù che
si convengono a un buon principe; e, al contrario,
20 quanta infamia e danno provengono dai vizi opposti
a queste virtù. Perciò io credo che come la musica,
le feste, i giuochi e le altre cose piacevoli sono quasi
il fiore, così l'indurre o l'aiutare il suo principe al
bene, e spaventarlo dal male, sia il vero frutto della
25 Cortegianeria.

E siccome la lode del ben fare consiste princi-
palmente in due cose, dalle quali una è lo scegliersi
un fine dove tenda la nostra intenzione, che sia
veramente buono, e l'altra è il saper trovare mezzi
30 opportuni ed atti per raggiungere questo buon fine
designato: è certo che tende ad ottimo fine l'animo
di colui il quale pensa di far sì che il suo principe
non sia ingannato da nessuno, nè ascolti gli adulatori, nè i maldicenti e bugiardi, e conosca il bene e
35 il male, portando amore all'uno e odio all'altro.

Libro IV, capitolo V.

159

Cortegiano   *Courtier*

guadagnarsi   *to gain for him-*
self
animo   *mind*
dica   *shall say*
convenga   *is fitting*
timore   *fear*

non conveniente   *wrongful*

grazia   *favor*
con   *through*
viziosa   *evil*
cammino   *path*
prontezza . . . piacevolezza
   a pleasing and ready wit

provengono   *come*

suoi   *his dynasty*

mansuetudine   *gentleness*

si convengono   *are becoming to*

vizi   *defects*

giuochi   *physical exercise*

al bene   *to do good*

dal male   *from doing evil*

Cortegianeria   *Courtiership*

lode   *merit*

tenda   *is directed*

ad ottimo   *to the best*

pensa   *intends*

adulatori   *flatterers*
maldicenti   *slanderers*

2. La Donna di Corte

poi *yet*

in tutto essere aliena *in everything abstain completely*
modi *ways*
portamenti *bearing*
dissimile *unlike*

. . . benchè alcune qualità siano comuni e necessarie così all'uomo come alla donna, poi ce ne sono alcune altre che più si convengono alla donna che all'uomo, ed alcune convenienti all'uomo, dalle quali essa deve in tutto essere aliena. Il medesimo 5 dico degli esercizi del corpo; ma sopra tutto mi pare che nei modi, maniere, parole, gesti, porta- menti suoi, la donna debba essere molto dissimile dall'uomo; perchè come a lui conviene mostrare

160

una certa virilità soda e ferma, così alla donna sta
bene avere una tenerezza molle e delicata, con una
maniera di dolcezza femminile in ogni suo movimento, la quale, nell'andare e stare e nel dir ciò
5 che si voglia, la faccia sempre parere donna senza
similitudine alcuna d'uomo . . .

Io credo che molte virtù dell' animo siano
necessarie alla donna così come, all' uomo; per
esempio la nobiltà, il fuggire l'affettazione, l'essere
10 naturalmente aggraziata in tutte le sue operazioni,
l'essere di buoni costumi, ingegnosa, prudente, non
superba, non invidiosa, non maldicente, non vana,
non litigiosa, non inetta, sapersi guadagnare e
conservare la grazia della sua Signora e di tutti gli
15 altri, far bene e aggraziatamente gli esercizi che si
convengono alle donne. Mi par bene inoltre che la
bellezza sia più necessaria a lei che al Cortegiano,
perchè in vero molto manca a quella donna a cui
manca la bellezza. Deve anche esser più circospetta,
20 ed aver più riguardo di non dar occasione che si
dica male di sè, e fare in modo che non solamente
non sia macchiata di colpa, ma nemmeno di
sospetto, perchè la donna non ha tante vie da
difendersi dalle false calunnie come ha l'uomo . . .
25 Lasciando dunque quelle virtù dell'animo che
lei ha da avere in comune con il Cortegiano . . . e
anche quelle condizioni che si convengono a tutte
le donne, come l'esser buona e discreta, il saper
governare i beni del marito, la casa e i figliuoli se
30 è maritata, e tutte le cure che si richiedono ad una
buona madre di famiglia . . . ; voglio che questa
Donna abbia conoscenza di lettere, di musica, di
pittura, e sappia danzare e festeggiare; accom-
pagnando gli altri precetti che sono stati insegnati
35 al Cortegiano con discreta modestia e con il dare
buona opinione di sè. E così nel conversare, nel
ridere, nel giocare, nel motteggiare, in somma in
ogni cosa sarà aggraziatissima; e converserà digni-
tosamente, e con motti e facezie convenienti a lei
40 con ogni persona che le sarà presentata.

Libro III, capitoli IV, V, IX.

virilità soda e ferma	*sturdy and solid manliness*
sta bene	*it is proper*
maniera	*air*
ciò che si voglia	*whatever she may wish*
similitudine	*likeness*
virtù dell' animo	*faculties of the mind*
nobiltà	*gentle birth*
il fuggire	*the avoidance of*
aggraziata	*graceful*
operazioni	*actions*
costumi	*manners*
ingegnosa	*clever*
superba	*haughty*
litigiosa	*quarrelsome*
grazia	*favor*
Signora	*Mistress (here, wife of the Prince)*
Mi par bene	*I am quite of the opinion*
aver più riguardo di	*take greater care*
macchiata	*stained*
condizioni	*qualities*
buona	*kind*
beni	*estate*
festeggiare	*make merry*
con il dare buona opinione	*creating a good opinion*
nel conversare	*in conversing*
motteggiare	*jesting*
motti	*witticisms*
facezie	*pleasantries*

XVIII

Luigi da Porto

(1485–1529)

One of the richest fields of Italian literature is without doubt that popular branch of fiction known as the *novella* or short story, which generated spontaneously during the 13th century with the *Novellino* or *Cento novelle*, came rapidly into full fruition with the *Decamerone*, and propagated thereafter over the entire peninsula. Brief, spontaneous, realistic, and concerned with a compact plot and point, the *novella* appealed to all classes of people and was cultivated not only by writers of fiction but by poets, scholars, chroniclers and biographers. It can be found in the *Fioretti di San Francesco*, *Il milione* and the *Divina Commedia*, in the romances of chivalry and in *Il Cortegiano*. Even Leonardo da Vinci and Machiavelli were tempted by it and became occasional short story writers. Beginning with Cimabue and Giotto, the *novella* found its greatest illustrators in the painters of storied frescos which, like colored picture books, could be read by the illiterate multitudes on the walls of churches and cloisters.

While historians and poets immortalized great events and described aristocratic life or an ideal of life, the *novellieri* or short story writers recorded and handed down to posterity everyday events in the social and domestic life of all classes. This vast and impressive mass of raw material supplied generations of Italian and foreign playwrights, novelists, composers and librettists with a storehouse of plots, and students of contemporary customs and manners with a mine of invaluable information.

The most distinguished of the *novellieri* who, during the 14th century, followed closely in the wake of Boccaccio, but without ever surpassing him, include Giovanni Fiorentino, one of whose novellas inspired Shakespeare's *Merchant of Venice*, Giovanni Sercambi and Franco Sacchetti; and in the 15th century, Gentile Sermini, Masuccio Salernitano, Sabbadino degli Arienti and Piovano Arlotto. Unquestionably, however, the *novella* yielded its most luxurious harvest during the 16th century. By that time it had become the prevailing literary fashion and writers from every region used this genre, whence its variety of form, style, subject matter and folklore. Some of these stories are short and simple, others take on the proportions of a short novel. Most are comic, satirical and licentious with a pretense at moralization; or

Nouella nouamente ritroua-
ta d'uno Innamoramento: Il qual fuc
cesse in Verona nel tempo del
Signor Bartholomeo de
la Scala: Hystoria Iocondissima.

again, fantastic, pathetic and tragic, each containing in latent form all the elements from which romantic comedies and tragedies can later be developed. Their authors were without artistic ambitions, their sole purpose being to amuse and thrill the reader or listener by arousing his passions. The best collections of this period are those of Matteo Bandello, Agnolo Firenzuola, Anton Francesco Grazzini, Giambàttista Giraldi Cintio and Gian Francesco Straparola.

One of the occasional short story writers was the poet and historiographer Luigi da Porto, born in Vicenza. Forced to lead an inactive life because of war wounds, he retired to his nearby villa Montarso where he wrote a history covering the events of the republic of Venice from 1509 to 1513. It was probably under the influence of his friend Bandello that da Porto composed a short story, the first edition of which appeared in Venice about 1530 and the second in 1535. It bears the title *Historia novellamente ritrovata* (recently rediscovered) *di due nobili amanti* and is the only *novella* he ever wrote. Had da Porto not written it, it is quite likely that Shakespeare might never have written his *Romeo and Juliet*, and the world would have been deprived of this theatrical masterpiece, in addition to the more than twenty operas and symphonic compositions which it inspired.

In 1554, Bandello, following da Porto's text very closely, also published a story on Romeo and Juliet which was very badly translated into French in 1560, and from French into English in 1569. This is the version that Shakespeare must have used as the plot for his tragedy, although Arthur Brooke had versified the story in English in 1562 from Bandello's original.

163

ROMEO E GIULIETTA

1. Prologo

Signore *Lord*
stringeva e rallentava a sua bella posta *pulled and slackened as he saw fit*
patria (*Verona*)

Udine (*city northeast of Verona*)

quello (*the power*)

Nel tempo in cui Bartolomeo della Scala, Signore cortese e umanissimo, stringeva e rallentava a sua bella posta il freno alla mia bella patria, ci furono, secondo quanto mio padre diceva di avere udito, due nobilissime famiglie nemiche perchè 5 appartenenti a fazioni contrarie o per odio particolare. L'una nominata i Cappelletti, l'altra i Montecchi. A una delle quali si crede certo che appartengono questi che ora dimorano in Udine; cioè messer Niccolò e messer Giovanni, ora nomi- 10 nati Monticoli di Verona che per strano caso vennero ad abitare qui. Benchè loro abbiano portato seco poco di quello che avevano i loro antenati, eccetto la loro cortese gentilezza; e benchè io, leggendo alcune vecchie cronache, abbia trovato 15 che queste due famiglie unite sostenevano lo stesso partito; nondimeno questa storia come io la udii, senza mutarla, a voi la esporrò.

EL TEMpo che Bartholo meo dalla Scala signore cor tese & humanissimo il freno alla mia bella patria a sua po sta & strignea & rallentaua, furono in lei, secondo chel mio patre dicea hauer udito

[Having told how much blood had been shed on both sides as a result of their enmity, da Porto narrates how at a ball during the carnival season, Romeo, the handsome young heir of the Montecchi, meets and becomes enamoured of Giulietta of the Cappelletti family, a girl of exquisite beauty and charm. Both soon realize that they cannot live without one another. Romeo, at the risk of his life, climbs to the balcony of Giulietta's room at night to converse with her.

Knowing full well that their parents will never consent to their marriage, they are secretly wed by Frate Lorenzo, their confessor. Shortly thereafter, Romeo, provoked by Giulietta's cousin, kills him and is forced to flee to Mantua, far from his beloved. Meanwhile, Giulietta's parents decide to marry her off to a kinsman. To avoid this, Giulietta convinces Frate Lorenzo to give her a potion which will put her in a state akin to death for forty-eight hours. After having been borne to the cemetery and placed in the family vault, the monk will come for her and take her to Romeo in Mantua. They agree that Giulietta will write her young husband and tell him of this plan. Unfortunately, the letter never reaches him. Instead, his servant Pietro, learning of Giulietta's death, hastens to Mantua to inform his master who, ignorant of the truth, returns to Verona in despair to see his beloved and die beside her.

At the beginning of this passage we find Romeo, disguised as a peasant, back in Verona, in the churchyard of San Francesco. He has removed the tombstone and has just descended into the Cappelletti family vault where Giulietta's body lies in state.]

2. Romeo nella Tomba di Giulietta

Romeo, lo sventurato giovane, aveva portato
seco una lanterna cieca per poter vedere la sua   lanterna cieca   *dark lantern*
donna. Rinchiusa la tomba, subito tirò fuori la   donna   *wife*
lanterna e l'accese. E lì vide giacere, tra ossa e
5 stracci di molti morti, come morta, la sua bella   stracci   *rags*
Giulietta. Immediatamente, piangendo forte, così   forte   *bitterly*
cominciò: "Occhi, che agli occhi miei foste, mentre
che piacque al cielo, chiare luci! O bocca, da me   bocca   *lips*
mille volte sì dolcemente baciata! O bel petto, che   petto   *bosom*
10 il mio cuore in tanta letizia albergasti! Dove ciechi,   albergasti   *lodged*
muti e freddi vi ritrovo? Come, senza di voi, vedo,
parlo e vivo? O misera mia donna, dove sei stata da   misera   *hapless*

165

Amore condotta? . . . O sventurata mia vita, a che
scopo continui a vivere?"

E così dicendo, le baciava gli occhi e la bocca
piangendo sempre più forte. E nel pianto diceva:
"O muri che sopra me state, perchè, cadendomi 5
addosso, non fate ancor più breve la mia vita? Ma
poichè ognuno è libero di darsi la morte, vilissima
cosa è desiderarla e non prenderla." E così, tirata
fuori dalla manica l'ampolla di acqua velenosissima,
soggiunse: "Io non so quale destino mi conduce a 10
morire nel sepolcro dei miei nemici da me uccisi,
ma poichè, o anima mia, è bene morire presso alla
nostra donna, ora moriamo." E così portando
l'ampolla alle labbra ingoiò tutta l'acqua velenosa.
Quindi, presa l'amata giovane fra le braccia . . . e 15
tenendola molto stretta, aspettava la morte.

nel pianto   *weeping*

addosso   *upon*

prenderla   *to act*

fra   *in*

stretta   *close*

166

Già era giunta l'ora quando il calore del corpo
di Giulietta dovesse estinguere la fredda e potente
virtù della polvere ed ella dovesse svegliarsi. Scossa
e stretta da Romeo, la giovinetta si destò fra le sue
5 braccia e rinvenuta, dopo un gran sospiro, disse:
"Ohimè, dove sono? Chi mi stringe? Misera me!
Chi mi bacia?" . . . Romeo, sentendo viva la sua
Giulietta, molto si meravigliò e disse: "Non mi
conoscete, o dolce donna mia? Non vedete che io
10 sono il vostro triste sposo venuto solo e in segreto
da Mantova per morire accanto a voi?"
La Giulietta, vedendosi dentro la tomba e
sentendosi nelle braccia di uno che diceva essere
Romeo, era quasi fuori di sè stessa e, sospintolo
15 alquanto da sè e guardatolo nel viso, gli diede mille
baci, e disse: "Quale sciocchezza vi fece entrare qui

polvere *potion*

stretta *held close*

gran *deep*

mi stringe *is holding me fast*

Mantova *Mantua* (*city in Lombardy*)

sospintolo *having pushed him away*

sciocchezza *folly*

167

dentro e con tanto pericolo? Non vi bastava per le mie lettere avere saputo che io con l'aiuto di frate Lorenzo mi dovevo fingere morta, e che in breve sarei stata con voi?"

Allora l'infelice giovane, accortosi del suo grande errore, cominciò: "O miserissima mia sorte! O sfortunato Romeo! . . . Io non ricevei le vostre lettere." E così le raccontò come Pietro, il suo servo fedele, gli aveva portato per vera la notizia della sua finta morte per cui, credendola morta, per farle compagnia, lì accanto a lei aveva bevuto il veleno, il quale, essendo potentissimo, già cominciava a mandare i segni della morte per tutte le membra.

La sventurata fanciulla, udendo questo, restò così vinta dal dolore che non faceva altro che strapparsi i bei capelli e battersi l'innocente petto, coprendo di baci e di lagrime il giovane amato che già giaceva supino . . .

. . . Romeo alzò alquanto gli occhi languidi, già gravati dalla vicina morte, verso la sua donna, e vedutala, li richiuse. Subito dopo, scorrendo la morte per le sue membra, torcendosi tutto, fatto un breve sospiro, morì. Allora Giulietta, avendogli

mi dovevo fingere morta *had to feign death*

accortosi del *realizing*

per *as*

strapparsi *tear out*

gravati dalla *heavy with*
scorrendo la morte per le *with death running through*
tutto *in all his body*

168

rinchiusi meglio gli occhi, e bagnando il freddo
volto di lagrime, disse: "Che devo io fare in vita
senza di te, mio signore? E che altro mi resta di
fare verso di te, se non seguirti? Niente altro certo;
5 affinchè da te, dal quale solo la morte mi poteva
separare, essa morte separare non mi possa." E
detto questo, recatasi nel suo animo la grande
sciagura e ricordandosi la perdita del caro amante,
deliberando di non vivere più, raccolto dentro di
10 sè il fiato, e tenutolo alquanto tempo, emettendolo
poi fuori con un gran grido, sopra il morto corpo
morta cadde.

[When the constables discover the bodies of the two lovers, frate Lorenzo
reveals their story to Bartolomeo della Scala, lord of Verona.]

Udendo questo, Bartolomeo della Scala, quasi
mosso a piangere dalla gran pietà, volle egli stesso
15 vedere i morti corpi e con grandissima quantità di
popolo andò a visitare il sepolcro. Fatti portare i
due amanti nella chiesa di San Francesco, li fece
deporre sopra due tappeti. In questo tempo vennero
anche nella chiesa i due padri, i quali, piangendo
20 sopra i loro morti figliuoli, vinti da doppia pietà,
benchè fossero nemici, si abbracciarono. E così la
lunga inimicizia, che tra essi e le loro case era
regnata, e che nè preghiere di amici, nè minacce
del Signore, nè danni ricevuti, nè tempo avevano
25 potuto estinguere, per la misera e pietosa morte di
questi due amanti, ebbe fine. E ordinato un bel
monumento, sopra il quale la causa della loro morte
fu scolpita, i due amanti con grandissima e solenne
pompa, accompagnati e pianti dal Signore, dai
30 parenti e da tutta la città, furono sepolti.

E che ... seguirti? *And what else is left me to do for you but to follow you?*

essa *that same*

recatasi nel suo animo *fixing her mind on*

quantità *numbers*

per *because of*
ebbe fine *came to an end*

XIX

Giambattista Giraldi Cintio

(1504–1573)

In addition to *Romeo and Juliet*, Shakespeare derived, both directly and indirectly, the plots for about eight other of his plays from Boccaccio, Giovanni Fiorentino, Ariosto, Bandello and Giambattista Giraldi Cintio whose works furnished him with the plot of *Measure for Measure* and that of *Othello*, one of his greatest tragedies.

Giraldi was secretary to the Dukes of Ferrara as well as a physician and teacher of philosophy. He wrote treatises on the technique of play and novel writing, besides poems in Latin and Italian, nine tragedies and one hundred and thirteen short stories. His influence as a dramatist was felt by Italian and foreign playwrights, particularly through *Orbecche*, his most celebrated tragedy, and *Epitia* upon which *Measure for Measure* was patterned.

Adapting Aristotle's principles on the nature of tragedy to the tenets of the Counter-Reformation, Giraldi stressed the ethical-religious purpose of tragedy, maintaining that horror must be used as an antidote to vice and sin, that is to say, it must serve as a salutary example to man, inducing him to purge himself of error and long only for virtue. Deducing from his premise that the more horrendous the example the more salutary its effects, some of Giraldi's tragedies and others of his contemporaries offer the spectacle of a slaughterhouse or of a graveyard.

170

Giraldi's major work is the *Ecatonmiti*, a collection of a hundred stories told by a group of men and women who are sailing toward Marseilles after having fled from the sack of Rome. The most celebrated of these tales is *Il Moro di Venezia*. In re-elaborating the plot, Shakespeare kept six of Giraldi's original characters: Il Moro (the Moor, Othello); Disdemona, his wife (Desdemona); l'Alfiere, his Ensign (Iago, the Ancient) with his wife (Emilia); the Caposquadra, the Lieutenant (Cassio), and his wife (Bianca).

IL MORO DI VENEZIA

[There was in the service of the army of the republic of Venice a noble Moor, wise and brave. Disdemona, a Venetian girl of rare beauty and virtue, fell in love with him. Attracted by her exceptional qualities, he returned her love. Despite her parents' strong opposition to a mixed marriage, Disdemona and the Moor became man and wife and lived happily together.

One day the republic, in recognition of his gallantry, promoted the Moor to the rank of captain and appointed him governor of the island of Cyprus where he and his wife went to live.

The Moor had two trusted friends among his officers: the lieutenant (il Caposquadra) and the ensign (l'Alfiere), the latter a handsome but evil man who had succeeded in concealing his real nature from the Moor.]

sciagurato Alfiere *wicked ensign*
fede data *vow made*
avesse *owed*

ardentissimamente *madly*

quanto più . . . poteva *as . . . as possible*

punto *at all*

Lo sciagurato Alfiere, non curando la fede data a sua moglie, nè amicizia, nè fede, nè obbligo che egli avesse al Moro, s'innamorò di Disdemona ardentissimamente. Ma non ardiva di dimostrarle questo amore, temendo che se il di lei marito, il 5 Moro, lo sapesse l'ucciderebbe subito. Egli cercò con vari modi, quanto più segretamente poteva, di far notare a Disdemona che egli l'amava. Ma ella, ch'aveva nel Moro ogni suo pensiero, non pensava punto nè all'Alfiere, nè ad altri. E tutte le cose che 10 l'Alfiere faceva per farla innamorare di lui era come se non le avesse fatte. Perciò costui s'immaginò che ciò avvenisse perchè ella fosse innamorata del

172

Caposquadra; e pensò di sbarazzarsi di lui. E non
solo decise di fare questo, ma mutò in acerbissimo
odio l'amore che egli portava a Disdemona.

    E dopo di aver pensate varie cose tutte
5 scellerate e malvage, alla fine deliberò di volerla
accusare di adulterio al marito e dargli a intendere
che l'adultero era il Caposquadra. Ma sapendo il
grande amore che il Moro portava a Disdemona e
l'amicizia che egli aveva col Caposquadra, capiva
10 bene che ci voleva una frode molto astuta per far
cadere il Moro nell'inganno. Perciò aspettò che il
tempo e il luogo gli facilitassero la scellerata
impresa. E non passò molto tempo che, avendo il

Caposquadra *lieutenant*
di sbarazzarsi *to get rid*

scellerate *iniquitous*
malvage *wicked*

ci voleva *it would take*
inganno *trap*

Caposquadra ferito un soldato, il Moro lo privò del grado: ciò dispiacque molto a Disdemona, la quale molte volte cercò di rappacificare il marito con lui. Un giorno il Moro disse all'Alfiere che la moglie gli dava tante seccature per il Caposquadra e 5 temeva che lui sarebbe stato costretto a ripigliarlo. Il mal'uomo pensò che questa era una buona occasione per eseguire gli orditi inganni e disse: "Forse Disdemona ha motivo di vederlo volentieri".

—E perchè? disse il Moro. 10

—Io non voglio, —rispose l'Alfiere, —metter male tra marito e moglie, ma se terrete gli occhi aperti, ve ne accorgerete voi stesso . . .

Tali parole lasciarono una spina così pungente nell'animo del Moro, che si mise a pensare seria- 15 mente quel che volessero dire, e così se ne stava molto malinconico . . .

La moglie del Moro andava spesso a casa della moglie dell'Alfiere e se ne stava con lei buona parte del giorno. Vedendo l'Alfiere che ella qualche 20 volta portava un fazzoletto donatole dal marito, e che questo fazzoletto era lavorato alla moresca sottilissimamente ed era carissimo tanto alla donna quanto al Moro, pensò di toglierglielo segretamente, e quindi preparare l'ultimo danno. 25

Egli aveva una fanciulla di tre anni, la quale era molto amata da Disdemona. Un giorno che la misera donna stava nella casa di questo malvagio, egli prese la fanciulla in braccio e la porse alla donna, la quale la prese e se la tenne al petto. 30 Questo ingannatore che era lesto di mano, le levò il fazzoletto dalla cintola così cautamente che ella non se ne avvide punto e tutto allegro andò via. Passati alcuni giorni Disdemona cercò il fazzoletto e non trovandolo stava tutta timida temendo che il 35 Moro, come spesso faceva, glielo chiedesse. Lo scellerato Alfiere se ne andò dal Caposquadra e con molta astuzia gli lasciò il fazzoletto a capo del letto.

La mattina seguente il Caposquadra, levandosi dal letto, trovò il fazzoletto e non poteva immagi- 40 nare come l'avesse in casa, ma riconoscendo essere

quello di Disdemona deliberò di darglielo e,
aspettando che il marito fosse uscito di casa, andò
all'uscio di dietro e picchiò.

La fortuna, la quale pareva che assieme
5 all'Alfiere avesse congiurato la morte della meschina, volle che in quell'ora il Moro fosse già
tornato in casa, e sentendo picchiare all'uscio, si
fece alla finestra, e tutto cruccioso, disse:

—Chi picchia là?

10 Il Caposquadra, udita la voce del Moro, senza
rispondere si mise a fuggire. Il Moro scese le scale,
e aperto l'uscio, uscì nella strada, ma non trovò
nessuno. Per cui, entrato in casa, tutto arrabbiato,
domandò alla moglie chi fosse colui che aveva
15 picchiato. La moglie rispose quel che era vero, che
non sapeva. Ma il Moro disse:

—A me è parso il Caposquadra.

—Io non so, disse ella, se sia stato lui o altri.

Rattenne il Moro il furore, benchè ardesse
20 d'ira. Però non volle far nulla se prima non avesse
parlato con l'Alfiere, dal quale egli subito andò.
Gli disse quanto era accaduto e lo pregò di farsi
dire dal Caposquadra tutto quanto egli poteva
intorno a ciò. Costui, lieto di sì grande avveni-
25 mento, gli promise di farlo. Un giorno egli parlò
con il Caposquadra in un luogo dove potevano
essere visti dal Moro e, parlandogli di ogni cosa
tranne di Disdemona, faceva le più grandi risate
del mondo come se udisse cose meravigliose. Il
30 Moro, appena li vide separarsi, andò verso l'Alfiere
per sapere ciò che il Caposquadra gli avesse detto.
Questi, dopo essersi fatto lungamente pregare, alfine
gli disse:

—Egli non mi ha celato nulla: e mi ha detto
35 che l'ultima volta che è stato con lei, ella gli ha
regalato quel fazzoletto che voi le deste in dono
quando la sposaste.

Il Moro ringraziò l'Alfiere, e pensò che se
trovava che sua moglie non avesse il fazzoletto,
40 poteva esser sicuro che così fosse, come gli aveva
detto l'Alfiere. Perciò un giorno, dopo desinare,

uscio di dietro *back door*

La fortuna *Luck*

congiurato *plotted*
meschina *unfortunate Disdemona*
si fece alla *went to look out of
the*
tutto cruccioso *very angrily*

si mise a fuggire *ran away*

Per cui *Wherefore*

Rattenne *restrained*

di farsi dire dal Caposquadra
to have the lieutenant tell him

faceva le più grandi risate del
mondo *burst into loud fits of
laughter*

dopo essersi fatto lungamente
pregare *after having had the
Moor urge him several times*

desinare *dinner*

175

parlando di varie cose con sua moglie, le chiese il
fazzoletto. La infelice, che di questo aveva molto
temuto, a tale domanda divenne tutta di fuoco nel
viso; e per celare il rossore, il quale molto bene
notò il Moro, corse alla cassa, e finse di cercarlo. 5
E dopo di averlo cercato per molto tempo:

—Non so, — disse, — come ora non lo trovi?
L'avreste forse preso voi?

—Se l'avessi preso io,—disse egli,—perchè te lo
chiederei? Ma lo cercherai più comodamente 10
un'altra volta.

E, andatosene, cominciò a pensare come dovesse
far morire Disdemona, e insieme il Caposquadra,
sì che a lui non fosse data colpa della loro morte . . .

infelice   unfortunate woman

*divenne tutta di fuoco nel viso
  blushed all over*
rossore   blush
cassa   chest
e finse   pretending

comodamente   easily

far morire   to do away with
insieme   with her
*a lui non fosse data colpa   he
  would not be accused*

The ensign, with diabolic art, drives the Moor to such a pitch of jealous
frenzy that the latter urges him to murder both the lieutenant and Disdemona.
The lieutenant barely escapes with his life, while Disdemona is beaten to
death in her bedroom with sandbags, to create the impression that her death
has been caused by a beam that has fallen from the ceiling. After his wife's
death, the Moor's love and anguish for her increase, while his anger and
hatred turn against her accuser whom he dismisses from the service. The
ensign takes his revenge by accusing the Moor of Disdemona's murder.
Recalled to Venice, the Moor is tried and tortured but stubbornly denies
the crime of which he is accused, whereupon he is banished and is later
murdered by Disdemona's relatives. The ensign continues on his evil way
until, falling in the hands of the law, he dies under torture. "Tale vendetta
fece Iddio dell'innocenza di Disdemona."

From: *Ecatonmiti*, III decade, novella VII.

176

XX

Benvenuto Cellini

(*1500–1571*)

The history of the rise and triumph of the individual from the advent of humanism to the peak of the Renaissance was profusely illustrated by the contemporary arts, but most especially by portrait painting. Admiration for the man of superior mental and physical endowments had evolved into a sort of hero worship which spurred artists to immortalize princes, popes, men of letters and men of arms. In the same spirit and in emulation of the examples left by classic writers, the historiographers of the Renaissance wrote biographies of the great artists and thinkers. By placing in high relief the character of the subject through a description of his actions, works and personal habits and by highlighting it with amusing episodes, they filled the gap left by the portrait painter and rounded out a complete personality. Thus, biography acquired the importance of a written portrait or of a personal history.

It is significant that the most celebrated and important work of this kind was compiled by Giorgio Vasari (1511–1574) of Arezzo, himself a painter and architect. Genuinely convinced that the fine arts had already reached the limits of human potentiality, he wrote during his spare time the history of the Italian arts: *Vite de' più eccellenti pittori, scultori e architetti*, which consists of over two hundred biographies divided into three periods: that of the innovators, from Cimabue to Jacopo della Quercia; that of maturity, from della Quercia to Leonardo; and that of the great masters, from Leonardo to—and including—himself. In spite of Vasari's inaccuracies and his partiality toward Tuscan artists, the *Vite* is invaluable to the student of art for the precious information it contains on the careers of the artists, its picturesque anecdotes and the detailed descriptions of paintings, sculptures and buildings.

One of the by-products of the custom which developed among prominent citizens of recording their personal experiences, thoughts and comments in the form of diaries or mémoirs was the autobiography or self-portrait. The unrivaled master in this field was Benvenuto Cellini, the greatest goldsmith of his day and a distinguished sculptor, who dictated the story of his life, *La vita di Benvenuto Cellini scritta da lui medesimo*, to a fourteen-year-old apprentice while attending to the labors of his craft.

Cellini was a genius and a madman, a viper and an eagle, an egocentric and an extrovert, a fanatic in religious matters and a profligate. A man of indomitable spirit, courageous, impetuous, vengeful and superstitious, he believed that an artist of his caliber should be bound neither by divine nor human law. So he fashioned a God and a law of his own. He determined to be and succeeded in being himself for good or for evil. He thus passed through the major courts of his time equipped with a chisel for his work and a dagger, a sword and a sharp-edged tongue to do justice to himself. The number of murders, stabbings, duels and fights in which he claims he was involved defy enumeration. He was submissive and loyal only to art, family and self.

He produced an astonishing number of jewels, *objets d'art*, and articles of personal adornment of intricate detail and exquisite workmanship while the courts of Rome, Paris and Florence vied with each other to secure his services. Most of his masterpieces have been lost save for a gold and enamel salt-cellar now in Vienna, a bronze statue of Diana at the Louvre, the bust of Cosimo I and the celebrated statue of Perseus, both of which are in Florence. He also left a collection of over-elaborate poems, *Rime*, and two valuable volumes of essays, *Trattati e Discorsi*, on the technique of the fine arts.

Interestingly enough, more than to his works of art, Cellini owes his fame to his autobiography considered one of the most enjoyable and artless accounts of the life, arts and mores of the 16th century. He relates his turbulent life with utmost candor and even complacency. Far from trying to conceal his homicidal quarrels and vendettas, he delights in embellishing and in trying to justify them, sometimes most callously. In the process he portrays not only himself but his contemporaries. Since his work took him to the most important courts and put him in close contact with Popes, kings and princes during one of the stormiest periods of history, his autobiography gives the impression of an immense stage on which the great events of that era evolve and the major actors of the times play out their own roles in the privacy of their chambers, completely unaware of the audience. Important though they are, scenery and actors merely form the background for Cellini's singular and spectacular performance. The whole is highlighted by memorable and often hilarious interludes such as the incantation performed by a priest and necromancer in the dead of night in the Colosseum, Cellini's own imprisonment and escape from Castel Sant'Angelo, his trial in a French courthouse, and the thrilling account of the casting of the Perseus. The action is dominated at all times by Cellini's volcanic personality which is the fullest expression of the individual uncurbed by tradition, an amalgam of all the virtues and vices of the Renaissance.

ALINARI   179

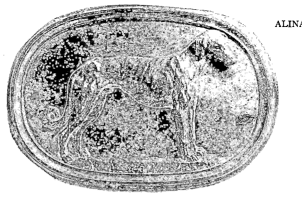

LA VITA

La famiglia e la nascita del Cellini
descritte da lui medesimo

Andrea Cellini (*Benvenuto's grandfather*)
s'intendeva assai dell' *knew a great deal about the*

Vitruvio (*Roman architect, 1st century B.C., author of " Treatise on Architecture"*)

la chiese per moglie *asked for her hand*

Questo Andrea Cellini, s'intendeva assai dell'architettura di quei tempi, e, siccome era la sua arte, viveva di essa. Giovanni, che fu mio padre, vi si dedicò più dei suoi fratelli. E perchè, come dice Vitruvio, volendo fare bene detta arte bisogna 5 aver conoscenza fra l'altre cose di musica e di disegno; mio padre, che era già buon disegnatore, cominciò a studiare la musica. Insieme con essa imparò a suonare molto bene la viola e il flauto; ed essendo persona molto studiosa, usciva poco di 10 casa. Accanto alla casa dei miei nonni abitava uno che si chiamava Stefano Granacci, il quale aveva parecchie figliuole tutte bellissime. Così come piacque a Dio, Giovanni vide una di queste figliuole che aveva nome Elisabetta; e tanto gli 15 piacque che lui la chiese per moglie. E perchè l'uno e l'altro padre si conoscevano benissimo a causa della stretta vicinanza, fu facile fare questo matrimonio; e a ciascuno di loro gli pareva di avere acconciato le cose sue molto bene. Quei due buoni 20 vecchioni prima conclusero il matrimonio, e poi

180

cominciarono a ragionare della dote. Ma essendo
sorta fra di loro una piccola disputa, Andrea diceva
a Stefano:

—Mio figlio Giovanni è il più valente giovane
5 di Firenze e d'Italia, e se io gli avessi voluto dar
moglie prima, avrei avuto la maggior dote che si
dia a Firenze ai nostri pari.

E Stefano diceva:

—Tu hai mille ragioni, ma io mi trovo con
10 cinque fanciulle e con tanti altri figliuoli e, fatti i
conti, questo è fin dove posso arrivare.

Giovanni, che era stato un pezzo a udire
nascosto da loro, improvvisamente li interruppe
dicendo:

15 —O padre mio, io ho desiderato e amato
quella fanciulla, e non i loro denari. Guai a coloro
che si vogliono rifare con la dote della loro moglie!
Se è vero, come voi vi siete vantato, che io sia così
valente, non potrò io mantenerla e soddisfare ai
20 suoi bisogni con una somma minore di quanto voi
vogliate? Ora io vi voglio dichiarare che la donna
è la mia e la dote voglio che sia la vostra.

Andrea Cellini, che era un po' irascibile,
rimase sdegnato a queste parole; ma pochi giorni
25 dopo, Giovanni portò la donna a casa e non chiese
mai più altra dote. Si godettero la loro giovinezza
e il loro santo amore per diciotto anni sempre con
gran desiderio di aver figliuoli.

Dopo diciotto anni la sua donna perdette in
30 sul nascere due figli maschi a causa della poca
intelligenza dei medici; poi ebbe una femmina alla
quale posero il nome di Cosa per ricordare il nome
della madre di mio padre. Dopo due anni ingravidò
di nuovo e siccome aveva delle voglie simili a quelle
35 del parto precedente, si credette che dovesse avere
un'altra femmina come la prima e le avevano
d'accordo dato il nome di Reparata per la madre
di mia madre. Avvenne che partorì la notte di
Tutti i Santi a quattro ore e mezzo del mille
40 cinquecento. La levatrice, che sapeva che loro
aspettavano una femmina, pulita la creatura e

ai nostri pari   *to people of our standing*

fatti i conti   *having figured it out*

un pezzo   *a while*

che si vogliono rifare   *who want to repair their fortune*

di quanto   *than the one*

in sul nascere   *at birth*

Cosa   *Nicky*
ingravidò   *was with child*
voglie   *longings*

partorì   *gave birth*
Tutti i Santi   *All Saints Day (Nov. 1st)*
levatrice   *midwife*

181

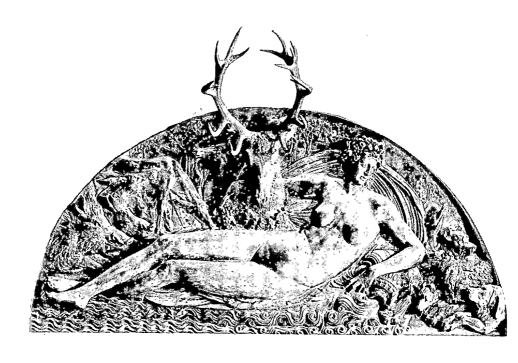

avvoltala in bellissimi panni bianchi, andò cheta da Giovanni, mio padre, e disse:

—Io vi porto un bel presente, il quale voi non vi aspettavate.

Mio padre, che era filosofo, stava passeggiando e disse:

—Quello che Dio mi dà, sempre m'è caro.

E, scoperti i panni, vide con i propri occhi l'inaspettato figliuolo maschio. Congiunte le vecchie palme, alzò gli occhi a Dio, e disse:

—Signore, io ti ringrazio con tutto il mio cuore. Questo m'è molto caro, e sia il Benvenuto.

Tutte le persone che erano lì gli domandarono che nome gli si dovesse dare. Giovanni non rispose altro che:

—Egli sia il Benvenuto.

E avendo tutti così deciso, il santo battesimo mi diede tale nome e così io vo vivendo con la grazia di Dio.

From: *La vita di Benvenuto Cellini scritta da lui medesimo:* Libro I, capitolo I.

filosofo *of a philosophical disposition*

il Benvenuto *Welcome*

5

1

1

IL SEICENTO

Characteristics of the Century

When the 17th century dawned, the political life of Italy was in the grip of her Spanish dominators; the free expression of Italian thought was rigidly curtailed by the Tribunal of the Holy Inquisition, and the multiform spirit of the Renaissance was already spent. Fear, silence, uncertainty and conformism shackled spiritual and intellectual life.

New outlets had to be found, of course, through which the Italian genius might flow and express itself without being either obstructed by limitation of thought or crushed by the towering achievements of the Renaissance. As it happened, one outlet was found for the figurative arts and poetry, and others opened up for those branches of the arts and fields of human knowledge —such as music, drama, and experimental science—which had been little exploited up to that time.

Whereas the artists of the Renaissance, as exemplified by Michelangelo, had attained perfect harmony between form and content, the artists of the *Seicento* found the classical style too static and austere. While they sought a

184

new and freer style, they continued to imitate Michelangelo, the great master, whose spell they could not throw off. But in so doing they lost sight of content and were carried away by their concern with form. Some of the artists of the early transitional period, who succeeded in developing and controlling form, produced works of remarkable originality, beauty and dignity. The majority, however, seemed to find in the new freedom from rigid classic rules a release for their pent-up inspiration, pursued to extremes their love of grandiose and restless forms, and by allowing this to become a fetish ended by losing all contact with life and reality.

The new style was called baroque. Rome was its center. Its development was encouraged by the Spanish rulers who loved pomp and grandeur; by the papacy which expected from artists a glamorous celebration and interpretation of the victories won over the Reformation; and by a frivolous and corrupt nobility that demanded excessive luxury and embellishments, luster and magnificence in their palaces, festivals and dress. The baroque spread throughout Europe and South America, affected all artistic manifestations, and became the acknowledged fashion of the *Seicento*, assuming the general name of *Secentismo*.

In architecture and sculpture *Secentismo* was characterized by freedom of design and movement, by a strong propensity for rich decoration, external beauty, effects and illusions, by a tendency toward the extravagant, the awesome and often the absurd which, as a rule, covered up lack of content and originality, and paucity of spiritual and intellectual motivation. In the disorderly search for the new, the plastic arts assumed the characteristics of painting, and painting those of the plastic arts. The outstanding representative of the best in Italian baroque art was Gian Lorenzo Bernini (1598–1680) who gave to Rome the solemn magnificence of her churches, palaces, monuments and statues and enriched her with the sumptuous gaiety of innumerable fountains whose rippling, cascading waters are one of the Eternal City's chief delights.

Strong resistance to the extravagant search for the new was put up by the major painters of the century, particularly by the Bolognese School under Ludovico Carracci (1555-1619) and his two cousins, Agostino and Annibale, whose eclecticism tried to combine and express the best characteristics of Michelangelo, Raphael and the Venetian masters. Their most renowned disciples were: Guido Reni (1575-1642), whose works are impressive for their luminosity and fantasy; Domenichino (1581-1641), painter of dramatic religious subjects and frescoer of Roman churches, palaces and villas; and Guercino (1591-1666), who painted in flamboyant colors vigorous figures emerging from deepest obscurity. A place of his own is occupied by Caravaggio (1575-1610), the tormented, impulsive and aggressive master of the chiaroscuro, whose influence was felt by Ribera, Velazquez and Rembrandt, and whose forceful and plebeian subjects make him a forerunner of realism in painting.

The baroque as a literary style was called "marinismo" after its supreme exponent, Giambattista Marino (1569–1625), a lascivious and adventurous poet born in Naples, twice imprisoned. Endowed with a facile and abundant poetic vein, Marino achieved renown while still in his twenties for his *Canzone dei baci*. Later, with the publication of woodland sonnets, madrigals and mythological idylls, his fame spread to the courts of Europe and he became the protégé of cardinals, princes and queens. His major work, commissioned by Maria de' Medici, Queen of France, is *Adone*, a mythological poem celebrating the love of Venus for Adonis, thwarted by the jealousy of Mars.

Totaling no less than 50,000 verses, the *Adone* is replete with endless descriptions, episodes and digressions of the most disparate nature, the whole interspersed with metaphors, antitheses, puns and hyperboles, often scintillating with color and imagery and couched in voluptuous and melodious verse. However, this extravagant style was not peculiar to Italy but manifested itself under different names in other literatures: In England it was called "Euphuism," in France "Préciosité" and in Spain "Gongorism." According to Marino, the object of the poet must be to astonish the reader, to captivate and "tickle" his ear with bizarre novelties. Words were no longer chosen or used for their content or meaning but for the musical effects they might produce. To charm the senses, especially the ear and the eye, at the expense of mind and soul, seems to have been the guiding principle of the *marinisti* poets and baroque artists.

This phenomenon may better be understood if we review briefly the slow birth and development of music, which had been almost choked by the rapid and vigorous growth of its sister arts. During the first part of the 11th century, Guido d'Arezzo, as we have seen, conceived the solmization syllables on which modern musical annotations were later based; in the early 13th century, the *ars nova*, in Florence, originated secular music; in 1480, Poliziano's *Orfeo* demonstrated the irresistible power of music and, in 1498, Ottaviano dei Petrucci, a Venetian printer, invented the printing of music

ALINARI

by movable steel type. By the beginning of the 16th century, under the influence of Flemish composers, Venice, Rome and Naples had already established, each with a characteristic style, their own schools of music which soon became national and universal. Once the figurative arts had reached their apogée, Italian music developed rapidly. Palestrina (1524?-1594), recognized as the first great Catholic musician, reformed sacred music and brought vocal polyphony to heights of beauty never since equaled. Vincenzo Galilei (1533–1591), father of Galileo, a musician, composer and mathematician, published his *Dialogo della musica antica e moderna* (1581), the first important contribution to the foundation of modern music; and the *Camerata fiorentina*-introduced musical drama in October 1600, with the first performance in the Pitti-Palace of Ottavio Rinuccini's *Dafne* which had been set to music by Jacopo Peri, and shortly thereafter with *Euridice* by the same composer on a text by Ottavio Rinuccini and Giulio Caccini. This new interest in music stimulated the invention and development of such new musical instruments as the viola da gamba, the violoncello and the violin which were brought to unsurpassed perfection in Cremona by the Amatis, the Guarnieris, and particularly by Antonio Stradivari (1644–1737). To these new instruments Bartolomeo Cristofori added in 1709 the first pianoforte ever built and which he had developed from the Venetian *gravicembalo* (spinet).

By the beginning of the 17th century, music becomes a new vehicle of expression for man's innermost emotions and one of mankind's greatest joys and consolations. The delirious fervor it aroused inspired an ever increasing number of composers and musicians and a prodigious musical production. Claudio Monteverdi (1547–1643), leader of the Venetian School, becomes

188

the creator of modern music and his *Orfeo*, presented in Mantua on February 6, 1607, marks the beginning of modern opera; Venice builds the first public opera house in the world, the San Cassian theater (1637); Gerolamo Frescobaldi (1583–1643) excels among the madrigalists and organists; Giacomo Carissimi (1605–1674), reformer of modern music, sets the style of the oratorio; Arcangelo Corelli (1653–1713) composes instrumental music and establishes a definite form and style for the concerto grosso; lastly, Alessandro Scarlatti (1660–1725), called the father of modern Italian opera, gives permanent form to the melodrama and founds the Neapolitan school whose influence was left in all European theaters for centuries.

The literati had discovered in the meantime that their own language, thanks to its structure, was extraordinarily musical. Small wonder, therefore, that Marino's poetry is impregnated with music.

Thus, music not only takes the lead in the Seicento, subjugating the other arts, but inspires poetry, painting and even sculpture and becomes the most original and powerful expression of Italian artistic life. Together with the Commedia dell'arte and the experimental method in science, it is one of the three impressive contributions that Italy, in a tragic period of political servitude, made to civilization.

189

ANDERSON

XXI

Galileo Galilei

(*1564–1642*)

While Italian musicians and composers were discovering the harmony of sound, Galileo Galilei, philosopher, astronomer, mathematician and physicist, was discovering the harmony of the universe. Unlike the composers whose works were warmly received and played everywhere, Galileo and his scientific theories were bitterly and mercilessly opposed. The struggles and humiliations which he had to endure during his life in order to uphold freedom of thought constituted a cause célèbre, the interest of which is still alive today. It represented the first major collision between light and darkness, present and past, reason and tradition, science and blind faith.

It was while studying medicine and philosophy at the University of Pisa, his native city, that Galileo developed a passionate interest in mathematics and the physical sciences to which he was to devote his whole life. The incredible precocity of his mind and the absolute independence of thought and judgment expressed in his early writings presaged an inevitable clash with the conformism of his times. He accepted experimentation and careful reflection as the criteria of truth. He also believed that the human mind, being created by God, should not submit basely to the arbitrary whims of others, because when men without competence are given authority to judge the experts and to treat them with reckless irresponsibility, there can be no other outcome than the ruin of the nation and the subversion of the state.

190

It is said that he discovered the isochronism of the pendulum while observing the oscillations of a lamp in the Cathedral of Pisa. At the age of 22 he published his first scientific work, *La bilancetta,* an account of his invention of the hydrostatic balance, and in recognition of its merits he was given a teaching position at the University. Some years later he discovered and demonstrated the correct law of falling bodies by experimenting with two balls of unequal weight which he dropped from the Leaning Tower of Pisa. The success of his scientific discoveries having spread abroad, he was appointed in 1592 professor of mathematics at the University of Padua which was frequented by students from all parts of Europe.

It was here that Galileo became interested in Nicolas Copernicus (1473–1543), whose treatise on the *Revolutions of the Celestial Orbs* (1543) suggested that the theories of Aristotle and Ptolemy, which claimed that the earth was at the center of the universe and that the heavens revolved around it, might prove to be an optical illusion if it could be proved that the sun occupied the center of the universe and that the earth, with all the other planets, revolved around it. No one for about a half a century had given serious thought to the theory of Copernicus except Galileo who, having formulated a new natural philosophy based on mathematics, found it very reasonable. But it remained to be proved. Galileo had been working to this end for some twenty-five years when, in 1610, he finished the construction of his first astronomical telescope. This wondrous invention made it possible for him to conduct unexpected and unprecedented astronomical observations which convinced him that Copernicus was right: the sun and not the earth was the center of the universe; the earth moved and not the sun. What philosophers and laymen had believed for centuries to be the truth was nothing more than an optical illusion.

The announcement of the discovery shook to their very foundations Aristotle's natural philosophy and Ptolemy's astronomical system. Galileo became the target of bitter denunciations on the part of professional scholars and ecclesiastics, while writers, artists, foreign scholars and public opinion praised him. Galileo's enemies declared his doctrine subversive, contrary to the Scripture and inspired by the Devil. Is it not said in the Holy Scripture, they claimed, that Joshua commanded the sun to stand still over Gideon: "And the Sun stayed in the midst of heaven, and hastened not to go down about a whole day"? (*Joshua* 10, XII–XIV.) Galileo held that part of the Scripture had to be interpreted figuratively and not to the letter; that the Scripture does not teach us about nature but only about supernatural things; "it teaches us how to go to heaven, not how the heavens go." He continued with his research, publications and new discoveries until 1615 when, having been denounced to the Holy Inquisition, he went to Rome in the hope of proving his theories and securing the favor of the Pope. He was well received. Nonetheless, one year later, the Congregation of the Index decreed the prohibition of the Copernican system and warned Galileo not "to hold, teach or defend" such a doctrine thereafter. Disheartened, he went to Florence where he had been appointed mathematician and philosopher to the Grand Duke of Tuscany, resumed his work in physics and did his best to be circumspect.

In 1623, he published *Il Saggiatore* (The Precision Scale), a masterpiece in the philosophy of science, and in 1630, finished his *Dialogo dei due massimi sistemi del mondo, tolemaico e copernicano*, which, after several revisions, received the necessary imprimatur of the Church, and appeared in print in 1632. The *Dialogo* consists of a lively, astute and profound discussion between two learned gentlemen on one side, and a literal-minded Aristotelian professor, aptly named Simplicio, on the other. They hypothetically attack and defend the Ptolemaic and Copernican systems. By the time the discussion ends, the hapless Simplicio is left with no ground to stand on and the reader recognizes easily the merits and superiority of the Copernican system. By resorting to this device, Galileo thought that he might be able to avoid being accused of holding, teaching or defending the theories of Copernicus. To all appearances he had complied with the order, but in fact, i.e., by hypothetically defending Copernicus, he had disregarded it.

The *Dialogo* was immensely successful. Unfortunately, it set Galileo's enemies against him once again. They accused his book of being a compelling and underhanded vindication of the Copernican system. They succeeded in having it banned and Galileo, now seventy years old, was ordered to appear in Rome before the Tribunal of the Holy Inquisition. He was tried and, on June 22, 1633, was ordered to read aloud, on his knees, and sign the following abjuration:

"I, Galileo, son of the late Vincenzo, Florentine, aged seventy years . . . having been pronounced by the Holy Office to be vehemently suspected of heresy, that is to say, of having held and believed that the Sun is the center of the World and immovable and that the Earth is not its center and moves

. . . with sincere heart and unfeigned faith, I abjure, curse and detest the aforesaid errors and heresies . . . and I swear that in the future I will never again say or assert verbally or in writing, anything that might furnish occasion for a similar suspicion regarding me; but should I know any heretic or person suspected of heresy, I will denounce him to the Holy Office . . ."*

It is said that Galileo, having signed his abjuration, murmured: "Eppur si muove!" (Nevertheless, it moves!)

Born in a century when the scientist was forced to believe in what he could not accept and was constrained to resort to double truths and mental reservations to be able to conduct his work, Galileo was compelled to bend in order not to be broken. It did not matter much what his enemies did to him. He knew that he was right: the earth did move and would continue to move. The important thing was for his ideas to continue to circulate and attract the attention of the scientific world. Nothing but the dissemination of scientific truth would break down the ecclesiastical and academic barriers set up against free and unfettered scientific thought.

The Holy Office condemned Galileo to prison, but his sentence was commuted to perpetual house arrest in his little villa at Arcetri outside Florence. It was there that he finished the *Discorsi sopra due Nuove Scienze*, his major contribution to physics. Smuggled out of Italy by a prince of the Medici family, this treatise was published in Holland in 1638. Thereafter, the astronomer who, to use the words of Ugo Foscolo,

> . . . . vide
> Sotto l'etereo padiglion rotarsi
> Più mondi, e il sole irradiarli immoto,

became totally blind. Consumed by overwhelming sadness and melancholy, he died on January 8, 1642, still a prisoner. It was not until 1737 that his body was allowed to find final rest in the Church of Santa Croce in Florence.

In 1893, the Church, through the Encyclical of Leo XIII, *Providentissimus Deus*, adopted Galileo's views that certain parts of the Holy Scripture may be given a figurative interpretation.

Creator of the experimental method and founder of modern physical science, Galileo gave mathematical formulations to many physical laws. In rehabilitating the science of astronomy and proving that the sun is the center of our universe and immovable with relation to it, he enlarged immeasurably man's vision and concept of the world he lives in and pointed out the place it occupies in the cosmos. Just as Columbus and Vespucci broadened man's knowledge of the earth, so did Galileo broaden his knowledge of the universe.

* From: *The Crime of Galileo*, by Giorgio de Santillana, page 312. The University of Chicago Press, 1955.

IL SAGGIATORE

L'autorità e l'esperienza

[If Machiavelli is the master of political prose, then Galileo is the master of Italian scientific prose. His style is lucid, simple and precise. It has both flexibility and elegance. Words and ideas form a cohesive entity. The subject matter is often lightened and brightened by topical anecdotes and humorous remarks. In polemical writings his style becomes tense; it erupts with the heat of passion and conviction, and lashes out with withering irony and even sarcasm. However, when he describes natural phenomena his prose is suffused with a sense of religious wonder and a lyrical ecstasy which makes it almost mystical scientific poetry.

The two chapters which we have culled from *Il Saggiatore* offer a clear idea of Galileo's polemic and scientific style. But to fully enjoy his pressing argumentations it is essential to have a brief background to the controversy.

In 1618, three comets made their appearance. Father Orazio Grassi, a member of the Jesuit Order, professor of mathematics and a bitter opponent of Galileo, published an essay on the nature and movements of the comets, which contained, besides, an indirect attack on Galileo's doctrine. One year later, Mario Guiducci, one of Galileo's disciples, wrote another essay confuting Padre Grassi's theories. The latter, convinced that Galileo was the real author of the confutation, published under the pseudonym of Lotario Sarsi a Latin dissertation entitled *Libra Astronomica* (The Astronomic Scale) in which he assailed Galileo, the experimental method and the Copernican System.

It was obvious that Padre Grassi was taking advantage of the ecclesiastical injunction of 1616 which forbade Galileo "to hold, teach or defend" the Copernican system, to provoke him without injury to himself. Galileo, nevertheless, felt duty-bound to step forward and vindicate himself and the honor of science. Unmindful of possible consequences, he published in 1623, *Il Saggiatore*, a masterpiece of polemic prose.

One of the points brought forward by Padre Grassi to corroborate his views on the nature of comets was that the friction of the air can ignite and destroy a body, such as an arrow or a cannon ball. To prove his assertion he adduced besides the authority of Aristotle, that of Ovid, Lucan, Lucretius, Statius and Virgil, to mention but a few, who, according to him, were trustworthy even on natural and philosophical questions.

In the following passage Galileo, while he atomizes his opponent's arguments, demonstrates why the scientist must not believe the ancients

IL SAGGIATORE

Nel quale
Con bilancia esquisita e giusta
si ponderano le cose contenute
nella

LIBRA ASTRONOMICA E FILOSOFICA
DI LOTARIO SARSI SIGENSANO
Scritto in forma di lettera

All'Ill.mo et Reuer.mo Mons. D.

VIRGINIO CESARINI

Acc.º Linceo M.º di Camera di N.S.

Dal Sig.

GALILEO GALILEI

Acc.º Linceo Nobile Fiorentino
Filosofo e Matematico Primario
del
Ser.mo Gran Duca di Toscana.

FILOSOFIA
NATVRALE

MATEMATICA

IN ROMA. M.DC.XXIII.
Appresso Giacomo Mascardi.

195

blindly if their theories prove to be false when subjected to our reasoning power and to scientific experimentation. Moreover, he asserts his unwavering faith in the experimental method as against authority and tradition.]

esperienza *experiment*

. . . Ora passiamo a esaminare l'esperienza della freccia tirata con l'arco, e della palla di

piombo *lead*
per *through*

piombo tirata col cannone, le quali si liquefanno per l'aria; esperienze confermate con l'autorità di Aristotile, di molti grandi poeti e di altri filosofi 5 e storici . . .

ci siamo risi . . . dell' *have laughed and poked fun at the*
e burlati dell' *and poked fun at the*

Che io o il signor Mario Guiducci ci siamo risi e burlati dell'esperienza narrata da Aristotile, è falsissimo, non essendo nel libro del signor Mario la minima parola di derisione. In esso c'è solamente 10 scritto che noi non crediamo che una freccia fredda tirata con l'arco s'infuochi, anzi crediamo che tirandola infocata si raffredderebbe più presto che tenendola ferma; e questo non è schernire, ma dire semplicemente il suo concetto. A quello poi che il 15 signor Sarsi soggiunge, cioè non esser noi riusciti a dimostrare falsa l'esperienza riferita da Aristotile, perchè non solo Aristotile, ma moltissimi altri grandi uomini hanno creduto e scritto la stessa cosa, rispondo che, se per dimostrare falso quello 20 che ha detto Aristotile è necessario far sì che gli altri grandi uomini non l'abbiano creduto nè scritto, nè io nè il signor Mario nè tutto il mondo insieme lo potranno mai dimostrare falso, perchè non sarà mai possibile far sì che quelli che l'hanno 25 scritto e creduto non l'abbiano creduto e scritto. Ma mi pare cosa assai strana che, per giudicare un fatto reale si voglia preferire le attestazioni di uomini a ciò che mostra l'esperienza. Il portare tanti testimoni, signor Sarsi, non serve a niente, 30 perchè noi non abbiamo mai negato che molti abbiano scritto e creduto tale cosa, ma abbiamo detto che tale cosa è falsa.

s'infuochi *ignites*

infocata *red-hot*
si raffredderebbe *it would become cold*
schernire *scoffing*
il suo concetto *one's opinion*
poi *moreover*
riusciti *succeeded*
dimostrare falsa *to prove false*

far sì *to show*

attestazioni *affirmations*

In quanto all' *As regards the*

In quanto all'autorità, per provare che la cosa sia vera o non vera, tanto vale la vostra sola quanto 35

tanto vale la vostra sola quanto *yours alone is worth as much as*

quella di cento persone insieme. Voi opponete l'autorità di molti poeti alle esperienze che noi produciamo. Io rispondo e dico: che se quei poeti fossero presenti alle nostre esperienze, cambierebbero opinione, e senza difficoltà direbbero di avere scritto iperbolicamente, e confesserebbero di essersi ingannati. Ma poichè non è possibile di avere i poeti presenti, noi possiamo trovare facilmente arcieri e scagliatori. Provate voi, se citando loro tutte queste autorità vi riesce a dar loro tanta forza che le frecce e le palle tirate da loro si infuochino e si liquefacciano per aria; e così capirete quanto influsso eserciti la forza delle umane autorità sopra gli effetti della natura, la quale rimane sorda e inesorabile ai nostri vani desideri . . .

    Io non posso non meravigliarmi che il Sarsi voglia persistere a provarmi per via di testimoni quello che io posso ogni ora vedere per via di esperienze. I testimoni si esaminano nelle cose dubbie, passate e non permanenti, e non in quelle che sono in fatto e presenti. Così è necessario che il giudice cerchi sapere per via di testimoni se è vero che ieri notte Pietro ferisse Giovanni, e non se Giovanni sia ferito, poichè ciò lui lo può ancora vedere e può accertarsene da sè. Ma dico inoltre che anche nelle conclusioni, delle quali non si potesse venire in cognizione se non per via di ragionamento, io stimerei meno l'attestazione dei molti che quella dei pochi, essendo sicuro che il numero di quelli che nelle cose difficili ragionano bene, è assai minore del numero di quelli che ragionano male . . .

    Se il Sarsi vuole che io creda a Suida, secondo cui i Babilonesi cocessero le uova facendole girare velocemente nella fionda, io lo crederò; ma dirò che la causa di tale effetto è lontanissima da quella che gli viene attribuita, e per trovare la vera causa di tale effetto io ragionerò così. Se a noi non riesce ottenere un effetto che ad altri, un'altra volta, è riuscito, vuol dire che a noi nel nostro esperimento manca ciò che fu causa della riuscita di questo effetto. Quindi non mancando a noi altro che una cosa sola, questa sola cosa è la vera causa. Ora a noi non mancano uova, nè fionde, nè uomini

Notes (right column):

di essersi ingannati *that they erred*

arcieri e scagliatori *bowmen and artillery-men*
citando *by quoting*
vi . . . loro *you succeed in giving them*

Io non posso non *I can't but*
per via *by means*

non permanenti *no longer existing*
in fatto *actually existing*

delle quali non si potesse venire in cognizione se non *about which one could obtain no knowledge except*

Suida (*Greek encyclopedist, 10th century, A.D.*)
facendole girare *by whirling them*
fionda *sling*

gli viene attribuita *is attributed to it*
a noi non riesce *we do not succeed*

riuscita *success*

eppure *and yet*

perchè *since*
di *from*
dunque *from it follows that*
attrizione *friction*
nel correr la posta *when traveling by stage-coach*
gli porti alla faccia *is felt by his face through*
mutamento *changing*

in sè stesso prova *can verify in his own person*

Seneca (*Roman philosopher, 1st century, A.D.*)

buona creanza *politeness*

io venga quasi a dar una mentita a *I virtually give the lie to*

detti *words*

sconoscenti *discourteous*

voglia posporre *should deliberately set less value on*
alle *than on the*
alla cieca e balordamente *blindly and blunderingly*
far serva *enslave*
a chi *to another who*

robusti che le girino; eppure le uova non si cuociono, anzi se fosser calde si raffredderebbero più presto. E perchè non ci manca altro che esser di Babilonia, dunque l'esser Babilonesi è la causa del cuocersi le uova e non l'attrizione dell'aria; che è quello che io volevo provare. È possibile che il Sarsi, nel correr la posta, non abbia osservato quanta freschezza gli porti alla faccia quel continuo mutamento di aria? Se egli l'ha sentito, vorrà egli credere più le cose di duemila anni fa accadute in Babilonia e riferite da altri, che le presenti le quali egli in sè stesso prova? . . .

All'invito che mi fa il Sarsi ad ascoltare attentamente Seneca, e alla domanda che egli poi mi fa, se si poteva dir una cosa più chiaramente e più sottilmente, io sono completamente d'accordo con lui, e confermo, che non si poteva nè più sottilmente nè più chiaramente dire una bugia. Ma non vorrei che egli mi costringesse, come egli cerca di fare, a credere per ragione di buona creanza, quel che io reputo falso, così che, negandolo, io venga quasi a dar una mentita a uomini che sono il fior dei letterati; perchè io penso che loro credesser di dire il vero, e così la loro bugia non è disonorevole. Mentre il Sarsi dice che egli non vuole essere uno di quelli che facciano un tale affronto, cioè di contraddire ad uomini sapienti e di non credere ai loro detti; io dico, che non voglio essere uno di quelli così sconoscenti ed ingrati verso la Natura e Dio, i quali, avendomi dato senso e ragione, io voglia posporre sì gran doni alle fallacie di un uomo, e alla cieca e balordamente credere ciò che io sento dire, e far serva la libertà del mio intelletto a chi può errare così bene come me.

Cap. 44, 45.

DIALOGO DEI MASSIMI SISTEMI

La mirabile potenza dell'ingegno umano

[During the Renaissance it was common practice to glorify man and the divine power of his mind. We have seen Leonardo da Vinci compare the painter to a god. In this passage from the *Dialogo dei massimi sistemi*, Galileo meditates with great humility and awe on the many, varied and wondrous inventions devised by man's intellect and, above all, on the formulation of the alphabet which drives home to him how small is his own store of knowledge. Not only is he unable to contribute new inventions, but he cannot master those which have preceded him. Whereupon, confused with wonderment and goaded by despair, he confesses his inadequacy.]

considerato fra me e me *wondered*
acutezza *keenness*
ingegno *mind*

come *as*
sapere *knowledge*
dallo sperare *from promising me*
dallo stupore *with wonder*

Quando sapresti tu levare il soverchio *Would you ever be able to remove the excess*
pezzo *block*
mescolare *mix*
distendere *spread*
tela *canvass*

udito *ear*
finire di stupirmi *cease being amazed*

di quanta *with what*

quale *what*

eminenza *sublimity*
s'immaginò di trovare il modo di *conceived the means of*
più reconditi *most hidden*
distante *separated*
per *by*

nè saranno se non di qua a *nor will be born for another*

col *by*
caratteruzzi *little letters*
Sia questo il sigillo *Let this be the seal*

Molte volte io ho considerato fra me e me quanto grande sia l'acutezza dell'ingegno umano; e, se dopo aver pensato alle tante e tanto meravigliose invenzioni fatte dagli uomini nelle arti come nelle lettere, rifletto sopra il mio sapere, mi 5 accorgo quanto esso sia lontano dallo sperare non solo di fare altre invenzioni, ma di conoscere quelle già fatte, allora, confuso dallo stupore e afflitto dalla disperazione, mi sento quasi infelice.

Se io guardo una statua eccellente, dico a me 10 stesso: Quando sapresti tu levare il soverchio da un pezzo di marmo, e scoprire sì bella figura, che vi era nascosta? Quando sapresti tu mescolare e distendere sopra una tela, o parete, colori diversi, e con essi rappresentare tutti gli oggetti visibili, come 15 un Michelangelo, un Raffaello, un Tiziano?

Se io guardo quello che gli uomini hanno inventato nel dividere gl'intervalli musicali, e nello stabilire regole per poterle adoperare con mirabile diletto dell'udito, quando potrei io finire di stu- 20 pirmi? Che dirò poi di tanti e sì diversi strumenti musicali?

La lettura dei poeti di quanta meraviglia riempe la mente di colui il quale considera attentamente l'invenzione dei concetti e il loro significato? 25

Ma sopra tutte le invenzioni stupende, quale eminenza di mente ebbe colui il quale s'immaginò di trovare il modo di comunicare i suoi più reconditi pensieri a qualsiasi persona, benchè distante per lunghissimo intervallo di luogo e di tempo? 30 poter parlare con quelli che sono nelle Indie; poter parlare a quelli che non sono ancora nati, nè saranno se non di qua a mille o diecimila anni? e con quale facilità? e far tutto ciò col mettere insieme venti caratteruzzi sopra una carta. Sia questo il 35 sigillo di tutte le ammirevoli invenzioni umane!

Giornata prima.

XXII
La Commedia
dell'Arte

comic plays — off the cuff; impromptu
scenario — basic plot

Another unique manifestation of Italian art which flourished during the
Seicento and spread rapidly beyond the Alps, was the *Commedia dell'Arte*, also
called *a soggetto* or *improvvisa*.

This dramatic form had first appeared in the middle of the 16th century
as an outgrowth of both the *Rappresentazione sacra* and the literary theater
largely as a popular reaction to the rigid, dry plays of classical imitation
which, by nature an admixture of ancient and modern forms, were neither
old nor new and were generally divorced from the realities of contemporary
life. This new genre was called *Commedia dell'Arte* because the comedies,
instead of being written by a playwright, were conceived, directed and acted
by the *artisti*, the actors themselves, who lived for their art.

For the first time in Europe, actors organized into traveling companies
or troupes, each composed of about ten comedians, seven men and three
women. For the first time, women appeared on the stage to play female
parts. There was nothing to memorize, since there was no script. Nothing
was written except the scenario, also called *soggetto* (plot) or *canovaccio* (canvas).

201

Signor Rahponelli   Signor Cascaretti

The *canovaccio*, divided into acts, outlined the various roles and indicated entrances and exits. Each company had a director or *corago* with whom the actors would meet before the performance to discuss, interpret and agree on the development of the *canovaccio*.

Besides the *canovaccio*, each actor had a kind of commonplace book which listed phrases, quotations and *lazzi* (jokes) that he kept ready in the fertile storehouse of his memory and could adapt at any moment to an infinite variety of plays. Once on stage, each actor, adjusting himself to the level and tastes of the audience, would weave the dialogue extemporaneously on the canvas, making his words and actions dovetail swiftly and perfectly with those of the other actors, thus creating the impression that the event acted was actually happening at that very moment on stage. Action, mimicry and diction were the very key of the success and popularity of the *Commedia dell'Arte*.

Since the dialogue changed with each performance, rich imagination, keen wit, quick invention and extraordinary powers of expression were required of the player. With continuing success, the plays became more spectacular and were interspersed with dancing, music and other forms of entertainment. The actor was therefore called upon to be dancer, singer, rhymester, gymnast and acrobat. This special type of acting thus gradually evolved into an art and profession requiring so many skills that it was always easier to find ten actors for a regular play than one for an impromptu comedy.

The *Commedia dell'Arte* originally addressed itself to the lower and middle classes for whom it had great appeal. It endeavored to mirror everyday public and private life, stressing the ridiculous, the unusual and the absurd. It often overstepped bounds and became ludicrous and at times, even obscene. The sets were at first simple and usually represented a public square, a street and two houses facing each other. Interior scenes were purposely excluded because they were considered unrealistic. Who has ever seen, they would say,

Signor Bambinelli

Signor Mascarillo

a room with only three walls? Through close observation and portraiture of local people, their mores and costumes, the *Commedia dell'Arte* developed and diffused throughout Italy a gallery of characters that typified the idiosyncrasies of certain Italian regions and cities. As time went on, actors who specialized in the personification of one of these characters, adopted a special mask and costume for each one. It was thus that Italian masks were born, and that Lombardy brought forth Arlecchino, Venice Pantalone and Corallina, Bologna the Dottore and Colombina, Tuscany Capitan Spaventa and Stenterello, Rome Pasquariello, Naples Tartaglia, Scaramuccia and Pulcinella, etc. Some of these masks, and others like Scapino, Pagliaccio (the Clown), Pedrolino (Pierrot), Burattino (Marionette), after undergoing a number of transformations, became both national and international characters which can still be seen in Elizabethan plays, in the marionette theater, in traditional puppet shows, or in the circus.

With the development of stage technique and the affirmation of the baroque towards the middle of the *Seicento*, the figurative arts began to play a role of increasing importance in the production of impromptu comedies. Sets became richer, more complex, more elaborate and spectacular. Regular tragedies, comedies and pastoral dramas were reduced to impromptu plays. Performances attained great artistic heights and the *Commedia dell'Arte* achieved its peak.

For over two centuries, beginning in 1527, when the first Italian company under the direction of Drusiano Martinelli went to play in England, to 1742, when Antonio Sacchi took his company on a three-year tour of Russia and some of the most celebrated Italian companies, such as Calderoni's, Ricciboni's, I Gelosi, I Confidenti, Gli Accesi and I Fedeli toured Europe, the *Commedia dell'Arte* ruled supreme. When a foreign audience failed to understand Italian, the actors resorted, with incredible success, to mimicry and pantomime. After 1660, the Italian companies performed more or less permanently in French and in Italian at the Hôtel de Bourbon or at the Palais Royal in Paris until they took over the Opéra Comique in 1762 and assumed its name.

Just as the Italian *novella* of the previous centuries had exercised widespread influence on European literature, the *Commedia dell'Arte* is similarly responsible for the development of the modern European theater to which it contributed the art of acting, the elaboration of stage technique, the organization of permanent professional companies of players, and the concurrence of Italian music and culture. It inspired some of the greatest of dramatists: Shakespeare, Molière, Lope de Vega and Goldoni. During the second half of the 18th century, following Goldoni's reform of the Italian theater, the *Commedia dell'Arte* slowly declined and left its place to the modern Italian theater, to the melodrama and to the opera, most particularly, to the opera buffa.

1. Del modo di concertare un soggetto

[Andrea Perrucci (1651–1704), librettist and playwright, also wrote a rare treatise on the technique of impromptu plays (*Dell'Arte rappresentativa, premeditata e all'improvviso*. Napoli, Muzio, 1699). In the following excerpt he gives a graphic idea of how to direct an impromptu play.]

corago *choragus (director)*	Il corago, guida, maestro o più pratico di
concertare il soggetto *direct the impromptu play*	conversazione deve concertare il soggetto prima che si reciti, affinchè si sappia da tutti gli attori il contenuto della commedia, dove devono terminare
battute *lines*	le battute e dove si possa introdurre qualche 5
arguzia *witticism*	arguzia o lazzo nuovo. L'ufficio, dunque, di chi
lazzo *joke*	
concerta *directs*	concerta non è solo di leggere il soggetto, ma di spiegare: i personaggi con i nomi e con le loro
qualità *characteristics*	qualità, l'argomento della commedia, il luogo dove
si recita *it is staged*	si recita, le case; chiarire i lazzi e tutte le altre 10 piccole cose necessarie, avendo anche cura di tutte quelle cose indispensabili per la commedia, come
stili *stilettos*	lettere, borse, stili, ed altro notato nella fine del
notato *listed*	soggetto . . .
	Stiano attenti gli attori sopratutto a non 15 sbagliare il paese dove si recita, da dove si viene, e per qual fine, e tengano bene in mente i nomi propri, essendo un errore imperdonabile che uno dica di essere in Roma ed un altro in Napoli;

204

dimenticarsi il padre il nome del figlio, l'innamorato
quello dell'innamorata . . .

Così anche si faccia attenzione nella distribu-
zione delle case, affinchè ognuno sappia la casa sua,
5 essendo ridicolo che uno bussasse o entrasse, invece   bussasse *should knock*
che nella casa sua, in quella d'altri. . . Qualche
errore di memoria o di lingua si può perdonare,
perchè la memoria è una trappola dove sono caduti   trappola *trap*
gli uomini più grandi, la lingua non è infallibile,
10 ma errori di case, di nomi, e di scene vuote non   scene vuote *empty stage*
sono perdonabili . . .

Avendo gli attori ascoltato ciò che hanno da
fare nell'uscire come nel rappresentare e terminare   nell'uscire *in coming on or*
la scena, potranno andare a ripetere con i loro   *going off stage*
15 compagni le scene e introdurvi d'accordo qualche
nuovo lazzo, o qualche cosa a capriccio. Si procuri   a capriccio *ad lib (ad libitum)*
però di non uscire troppo dal soggetto, affinchè   uscire *to stray*
l'udienza non perda il filo dell'intreccio, e l'attore   filo *thread*
non dimentichi il soggetto, altrimenti la commedia   intreccio *plot*
20 diventa un caos di confusione . . . Stiano tutti i
personaggi in circolo a sentire assieme, non si fidino
di sapere a memoria o di avere altre volte recitata
quella commedia, perchè potrebbe essere che sia
diretta diversamente da diversi coraghi nell'in-
25 treccio e che i nomi e i luoghi siano anche diversi. . .

Udito il soggetto, pensino gli attori di aggiun-
gervi qualche cosa preparata apposta per quella
commedia avendo cura di saperla collocare di
modo che sembri naturale . . .

30 Quando a qualche scena segue la notte, procuri chi è nella scena precedente d'accennarlo
dicendo: "Già si fa notte" o, come dice Virgilio:

Cadunt altis de montibus umbrae . . .   Cadunt altis de montibus
  umbrae *The shadows are fall-*
Se vi saranno due notti (benchè ciò venga   *ing from the high mountains*
35 proibito da Aristotile) . . . si accenni dove fa giorno,   dove fa *when it is*
dove notte, dove torni giorno e dove torni notte,
affinchè l'uditore possa capirlo. . . Chi recita non   uditore *spectator*
si serva per leggere lettere o altro dei lumi posti   altro *something else*
per illuminare il teatro, perchè quelli è come se   lumi *lamps*
40 non ci fossero.

2. Scenario

[About a thousand scenari have been discovered, most of them in Italian, a number in French, others in English and Russian. Since they contain only the skeleton of the plays, they are of little literary significance. They are invaluable, however, as documents for the history of modern drama. We give here the first half of Act I of an old scenario, *Il Dottor Bacchettone* (Doctor Bigot), found and published by Adolfo Bartoli (*Scenari inediti della Commedia dell' Arte*. Firenze, Sansoni, 1880).]

Il Dottor Bacchettone

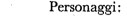

Personaggi:

Florindo, amante di Lucinda.
Silvio, amante di Flaminia.
Flaminia, figlia del Dottore, amante di Silvio.
Lucinda, amante di Florindo.
Corallina, povera, moglie di Trivellino.   5
Ragazza, sua figlia.
Graziano, il Dottore, bacchettone.
Stoppino, suo servo.
Trivellino, marito di Corallina.
Pantalone, padre di Lucinda.   10

Attrezzi *properties*

Attrezzi

argenteria *silverware*

Borsa con monete d'oro; argenteria con altri articoli da mettere nel sacco; la lista degli articoli che il Dottore consegna a Pantalone; tavola e un tavolino coperto con un tappeto rotto; articoli diversi che il ladro vende al Dottore; carte da 15 giuoco.

si finge *is laid*

La scena si finge a Bologna.

Atto primo

paniere *hand basket*
padrone *master*

Stoppino, con dei pezzi di pane in un paniere, esalta la bontà del suo padrone; benedicendo l'ora quando entrò al suo servizio per avere 20 mutato vita; dice che il padrone non parla mai in casa e che sta sempre contemplando; ora gli ha ordinato di distribuire il pane ai poveri. In questo momento arrivano i

Poveri, chiedono il pane; lui lo distribuisce con
 lazzi; alle insistenze di Trivellino, che gli chiede
 qualche cosa, Stoppino va in casa, torna con un
 piatto di farina, glielo dà e parte; Trivellino fa il
 lazzo della farina e tutti partono.   5
Pantalone entra, e dice che sta maritando sua figlia
 con Florindo con dieci mila scudi di dote, ma
 gliene mancano ancora mille; non sa come fare
 a trovarli e non vorrebbe far sapere agli estranei
 i fatti suoi; finalmente decide di chiederli al 10
 Dottore, perchè ha sentito dire che sia uomo
 buono. Picchia alla porta del Dottore, e in
 questo momento s'affaccia
Stoppino, gli domanda che vuole; Pantalone, dopo
 molte cerimonie, dice a Stoppino che gli darà 15
 una mancia se lui lo aiuterà a convincere il
 Dottore di prestargli i mille scudi; in questo
 momento il
Dottore, esce di casa parlando delle cose del mondo,
 della salvezza dell'anima e della bruttezza del 20
 peccato. Vede il servo: si salutano; gli domanda
 che ha fatto; Stoppino risponde che ha dato il
 pane ai poveri; gli dice che ha fatto bene e vuol
 sapere se dopo di essersi levato ha ringraziato il
 cielo; Stoppino dice che prima ha fatto colazione; 25
 lui esclama: "Non si deve pensare prima al
 corpo, ma all'anima!", e da qui in avanti non
 faccia come per il passato: cerchi di non mangiar
 troppo per non peccare. Stoppino promette, e poi
 gli annuncia che Pantalone è lì e desidera parlar- 30
 gli; lui va verso Pantalone facendo cerimonie;
 Pantalone gli chiede scusa; il Dottore sgrida
 Stoppino perchè gli ha fatto commettere un
 peccato di superbia poichè lui doveva essere il
 primo a salutare Pantalone, si scusa; Pantalone 35
 gli dice che uomini come lui non peccano; il
 Dottore si dichiara il maggior peccatore di
 questo mondo, e poi dice che Pantalone è il suo
 vero padrone; Pantalone accetta il complimento
 e gli dice che vorrebbe da lui un favore, ma non 40
 ha il coraggio di chiederglielo; glielo dirà

Stoppino; il Dottore chiama da parte Stoppino; Stoppino gli dice dei mille scudi; il Dottore dice che non li ha; Stoppino riferisce a Pantalone, il quale dice che gli darà un mallevadore; Stoppino lo dice al Dottore; lui: "Ci penserò", ma crede di non poterlo servire; Stoppino lo riferisce a Pantalone; Pantalone dice che oltre al mallevadore, darà in pegno molta argenteria; Stoppino lo dice al Dottore; il quale differisce la risposta, dicendo che vedrà se gli può fare questo servizio; Stoppino propone un interesse del 5 per 100; il Dottore grida che ciò è usura marcia e che non vuol macchiare la sua coscienza, perchè il denaro non può far denaro. Pantalone si scusa, che non sgridi Stoppino, è stato lui, Pantalone, a proporre l'interesse; il Dottore esagera sulla sua coscienza con Pantalone; dice a Stoppino che ringrazi Pantalone e lo licenzia. Pantalone s'inginocchia avanti al Dottore, gli chiede perdono e gli bacia il piede; il Dottore dice che lo vuol servire gratis e che, in quanto al mallevadore, lui non l'ha chiesto, ma lo accetta perchè non si abusi della sua cortesia; in quanto all'argenteria non la vuole in pegno, ma la prende lo stesso, perchè crede che in giorni di matrimonio essa sarà più sicura a casa sua che in quella di Pantalone; dice che si vada in Corte a fare la scritta di scudi mille e duecento; Pantalone dice che ne vuole solo mille; il Dottore che gliene darà solo mille, ma farà la scritta per mille e duecento; Pantalone non capisce; il Dottore finalmente va via, dicendo che i duecento scudi serviranno per un poco d'amorevolezza per il prestito, e partono. . . . . Silvio, forestiero, esce con Florindo, suo amico, al quale dice che era ricco e che il giuoco l'ha ridotto povero; Florindo fa complimenti e gli dice che tutto quello che lui ha è a sua disposizione; Silvio ringrazia e dice che è innamorato di Flaminia, figlia del Dottore; Florindo risponde che Stoppino è la persona che lo può aiutare; che finga di essere un gran barone napoletano.

da parte *aside*

mallevadore *guarantor*
"Ci penserò" *I'll think it over*

in pegno *as collateral*

marcia *downright*
macchiare *to soil*

esagera sulla *breaks into a bombastic speech about*

fare la scritta *draw up the deed*

per un poco d'amorevolezza *as a token of appreciation*

il giuoco . . . povero *gambling has reduced him to poverty*
fa complimenti *ceremoniously offers to help*

209

In questo momento arriva

Stoppino dice di voler andare a casa perchè lo aspetta il padrone che deve mettere insieme il denaro; esagera la bontà del Dottore perchè ha favorito Pantalone senza aver voluto l'interesse. 5 Florindo lo chiama, e gli dice che quel signore è un ricco barone; che è innamorato della figlia del Dottore; Silvio gli offre venti doble. Stoppino chiede un anticipo, e Silvio, perchè non ha denari addosso, promette che glieli darà; Florindo 10 lo rassicura. Stoppino propone diversi modi ridicoli per introdurre Silvio in casa del Dottore a vedere Flaminia; non sono approvati; infine annunzia che ha trovato un modo che egli dice a tutti e due nell'orecchio. Questi, contenti, 15 partono. . .

doble   *gold coins*
anticipo   *advance*
addosso   *with him*

tutti e due   *both*

210

IL SETTECENTO

Characteristics of the Century

The 18th century is the Age of Reason and Enlightenment, with the predominating trends of European thought engaged in introducing a rationalistic approach to religious, political, social and economic problems. This movement, having gathered the dispersed spirit of humanism, was able to develop and spread it by taking advantage of the rapid evolution of philosophy and science to which the naturalistic philosophy of Bernadino Telesio (1509–1588), Giordano Bruno (1548–1600) and Tommasso Campanella (1568–1639) had given great impetus, and for which Galileo had opened the way. Unfortunately, the pursuit of independent speculation had become impossible in Italy. In fact, Bruno, condemned for heterodoxy, was burned alive when he refused to retract; Campanella was shut up for thirty years in prison for political reasons, and Galileo, as has already been seen, was sentenced to confinement for life. Thus Italy, notwithstanding the brilliant contributions of her thinkers, did not become the cradle of the new movement, her intellectual supremacy was lost and modern thought sought refuge in other countries where, in an atmosphere of relative intellectual freedom, Descartes,

212

Newton, Locke, Voltaire, Franklin, Diderot, Kant and Paine were able to continue and complete the philosophical and scientific exploits initiated by the Italians. Under the existing circumstances, Italy's contributions to the new European trends were restricted to the fields of historical and literary criticism and to that of jurisprudence.

In point of fact, Giambattista Vico (1668–1744), a Neapolitan writer of great thought and depth, was the originator of the philosophy of history. Through the application of scientific analysis to the study of history, he developed a cyclical interpretation of the eternal laws which govern the course of humanity called the law of occurrences and recurrences (*Principi di una scienza nuova intorno alla natura delle nazioni*, 1730). According to this theory society develops through three epochs: The Age of the Gods (Theocracy), the Age of Heroes (Aristocracy) and the Age of Men (Democracy). A series of excesses develops within each age, bringing about its end and the beginning of another age. When the cycle is completed, society decays and may either fall into anarchy, reform under a despot, or be assimilated by a younger society, thus giving rise to a new cycle.

The method of historical criticism based on the methodical investigation of every aspect of the past conducted through a scrupulous analysis of existing facts, documents and monuments was initiated by L. A. Muratori (1672–1750), a Milanese priest who figures among the foremost scholars of his age. His major opus, *Rerum Italicorum Scriptores*, is a monumental 28-volume history of the Middle Ages which remains still today a mine of historical data.

Following in the trail blazed by Muratori, Girolamo Tiraboschi (1731–1794), a Jesuit historian and scholar, composed his elaborate and comprehensive 13-volume *Storia della Letteratura Italiana* delineating the manifestations of Italian culture from the Etruscan period to the 18th century.

Among the outstanding economists, jurists and criminologists the most famous and influential was Cesare Beccaria (1738–1794) whose *Dei delitti e delle pene*, a powerful treatise against capital punishment and the inhuman treatment of criminals, paved the way for penal reforms throughout Europe.

The literature of the *Settecento* may be divided into two periods corresponding to each half of the century. The first is dominated by the Accademia dell'Arcadia, founded in Rome in 1690, to counter the artificiality and extravagance of *secentismo* and *marinismo*. This it hoped to bring about through a new approach to poetry inspired by the tranquility of the fields and the humble but serene bucolic existence of shepherds, in imitation of ancient Greek Arcadia where, it was believed, life was spent in making idyllic love and in writing poetry. The Arcadian poet of the *Settecento* was given complete freedom in his choice of poetical forms, but the content of his compositions was rigorously restricted to pastoral themes. It was this disregard for content,

in particular, which vitiated the projected reform of Italian poetry from the very start. Eighteenth century Italy was not the legendary land of Arcadia, nor could its poets live as simple shepherds. Italian society was effete and sterile. Life was an endless minuet. Far from being shepherds, the Italians of the period were *cicisbei* (gentlemen-in-waiting) who fulfilled for the ladies the duties of husbands, lovers and friends: perfumed fops dripping with fine laces, in curled wigs, and silk breeches. The shepherdesses wore elaborate hoop-skirts, over-decorated and complicated headdresses and were subject to periodical migraines and fainting spells. Vanity, frivolity and conventionality were the main characteristics of this society. It was the antithesis of that humble, peaceful pastoral life declaimed by the neo-Arcadian poets, whose poetry, lacking substance, genuine motivation and inspiration, deteriorated into a cold, languid and mellifluous babbling. The Arcadia died slowly of consumption. Its only merits were the founding of the first National Academy and the revival, with Pietro Metastasio, of the melodrama.

The second period may be encompassed between the Peace of Aix-la-Chapelle (1748), which marked the end of the Spanish and the beginning of the Austrian domination over Italy, and the first descent of Napoleon into Italy (1796). This was an era of economic, cultural and spiritual revival which was, in the main, an outgrowth of the broad influence of the illuministic movement and of foreign culture. From then on, Italy awakens to a new national life and participates more closely in the political and intellectual life of Europe. The three major initiators of the literary revival were Parini, Goldoni and Alfieri who, each in his own field, injected a new spirit into

poetry, comedy and tragedy, and contributed greatly to the reform of the moral, social and political life of the country.

Giuseppe Parini (1729–1799), a priest of liberal principles and rigorous intellectual integrity, was a keen observer and castigator of the corrupt and pretentious society of the century. With his *Odi*, which are inspired by noble social and moral ideals, he infused new vigor into lyrical poetry and in his masterpiece, *Il Giorno*, he gave in polished, exquisitely ironical verse, a graphic picture of the life of fashionable idleness and mental lethargy led by the aristocracy and the contrast it provided with the laborious poverty of the humble. He tried all his life to reconcile the social principles of the Enlighten-

S MARIA MAGGIORE

ment with those of Christianity. As he had predicted in one of his poems, *La vita rustica*, he lived and died poor, but free from servility and adulation:

>Me non nato a percuotere
>Le dure illustri porte
>Nudo accorrà, ma libero,
>Il regno della morte.

Carlo Goldoni (1707–1793), the son of a Venetian physician, had an inborn vocation for the theater. He wrote his first play at the age of nine and, as a student, ran away from school to join a troupe of players. To please his father, he became a lawyer, but upon the latter's death dedicated himself wholly to playwriting for the Venetian theater. Goldoni wrote over 350 dramatic works, including more than a hundred comedies. Direct, lively, fluent and scintillating with humor, they are a sparkling mirror of contemporary life, yet they contain such profoundly timeless truths that they still captivate and delight audiences today. The eminent position that Goldoni occupies in the history of Italian drama is not limited to his playwriting, but extends to the reforms he introduced in the theater despite the stubborn and bitter resistance of actors, playwrights and the public. For the impromptu comedy, which had gone into an artistic decline, he substituted

216

ALINARI   ALINARI

the written comedy; he eliminated masks, which standardized characters, introduced real types sketched from life, and also abolished all forms of entertainment extraneous to the drama. In short, by eliminating vulgarity, complex plots, nonsense and horseplay from the *Commedia dell'Arte*, he restored classic literary dignity to comedy. In 1762, Goldoni was invited to Paris to direct the Comédie Italienne and, in 1764, was appointed teacher of Italian to the royal princesses at Versailles, a position he kept until 1774, when he retired. During this period, Goldoni wrote in French two more comedies and his *Mémoirs*, a valuable document relating the history of his life and his theater and giving a graphic picture of the customs of contemporary society. He died in Paris in abject poverty in 1793.

Count Vittorio Alfieri (1749–1803) was born at Asti in Piedmont. When he was eight years old, he was sent to the Military Academy of Turin where, as he wrote later, he went through "eight years of uneducation, a jackass among jackasses under a jackass." During the following ten years he traveled throughout Italy, took the usual "grand tour of Europe", leading a gay life and becoming involved in the strangest and most romantic adventures. He was obsessed by the desire to do something great and extraordinary but, plagued by a headstrong, forthright, quick-tempered disposition, and subject to outbursts of scorn and disdain, he feared he would be incapable of accomplishing anything. Yet by the time he was 25, he had developed an iron will power. He plunged for several years into serious studies of Italian and classic literatures and then devoted himself to the writing of tragedies whose plots he drew from Greek, Roman and medieval history. Among his best are *Oreste, Saul* and *Merope. Mirra* is his masterpiece. His are mostly tragedies on the theme of freedom, solidly constructed, straightforward, concise and powerful. They deal with the struggle between the tyrant and his victim, the strong and the weak, right and wrong. His heroic characters are tormented by an inner passion which builds up slowly until it finally explodes with a logical and terrifying impact. The love of liberty and hatred of tyranny which they inspire aroused the patriotic spirit of the Italians and incited them to join in insurrections and battles for the independence, freedom and unification of their country.

In the figurative arts the baroque lingered through the second part of the century, producing such characteristic works as the grandiose Fontana di Trevi, the picturesque staircase of Trinità dei Monti, and the imposing façades of San Giovanni in Laterano and Santa Maria Maggiore, all in Rome. But it was soon supplanted by the neo-classic style which combined severity of lines with simple and harmonious forms. The outstanding architects of this school, Filippo Iuvara (1676–1736) and Luigi Vanvitelli (1700–1773), produced the Castello di Stupinigi in Turin and the Palazzo Reale of Caserta. Even sculpture, once the vogue of Bernini had spent itself, returned with Antonio Canova (1757–1822) to classic purity. Painting found a new field of expression in the decoration of theaters, palaces, and villas or portrayed the life, festivals and mores of the period. The great masters of the century all belong to the Venetian school. Outstanding among them were: Giambattista Tiepolo (1696–1770), poet of space and color, who celebrated the triumph of heaven and earth in his spectacular frescos; Antonio Canaletto (1697–1768), who depicted with precise and delicate realism, the canals, palaces and squares of Venice; and Francesco Guardi (1712–1793), whose small canvasses immortalized in a naturalistic vein picturesque indoor and outdoor Venetian life.

During the Age of Enlightenment Italy held undisputed supremacy over all of Europe in the field of music, just as she had in the Seicento. Italian opera became a synthesis of all the arts. Drama, music, poetry, singing, dancing, architecture and painting all contributed to the triumph of the new musical artistic expression. Throughout the century, Italian architects, painters, composers, musicians and singers were in great demand everywhere and could be found in the most important European cities building opera houses, establishing opera companies, concert orchestras and schools of music in order to brighten, enlighten and delight the human soul.

XXIII

Pietro Metastasio

(*1698–1782*)

Rinuccini, Monteverdi and Scarlatti left no great successors. The melodrama, having fallen under the influence of the baroque, was already deteriorating as a result of abuse in the portrayal of vulgar passions, and in the introduction of extraneous comic eposides and over-elaborate stage settings. This deterioration was aggravated by the very nature of opera which requires perfect cooperation between composer and poet or librettist. But as often happens, the composer tries to subordinate the poetry to his music while the poet wants to do the very opposite; besides, during the performance of an opera the orchestra at times tends to drown out the singers and the singers the orchestra. While Italian melodrama was triumphant in the capitals of Europe during the second half of the 18th century, composers in Italy were unable to find poets willing to write librettos and, in order to meet the ever-increasing demand for new operas, were forced to use inferior ones. An effort toward remedying this situation was made by Apostolo Zeno, (1668–1750), then court poet in Vienna, but the real reform and revival of melodrama were brought about by Pietro Metastasio.

Born in Rome in 1698, Metastasio soon revealed himself a poet by instinct. At the age of nine he improvised poetry to the delighted astonishment of his public. After a period of serious studies during which he also wrote poems and a tragedy, he practiced law in Naples where his poetic works attracted the attention of the court and he was asked to write several musical dramas. He became the protégé of the great diva, Marianna Bulgarelli, who induced him to study music. In 1723, when he was twenty-five years old, Metastasio wrote his first melodrama, *Didone abbandonata*, which was performed in Naples with Marianna Bulgarelli singing the leading role. Its immediate and unanimous success marked the beginning of Metastasio's spectacular career and the revival of melodrama.

In 1730, Metastasio was invited by Charles VI to the court of Vienna. There he became poet laureate, reached the perfection of his art and was acclaimed and honored as few other poets had ever been. Before he died there in 1782, he wrote twenty-six melodramas as well as a considerable number of essays, oratorios and songs.

Metastasio drew his plots mainly from Greek and Roman history. He handled his characters with a deft, modern, human touch yet charged them, in accordance with the taste of the century, with powerful heroic and sentimental passions. His great contribution, however, was his significant reform of the melodrama. He asserted the supremacy of poetry over musical score and cut down the number of arias and the length of the recitatives. He eliminated all superfluous comic episodes, grandiloquent tirades and mechanical contrivances; he reinstated the chorus; gave lyrical and dramatic movement to the scenes; and conferred melody, fluidity and variety upon his poetry, thus bringing into being the serious, unified three-act opera. His dramas, which inspired such great composers as Gluck, Händel and Mozart, were set to music by more than one composer: his *Artaserse*, for instance, more than a hundred times and *Didone* over sixty.

220

DIDONE ABBANDONATA

[Dido, Queen of Carthage, is enamoured of Aeneas, a Prince of Troy, who, after the fall of his city, had escaped and wandered about the Mediterranean until, shipwrecked during a terrible storm, he had found refuge in Dido's palace. He is torn between his love for Dido and his impelling duty, dictated to him by the gods, his dying father, conscience and a desire for fame, to go to the coast of Latium to found a new city, Rome, and the Roman Empire. Meanwhile, Iarba, King of the Moors, who also loves Dido and is jealous of Aeneas, comes in disguise to the royal palace to kill him, but fails in his attempt.

In the final scenes of Act I given below, Dido rejoices that the life of Aeneas has been spared while Aeneas, caught between two conflicting impulses, tries to explain to her why he cannot return her love.]

ATTO I

Scena XVII

L'amore e il dolore di Didone

Didone.	Enea, salvo già sei	salvo *cured*
	Dalla crudel ferita.	
	Per me serban gli Dei sì bella vita.	
Enea.	Oh Dio, regina!	
5 *Didone.*	Ancora	
	Forse della mia fede incerto stai?	
Enea.	No: più funeste assai	
	Son le sventure mie. Vuole il destino. . .	
Didone.	Chiari i tuoi sensi esponi.	sensi *feelings*
10 *Enea.*	Vuol . . . (Mi sento morir) ch'io t'abbandoni.	
Didone.	M'abbandoni! Perchè?	
Enea.	Di Giove il cenno,	cenno *sign*
	L'ombra del genitor, la patria, il Cielo,	del genitor *of my father (Anchises)*
15	La promessa, il dover, l'onor, la fama	promessa *(made to his dying father)*
	Alle sponde d'Italia oggi mi chiama.	sponde *shores*
	La mia lunga dimora	dimora *sojourn*
	Purtroppo degli Dei mosse lo sdegno.	Dei *gods*

221

fin ad ora *until now*	*Didone.*	E così fin ad ora,
		Perfido, mi celasti il tuo disegno?
	Enea.	Fu pietà.
	Didone.	Che pietà? Mendace il labbro
		Fedeltà mi giurava, 5
		E intanto il cor pensava
Come lunge da me volgere il piede *How to run away from me*		Come lunge da me volgere il piede!
		A chi, misera me! darò più fede?
onde *sea*		Vil rifiuto dell'onde
l' *him (Aeneas)*		Io l'accolgo dal lido; io lo ristoro 10
		Dalle ingiurie del mar; le navi e l'armi
loco *a place*		Già disperse io gli rendo, e gli do loco
		Nel mio cor, nel mio regno; e questo
		è poco.
		Di cento re, per lui, 15
gli sdegni irrito *I arouse the wrath*		Ricusando l'amor, gli sdegni irrito:
mercede *reward*		Ecco poi la mercede.
		A chi, misera me! darò più fede?

Enea.	Fin ch'io viva, o Didone,	
	Dolce memoria al mio pensier sarai;	
	Nè partirei giammai,	
	Se per dover de' Numi io non dovessi	per dover de' Numi *by order of the gods*
5	Consacrare il mio affanno	consacrare *dedicate*
	All'impero latino.	affanno *distress*
Didone.	Veramente non hanno	
	Altra cura gli Dei che il tuo destino.	
Enea.	Io resterò, se vuoi	
10	Che si renda spergiuro un infelice.	Che si renda spergiuro un infelice *an unhappy man to become a perjurer*
Didone.	No: sarei debitrice	debitrice *answerable*
	Dell'impero del mondo a' figli tuoi.	Dell' *for the*
	Va' pur, segui il tuo fato:	pur *please*
	Cerca d'Italia il regno; all'onde, ai venti	
15	Confida pur la speme tua; ma senti:	speme *hope*
	Farà quell'onde istesse	Farà (*the subject of this verb is* cielo)
	Delle vendette mie ministre il Cielo;	istesse *very same*
	E tardi allor pentito	
	D'aver creduto all'elemento insano	elemento insano *supernatural forces*
20	Richiamerai la tua Didone invano.	
Enea.	Se mi vedessi il core . . .	
Didone.	Lasciami, traditore.	
Enea.	Almen dal labbro mio	
	Con volto meno irato	
25	Prendi l'ultimo addio.	
Didone.	Lasciami, ingrato.	
Enea.	E pur con tanto sdegno	E pur *And yet*
	Non hai ragion di condannarmi.	
Didone.	Indegno!	
30	Non ha ragione, ingrato,	
	Un core abbandonato	
	Da chi giurogli fè?	giurogli (gli giurò) fè *swore to remain faithful*
	Anime innamorate,	
	Se lo provaste mai,	
35	Ditelo voi per me.	
	Perfido! Tu lo sai	
	Se in premio un tradimento	
	Io meritai da te.	
	E qual sarà tormento,	
40	Anime innamorate,	
	Se questo mio non è? (Parte)	Parte *Exit*

223

Il dilemma di Enea

soffrirò *shall I tolerate*	*Enea.*	E soffrirò che sia
mercede *requital*		Sì barbara mercede
		Premio della tua fede, anima mia!
		Tanto amor, tanti doni . . .
pria ch' *before*		Ah! pria ch'io t'abbandoni, 5
Pera (Perisca) *let . . . perish*		Pera l'Italia, il mondo,
		Resti in oblio profondo
sepolta *buried*		La mia fama sepolta;
Vada in cenere *Let . . . burn to ashes*		Vada in cenere Troia un'altra volta.
		Ah, che dissi! Alle mie 10·
		Amorose follie,
io . . . rossore *I blush with shame*		Gran genitor, perdona: io n'ho rossore:
		Non fu Enea che parlò, le disse Amore.
empio Moro *merciless Moor (Iarba)*		Si parta . . . e l'empio Moro
Stringerà *will hold in his arms*		Stringerà il mio tesoro? 15
tesoro *love*		No . . . Ma sarà frattanto
		Al proprio genitor spergiuro il figlio?
		Padre, Amor, Gelosia, Numi, consiglio!
sul lido *ashore*		Se resto sul lido,
sciolgo le vele *unfurl the sails*		Se sciolgo le vele, 20
		Infido, crudele
		Mi sento chiamar:
		E intanto, confuso
Nel *by*		Nel dubbio funesto
		Non parto, non resto, 25
martire *torment*		Ma provo il martire,
		Che avrei nel partire,
		Che avrei nel restar. (Parte)

Fine dell'Atto Primo.

[The Hamlet-like indecision of Aeneas comes to an end in Act III when he decides to sail; whereupon Iarba assaults and sets fire to Carthage and Dido, in despair, throws herself into the flames and dies.]

XXIV

Cesare Beccaria

(1738–1794)

The despotism with which European sovereigns ruled over their subjects during the 18th century, the confusion and obscurity of feudalistic laws arbitrarily interpreted and inhumanly administered, the widespread use of all sorts of instruments of torture devised to extract confessions from the accused, together with the appalling number of death penalties carried out in every state, gave pause to many European thinkers who realized that the existing code of penal laws and the treatment meted out to criminals were the antithesis of the humanitarian principles advocated by the Enlightenment, and several centuries behind the refinement of social life in all nations.

The most eloquent and effective voice raised in Italy against this barbarous system was that of Cesare Beccaria, jurist, criminologist and economist. Born in Milan of a noble family, he received his early education in a Jesuit school and his law degree from the University of Pavia. After his return to his native city he read widely and deeply and meditated upon the works of the French Encyclopedists, particularly those of Montesquieu. These readings aroused his humanitarian feelings which, as he stated, "had been repressed by eight years of fanatical education," caused a radical upheaval in his thinking, and converted him to the liberal principles of the Illuminists. During this moral crisis, Beccaria joined a group of Milanese intellectuals who met every evening to read, discuss and work together. At the insistence of his friends, he wrote his first work, a critical study on the financial system of the state of Milan which was instrumental in bringing about badly needed local economic reforms. By the time he was twenty-five, he wrote *Dei delitti e delle pene*, a treatise which was to give him sudden and lasting fame. It was first published in 1764 at Leghorn (Tuscany) to circumvent censorship and avoid eventual reprisals on the part of the Austrian rulers of Milan.

The wonder and interest aroused by the young author's courageous, eloquent and revolutionary opinions were such that the book, soon reprinted and translated, was highly praised at home and abroad and bitterly attacked by political and religious groups. The first English edition appeared in 1767 and was prefaced by the following statement:

> "It is not surprising that this little book hath engaged the attention of all ranks of people in every part of Europe. It is about eighteen months since the first publication; in which time it hath passed no less than six editions in the original language . . . It hath been translated into French; that translation hath also been several times reprinted, and perhaps no book, on any subject, was ever received with more avidity, more generally read, or more universally applauded."

Since then the book has had numberless translations and editions. In the United States alone seven editions appeared between 1773 and 1872. John Adams, John Quincy Adams and Thomas Jefferson in particular were among the most ardent advocates of Beccaria's principles. In Paris, the author was received triumphantly by the Encyclopedists. Diderot and Voltaire each published a commentary on his treatise, and Empress Catherine II offered him a position, which he declined, in the Russian capital.

In his essay Beccaria reaffirmed in an unpolished but concise and powerful style the sacred and moral worth of the human personality. He was the first to formulate the principle that laws must have as their sole purpose the pursuit of "the greatest happiness of the greatest number," and to enunciate the tenet that no man be considered guilty unless it has first been proved that he is so. Punishment, according to him, should not be imposed upon a criminal as retribution and expiation of the irreparable crime committed; its purpose should be to prevent criminals and potential criminals from committing new crimes; it should also make it possible for the criminal to redeem himself and to become a better member of society. In any case, the punishment of a crime cannot be considered just or necessary if the laws have not provided, through every possible means permitted by times and circumstances, for the prevention of that crime.

He denounced the system of secret accusations since it leads unscrupulous men to be false and treacherous while it robs society of its rightful sense of tranquillity and security. The use of torture as a means of wresting confessions was deprecated by him as savage and useless because it serves to determine not who is guilty or innocent, but only who can withstand the greatest physical pain, with the result that the guilty and strong often triumph over the innocent and weak.

He pleaded with force and eloquence against capital punishment, demonstrating that it has never prevented determined men from injuring society, nor has it ever made men better. It is neither just, necessary nor

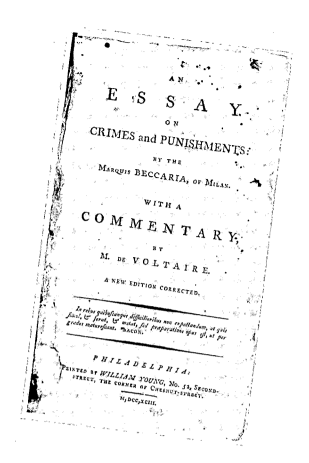

useful. On the contrary, he stated, it is pernicious to society because of the example of barbarity it affords. In Italy the death penalty was abolished in 1889, re-established by Fascism in 1926 and again abrogated in 1948.

The influence of this epoch-making treatise throughout Europe and North America toward the end of the 18th century was enormous and lasting. It induced many countries to mitigate punishment, to abolish completely or limit torture and capital punishment, to consider criminals as salvageable citizens and to improve living conditions in the prisons. Besides being introduced in the *Déclaration des Droits de l'Homme* which was drafted by the French Assembly in 1789, Beccaria's principles have inspired many modern constitutions and—what is even more important—have paved the way for modern penal science. Still today, whenever wars, revolutions and tyranny embitter men's minds and souls and provoke waves of violence, mercilessness and injustice, it is still Beccaria with his booklet who points the way that legislation on crime and punishment should take to restore security to the state and tranquillity to society.

227

DEI DELITTI E DELLE PENE

1. Della tortura

consacrata *sanctioned*
reo *accused*
mentre si forma il processo
 during the preparation of his trial
delitto *crime*

incorre *he may fall*

purgazione d' *redemption from*

reo *guilty*

se non quando *until*

accordata *granted*

Una crudeltà, consacrata dall'uso della maggior parte delle nazioni, è la tortura del reo mentre si forma il processo. Essa viene inflitta, o per costringerlo a confessare un delitto, o per le contraddizioni nelle quali incorre, o per scoprire 5 dei complici, o per non so quale immaginaria e incomprensibile purgazione d'infamia, o finalmente per scoprire altri delitti, di cui potrebbe esser reo, ma dei quali non è accusato.

Un uomo non può chiamarsi reo prima della 10 sentenza del giudice. La società non può togliergli la pubblica protezione, se non quando sia deciso che egli abbia violato i patti con i quali gli fu accordata.

Qual'è dunque quel diritto, se non quello della forza, che dia autorità a un giudice di dare una pena a un cittadino, mentre si dubita se sia reo o innocente? Non è nuovo questo dilemma: o il
5 delitto è certo, o incerto. Se certo, non gli si deve dare altra pena che quella stabilita dalle leggi, e inutili sono i tormenti, perchè è inutile la confessione del reo. Se il delitto è incerto, non si deve tormentare un innocente, perchè tale è, secondo le
10 leggi, un uomo, i cui delitti non sono provati . . .

L'uso della tortura è il mezzo sicuro di assolvere i robusti scellerati, e di condannare i deboli innocenti . . . Di due uomini ugualmente innocenti, o ugualmente rei, il robusto e il coraggioso sarà
15 assolto, mentre il fiacco e il timido sarà condannato . . . L'esito dunque della tortura è un affare di temperamento e di calcolo, che varia in ciascuno individuo in proporzione della sua robustezza e della sua sensibilità; così che un matematico
20 solverebbe questo problema meglio che un giudice: data la forza dei muscoli e la sensibilità delle fibre d'un innocente, trovare il grado di dolore che lo farà confessare reo di un delitto.

di dare *to inflict*
pena *punishment*

tormenti *torture*

scellerati *criminals*

fiacco *feeble*
esito *outcome*
affare *matter*
calcolo *calculation*
robustezza *strength*

data *being given*
fibre *nerves*

Cap. XII.

ANDERSON

229

2. Della pena di morte

supplizi *torture*

spinto *induced*

si attribuiscono *arrogate unto*
  themselves
trucidare *put to death*
simili *fellow-men*
somma *sum total*

Chi . . . lasciare ad *Who has*
  ever been willing to grant
Come mai nel *How is it that*
  in the
quello del massimo fra tutti i
  beni *that (the sacrifice) of*
  man's most precious possession
accorda *reconcile*
non è padrone *has no right*
dare altrui *to give away to*
  another

intera *as a whole*

essere *life*

regno *rule*

L'inutile abuso di supplizi che non ha mai resi gli uomini migliori, mi ha spinto ad esaminare se la pena di morte sia veramente utile e giusta in un governo bene organizzato.

Quale può essere il diritto che si attribuiscono 5 gli uomini di trucidare i loro simili? Non certamente quello su cui sono basate la sovranità e le leggi. Esse non sono che una somma di minime porzioni della libertà privata di ogni individuo. Esse rappresentano la volontà generale, che è la somma 10 delle volontà individuali. Chi è mai colui che abbia voluto lasciare ad altri uomini il diritto di ucciderlo? Come mai nel minimo sacrificio della libertà di ognuno vi può essere quello del massimo fra tutti i beni, la vita? E se ciò fu fatto, come si 15 accorda tale principio con l'altro, che l'uomo non è padrone di uccidersi? Egli doveva esserlo, se ha potuto dare altrui questo diritto o alla società intera.

Non è dunque la pena di morte un diritto, 20 poichè ho dimostrato che non può esser tale; ma è una guerra della nazione contro un cittadino, perchè essa giudica necessaria o utile la distruzione del suo essere. Ma se dimostrerò che la pena di morte non è nè utile nè necessaria, avrò vinto la 25 causa dell'umanità.

La morte di un cittadino può credersi necessaria in un solo caso. Quando egli, benchè privo di libertà, abbia ancora tali relazioni e tal potenza che possono mettere in pericolo la sicurezza della 30 nazione; quando la sua esistenza possa produrre una rivoluzione pericolosa nella forma di governo stabilita. La morte di qualche cittadino diventa dunque necessaria quando la nazione ricupera o perde la sua libertà, o in tempi di anarchia, quando 35 gli stessi disordini tengono luogo di leggi. Ma durante il tranquillo regno delle leggi, io non vedo nessuna necessità di distruggere un cittadino.

Se l'esperienza di tutti i secoli non basta a
provare che la pena di morte non ha mai distolti   distolti *prevented*
gli uomini determinati dall'offendere la società . . .   dall'offendere *from offending*
basta consultare la natura dell'uomo per provare
5 la verità della mia asserzione.

     Non è l'intensità della pena, che fa maggiore
effetto sull'animo umano, ma la lunghezza di essa;   animo *mind*
perchè la nostra sensibilità è più facilmente e forte-
mente mossa da minime, ma ripetute impressioni,   mossa *affected*
10 che da un forte e passeggero movimento. Il freno   freno *deterrent*
più forte contro i delitti non è il terribile, ma
passeggero spettacolo della morte di uno scellerato,
ma il lungo e continuo esempio di un uomo privo

di libertà, che divenuto bestia di servizio, ricompensa con le sue fatiche, quella società che egli ha offesa . . .

Non è utile la pena di morte, per l'esempio di atrocità che dà agli uomini. Se le passioni, o la 5 necessità della guerra, hanno insegnato a spargere il sangue umano, le leggi, fatte per moderare la condotta degli uomini, non dovrebbero aumentare il feroce esempio, tanto più orribile poichè la morte legale è data con studio e con formalità . . . 10

Se mi si oppone l'esempio di quasi tutti i secoli, e di quasi tutte le nazioni, che hanno adottato la pena di morte per alcuni delitti, io risponderò che tale esempio svanisce in faccia alla verità, contro la quale non c'è autorità; e che la storia 15 degli uomini è come un immenso mare di errori fra i quali galleggiano poche, confuse e distanti verità . . .

La voce di un filosofo è troppo debole contro i tumulti e le grida dei molti, che son guidati dalla 20 cieca consuetudine, ma i pochi saggi, che sono sparsi sulla faccia della terra, mi faranno eco nell'intimo dei loro cuori. E se la verità potesse, fra gl'infiniti ostacoli che l'allontanano dai regnanti, giungere fino al loro trono, sappiano loro 25 che essa verità vi arriva con i voti segreti di tutti gli uomini.

Cap. XVI.

L'OTTOCENTO

Characteristics of the Century

The ideals of liberty, equality and fraternity proclaimed by the French Revolution, and the spirit of freedom propagated by Napoleon Bonaparte during his occupation of northern Italy, spread rapidly throughout the peninsula where the ground had already been prepared morally by Parini and politically by Alfieri.

The diffusion of these ideals was intensified by the development of romanticism which manifested itself in Italy both as a literary and a political movement aimed at freeing literature from mythology and classicism and liberating the country from foreign domination.

The struggle for independence began around 1821, when the country was still broken up into eight separate states, and ended in 1870 when Rome became the capital of unified Italy. It was called the "Risorgimento". Its greatest architects and builders were Mazzini, the thinker, Garibaldi, the warrior, and Cavour, the statesman.

The *Risorgimento* may be divided into three periods. The first (1821–1849), begins with the constitution of secret societies such as *La Carboneria* and *La Giovine Italia* and the rebellions they organized, and ends with the popular revolts which broke out all over Italy in 1848. These sporadic outbreaks were all suppressed after the first war of independence in which the Piedmontese army, reinforced by thousands of volunteers coming from all parts of Italy, despite a series of initial victories, was finally defeated by the Austrians.

The second period (1849–1862) is marked by the second war of independence (1859), which was fought by Piedmontese and French troops against Austria, and culminated in the liberation of Lombardy; by revolts in the states of central Italy which held plebiscites favoring their union with Piedmont; and by the expedition of Garibaldi with his *Mille* (One Thousand Men) who liberated southern Italy, all the way from Sicily to Naples. On March 17, 1861, Victor Emmanuel II was proclaimed King of Italy.

During the third period (1863–1870), Venetia won her freedom as an outgrowth of the third war of independence and proclaimed her union with Italy. On September 20, 1870, with the fall of Napoleon III, the defeat of the French empire in the war against Prussia, and the withdrawal of the French garrison from Rome, the Italian army, after a brief encounter with the papal troops, entered Rome which finally became the capital of Italy. Thus Italy, once more resurrected, became the oldest of the youngest nations.

9/20/1870 final date
of the Risorgimento

The *Risorgimento* may be considered the most significant and happiest political event in the history of Italy particularly if one bears in mind that never, after the fall of the Western Roman Empire during the fifth century, had she been a political unit. She already had a language, a world-famous art and literature; she had brought forth humanism and the Renaissance and yet her name was nothing more than "a geographical expression". Although invaded, devastated, ruled and oppressed for fifteen centuries by foreign conquerors whom she had civilized, the ideal of a united and free Italy, however repressed, had never been extirpated from the hearts and minds of her great thinkers.

When, at last, the time seemed propitious, the name of Italy and the concept of Fatherland were welded by the men of the *Risorgimento* into a new religion which inspired a whole generation of Italians to work, fight and die for their country.

Literature was the most powerful single agent in promoting the *Risorgimento*, with music a strong ally. Ugo Foscolo (1778–1827), soldier, critic, dramatist and poet of distinction, was the bard who inaugurated patriotic literature. He is the author of *Le ultime lettere di Jacopo Ortis*, a taut and moving semi-autobiographical romantic novel, centering on the anguish of a young Italian patriot who is driven to suicide when he loses both his fatherland and the girl he loves. Foscolo's poetical masterpiece is *Dei Sepolcri*. Its magnificent blank verse, ringing with patriotic fervor, extols the civic and moral significance of the tombs of Italy's immortals whose memory inspires mortals with strong and noble hearts to lofty thinking and great deeds:

A egregie cose il forte animo accendono
l'urne dei forti . . . .

Manzoni and Leopardi, although they remained aloof from the political scene, could not refrain from singing the name of Italy and comparing her past glory with her present misery. Gabriele Rossetti (1783–1854), Giovanni Berchet (1783–1851) and Giovanni Prati (1815–1884), all exiled, exalted the heroism of the patriots in the struggle for the liberation of Italy while the impassioned political satires of Giuseppe Giusti (1809–1850) lashed out against the truculence of foreign oppressors. Silvio Pellico (1789–1854), a poet and dramatist of the romantic school, who had spent ten years in the dungeons of Austria for having belonged to *La Carboneria*, wrote without rancor *Le Mie Prigioni*, a stirring account of the inhuman sufferings inflicted upon him and his political friends. The book aroused everywhere such a wave of sympathy for the Italian cause that its publication was said to have cost Austria more than a lost battle.

The novelists, following the example set by Manzoni's masterpiece, *I Promessi Sposi*, eluded censorship by selecting for their historical novels characters, situations and backgrounds which portrayed man's struggle against tyranny and obscurantism, and thus aroused and fired the moral conscience of the Italians. A similar mission was assumed by the romantic theater, through historical and classical-romantic tragedies which are a poignant and eloquent expression of the ideals of the period.

The outstanding literary critic of this period was Francesco De Sanctis (1817–1883), eminent educator and patriot, imprisoned in, and later exiled from Naples, founder of aesthetic criticism and author of the *Storia della Letteratura Italiana*, a literary and historical masterpiece which embraces the history of Italian thought in all its manifestations.

It was Italian music, especially opera, that played the most spectacular role among the arts. Because of its popularity and the relative safety afforded by the crowded and darkened theater, delirious applause and patriotic

demonstrations on the part of the audience would invariably greet such words as "patria, libertà, guerra and oppressori" whenever they were sung. The censor would usually compel the composer to change the fiery words, as in the case of Bellini whose "Gridando libertà" in *I Puritani* had to be changed to "serbando fedeltà", but to no avail. Such operas as *L'Italiana in Algeri* and *Guglielmo Tell* by Gioacchino Rossini (1792–1868); *Lucrezia Borgia* by Gaetano Donizetti (1797–1848); *Norma* by Vincenzo Bellini (1801–1835); and *Nabucco, I Lombardi, Ernani, Attila, I Vespri Siciliani, La Battaglia di Legnano* and *Alzira* by Giuseppe Verdi (1813–1901) all voiced the grief of the Italian people for their oppressed country and incited the youth of Italy to fight and die for their fatherland.

Receiving fresh impetus from the discovery of the art treasures of Herculaneum and Pompei, the figurative arts during the *Risorgimento* adopted the neo-classical style introduced by the sculptor Canova toward the end of the previous century as a reaction to the extravagances of the baroque and the rococo. The most striking examples of this type of neo-classical architecture include the great opera houses of La Scala in Milan and the San Carlo in Naples, the church of San Francesco da Paola also in Naples, the Caffè Pedrocchi of Padua, the Piazza del Popolo in Rome and the Arco della Pace in Milan. Painting revealed little originality in the many frescos on mythological, historical and sacred subjects because of lack of inspiration and traits of pomposity inherited from the preceding century. The most original contribution was made by the portrait painters who rose to the demands that life and reality made on them.

The new Italian state was confronted during the immediate *post-Risorgimento* with the vast problems of national reconstruction left by the foreign dominators. The country was terribly poor and years of misrule and mismanagement, of war and rebellions had aggravated the already bad conditions. The government therefore embarked on a vast program to organize and unify the army, the codes of law, local governments, education, transportation and communications in order to give a tangible sense of unity to populations which for centuries had been kept separated in different states.

The last thirty years of the 19th century produced three great poets—Carducci, Pascoli and D'Annunzio—and two influential novelists—Fogazzaro and Verga.

Giosuè Carducci (1835–1907; see Chapter I) was the greatest of the poets of the new Italy. His poetry is classical in form yet modern in feeling; limpid and vigorous, its eloquence is tempered by prodigious restraint. Although rooted in the great memories of antiquity and in a pantheistic sense of nature, it gives expression to the political passions of the times and to the poet's ardent love of justice and liberty.

Giovanni Pascoli (1855–1912) succeeded Carducci in the chair of Italian literature at the University of Bologna. Although he inherited his predecessor's classicism, Pascoli substituted for Carducci's paganism a mystic sense of life which he moulded into exquisite idylls that express the awe and tremulous bewilderment of man and nature before the mysteries of life and death. Sorrow is for him a source of love and goodness which binds man and the universe in a common brotherhood. Pascoli also wrote Latin poems of such excellence that he was fourteen times awarded the Amsterdam Prize for Latin Poetry.

Gabriele D'Annunzio (1863–1938) made his début as a poet at the age of sixteen while still a student. Like Pascoli, he strives in his early poems to imitate Carducci whose paganism he retained but whose moral classical vigor becomes transformed into powerful expressions of panic sensuality and whose

(handwritten marginal notes:)
romanticism – opposite of classicism
1. freedom from restraint
2. emotional mentality

Classicism – geometric simplicity + symmetry
rules.
unity of time, place, + action
rational mentality

ALINARI

austere patriotism he perverted into a mad exaltation of imperialistic dreams and an apotheosis of hollow supermen. D'Annunzio reached the peak of his lyrical production with *Alcione*, the third and best of his four volumes of *Laudi del cielo, del mare, della terra e degli eroi*. In his novels such as *Il Fuoco*, which describe with cruel candor the details of his love affairs, there is an exuberant, intoxicating wealth of sensuous imagery and musical verbosity.

In striking contrast to D'Annunzio, the novelist, stands solitary, stately Giovanni Verga (1840–1922), one of the great modern European prose writers who developed a narrative style called "verismo" which is characterized by the stark simplicity and scrupulous accuracy with which he treats a completely new milieu, the world of the humble.

Half way between D'Annunzio and Verga yet closer perhaps to Manzoni stands Fogazzaro (1842–1911), a distinguished novelist, advocate of religious reform, and a sincere interpreter of some of the most perplexing problems of the new Italy. His characters are enmeshed in a conflict between reality and fantasy, faith and reason, mysticism and sensuality, duty and instinct. (*Daniele Cortis, Piccolo Mondo Antico, Piccolo Mondo Moderno, Il Santo*).

240

A notable influence was exercised on the Italian theater by the *verismo* of Verga who also wrote several one-act plays, the most noted being *Cavalleria Rusticana* which was given operatic form in 1890 by Mascagni. The verist theater reflected either the regional life and customs of the middle class in the manner of Goldoni or those of the lower classes along the lines set by Verga, and was often written in dialect (Gallina, Di Giacomo and Novelli). The influx of the various European currents, from the naturalistic to the moralistic and from the late-romantic to the psychological, is represented in the theater of the versatile Paolo Giacometti (1817–1882), Paolo Ferrari (1822–1889) and Giuseppe Giacosa (1847–1906). Great popularity was also enjoyed by Girolamo Rovetta (1854–1906), especially for his historical and psychological plays.

With the passing of romanticism and neo-classicism, the fine arts, following prevailing European trends, branched off toward the end of the century into the various schools which fall under the general name of modern art.

Three important painters stand out above all others: Giovanni Segantini (1858–1899), who applied the technique of *divisionismo* in his canvasses, inspired by the majestic beauty of the Alps; Giovanni Fattori (1825–1908), founder of a school of considerable originality known as the *Macchiaioli fiorentini* (Florentine spot painters); and Telemaco Signorini (1835–1901), who became the best exponent of that school.

Sculpture fluctuated between idealization, allegory and realism. Architecture produced an eclectic style compounded of Roman and Renaissance elements, expressed with considerable freedom and harmony to meet requirements of modern life. Typical of this genre are the Teatro Massimo of Palermo, the Victor Emmanuel Gallery and the Railroad Station of Milan, and the Mole Antonelliana of Turin.

XXV

Alessandro Manzoni

(*1785–1873*)

The romantic movement which originated in Germany at the end of the 18th century was introduced into Italy by Giovanni Berchet. Since it represented a crusade against classicism it was bitterly attacked in Italy where the classic tradition was indigenous, and ran deep and strong. The debate between classicists and romanticists was long and sharp but finally culminated in a judicious combination of the two schools which may be summarized as follows: poetry and literature must generally aim at being useful, adopting the truth as subject matter and the interesting as medium; the artist must be an interpreter of the customs, beliefs and thoughts of his times; he must seek and find inspiration in the chivalrous and religious traditions of the Middle Ages and not in mythology which no one believes in, nor in the classic world that is now dead; his works must move and educate not only a small learned class but the people as well. The Italian romanticists were opposed to the imposition of the aesthetic rules of the ancients, particularly the so-called dramatic unities of time and place, but they did favor the study of the classics for their cultural values.

The most significant representative of Italian romanticism is Alessandro Manzoni, born in Milan of Count Piero Manzoni and Giulia Beccaria, daughter of the celebrated penologist who wrote *Dei delitti e delle pene*. Brought up in religious schools, he lost his faith in early youth when he fell under the influence of the French rationalists and sensists, and went through a short period of dissipation. In 1808, he was married in the Protestant church to Enrichetta Blondel, a Calvinist who, that same year, was converted to Catholicism. After two years of profound religious crisis and deliberation, Manzoni became a Catholic. This experience brought about a complete transformation of his spirit and left its mark on him throughout the long journey of his life which encompassed the French Revolution, the Napoleonic Era, the Holy Alliance, the revolutions of 1848 with all the events leading to the *Risorgimento* and the unification of Italy. Moreover, he bore with fortitude the death of his first and second wives and the loss of six of his children. In 1860 he was made senator of the new kingdom of Italy and in 1861, he, a Catholic and patriot, cast his vote in favor of Rome as the capital of Italy and against the temporal power of the Church. He died in Milan in 1873 and was buried in the Famedio (Temple of Fame) of the Cimitero Monumentale.

Of cautious, serene, contemplative mind, Manzoni considered himself inept in political matters and thus never played an active role in the struggles of the *Risorgimento*. He was first and foremost an artist and a novelist.

Two years after his conversion he began to write his five *Inni Sacri*, each dedicated to one of the major religious celebrations of the Church. They are a fervid poetical exaltation of the Christian religion in which the oppressed may find hope, the oppressors forgiveness and the afflicted consolation. In them Manzoni blends felicitously human pessimism and religious optimism as he muses on the mystery of the hereafter which his poetry glorifies. Few other poets have succeeded so well in translating faith in terms of images and words. In this sense Manzoni's poetry may be compared, for the sublimity of the sensations and impressions it evokes, to St. Francis' *Laude delle Creature a Dio* and to the final scenes of Dante's *Paradiso*.

While in his *Inni Sacri* Manzoni contemplates humanity from the vantage point of Heaven, in his historical tragedies (*Il Conte di Carmagnola* and *Adelchi*) —which are great literary monuments though unsuited to the stage—and in some of his odes, for instance, the celebrated *Cinque Maggio* on the death of Napoleon I, he treats the ascension of man to God. And the tragedy of his characters, although it is suffered on earth, finds its logical conclusion only in the immense peace of a timeless spiritual world.

The work that gives the full measure of Manzoni's moral and artistic genius is *I Promessi Sposi* (The Betrothed), one of the world's great novels. He was inspired to write it one day when, reading the political and economic history of Milan under the Spanish domination of the 17th century, he came across a proclamation announcing penalties for using violence to keep a priest from performing a marriage. This document so fired his imagination, which had been under the spell of Sir Walter Scott's historical romances, that he plunged into historical and linguistic research which lasted from 1821 to 1842, the year that the final edition of the third and last volume of *I Promessi Sposi* came off the press.

I Promessi Sposi is the only novel that Manzoni ever wrote, but it was enough to assure his immortality. The story is laid in Lombardy between 1628 and 1630, during the Spanish domination. It is divided into two parts: in the first Don Abbondio, the curate of a small village church, is stopped while taking his customary late-afternoon stroll by two fierce *bravi* who, in the name of their master, Don Rodrigo, the local petty tyrant, threaten him with death if he dares perform the next day the marriage of Renzo and Lucia, two young village lovers. The all-powerful and iniquitous Don Rodrigo has set eyes on Lucia and wants her for himself. Don Abbondio, timid by nature

Renzo about for Lorenzo

244

and concerned rather with saving his skin than with performing his ecclesiastical duties, puts off the marriage. Neither the religious nor the civil authorities wish, or are in a position to protect the humble lovers who are forced to flee from their home town with the help of Fra Cristoforo, a monk who is now expiating a murder committed in his turbulent youth by devoting his life to charity. From that moment on, all manner of misfortunes and complications harass the luckless young couple. Arriving in Milan during a bread riot, Renzo is arrested but manages to escape to nearby Bergamo. Lucia finds refuge in a convent where she is betrayed by an unscrupulous nun into the hands of the Innominato (the Unnamed), a nefarious blackguard who locks her up in his castle for Don Rodrigo.

In the second part of the novel the vicissitudes of the two unhappy lovers undergo a change for the better thanks to the intervention of Divine Providence. Lucia's candor and innocence touch the heart of the Innominato who experiences a spiritual crisis and releases the girl who goes to Milan where she is taken in by a friendly family.

At this point war breaks out and is followed by the terrible plague of 1630. Thousands of people die daily. When Renzo recovers from a case of the plague, he hastens to the death-ridden city of Milan in the hope of finding Lucia. While looking for her in the public pesthouse he meets Fra Cristoforo who is nursing the sick, and the dying Don Rodrigo to whom he gives his forgiveness. At last he comes upon Lucia who is convalescing. But she can no longer marry him because, while a prisoner of the Innominato, she had made a vow of chastity to the Virgin and had therefore renounced her lover. Fra Cristoforo succumbs to the plague, but before breathing his last frees Lucia from the bonds of her vow. Thus, all obstacles having been removed, the betrothed return to their native town, are married by Don Abbondio and live a happy life.

This simple tale of two humble lovers serves as a pivot around which unfolds 17th-century Italian life, with its rotting institutions based on violence under the mask of legality, and its externalized religion put at the service of the state. Above the unrest, misery and corruption emerge a few courageous and selfless servants of Christ at the head of their humble and oppressed flocks.

The novel has two purposes: one religious and the other political. Manzoni wished primarily to demonstrate his profound conviction that resignation and faith in God could end by helping the victims of oppression and misfortune; secondly, by laying bare the iniquities of 17th-century Spanish domination, he was able to point out to the Italians the evils of the existing Austrian oppression. In fact, in the misadventures of the two hapless lovers, the readers saw reflected the tragedy of a whole nation.

The characters, both historical and imaginary, are so fully and skilfully drawn that they have become immortal. The action, though slow-paced, is varied, colorful and rich in unforgettable episodes and stupendous descriptions. The style is clear, concise and sparkling. While the author's mild and indulgent humor predominates, all other shades of human emotions and artistic expression are represented, from the comic to the tragic, the dramatic to the epic, the human to the divine. The work as a whole is infused with Manzoni's ideal of justice and faith. As no other among his contemporaries, Manzoni imparted to romanticism an aesthetic and moral harmony that successfully fused the conflicting trends of two centuries: rationalism and Christianity, classicism and romanticism, Catholicism and democracy.

I PROMESSI SPOSI

L'incontro di don Abbondio coi bravi

Per una di queste stradicciole, tornava bel
bello dalla passeggiata verso casa, sulla sera del
giorno 7 novembre dell'anno 1628, don Abbondio,
curato d'una delle terre accennate di sopra,
5 Diceva tranquillamente il suo ufizio, e talvolta, tra
un salmo e l'altro, chiudeva il breviario, tenendovi
dentro, per segno, l'indice della mano destra, e,
messa poi questa nell'altra dietro la schiena,
proseguiva il suo cammino, guardando a terra, e
10 buttando con un piede verso il muro i ciottoli che
facevano inciampo nel sentiero: poi alzava il viso,
e girati oziosamente gli occhi all'intorno, li fissava
alla parte di un monte . . . Aperto poi di nuovo il
breviario, e recitato un altro squarcio, giunse a una
15 voltata della stradetta, dov'era solito d'alzar sempre
gli occhi dal libro, e di guardarsi dinanzi: e così
fece anche quel giorno . . . Il curato, voltata la
stradetta, vide una cosa che non s'aspettava, e che
non avrebbe voluto vedere. Due uomini stavano,
20 l'uno dirimpetto all'altro, al confluente, per dir
così, delle due viottole: un di costoro, a cavalcioni
sul muricciolo basso; il compagno, in piedi,
appoggiato al muro, con le braccia incrociate sul
petto. L'abito, il portamento, e quello che, dal
25 luogo ov'era giunto il curato, si poteva distinguer
dell'aspetto, non lasciava dubbio intorno alla loro
condizione . . . a prima vista si davano a conoscere
per individui della specie de' bravi. . . .
Che i due stessero ivi ad aspettar qualcheduno,
30 era cosa troppo evidente; ma quel che più spiacque
a don Abbondio fu il dover accorgersi, per certi
atti, che l'aspettato era lui. Perchè, al suo apparire,
coloro s'eran guardati in viso, alzando la testa, con
un movimento dal quale si scorgeva che tutt'e due
35 a un tratto avevan detto: è lui; quello che stava a
cavalcioni s'era alzato; l'altro s'era staccato dal

(glossa a margine)

stradicciole *lanes*
bel bello *at a leisurely pace*
sulla sera *at dusk*

terre *towns*

ufizio *office*

il suo cammino *on his way*
buttando con un piede *kicking*
ciottoli *pebbles*
inciampo *obstacle*
sentiero *path*

squarcio *passage*

voltata *turn*
solito *accustomed*

viottole *paths*
costoro *them*
a cavalcioni *astride*
muricciolo basso *low wall*

si davano a conoscere . . .
bravi *showed themselves to be individuals belonging to the category of hired assassins*
ivi *over there*

l'aspettato era lui *it was he they were expecting*

s'era staccato *had walked away*

247

ispiar le mosse *watch the moves*

vedendoseli venir proprio incontro *seeing them head straight toward him*

uscita di strada *side road*
gli sovvenne subito di no *he recalled in a flash that there was none*

raccomodarlo *fix it*

fuorchè *except*
non era a tempo *it was too late*
darla a gambe *to take to his heels*
schivare *to avoid*

su due piedi *short*
Signor curato *Reverend Father*

spalancato *wide open*
leggìo *reading stand*

Cioè *That is*

muro; e tutt'e due gli s'avviavano incontro. Egli, tenendosi sempre il breviario aperto dinanzi, come se leggesse, spingeva lo sguardo in su, per ispiar le mosse di coloro; e, vedendoseli venir proprio incontro, fu assalito a un tratto da mille pensieri. 5 Domandò subito in fretta a sè stesso, se, tra i bravi e lui, ci fosse qualche uscita di strada, a destra o a sinistra; e gli sovvenne subito di no. Fece un rapido esame, se avesse peccato contro qualche vendicativo; ma, anche in quel turbamento, il testimonio 10 consolante della coscienza lo rassicurava alquanto: i bravi però s'avvicinavano, guardandolo fisso. Mise l'indice e il medio della mano sinistra nel collare, come per raccomodarlo; e, girando le due dita intorno al collo, volgeva intanto la faccia 15 all'indietro, torcendo insieme la bocca, e guardando con la coda dell'occhio, fin dove poteva, se qualcheduno arrivasse; ma non vide nessuno. Diede un'occhiata, al di sopra del muricciolo, ne' campi: nessuno; un'altra più modesta sulla strada dinanzi; 20 nessuno, fuorchè i bravi. Che fare? tornare indietro, non era a tempo; darla a gambe, era lo stesso che dire, inseguitemi, o peggio. Non potendo schivare il pericolo, vi corse incontro, perchè i momenti di quell'incertezza erano allora così penosi per lui, che 25 non desiderava altro che d'abbreviarli. Affrettò il passo, recitò un versetto a voce più alta, fece ogni sforzo per preparare un sorriso; quando si trovò a fronte dei due galantuomini, disse mentalmente: ci siamo; e si fermò su due piedi. 30

"Signor curato," disse un di quei due, piantandogli gli occhi in faccia.

"Cosa comanda?" rispose subito don Abbondio, alzando i suoi dal libro, che gli restò spalancato nelle mani, come sur un leggìo. 35

"Lei ha intenzione," proseguì l'altro con atto minaccioso e iracondo di chi coglie un suo inferiore sull'intraprendere una ribalderia, "lei ha intenzione di maritar domani Renzo Tramaglino e Lucia Mondella!" 40

"Cioè . . ." rispose, con voce tremolante, don

248

Abbondio: "cioè. Lor signori son uomini di mondo, e sanno benissimo come vanno queste faccende. Il povero curato non c'entra: fanno i loro pasticci tra loro, e poi : . . . e poi, vengono da noi, come s'an-
5 drebbe a un banco a riscuotere: e noi . . . noi siamo i servitori del comune."

"Orbene," gli disse il bravo, all'orecchio, ma in tono solenne di comando, "questo matrimonio non s'ha da fare, nè domani, nè mai."

10 "Ma, signori miei," replicò don Abbondio, con la voce mansueta e gentile di chi vuol persuadere un impaziente, "ma, signori miei, si dégnino di mettersi nei miei panni. Se la cosa dipendesse da me . . . vedon bene che a me non me ne vien nulla
15 in tasca . . ."

"Orsù," interruppe il bravo, "se la cosa avesse a decidersi a ciarle, lei ci metterebbe in sacco. Noi non ne sappiamo, nè vogliam saperne di più. Uomo avvertito . . . lei c'intende."

20 "Ma lor signori son troppo giusti, troppo ragionevoli . . ."

"Ma," interruppe questa volta l'altro com-pagnone, che non aveva parlato fin allora, "ma il matrimonio non si farà, o . . ." e qui una buona
25 bestemmia, "o chi lo farà non se ne pentirà, perchè non ne avrà tempo, e . . ." un'altra bestemmia.

"Zitto, zitto," riprese il primo oratore, "il signor curato è un uomo che sa il viver del mondo; e noi siam galantuomini, che non vogliam fargli del
30 male, purchè abbia giudizio. Signor curato, l'illus-trissimo signor don Rodrigo, nostro padrone la riverisce caramente."

Questo nome fu, nella mente di don Abbondio, come, nel forte d'un temporale notturno, un lampo
35 che illumina momentaneamente e in confuso gli oggetti, e accresce il terrore. Fece, come per istinto, un grand'inchino, e disse: "se mi sapessero suggerire . . ."

"Oh! suggerire a lei che sa di latino!" inter-
40 ruppe ancora il bravo. "A lei tocca. E sopra tutto, non si lasci uscir parola su questo avviso che le

---

uomini di mondo *men of experience*
faccende *affairs*
non c'entra *has nothing to do with it*
pasticci *silly plans*
banco *bank*
riscuotere *draw money*
comune *town*
Orbene *Very well*

non s'ha da fare *must not be performed*

mansueta *subdued*

panni (clothes): shoes

a me non me ne vien nulla in tasca *I do not get anything out of it*
Orsù *Come now*
a ciarle *with idle talk*
ci metterebbe in sacco *would outwit us*
Uomo avvertito *A word to the wise*

buona bestemmia *dreadful curse*

il viver del mondo *the ways of the world*

abbia giudizio *he uses his head*

riverisce caramente *sends his kindest regards*

temporale notturno *night storm*
lampo *flash of lightning*

inchino *bow*

A lei tocca *it's up to you*

249

abbiam dato per suo bene: altrimenti. . . ehm. . .
sarebbe lo stesso che fare quel matrimonio. Via, che
vuol che si dica in suo nome all'illustrissimo signor
don Rodrigo?"

"Il mio rispetto . . ."   5
"Si spieghi meglio!"
". . . Disposto . . . disposto sempre all'ubbi-
dienza." E, dicendo queste parole, non sapeva
nemmeno lui se faceva una promessa, o un complimento. I bravi le presero, o mostraron di prenderle 10
nel significato più serio.

"Benissimo e buona notte, messere," disse l'un
d'essi, in atto di partire col compagno. Don
Abbondio, che, pochi minuti prima, avrebbe dato
un occhio per iscansarli, allora avrebbe voluto 15
prolungar la conversazione e le trattative. "Signori . . ." cominciò, chiudendo il libro con le due
mani; ma quelli, senza più dargli udienza, presero
la strada dond'era lui venuto, e s'allontanarono,
cantando una canzonaccia. Il povero don Abbondio 20
rimase un momento a bocca aperta, come incantato;
e poi prese quella delle due stradette che conduceva
a casa sua, mettendo innanzi a stento una gamba
dopo l'altra, che parevano aggranchiate.

Cap. I.

XXVI

Giacomo Leopardi

(1798–1837)

Unlike Manzoni whose faith was deeply rooted in God and who was loved, admired and honored during a long and full life, Giacomo Leopardi lived but a short time, bereft of faith, health, love and fame. The unhappiest as well as the greatest poet of his age, the misfortunes of his life were the fortune of his poetic genius.

He was born in the little hill town of Recanati not far from Ancona on the Adriatic. His parents, Count Monaldo and Countess Adelaide, were opinionated, bigoted and reactionary. An abyss divided the Leopardi household. On one side were arrayed the parents and close relatives who stood for inflexible parental authority, political and clerical servitude, while on the other were the children who believed in and struggled to achieve an ideal of personal and general happiness and freedom. As the poet later wrote to his father, his parents "required of their children the sacrifice, not only of their physical welfare, but of their natural desires, their youth, their whole life."

Leopardi grew up and died a liberal and an agnostic. From his twelfth to his nineteenth year he lived like a caged bird in his family's ancestral palace. His only solace was his father's vast library where he buried himself and devoured books. In seven years he learned Latin, Greek and Hebrew in addition to a number of modern languages and translated and composed Greek and Latin poems, besides writing a tragedy and several critical essays on the classics, history and astronomy. Unfortunately, the toll was high. The incredible rigors of study permanently impaired his already frail constitution and brought on terrible attacks of melancholy. Only briefly in 1817 did love and the thought of his oppressed country draw him from his depression. At about the same time he began corresponding with Pietro Giordani, a philologist, who had read and admired his poems. Sensing Leopardi's extraordinary talent he urged him in frequent letters to write, and kept him in touch with the world beyond Recanati.

But despair stalked the young poet incessantly. He tried to break his bonds but since his father kept him without funds and under close surveillance his attempt at flight came to nothing. Forced to lead a "bodiless, soulless, lifeless existence," he lost all shadow of hope and with it, faith. Rejecting all consolation, he refused to believe in what his intellect could not confirm and accepted the bitter consequences of this philosophy as the sole truth. He described himself as "nothing but a trunk that feels and suffers," "nothing in the midst of nothingness." The only faith he had left was that of poetry which remained his one consolation to the very end of his life.

When he was finally allowed to leave Recanati to go to Rome, it was too late. His health was gone and he had become a hunchback. Worst of all, in his solitude he had fashioned unknown worlds for himself and had hoped that once away from home a mysterious happiness would fill his empty life with new meaning. Reality proved a bitter disillusionment and a few months later, he returned to his "wild native town".

Twice more he succeeded in getting away from Recanati, subsisting on the modest salary and advances that his publishers and friends sent him for works written in Milan, Bologna, Pisa and also in Florence, where he met Manzoni. Twice, at least, he fell desperately in love but his love was unrequited and brought him nothing but pity, ridicule and disillusionment. In 1828, the University of Bonn offered him the Dante Chair which he was forced to decline because of poor health. In 1832, his devoted friend, Antonio Ranieri, finding him ill and penniless, took him to Naples in the hope that the mild climate might restore his health. But to no avail. On June 14, 1837, Leopardi prematurely breathed his last.

No less unfortunate than his life was the fate of his mortal remains which, after having been moved a number of times, were finally given permanent

ANDERSON

rest in 1939, not far from the supposed tomb of Virgil, on the laurel-covered
hillside of Posilippo, overlooking the Bay of Naples and Vesuvius, the

> . . . . formidabil monte
> sterminator Vesevo . . . .

which had inspired his most grandiose poem, *La Ginestra.*

Leopardi's major claim to glory lies in his collected poems, *I Canti*, which
are a distillation of the few dreams and numberless sorrows of his intolerably
sad and lonely life. *I Canti* may well be compared to an unfinished *Symphonie
Pathétique* in three movements. The first—an allegro con spirito—comprises
the poems of his youth in which, forgetful of his physical handicaps and as

yet unaware of the cruelty of the world, hope and faith inspired him to sing of love and patriotism. The second and longest, a powerful largo-like movement, has as its leit-motif the profoundly pessimistic universal sorrow which surged in his soul when the harsh realities of his life and his bitter contacts with society led him to conclude that his dreams had been mendacious, that man was born to suffer and that disillusion and melancholy were his inescapable lot.

> . . . . Amaro e noia
> [è] la vita, altro mai nulla; e fango è il mondo.

> . . . . Al gener nostro il fato
> non donò che il morire . . . .

The third—in two parts—consists of his two last poems, composed in Naples (1836–37), just before his death. The first, *Il Tramonto della Luna*, is an elegiacal nocturne on the theme of the poet's last lament over his lost youth: Like the earth that fades from view when the moon descends, so vanishes youth. Yet the hills will not long remain widowed, for the sun will flood them again with its torrents of light. But not so with mortal life. Once youth has fled, it remains bereft to the end since the gods have set the tomb as its goal. The second is *La Ginestra*, a *canto* which restates in counterpoint the principal motifs of the poet's philosophy of art and life. It was suggested to him by the contemplation of the supple, golden broom plant that springs from black, arid lava and blooms in solitary splendor: the symbol of man's undaunted vitality and of his frailty and impotence when he is pitted against the blind, annihilating forces of nature, symbolized by Vesuvius which can, at any moment, sear and bury the cities lying at its feet. There follows the poet's conclusion in which a new note of serenity, resignation and tolerance is heard. Man should blame not his fellow man for his woes, but iniquitous nature against which he is powerless. To better its wretched lot, the family of man must federate so that united, men may effectively oppose inimical nature with the forces of enlightened citizenship, rectitude, justice and mercy. Thus, the poet's sorrow, transformed from the purely personal in youth to the universal in maturity, evolves as he stands on the threshold of death into an ideal of human brotherhood and regeneration.

While Leopardi, the poet, owes his undying fame to *I Canti*, his reputation as a prose writer comes to him from his *Operette morali*, twenty-five dialogues which are, in substance, a definition and defense of his universal philosophy of pessimism. Together with his *Zibaldone*, a diary of his psychological life, and his copious *Epistolario*, they constitute a vital and illuminating commentary to his *Canti* and provide us with a key to understanding that starless wintry night which was his life.

254

CANTI

1. All'Italia

O patria mia, vedo le mura e gli archi
e le colonne e i simulacri e l'erme
torri degli avi nostri,
ma la gloria non vedo,
5 non vedo il lauro e il ferro ond'eran carchi
i nostri padri antichi. Or fatta inerme,
nuda la fronte e nudo il petto mostri.
Ohimè quante ferite,
che lividor, che sangue! Oh qual ti veggio
10 formosissima donna! Io chiedo al cielo
e al mondo: dite dite;
chi la ridusse a tale? E questo è peggio,
che di catene ha carche ambe le braccia;
sì che sparte le chiome e senza velo
15 siede in terra negletta e sconsolata,
nascondendo la faccia
tra le ginocchia, e piange.
Piangi, che ben hai donde, Italia mia,
le genti a vincer nata
20 e nella fausta sorte e nella ria.
    Se fosser gli occhi tuoi due fonti vive,
mai non potrebbe il pianto
adeguarsi al tuo danno ed allo scorno;
ché fosti donna, or sei povera ancella.
25 Chi di te parla o scrive,
che, rimembrando il tuo passato vanto,
non dica: già fu grande, or non è quella?
Perchè, perchè? dov'è la forza antica,
dove l'armi e il valore e la costanza?
30 chi ti discinse il brando?
chi ti tradì? qual arte o qual fatica
o qual tanta possanza
valse a spogliarti il manto e l'auree bende?
come cadesti o quando
35 da tanta altezza in così basso loco?

simulacri statues
erme lonely
avi ancestors

ferro ond'eran carchi armor with which were burdened
inerme defenseless

Ohimè Alas

lividor bruises
qual ti veggio in what state do I behold you
formosissima most comely

a tale to such a state

ambe both
sì che so that
sparte le chiome dishevelled

Piangi . . . nella ria Weep, for you have good reason to, my Italy, (who were) born to surpass all nations both in times of good and evil fortune
fonti vive overflowing fountains

danno misery
scorno shame
ché because
donna queen
ancella servant girl
vanto pride
non è quella she no longer is
forza might

discinse il brando disarmed

arte craftiness
fatica feat
tanta possanza overpowering force
valse was needed
l'auree bende golden crown

255

combatte

pugna *fights*	Nessuno pugna per te? non ti difende
tuoi *your sons*	nessun de' tuoi? L'armi, qua l'armi: io solo
qua *bring*	
procomberò *perish*	combatterò, procomberò sol io.
Dammi *Grant me*	Dammi, o ciel, che sia foco
foco *fire*	
italici petti *Italian hearts*	agl'italici petti il sangue mio . . . 5

Grant me oh heaven that my
blood will inspire the Italians   (1818)

purpose to fight (never used)

2. Il sabato del villaggio

donzelletta *peasant maiden*	La donzelletta vien dalla campagna,
in sul calar del sole *at sunset*	in sul calar del sole,
fascio *sheaf*	col suo fascio dell'erba; e reca in mano
	un mazzolin di rose e di viole,
onde, siccome suole *with which, as is her habit*	onde, siccome suole, 10
si appresta *intends*	ornare ella si appresta
crine *hair*	domani, al dì di festa, il petto e il crine.
	Siede con le vicine
a filar *spinning*	su la scala a filar la vecchierella,
incontro là *facing*	incontro là dove si perde il giorno; 15
si perde *fades away*	
novellando vien *she keeps telling tales of*	e novellando vien del suo buon tempo,
buon tempo *youth*	quando ai dì della festa ella si ornava,
sana *young*	ed ancor sana e snella
solea *she used to*	solea danzar la sera intra di quei
intra di quei *with those (young men)*	ch'ebbe compagni dell'età più bella. 20
imbruna *grows dark*	Già tutta l'aria imbruna,
sereno *sky*	torna azzurro il sereno, e tornan l'ombre
tetti *housetops*	giù dai colli e dai tetti,
recente *new-risen*	al biancheggiar della recente luna.
squilla *bell*	Or la squilla dà segno 25
	della festa che viene;
	e da quel suon diresti
	che il cor si riconforta.
	I fanciulli gridando
frotta *groups*	su la piazzuola in frotta, 30
	e qua e là saltando,
romore *din*	fanno un lieto romore:
riede *returns*	e intanto riede alla sua parca mensa,
parca mensa *frugal table*	fischiando, il zappatore,
zappatore *farmer*	e seco pensa al dì del suo riposo. 35

Poi quando intorno è spenta ogni altra face,   face *light*
e tutto l'altro tace,   tutto l'altro *everything else*
odi il martel picchiare, odi la sega   martel *hammer*
del legnaiuol, che veglia   sega *saw*
   legnaiuol *carpenter*
5 nella chiusa bottega alla lucerna,   veglia *is working late*
e s'affretta e s'adopra   lucerna *oil lamp*
   s'adopra *strives*
di fornir l'opra anzi il chiarir dell'alba.   fornir l'opra *finish his task*
   anzi *before*

Questo di sette è il più gradito giorno,
pien di speme e di gioia:
10 diman tristezza e noia
recheran l'ore, ed al travaglio usato   travaglio usato *usual (accus-*
   tomed) work
ciascun in suo pensier farà ritorno.

Garzoncello scherzoso,   Garzoncello scherzoso *Playful*
   boy
cotesta età fiorita   fiorita *blossoming*
15 è come un giorno d'allegrezza pieno,
giorno chiaro, sereno,
che precorre alla festa di tua vita.   precorre *precedes*
Godi, fanciullo mio; stato soave,   stato soave *a sweet estate*
stagion lieta è cotesta.
20 Altro dirti non vo'; ma la tua festa   vo' *(voglio)*
ch'anco tardi a venir non ti sia grave.   ch'anco tardi a venir non ti sia
   grave *even if it be late in coming,*

(1829)   *may it not be a burden to you*

257

3. Il tramonto della luna

piagge *slopes*	. . . Voi, collinette e piagge,
splendor (*of the moon*)	caduto lo splendor che all'occidente
	inargentava della notte il velo,
orfane . . . resterete *not much*	orfane ancor gran tempo
longer will you be bereft	
ché *since*	non resterete; ché dall'altra parte 5
altra parte (*East*)	tosto vedrete il cielo
sorger l' *the breaking of*	imbiancar nuovamente, e sorger l'alba:
poscia *soon*	alla qual poscia seguitando il sole,
folgorando intorno *lighting*	e folgorando intorno
up everything about	con sue fiamme possenti, 1‣
	di lucidi torrenti
eterei campi (*air and sky*)	inonderà con voi gli eterei campi.
poi che *after*	Ma la vita mortal, poi che la bella
	giovinezza sparì, non si colora
	d'altra luce giammai, nè d'altra aurora. 1‣
Vedova è insino al fine	Vedova è insino al fine; ed alla notte
Widowed (*of light*) *it remains*	
to the end	che l'altre etadi oscura,
etadi (*phases of our life*)	segno poser gli Dei la sepoltura.
segno *as a goal*	

(1836)

XXVII

Giuseppe Mazzini

(1805–1872)

When Mazzini was born Manzoni was twenty years old and Leopardi seven. They were contemporaries, patriots and products of the same culture. Yet all three stand far apart, each embodying a different philosophy of life.

Mazzini's ethical code was based on his unflinching faith in "Dio e Popolo". God is, for him, the eternal fount of progress and man the interpreter and executor of God's law of progress. He considered resignation and expiation the enemies of progress. Man must find redemption not from original sin but from his original moral and intellectual imperfection. The world is not a desert, as Leopardi believed, but a place to work toward the realization of an ideal of truth and justice, a battlefield on which man must fight against evil. It is true that evil cannot be rooted out, but one must wage undying battle upon it and everlastingly weaken its dominion. Life is neither a valley of sorrow nor a retreat for contemplation; it is a mission bestowed upon man by God, to be used in the collective task of bettering humanity which is like a man who lives indefinitely and who always learns and perfects himself. The supreme virtue is sacrifice: to think, work, fight and suffer where our lot lies, not for ourselves but for others, for the victory of good over evil. One must, so run Mazzini's arguments, do his duty for duty's sake, and be good for the sake of goodness alone. It is not success that matters but effort in the right direction. However, in order to do his duty man must have a country, which is a stepping stone to world federation. Without a country he has neither name, flag, voice, rights nor even admission into the fellowship of peoples. Besides, he must have liberty for without it there can be no true

society or morality. Liberty is as sacred as the individual, and man is in duty bound to wrest it by any means from any power which denies it to him.

It is on these universal principles of humanism that Mazzini based his apostolate of education and revolution among the Italians. To these ideals he dedicated his whole life and on them he planned, willed and unified Italy.

There are striking similarities between the early years of Mazzini and Leopardi. Both were in poor health. Delicate, sensitive, incredibly precocious, they reacted with pessimism and skepticism toward official religion. Both lived retired lives and were beset by failure and weariness; both were denied the love of wife and family. Mazzini might in all likelihood have succumbed to the same kind of black pessimism which had engulfed Leopardi had it not been for the faith in God and love of mankind which had been instilled in him by his parents.

He was born in Genoa in 1805. His father, a physician and professor of anatomy, and his remarkable mother were both deeply religious, liberal and republican. When only sixteen Mazzini came to full political consciousness and decided that something had to be done to liberate Italy from foreign tyrants. It was then that he began to wear black as a sign of mourning for the plight of his country, a habit he was to keep until he died. He also became the leader of a group of revolutionary students. Although he admired Manzoni's works and respected his beliefs, Dante, Alfieri, Foscolo and Byron were his favorite authors along with Aeschylus and Tacitus among the classics.

Mazzini became a lawyer and practiced especially on behalf of the poor. He also wrote on literary and historical subjects for liberal magazines which were sooner or later suppressed by the censors. Meanwhile, he joined the secret revolutionary society *La Carboneria*, which organized insurrections aimed at overthrowing the local absolutist governments. Having initiated into the society a new member, who turned out to be a government spy, Mazzini was arrested and jailed in the fortress of Savona from which he was released after six months on condition that he choose between confinement in a small town or exile. He chose exile. It was a momentous decision that affected not only his whole life but the destiny of Italy. This happened in 1831. From that year until he died in 1872, Mazzini dedicated himself with messianic faith to Italy and to humanity.

Mazzini went next to Marseilles where he organized a new secret society, *La Giovine Italia*, based on a new creed rooted in principles of political, social, economic and religious reforms. Its recruits were young people who spoke to the masses of fatherland and humanity, of freedom, justice and brotherhood, of duty and sacrifice, and who were pledged to lead them in the fight for a united and republican Italy.

Through a journal also called *La Giovine Italia* which was smuggled into Italy, Mazzini was able to communicate his ideas to his countrymen and to influence the trends of Italian thought. Between 1831 and 1848 his principles had spread from the Alps to Sicily. In every city, chapters of *La Giovine Italia* were formed to which flocked young people, intellectuals, army officers and workers ready to devote themselves to the dangerous life of conspirators. Wherever there were Italians in Europe and even in the Americas, new chapters of *La Giovine Italia* were established.

Fired by Mazzini's faith, these selfless men became apostles of the new faith, of a united Italy and of the brotherhood of nations. Their mottos were: "Dio e Popolo; Pensiero e Azione; Educazione e Rivoluzione; Dovere, Sacrificio, Umanità." Military expeditions, insurrections, uprisings and outbreaks were organized and carried out in all parts of Italy. Reprisals against them were immediate and ferocious. Thousands of patriots were imprisoned, executed or forced into exile. Confident that the seed they were sowing would propagate, their ardor could not be extinguished.

Meanwhile Mazzini's life became even more difficult. Expelled from one country after another, he went into hiding for months on end to continue directing his conspiratorial work through his emissaries abroad or in Italy. He was sentenced to death in absentia by the Piedmontese government. The police and spies of several nations were on his trail, but he managed always to elude them. He was nowhere and everywhere. When they sought him in France or Switzerland he was hiding in Italy under disguise, and the vain efforts of the international police were lampooned by Italian and English poets. Here is a characteristic popular rhyme:

> Where is Mazzini? Ask it of the pine
> that guards the slope of Alps and Apennine.
> In every spot where trembling tyrants fear
> the dawn of freedom, seek Mazzini there!

England, which he came to love as his second motherland, was the only country where, after a period of poverty and hardship, Mazzini found warm and friendly hospitality. Here he spent most of his exile. Through his unceasing activity he won the most influential British intellectuals and statesmen over to the Italian cause. Besides directing *La Giovine Italia,* he established contacts with other European exiles and with them founded *La Giovine Europa,* constituting the basis of the second portion of his political program, the Federation of Europe, which would some day, he hoped, lead to a universal alliance.

The unending insurrections from below and the willingness of the Italians to die for their country revealed the profound changes which had taken place in the conscience of the people and convinced the Italian and foreign governments that the Italians were resolved to free their fatherland regardless of cost. Moreover, they roused the Italian aristocracy and upper conservative classes which, though they did not believe in unification, were forced to put forth a program of their own in order to counterbalance Mazzini's revolutionary and republican plans. Thus, two different currents emerged: the neo-Guelf, led by Vincenzo Gioberti (1801–1852), which advocated a federation of Italian states under the presidency of the pope; and a liberal-moderate current, represented by Count Camillo Benso di Cavour (1810–1861), which, through diplomatic maneuvers, compromises and concessions to foreign powers, proposed to establish a Kingdom of Upper Italy under the rule of the House of Savoy. Mazzini and his followers fought both currents bitterly. They believed that Italy had to be liberated by her own people and united under a democratic republic. As political events began to unfold the struggle narrowed down between Mazzini's and Cavour's programs.

The outcome of the *Risorgimento* was the result of a general compromise, to which Mazzini never agreed, between Cavour's liberal-moderates who were forced to liberate all of Italy, and a considerable number of Mazzini's followers who accepted the monarchy for the sake of achieving unification.

In 1870 the Kingdom of Italy had already been proclaimed, and its capital had been transferred from Turin to Florence. Rome still remained under the Pope. Mazzini, impatient at government delay, had gone off to Sicily to lead a republican insurrection which should have spread upward through the peninsula and liberated Rome; but he was betrayed and, upon landing in Sicily, was arrested and sent to the fortress of Gaeta. By a strange coincidence, he had been imprisoned before in 1831 in his own country by the Piedmontese government in the fortress of Savona where he had conceived *La Giovine Italia* and the unification of Italy; when, nearly forty years later, as a result of the Franco-Prussian war and the withdrawal of the French troops from Rome the Italian government gave orders to its troops to occupy Rome, on December 20, 1870, Mazzini was again imprisoned by the government of Italy to whose liberation and unification he had dedicated his life.

A few weeks later an amnesty was granted, Mazzini was set free and the death sentences pending on him were withdrawn. He refused the amnesty. This was not the Italy he had dreamed, he said.

Two years later, on March 10, 1872, considering himself still an exile, under the assumed name of George Brown, he died in Pisa. He was laid to rest amidst national mourning in the Cemetery of Staglieno in Genoa near the tomb of his mother.

Mazzini's political, social and religious ideas are contained in his booklet *Doveri dell'uomo*, which he dedicated to the workers of Italy. The National Edition of his writings and correspondence consists of over a hundred volumes.

On June 2, 1946, Italy held a referendum to determine whether she would remain a monarchy or become a republic. She became a republic. On that day the thoughts of the Italians were directed toward Mazzini whose life's dream had finally been realized. For days thousands of men, women and children in reverent homage, filed past the tomb of the man who, as Carducci wrote, was:

L'ultimo

dei grandi italiani antichi
e il primo dei moderni
il pensatore
che de' romani ebbe la forza
de' Comuni la fede
de' tempi nuovi il concetto
il politico
che pensò e volle e fece una la nazione . . .

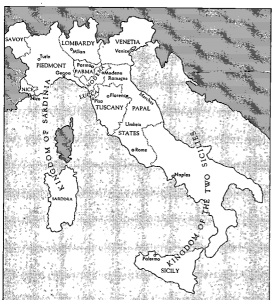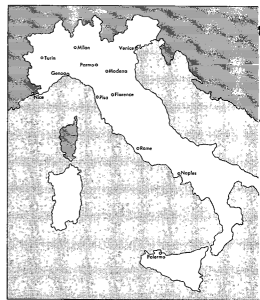

OPERE

1. Per i proscritti d'Italia!

Una domenica dell'aprile 1821, io passeggiavo, giovanetto, con mia madre e un vecchio amico della famiglia, Andrea Gambini, nella Strada Nuova in Genova. L'insurrezione Piemontese era in quei giorni stata soffocata dal tradimento, dalla 5 fiacchezza dei Capi e dall'Austria. Gli insorti si affollavano, cercando salvezza al mare, in Genova, poveri di mezzi, erranti in cerca di aiuto per recarsi nella Spagna dove la rivoluzione era tuttavia trionfante. . . Un uomo di sembianze severe ed 10 energiche, bruno, barbuto e con uno sguardo scintillante che non ho mai dimenticato, s'avvicinò

soffocata *crushed*

fiacchezza *weakness*
insorti *revolutionists*

poveri di *lacking*

tuttavia *still*

sembianze *countenance*

264

a un tratto fermandoci: aveva tra le mani un
fazzoletto bianco spiegato, e proferì solamente le
parole: "Per i proscritti d'Italia!" Mia madre e
l'amico versarono nel fazzoletto alcune monete; ed
5 egli si allontanò per incominciare con altri. Seppi
più tardi il suo nome. Era un Rini, capitano nella
Guardia Nazionale che s'era istituita, sul cominciar
di quel moto. Partì anch'egli cogli uomini per i
quali s'era fatto collettore, e credo morisse com-
10 battendo come tanti altri dei nostri, per la libertà
della Spagna. Quel giorno fu il primo in cui
s'affacciasse confusamente all'anima mia, non dirò
un pensiero di Patria e di Libertà, ma un pensiero
che si poteva e quindi si doveva lottare per la
15 libertà della Patria.

 Io ero già inconsciamente educato al culto
dell'Eguaglianza dalle abitudini democratiche dei
miei genitori e dai modi identici che essi usavano
col patrizio e col popolano. Evidentemente nell'in-
20 dividuo essi non cercavano che l'uomo e l'onesto. . .
Ma l'idea che v'era un guasto nel mio paese contro
il quale bisognava lottare, l'idea che in quella lotta
io avrei potuto far la mia parte, non mi balenò che
in quel giorno per non lasciarmi mai più.

25 L'immagine di quei proscritti, parecchi dei
quali mi furono più tardi amici, mi seguiva ovunque
nelle mie giornate, mi s'affacciava tra i sogni. Avrei
dato non so che per seguirli. . . Sui banchi dell'Università, in mezzo alla irrequieta tumultuante vita
30 degli studenti, io ero cupo, assorto, come invecchiato
anzi tempo. Mi diedi fanciullescamente a vestir
sempre di nero; mi pareva di portare il lutto della
mia patria. . . Dopo, quella prima tempesta si
racquetò e diede luogo a meno travolti pensieri. . .

From: *Note autobiografiche*. Edizione Nazionale delle
 Opere di Giuseppe Mazzini. Vol. 77.

2. Mazzini carbonaro

35 Scoppiava l'insurrezione francese del luglio
1830. I capi si agitavano senza intento determinato,

Glossary

a un tratto *suddenly*
spiegato *spread open*

versarono *dropped*

un *a certain*

moto *insurrection*

nostri *(compatriots)*

s'affacciasse *presented itself*
anima *mind*

popolano *common man*
essi . . . l'onesto *they sought only the man and what is decent (in him)*
v'era un guasto *something was wrong*
parte *bit*
balenò *flashed before my mind*

s'affacciava tra *crept into*

irrequieta *restless*

cupo *gloomy*
fanciullescamente *childishly*

si racquetò *quieted down*
travolti *troubled*

Scoppiava *was breaking out*

Luigi Filippo (*Louis Philippe,*
  King of France)
fondere palle *make bullets*

Tre Giornate *three glorious
  days (July 27–29)*

salita *slope*
Maggiore *Major*

a guisa di *like*

incarico *task*
colto *seized*

intimi *intimate friends*

da praticarsi *to be carried on*

antiveggenza *foresight*

"cugino" *fellow member*

cavata *having pulled out*

bastone *walking stick*
prestare *take*
giuramento *oath*
si schiuse *opened*
ignoto *unknown man*

lavorato *proselytized*

aspettando libertà da Luigi Filippo. Noi giovani ci demmo a fondere palle e a prepararci per un conflitto che consideravamo inevitabile e decisivo.

Non ricordo le date, ma poco dopo le Tre Giornate di Francia, ricevetti l'ordine di recarmi 5 ad un'ora determinata al Lion Rouge, albergo esistente allora nella salita di San Siro, dove avrei trovato un Maggiore Cottin di Nizza o di Savoia, il quale aveva ricevuto, dicevano, il primo grado di Carboneria e invocava il "secondo" che io 10 dovevo conferirgli. Noi giovani eravamo comandati dai Capi a guisa di macchine e sarebbe stato inutile chiedere perchè scegliessero me a quell'ufficio invece d'altri a cui il Maggiore fosse già noto. Accettai quindi l'incarico. Soltanto, colto da non 15 so quale presentimento, mi misi d'accordo, prima di compierlo, coi giovani Ruffini, intimi di mia madre, intorno a un modo di corrispondenza segreta da praticarsi per mezzo delle lettere della famiglia nel caso possibile d'imprigionamento. E 20 l'antiveggenza giovò.

Mi recai, nel giorno assegnato, all'albergo, chiesi del Cottin e lo vidi. Era un uomo piccolo di statura con uno sguardo errante che non mi piacque; vestiva abito non militare, parlava fran- 25 cese. Gli dissi, dopo d'essermi fatto riconoscere "cugino", ch'egli doveva sapere perchè io venissi. Introdottomi nella sua camera da letto, chiuso l'uscio, egli piegò un ginocchio ed io, cavata, com'era d'uso, una spada dal bastone, cominciavo 30 a fargli prestare il giuramento, quando si schiuse subitamente un piccolo uscio nel muro, accanto al letto, e s'affacciò da quello un ignoto. Mi guardò e richiuse. Cottin mi pregò di acquetarmi, dichiarò che colui era un suo fidatissimo domestico e si scusò 35 dell'avere dimenticato di chiudere l'uscio a chiave. Compìta l'iniziazione, il Maggiore mi disse che egli si recava per tre giorni a Nizza dove avrebbe lavorato utilmente fra la milizia, ma che la memoria lo tradiva e che io avrei fatto bene a dargli la 40 formula del giuramento in iscritto. Rifiutai, dicendo

266

che non era abitudine mia scrivere cose simili. Scrivesse egli sotto mia dettatura. Scrisse, e mi congedai, scontento di quella scena.

Scrivesse egli *I suggested that he write*

L'ignoto, come seppi dopo, era un carabiniere regio travestito.

carabiniere regio travestito *member of the Royal Police in disguise*

5 Trascorsi pochi giorni, io ero nelle mani della polizia.

Ibid.

3. L'individuo, la nazione e l'umanità

Da quando l'idea d'una vita collettiva e progressiva del genere umano—affermata in tanti 10 luoghi del poema e delle opere minori di Dante— diventò, per meditati lavori storici e filosofici, fede agli intelletti del nostro secolo, l'umanità fu riconosciuta come l'intento supremo ad ogni sforzo sulle vie del bene. E da quel giorno crebbe l'importanza 15 della nazione, termine intermedio tra l'umanità e l'individuo. . . Il culto della nazione venne opportuno a moltiplicare le forze dell'individuo e a insegnargli come il sacrificio e il lavoro di ogni uomo si possano rendere efficacemente giovevoli 20 all'umanità.

fede agli intelletti *the faith of the intellectuals*

termine intermedio *intermediate link*
opportuno *at a timely moment*

giovevoli *beneficial*

Senza patria non c'è umanità, come senza organizzazione e divisione di lavoro non esiste speditezza e fecondità di lavoro. Le nazioni sono gl'individui dell'umanità, come i cittadini sono 25 gl'individui della nazione. Come ogni uomo vive d'una vita propria e d'una vita di relazione, così vive ogni nazione. Come i cittadini d'una nazione devono farla prospera e forte con l'esercizio delle loro diverse funzioni, così ogni nazione deve com- 30 piere una missione speciale, una parte di lavoro a seconda delle proprie attitudini per lo sviluppo generale, per l'incremento progressivo dell'umanità. Patria e umanità sono dunque ugualmente sacre. Dimenticare l'umanità sarebbe sopprimere ogni

speditezza e fecondità di lavoro *expeditious and fruitful labor*

incremento *betterment*

intento *incentive*

raggiungere *achieve*
l'intento *the aim*
punto d'appoggio dato alla
  leva *fulcrum of the lever*

intento al lavoro. Cancellare, come alcuni vorreb-
bero, la nazione sarebbe sopprimere lo strumento
con il quale noi possiamo raggiungere l'intento. La
patria è il punto d'appoggio dato alla leva che deve
operare a pro dell'umanità.   5

"La Santa Alleanza dei Popoli," *Ibid.*
Vol. 39.

4. La Federazione Europea

ordinandovi *organizing*

La tendenza innegabile dell'epoca che ora
s'inizia è quella di ricostituire l'Europa ordinandovi,
a seconda delle vocazioni nazionali, un certo
numero di Stati uguali possibilmente per estensione
e popolazione. E questi Stati, divisi, ostili, gelosi 10
l'uno dell'altro finchè la loro bandiera nazionale
non rappresentava che un interesse di casta o di
dinastia, s'associeranno, per mezzo della demo-
crazia, sempre più intimamente. Le nazioni saranno
sorelle. Libere, indipendenti nella scelta dei mezzi 15
a raggiungere il fine comune e nell'ordinamento
delle loro forze per tutto ciò che riguarda la vita

vita interna *national affairs*

si stringeranno *will unite in*

interna, si stringeranno a una fede, ad un patto per
tutto ciò che riguarda la vita internazionale.

fuggendo a un tempo *avoiding
both*

L'Europa dei popoli sarà una, fuggendo a un tempo 20
l'anarchia di una indipendenza assoluta e il con-
centramento della conquista.

Ibid.

5. L'Associazione dei Popoli

Noi vagheggiamo da molto
tempo il pensiero *We have
been cherishing for a long time
the idea*

schierasse affratellati e ordinati *should group together and
organize*
ne avviasse . . . lavori *should
initiate its work with a general
plan*

Noi vagheggiamo da molto tempo il pensiero
d'una vasta associazione che, divisa in altrettante
sezioni e abbracciando in sè tutte le manifestazioni 25
dell'attività umana, schierasse affratellati e ordinati,
secondo le tendenze e le capacità individuali, tutti
i credenti della nuova era e ne avviasse con un
disegno generale i lavori. Pochi uomini venerandi
per dottrina e virtù, per intelletto ed amore, per 30

sacrifici intrepidamente sostenuti a pro della fede comune nei diversi paesi d'Europa e d'America, formerebbero il Consiglio Supremo dell'Associazione e la loro parola uscirebbe sempre collettiva
5 e sintetica al mondo. Altri uomini più intimamente affratellati per comunanza d'origine col pensiero e colle tendenze di ciascun popolo, costituirebbero una serie di Consigli Nazionali presieduti, per tutelare l'unità del concetto, ciascuno da un mem-
10 bro del Consiglio Supremo appartenente alla nazione rappresentata. Nel Consiglio Supremo avrebbe espressione il concetto della missione generale dei popoli; nei Consigli Nazionali quello della missione speciale che spetta ad ogni nazione.

Ibid.

intrepidamente sostenuti *nobly endured*

affratellati *related*

tutelare *guarantee*

avrebbe espressione *would be expressed*

ALINARI

XXVIII

Giuseppe Garibaldi

(1807–1882)

Mazzini's motto was "Pensiero e Azione". While he represented thought, it was Garibaldi who came to represent action.

Garibaldi was a born warrior for justice, liberty and humanity. A man with nerves of steel and with a granite-like faith in the unification of Italy, he could arouse the masses to magnanimous deeds. His life is unparalleled in the wealth of its experiences.

270

He was born in Nice in 1807, when it belonged to Piedmont. His father, a seaman, tried to give his son the best education he could afford but the boy was restless and had little use for his studies. When his mother tried to drive him into the priesthood, he rebelled and ran away from home. The sea was his element and his passion. At the age of fifteen he embarked as a cabin boy and for eleven years sailed the Mediterranean in this capacity and others until 1833, when he became captain of a brigantine.

One night, having laid anchor in a small port of the Black Sea, he overheard a group of sailors in an inn discussing the plight of Italy under the foreign yoke. He joined them and heard of the work that Mazzini and *La Giovine Italia* were doing towards its liberation. This incident was as decisive in Garibaldi's life as the meeting with the Italian refugees in the harbor of Genoa had been for the young Mazzini in 1821. Writing about this incident years later, Garibaldi said that his joy in discovering that there existed a man and an organization dedicated to the redemption of Italy was greater than that of Columbus upon the discovery of the new world. The same night, in that far-distant port of the Black Sea, Garibaldi took the oath of *La Giovine Italia*.

Some months later he met Mazzini in Marseilles and offered his sword to the common cause. Thought and action had come together and the destiny of the new Italy was sealed. Mazzini was preparing that year an insurrection in the Piedmontese navy aimed at seizing ships for the republican insurrectionists. But government spies got wind of the plot and the insurrection failed. Garibaldi and Mazzini were both condemned to death. But Mazzini was already in exile and Garibaldi a fugitive. Thus began a long series of adventures which skyrocketed Garibaldi among the makers of modern history and forged him into one of the world's legendary heroes.

Since the French police had orders for his deportation, Garibaldi found himself a job as a second mate on a ship and fled to Rio de Janeiro.

One of the basic principles in the moral education of the Italians enunciated by Mazzini in his *Doveri dell'uomo* stated: "In whatever land you may be, whenever a man is fighting for right, for justice, for truth, there is your brother. Whenever a man suffers through oppression of error, of injustice, of tyranny, there is your brother . . . Fight for him, but fight as Italians so that the blood you shed will bring honor not only to you but also to your country." Garibaldi became the embodiment of this principle. He established the Garibaldian tradition according to which for generations, freedom-loving Italians, obeying the dictates of conscience, have donned the traditional Red Shirt and gone to fight not only for the freedom of their own country but for that of the peoples of Uruguay (1842–1846), Greece (1866, 1879), France (1870, 1914–1915) and Spain (1936–1937).

Garibaldi spent the greater part of his twelve years in South America fighting first, as Fleet Commander of the Republic of Rio Grande do Sul which was rising against Brazil for its independence and, later, as Commander-in-Chief of the naval and ground forces of the Uruguayan republic, in revolt against the Argentinian dictatorship. It was during the latter campaign that Garibaldi organized the first Italian Legion and that the traditional Red Shirt was worn for the first time by his men. All of Garibaldi's actions had been crowned with success, and reports of his astonishing exploits attracted the attention of the world but most particularly of Italy where he was considered a popular hero and his name was on everyone's lips. During this period he had become expert in every phase of the art of warfare, had learned how to improvise armies and provide for their equipment, how to inspire his troops and inflame them with a courage and will power more effective than material strength.

In 1848, when news of the first revolts reached him in Montevideo, he went to Italy to which Mazzini had also returned from London. The two exiles met in Milan while the city was in revolt against the Austrians. Just as action very often fails to respond to thought, the meeting of the two leaders of the movement for Italian unification revealed a deep cleavage: Mazzini stood adamant on his republican principles; besides, past experience had taught him to have little trust in King Carlo Alberto and in the monarchy. Garibaldi, on the other hand, although a staunch republican, was ready "to serve the Italian cause even if led by the devil himself." Events were to bring these two men together at various times in later years, but perfect unity of thought and action was never realized between them. Mazzini, undeterred, went on working for the cause of Italy against the monarchy. Garibaldi did the same, but when he deemed it expedient he fought for the monarchy.

Thus in all three wars for Italian independence he led his volunteers victoriously on the side of the monarchy against the Austrians. In 1849 he was again with Mazzini and heroically defended the republic of Rome against the French, Austrian, Neapolitan and Papal armies. To avoid surrendering his army he accomplished a memorable retreat, hotly pursued through enemy territory from Rome to a place near Venice. During this operation he lost under tragic circumstances his Brazilian wife, Anita, who had courageously followed him during his battles in South America and Italy. After disbanding his troops, he sought refuge in Piedmont, Tunis, Gibraltar and Tangier, but expelled from every place, he came to the United States where he tried to earn a living as a candle-maker on Staten Island. In 1860, he was back in Italy and, despite Cavour's opposition, conducted the famous expedition of one thousand Red Shirts (*I Mille*), the greatest undertaking of his life, and liberated southern Italy, from Sicily to Naples, which he turned over to Victor Emmanuel II who, the following year, was proclaimed King of Italy.

Garibaldi decided that his next mission would be the liberation of Rome ("O Roma, o Morte!"). This dream became so obsessive that in 1861 he declined Abraham Lincoln's invitation to come to North America to assume command of the Federal army. To carry out his Roman undertaking he had to overcome both the French troops garrisoned in the city and the irresolution of the newly created Italian government. Three times he marched toward Rome. In 1862 he was stopped, wounded and arrested by the Italian army. In 1867 he was again arrested and confined by the same government to the island of Caprera from which he escaped a few weeks later, crossed the Tyrrhenian Sea and led 5,000 volunteers to capture the Eternal City. During the first encounters he defeated the papal troops, but having arrived in the town of Mentana, his men, armed with old guns and supplied with no more than twenty-four cartridges apiece, were confronted with 11,000 fresh French troops fully equipped with guns of the latest model. This time he was forced to retreat and, worse, was once more arrested on order of the government of the very Italy whose historical capital he had wished to restore.

This was not Garibaldi's last campaign. In 1870, Napoleon III brought France into war against Prussia, the country was invaded by the Germans, the emperor was overthrown and the republic re-established. Rome, liberated by the Italian army, became the capital of the united Italy. Garibaldi was sixty-three years old. His dream now realized, he might have spent the last years of his life on his island of Caprera. But he saw that the French people and their new republic were in danger and fighting for their freedom. He forgot the defeats that the French army had inflicted upon him in his attempts to liberate Rome, hastened to France and was put in command of a unit composed of 20,000 Italian and French volunteers. They fought so brilliantly that they won the admiration even of the Prussian commanders and, at Dijon, fought the only victorious battle of the war.

Although this was the last dramatic act of his tempestuous and colorful life, Garibaldi in his last years never lost touch with world events. Now that the wars of independence were over, he devoted himself to the maintenance of peace between nations and to the writing of his mémoirs. In letters, speeches and proclamations he passionately advocated universal suffrage, the abolition of all standing armies and a league of all nations. The complete national edition of his writings includes three historical novels and numerous poems.

He died in 1882 and was put to rest on the island of Caprera. His death was mourned by friend and foe the world over and he passed to history as the "Hero of Two Worlds" and "The Knight of Humanity".

MEMORIE AUTOBIOGRAFICHE

1. Prefazione

3 luglio 1872

Vita tempestosa, composta di bene e di male, come credo della maggior parte della gente. Coscienza di aver cercato il bene sempre, per me e per i miei simili. E se ho fatto il male qualche volta, certo lo feci involontariamente. Odiatore della tirannide e della menzogna, col profondo convincimento che esse sono l'origine principale dei mali e della corruzione del genere umano. Republicano quindi, essendo questo il sistema della gente onesta, sistema normale voluto dai più, e per conseguenza non imposto colla violenza e coll'impostura. . .

i miei simili my fellow-men
Odiatore Foe
menzogna falsehood

più majority
impostura deceit

2. Esilio a Staten Island

. . . A Tangeri, col generoso mio ospite Carpeneto, io passai vita tranquilla e felice, quanto lo può essere quella d'un esule italiano, lontano dai suoi cari e dalla patria sua. . .

Nella mia relegazione però non ero dimenticato da tutti i miei amici italiani. Francesco Carpanetto, a cui dovevo sin dal principio del mio arrivo in Italia nel 1848 un'infinità di favori e gentilezze, aveva ideato di raccogliere, per mezzo dei miei conoscenti e suoi, una somma sufficiente a costruire un bastimento destinato ad esser comandato da me per guadagnarmi la vita.

Questo progetto mi piaceva. Non potendo fare nulla per l'adempimento della mia missione politica, mi sarei almeno occupato, lavorando mercantilmente, ad acquistare un'esistenza indipendente,

Carpeneto (Piedmontese consul)
quanto lo as far as
cari dear ones
relegazione banishment
Francesco Carpanetto (a shipowner)
sin dal ever since the

raccogliere collecting

bastimento ship

vita living

adempimento accomplishment
mercantilmente in the merchant marine
esistenza livelihood

274

e non più stare a carico dell'amico generoso che mi aveva ospitato.

stare a carico *be a burden*
ospitato *given hospitality*

    Accettai immediatamente il progetto dell'amico mio Francesco, e mi disposi a partire per gli Stati Uniti ove doveva effettuarsi la compra del bastimento. Verso giugno 1850 m'imbarcai per Gibilterra, di là per Liverpool e da Liverpool a New York. Nella traversata per l'America fui assalito da dolori reumatici che mi tormentarono durante una gran parte del viaggio. Fui finalmente sbarcato come un baule, non potendo muovermi, a Staten Island, nel porto di New York.

disposi *prepared*
doveva effettuarsi *was to be effected*
di *from*

baule *trunk*

    I dolori mi durarono un paio di mesi, ch'io passai parte a Staten Island e parte nella città stessa di New York, in casa del mio caro e prezioso amico Michele Pastacaldi, ove godevo l'amabile compagnia dell'illustre Felice Foresti, uno dei martiri dello Spielberg.

Felice Foresti (*exile and teacher of Italian at Columbia University*)
Spielberg (*Moravian prison*)

    Il progetto del Carpanetto non poteva intanto attuarsi per mancanza di contribuenti. Egli aveva

275

azioni *shares*
diecimila lire *(then about $2,000)*
Bergamo *(city in Lombardy)*

Antonio Meucci *(he claimed the invention of the telephone)*
brav' *fine*
fabbrica di candele *candle factory*
Detto fatto *No sooner said than done*
interessarmi nella speculazione *take a share in the business*

qualunque *ordinary*

amorevolezza *kindness*

spinto *urged*

irrequietezza *restlessness*

proposito *intention*
mestiere *trade*
marinaio *a seaman*
sul litorale *along the shore*
navi da cabotaggio *tramp-ships*
merci *cargo*
Giunto *Reaching*
dettero retta *paid attention*

si stava lavorando a scaricare *they were unloading*

mercede *wages*

scuotere *shake off*

Meno ancora *Nothing doing*

Riandavo *went back*

squadra *fleet*
nonchè *not to speak of*
bellicoso *valiant*
Rintuzzai *I swallowed*

raccolto tre azioni di diecimila lire ognuna dai Fratelli Camozzi di Bergamo e da Piazzoni. Ma che bastimento si poteva comprare in America con trentamila lire? Inoltre, non essendo io cittadino americano, sarei stato obbligato di prendere un Capitano di quella nazione, e non conveniva.

Infine qualche cosa bisognava fare. Un mio amico, Antonio Meucci, fiorentino e brav'uomo, si decide a stabilire una fabbrica di candele e mi offre di aiutarlo.

Detto fatto. Non potevo interessarmi nella speculazione per mancanza di fondi, giacchè le trentamila lire, non essendo state sufficienti per la compra del bastimento, erano rimaste in Italia. Mi adattai quindi a quel lavoro colla condizione di fare quanto potevo. Lavorai per alcuni mesi con Meucci, il quale non mi trattò come un suo lavorante qualunque, ma come uno della famiglia e con molta amorevolezza.

Un giorno però, stanco di far candele e spinto forse da irrequietezza naturale ed abituale, uscii di casa col proposito di mutar mestiere. Mi rammentavo d'esser stato marinaio, conoscevo qualche parola d'inglese, e mi avviai sul litorale dell'isola, ove scorgevo alcune navi da cabotaggio occupate a caricare e scaricare merci.

Giunto alla prima, chiesi d'esser imbarcato come marinaio. Appena mi dettero retta coloro che scaricavano sulla nave, e continuarono i loro lavori. Feci lo stesso avvicinando una seconda nave, ed ebbi la medesima risposta. Infine passo ad un' altra, ove si stava lavorando a scaricare, e domando se mi si permette di aiutare al lavoro, e n'ebbi in risposta che non ne abbisognavano. "Ma non vi chiedo mercede," io insistevo. E nulla. "Voglio lavorare per scuotere il freddo." (Vi era veramente la neve). Meno ancora. Io rimasi mortificato.

Riandavo col pensiero a quei tempi quando ebbi l'onore di comandare la squadra di Montevideo, nonchè il bellicoso e immortale esercito. A che serviva tutto ciò? Non mi volevano. Rintuzzai

276

infine l'umiliazione e tornai al lavoro del sego. Fortuna ch'io non avevo palesato la mia risoluzione all'eccellente Meucci, e quindi, concentrato in me stesso, il dispetto fu minore. Devo confessare inoltre
5 non essere il contegno del mio buon principale verso di me che mi avesse indotto alla mia intempestiva risoluzione. Egli m'era prodigo di benevolenza e d'amicizia, come lo era la signora Ester, sua moglie.
10   La mia condizione non era dunque deplorabile in casa dei Meucci, ed era proprio stato un accesso di malinconia che m'aveva spinto ad allontanarmi da questa casa. In essa io ero liberissimo, potevo lavorare se mi piaceva: e preferivo naturalmente il
15 lavoro utile a qualunque altra occupazione; ma potevo andare a caccia qualche volta, e spesso si andava anche a pesca collo stesso principale, e con vari altri amici di Staten Island, che spesso ci favorivano colle loro visite. In casa poi non v'era
20 lusso, ma nulla mancava delle principali necessità della vita, tanto per l'alloggio quanto per il vitto. . .
    Finalmente giunse l'amico mio Francesco Carpanetto a New York. Egli aveva da Genova iniziato un commercio in grande per l'America
25 centrale. Il San Giorgio, nave a lui appartenente, era partito da Genova con parte del carico, ed egli stesso era passato in Inghilterra a preparare il resto ed inviarlo a Gibilterra, ove la nave doveva prenderlo. Deciso che io l'accompagnassi nel-
30 l'America centrale, facemmo subito i preparativi di partenza, e nel 1851 mi misi in viaggio con Carpanetto per Chagres con un vapore americano comandato dal Capitano Johnson.

3. Ritorno a New York

   . . . Rimasi alcuni giorni ancora a New York,
35 godendo la cara compagnia dei miei preziosi amici Foresti, Avezzana e Pastacaldi, ed essendo giunto

Glossary

sego *tallow*

palesato *revealed*

dispetto *resentment*

contegno *behavior*
principale *employer*
intempestiva *unreasonable*
la signora *Signora*

casa dei Meucci (*now "The Garibaldi and Meucci Memorial Museum"*)
accesso *attack*

a caccia *hunting*

a pesca *fishing*

in grande *on a large scale*
nave *ship*
carico *cargo*

mi misi in viaggio *set out*
Chagres (*Panamanian river*)
vapore *steamer*

in quel mentre *during the interval*
ebbi da lui proposta *he asked me*

veleggiai *sailed*

carbon fossile *coal*

di stringere al seno *to embrace*

in quel mentre nel porto il Capitano Figari con intenzione di comprare un bastimento, ebbi da lui proposta di comandarlo per condurlo in Europa. Io accettai e fummo col Capitano Figari a Baltimore, ove si acquistò la nave Commonwealth. 5 Caricatala di farina e grano, veleggiai per Londra, ove giunsi in febbraio del 1854.

Da Londra andai a Newcastle, ove caricammo carbon fossile per Genova, e giungemmo in quest'ultimo porto il 10 maggio dello stesso anno. 10

A Genova, essendo ammalato di reumatismi, fui trasportato in casa del mio amico il Capitano G. Paolo Augier, ove ricevetti ospitalità gentile per quindici giorni; quindi passai a Nizza, ove ebbi finalmente la fortuna di stringere al seno i miei 15 figli dopo un esilio di cinque anni.

From: *Memorie autobiografiche*. G. Barbera, Editore, Firenze, 1888.

278

ANDERSON

XXIX

Giuseppe Verdi

(*1813–1901*)

Giuseppe Verdi was born in the little village of Le Roncole, in the province of Parma, where his parents ran a small wine and grocery shop. The parish priest taught the three R's to the outwardly shy and uncommunicative boy who was easily disposed to anger and chafed under any sort of restriction. Very early in life he revealed an uncommon sensitivity to music, which he had first heard in the little church where he served mass, from strolling players and wandering minstrels.

Impressed by the young Verdi's musical talent, Antonio Barezzi, a wine merchant and amateur musician from the nearby town of Busseto, induced the child's father to buy him an old spinet. The village organist instructed the boy who practiced tirelessly for hours on end. When he replaced his old teacher as organist in the church of Le Roncole at the age of twelve, Verdi's

279

father decided to send him to the high school of Busseto where he also took private music lessons from the conductor of the local philharmonic orchestra which he subsequently joined. Here he learned to play the piano and wind instruments, to arrange opera selections and compose marches and ballet music. His local fame grew. Determined that the boy should be a musician, Barezzi again convinced Verdi's father to borrow the necessary money from the Monte di Pietà so that he might study music at the Milan Conservatory.

In 1832, young Verdi set out for Milan to take his entrance examinations. Either because his playing failed to impress the examiners or perhaps because of his uncouth appearance, he was refused admission. Disheartened but not crushed, Verdi, with Barezzi's financial help, remained in Milan where he took private lessons, studied composition and became acquainted with the works of Italian classic composers.

It was during this period that a completely fortuitous incident brought Verdi to the attention of the world's musical capital. One evening a group of musicians were rehearsing Haydn's *Creation* in a local theater. The conductor failed to turn up. The 20-year-old Verdi, who was sitting inconspicuously in a corner, was asked to substitute. He gave such a magnificent account of himself that he was invited to conduct other productions, among them Rossini's *La Cenerentola*.

After three years of hard study Verdi applied for the post of choir and music master at Busseto. He was turned down for reasons of petty local rivalries and politics, but when the townspeople rose in protest, the position was finally assigned to him.

The period running from 1836 to 1840 was the happiest and saddest of Verdi's life. He married Margherita Barezzi, the lovely and musical daughter of his old friend, and practiced, taught, directed and composed feverishly. Two children were born and, in November 1839, his first opera, *Oberto*, was performed at La Scala. Its great success brought him admiration and contracts as well as contacts with the most eminent personalities of Milan's artistic circles. Among these were two persons destined to have an enormous influence on his life and career: the great singer Giuseppina Strepponi, who later became his second wife, and Giovanni Ricordi, Verdi's publisher and son of the founder of the famous music publishing house.

But fortune soon deserted him. Within the brief span of three months, from April to June 1840, while hard at work on his second opera, *Un Giorno di Regno*, death claimed his beloved wife and two children. Overwhelmed by grief, he nonetheless drove himself mercilessly to finish the opera which was produced in September. It was a complete fiasco. Vowing to compose no more, he closed his apartment, shipped his household effects to Busseto and took a furnished room where he brooded over his sorrow.

The world might easily have lost one of its greatest musical geniuses if Domenico Morelli, impresario at La Scala, who was rushing to a rehearsal one snowy night, had not chanced to meet Verdi coming out of a *trattoria.*. Seizing "the temperamental boy"—in whom he had never lost faith—by the arm, he walked and talked with him and, before leaving him, thrust the manuscript of a new libretto into his pocket. Verdi went home and to bed determined not even to look at the libretto. But he could not resist. Waking during the night, he read it and liked it.

The evil spell was broken. He set to work and by the time the next theater season opened Verdi's new opera *Nabucco* was ready. Its première at La Scala was greeted with thunderous ovations. His reputation now securely re-established, Verdi felt reborn.

Nabucco was destined to be the first of a long series of operatic master-pieces which include: *Ernani, Rigoletto, Il Travotore, La Forza del Destino, Aida* and *Otello*. These were climaxed by *Falstaff*, a gem of operatic orchestration and one of the most perfect and complex works of art, written when Verdi was eighty years of age.

Verdi composed rapidly and at white heat. He would then rearrange, eliminate, add and polish. His style is a striking fusion of music and words which spring from a profound understanding of the passions of the human heart. Here is his advice to young artists: "Put your hand upon your heart and study that. If you have the soul of an artist, your heart will tell you all you need to know."

His operas have an inexhaustible range and give voice to every gradation of human feeling. They combine technical mastery and genuine inspiration with a grandiose but austere atmosphere. All bear the mark of painstaking research for perfection which Verdi would finally achieve by the felicitous blending of recitative and cantabile, of drama and lyricism in a new and full-flowing melody.

From Shakespeare, in whom he found a kindred soul, he drew the plots of some of his greatest operas. Like Shakespeare, he wrote not for the select few or for his countrymen alone, but for mankind. To quote the words which Alfredo sings in *La Traviata*, Verdi's music expresses "the heart beat of the entire universe"

> . . . . quell'amor ch'è palpito
> Dell'universo, dell'universo intero.

This is the key to Verdi's universal appeal and popularity and to the lasting magical enchantment which his operas create for audiences throughout the world.

I COPIALETTERE

1. Fiasco e successi della "Traviata"

[For over a century *La Traviata* has been one of Verdi's most acclaimed operas. Strange as it may seem today, its première was a complete fiasco. Realizing that the débacle was due to the baritone who had sung without feeling and to the hefty and vigorous soprano whose interpretation of the role of the gentle and consumptive Violetta had aroused hilarity in the audience, Verdi's friends insisted that the opera be performed again with a new cast to test its merits. Verdi made a number of small changes in the score and, one year later, in the very city of Venice where it had failed so dismally, *La Traviata* was hailed as a tremendous success. In the three letters which follow, Verdi, who had witnessed the première, gives a candid report of the fiasco to one of his former pupils; to his publisher; and to a friend.

In the fourth letter, written a year later, the publisher's secretary informs Verdi of *La Traviata*'s triumph.]

Venezia, 7 marzo 1853

Caro Emanuele,

La Traviata, ieri sera, fiasco. La colpa è mia
o dei cantanti? . . . Il tempo giudicherà.

Giuseppe Verdi 5

Venezia, 7 marzo 1853

Caro Ricordi,

Sono dolente doverti dare una triste notizia,
ma non posso nasconderti la verità. La Traviata ha
fatto fiasco. Non indaghiamo le cause. La storia è 10
così. Addio, addio.

Partirò dopodomani. Scrivere a Busseto.

Giuseppe Verdi

La storia è così These are the hard facts

Scrivere Please write

Venezia, 9 marzo 1853

Carissimo Luccardi, 15

Non ti ho scritto dopo la prima recita della
Traviata; scrivo dopo la seconda. L'esito è stato
fiasco! Fiasco deciso! Non so di chi sia la colpa: è
meglio non parlarne. Non ti dirò nulla della musica
e permettimi che nulla ti dica degli esecutori. 20

Addio; vogliami sempre bene. Parto domani
per Busseto.

Giuseppe Verdi

vogliami sempre bene continue to hold me in your affection

Milano, 9 maggio 1854

Illustre Maestro, 25

Accludo alla presente una lettera ricevuta ieri
tardi da Gallo. Oggi ne abbiamo ricevute delle
altre, e da lui e da Vigna, che parlano dell'inde-
scrivibile entusiasmo con cui fu accolta, meglio
ancora, se è possibile della prima sera, La Traviata. 30

Gallo (an impresario)

Vigna (an alienist)

È un successo senza esempio. Ella era profeta quando diceva: "La Traviata è caduta, di chi la colpa? Mia o dei cantanti? Non so nulla. Il tempo deciderà." Ed il tempo ha deciso, e nella stessa città, e con quegli stessi spettatori che prima l'avevano condannata, mentre ora, come scrive Vigna, ognuno si vanta d'averla giudicata per una bellissima opera fino dall'anno scorso!

senza esempio *unparalleled*

fino dall' *as early as*

p. (per) *for (on behalf of)*

p. Tito di Giovanni Ricordi
Girolamo Cerri, segretario

From: *I Copialettere di Giuseppe Verdi*, a cura della Commissione Esecutiva per le Onoranze a G. V. nel primo centenario della nascita. Milano, 1913.

2. Per il suocero

[Verdi's affection for and gratitude toward his father-in-law, Antonio
Barezzi, was to last all his life. Countess Clara Maffei, one of Verdi's most
devoted friends, whose salon was a rendezvous of distinguished artists and
patriots, had enquired about Barezzi's health and Verdi, in this letter,
announces to her the imminent death of the beloved old man.]

Sant'Agata   (*Verdi's villa*)

Sant'Agata, 30 gennaio 1867

Carissima Clarina,

Vi ringrazio, mìa graziosa buonissima Clarina
della vostra affettuosa lettera.

Oh, questa perdita mi sarà estremamente 5
dolorosa! Egli sta meglio da tre o quattro giorni;
ma vedo bene che non è che un sollievo per prolungare la vita di qualche giorno, e non di più!
Povero vecchio, che mi ha voluto tanto bene! E
povero me che per poco ancora, e poi non lo 10
vedrò più! ! !

Egli   (*Verdi's father-in-law*)

Voi sapete che a lui devo tutto, tutto, tutto.
Ed a lui solo, non ad altri, come han voluto far
credere. Mi par di vederlo ancora (e son ben molti
anni) quando, finiti i miei studi nel ginnasio di 15
Busseto, mio padre mi dichiarò che non avrebbe
potuto mantenermi nell'Università di Parma, e mi
decidessi di ritornare nel mio villaggio natio.
Questo buon vecchio, saputo questo, mi disse: "Tu
sei nato a qualche cosa di meglio, e non sei fatto 20
per vendere il sale e lavorare la terra. Domanda a
codesto Monte di Pietà una borsa di studio di 25
franchi al mese per quattro anni, ed io farò il resto;
andrai al Conservatorio di Milano e, quando lo
potrai, mi restituirai il denaro speso per te." 25

son . . . anni   *that was many
years ago*

Monte di Pietà (*public pawn-
broking institution*)

cuore   *kindheartedness*

Così fu! Vedete quanta generosità, quanto
cuore e quanta virtù! Io ne ho ben conosciuti degli
uomini, ma giammai uno migliore! Egli mi ha
amato quanto i suoi figli, ed io l'ho amato quanto
mio padre. . . 30

Giuseppe Verdi
Ibid.

286

3. Per fare della musica

[Verdi and Wagner were born the same year. Both dominated the world of music at the same time. But an unbridgeable chasm separated them, their art and musical worlds. Verdi was of the opinion that Wagner was a philosopher-composer who wrote with his brain alone and composed according to dogmatic tenets. Moreover, Verdi sensed in Wagner's musical apotheosis of the hero the germ of rising Pan-Germanism. On the other hand, Verdi considered himself an instinctive artist who sought the highest musical perfection through the union of heart and brain. As a matter of fact, each was the expression of two different temperaments: the German and the Latin. And each, in his own fashion, was great.

Verdi admired Wagner's genius but detested his music. He abominated even more Wagner's imitators whom he lumped together with all imitators and academicians who blindly follow artistic preconceptions. In one of his intimate letters written to Count Arrivabene, a journalist and old friend, Verdi, evidently in a belligerent mood, pokes fun at the sculptor Giovanni Dupré who was making in Florence a statue of Cavour wearing a Roman toga in the neo-classical style of the day. He takes the occasion to unleash his tongue against the *avveniristi* or Wagnerian composers who were writing "Music of the Future" without having music "in their hearts".]

Genova, 6 marzo 1868

Caro Arrivabene,

L'uomo propone e . . . dispone.   . . . *(God)*

È un fatto positivo che io non sono mai
5 riuscito a fare quello che ho voluto. Vedi, per
esempio, io vorrei essere o falegname o muratore;   falegname *carpenter*
no signore, sono un maestro di musica. Quando   muratore *mason*
spero una cosa me ne arriva un'altra; se temo una
disgrazia mi capita una fortuna; se mi decido andar   mi capita una fortuna *good*
10 a piedi uno mi porta via in carrozza; se voglio   *luck comes my way*
andar in carrozza si rompe una ruota e mi mette   uno *someone*
a piedi.

Immaginati poi quando si tratta di far un
viaggio, od anche un viaggetto. Tutta questa
tiritera è per dirti, cose che già sai, che non sono
venuto a Firenze. Perchè? Non lo so! Vi verrò più
5 tardi? Non oso rispondere. E sì che ho una gran
voglia di veder Firenze col suo Cavour vestito a la
romana! Ah, questi artisti sono una razza di bestie
curiose! Una volta che s'abbian formata una
reputazione hanno paura di loro stessi e diventano
10 scolastici. Dupré sa bene che fare un Cavour
vestito alla romana è cosa da pazzi, ma ciò gli
offrirà il mezzo di far delle pieghe e delle pose, ecc.
Gli accademici avran gridato bravo . . . la *claque*
e la *réclame* fanno il resto e i gonzi credono. Amen!
15 non voglio più dir niente degli artisti perchè temo
(sono in vena) di dirne male, e se prolungando il
discorso dovessi cadere sugli artisti-musici ne direi
male sicuramente. Oh questi sono ancora più
matti degli altri! Son ciechi che giocano al bastone.
20 Dove capita, capita. Non sanno cosa vogliono nè
dove vanno. Che bella novità! so anch'io che vi è
una Musica dell'avvenire, ma io presentemente
penso e penserò così anche l'anno venturo che per
fare una scarpa ci vuole del corame e delle pelli! . . .
25 Che ti pare di questo stupido paragone che vuol
dire che per fare un'opera bisogna aver in corpo
primieramente della musica! . . . Dichiaro che io
sono e sarò un ammiratore entusiasta degli avveniristi a una condizione: che mi facciano della
30 musica . . . qualunque ne sia il genere, il sistema
ecc. ma musica! . . . Basta, basta! perchè non vorrei
che parlandone troppo mi si attaccasse il male.
Sta' tranquillo. Mi possono benissimo mancare le
forze per arrivare dove io voglia, ma io so che
35 voglio. Addio. Addio. Sta' sano. Già so che stai
bene perchè lo desidero e lo sento. Dammi tue
notizie. La Peppina ti saluta.

Giuseppe Verdi

From: *Verdi intimo*, by Annibale Alberti.
A. Mondadori, Milano, 1931.

Glosses:

tiritera *long story*

E sì che *To be sure*

Cavour (*a monument to Cavour, now in Turin*)
vestito a la romana *wearing a Roman toga*

scolastici *traditionalists*
Dupré *Giovanni Dupré (1817–1882), Tuscan sculptor*
cosa da pazzi *stark madness*
claque *paid applauders*
réclame *advertising*
gonzi *fools*
più dir niente *to say anything else*
in vena *in the mood*

ciechi che giocano al bastone *like blind fencers*
Dove capita, capita *It does not matter where they hit*
Musica dell'avvenire (*Wagner's music*)

corame *hide*
pelli *skins*

in corpo *within oneself*

avveniristi (*Wagnerian composers*)

mi si attaccasse il male *I should fall prey to the contagion (of excogitating systems instead of writing music)*
Sta' tranquillo *Rest assured*

Dammi tue notizie *let me hear from you*
Peppina (*Giuseppina Strepponi, Verdi's second wife*)

288

4. La pubblicità

[Because Verdi considered the audience the sole and best judge of his works, he had little love for music critics. He also had nothing but contempt for all publicity which he considered a humiliation for the arts and the artist. He was determined to win recognition for his operas not through humbug, intrigue and favoritism but on the basis of merit alone. On the occasion of the première of *Aida* in Cairo, a music critic who had been invited by the Viceroy of Egypt to cover the event, wrote to Verdi offering his services. Verdi seized the opportunity to make a number of caustic remarks about success based on publicity.]

Genova, 8 dicembre 1871

Egregio Signor Filippi,   Signor Filippi   (*music critic*)

Le sembrerà strano, ben strano, quanto sto per   ben   *indeed*
dirle, ma perdoni se non posso tacerle tutte le   tacerle   *refrain from giving you*
5 impressioni dell'animo mio.
Ella al Cairo?—È questa una delle più potenti
réclames che si potessero immaginare per Aida!—A   réclames   *advertisements*

289

partita di piacere *game*
caccia *hunting party*
dietro *after*

a ricevere le fucilate *to be shot down*
destare *create*
apparato *fuss*
coristi *chorus-singers*

edifizio *temple*
piccole miserie *idle talk*

offuscano *obscure*

Bottesini (*orchestra conductor*)

di mise en scène *effective staging*
à la grâce de Dieu *I recommend myself to God's mercy*
ché *because*
Dev.mo (Devotissimo) *Sincerely*

me pare che l'arte in questo modo non sia più arte, ma un mestiere, una partita di piacere, una caccia, una cosa qualunque a cui si corre dietro, a cui si vuol dare, se non il successo, almeno la notorietà ad ogni costo! . . . Il sentimento che io provo è quello del disgusto, dell'umiliazione!—Io rammento sempre con gioia i miei primi tempi in cui senza quasi un amico, senza che alcuno parlasse di me, senza preparativi, senza influenza di sorta mi presentavo al pubblico con le mie opere pronto a ricevere le fucilate, e felicissimo se potevo riuscire a destare qualche impressione favorevole. Ora quale apparato per un'opera?! . . . Giornalisti, artisti, coristi, direttori, professori, ecc. ecc., tutti devono portare la loro pietra all'edifizio della *réclame*, a formare così una cornice di piccole miserie che non aggiungono nulla al merito di un'opera, anzi ne offuscano il valore reale.—Ciò è deplorabile: profondamente deplorabile!!!

La ringrazio delle cortesi offerte per il Cairo. —Scrissi l'altro ieri a Bottesini su tutto quanto riguardava l'Aida. Desidero solo per quest'opera una buona e sopratutto intelligente esecuzione vocale, strumentale e di *mise en scène*. Per il resto: *á la grâce de Dieu*, ché così ho cominciato, e così voglio finire la mia carriera.

Faccia buon viaggio e mi creda Suo Dev.mo

Giuseppe Verdi

From: *I Copialettere di Giuseppe Verdi*. Ibid.

290

XXX

Giovanni Verga

(1840–1922)

The story of Verga's life is as uneventful as the lives of the characters he portrays were eventful. He was born in Catania at the foot of Mount Etna. Abandoning his law studies to become a writer, he wrote during his early twenties four historical and psychological novels which served to give him entrée into the social and literary circles of Florence and Milan where he went to live. Under the influence of Italian romanticism he then wrote several successful novels of passion dealing mostly with the sentimental problems of the upper classes. Meanwhile, he had become interested in the French realistic and naturalistic schools of Flaubert and Zola which had developed as a reaction to romanticism. Through these influences he gradually fashioned and inaugurated a new style and a new way of seeing and portraying man's existence which, because of its austere impersonality and closeness to reality, became known as *verismo*.

Verga's *verismo* differs from French or Russian naturalism in a number of ways. To begin with, the characters think and see with their own mind and eyes, and speak with their own language in terms of their own culture, customs, traditions and environment and not in those of the author. While the naturalists tended to see and study man in his animality, Verga sought and studied man in his humanity, in his primeval and innate nobility. These he found most particularly among the humble peasants and fisherfolk of his native Sicily.

The *verismo* of Verga is abundantly evident in his collections of short stories—*Vita dei campi* (1880) and *Novelle rusticane* (1883)—which are true literary jewels. But it reaches its climax in his two novels, *I Malavoglia* (1881) and *Mastro Don Gesualdo* (1889).

Verga had planned to write a series of five novels describing man's eternal struggle for progress through five stages of his ascent and decline: the struggle for material existence; for wealth; for social pre-eminence; for political power and luxury. Once man reaches this ultimate stage, he is consumed by his own appetites and passions and sooner or later degenerates and reverts to his initial condition or stage.

Basing himself on this theory, which recalls Vico's law of occurrences and recurrences governing civilizations, Verga expected to trace "the fatal, ceaseless, often exhausting and fevered journey that humanity covers in its efforts to achieve progress."

He wrote only the first two novels of the proposed cycle. Soon after *Mastro Don Gesualdo* appeared, the reading public fell under the spell of D'Annunzio's melodious if magniloquent style and of his lustful, polished tales of love between aristocratic ladies and hedonistic supermen. By comparison, Verga's stories about the tribulations of humble men and women, narrated in a starkly simple and unconventional style, seemed uninteresting and barbaric.

Verga stopped writing, and with stoic dignity retired to Catania where, shut up within an enigmatic silence, he lived a solitary life for thirty years, a forgotten and unproductive writer.

The tragic years of the first World War, however, changed the outlook of many Italians who had been brought face to face with the bitter realities of life and death and felt an impelling need to know man's real condition. D'Annunzio's star began to wane. Critics undertook a reappraisal of Verga's work and came to appreciate the impact of its moral strength and the enduring vitality of its inspiration.

By 1920, the Italians discovered that Verga was not only the greatest Italian novelist after Manzoni but one of the great writers of Europe. National honors were showered upon Verga who was then eighty years old. Two years later he died. His reputation has continued to grow steadily in Italy and abroad. His works have been translated several times into English, some of them by D. H. Lawrence. The most recent and best translation of *I Malavoglia* (The House by the Medlar Tree) appeared in 1953.

La Donya è la moglie di Sebastiano

Modern American prose bears a striking resemblance to Verga's style, a coincidence which, in an indirect way, makes Verga responsible for the popularity which contemporary American writers enjoy at present in Italy.

I Malavoglia takes place in the picturesque fishing village of Aci Trezza that lies at the foot of Mount Etna, facing a group of high-pointed rocks called I Faraglioni or Scogli dei Ciclopi which rise from the sea and which, legend claims, are the very rocks that the blinded Poliphemus hurled at the fleeing Ulysses.

The story is concerned with the epic struggle against nature, fate and society of three generations of Malavoglias, a family of fisherfolk, who strive to pay off a crushing debt, recover their lost boat, La Providenza, the mortgaged homestead where all were born, and gather their scattered clan together again under the paternal roof. The family, which had enjoyed a certain measure of security and prosperity, is composed of a patriarchal grandfather, Old Master 'Ntoni; his only son Sebastiano, who also lives in the old house with his wife and their five children: three boys, young 'Ntoni, Luca and Alessi, and two girls, Mena (Philomena) and Lia (Rosalia).

Their troubles begin during the period of depression which followed in the wake of Garibaldi's liberation of Sicily. To make both ends meet, Padron 'Ntoni decides to buy on credit a load of edible white lupins which his son will then take by boat to a nearby city where he can sell them at a substantial profit. The Providenza, laden with the lupins and with Sebastiano at the helm, sails out of Aci Trezza but ship, cargo and men are engulfed by the sea in a storm. From then on the ill-starred Malavoglias, as they are commonly nicknamed in their village, are dogged by disaster. Aging Padron 'Ntoni resumes full control of the family and during his long, relentless efforts to pay off the debt on the lupins he loses his beloved house, Luca is killed in a

Master 'Ntoni of importance to working the family

293

naval battle and, what is perhaps even more irreparable in their conception of life, two of his grandchildren, tired of sweating and toiling endlessly, break the unity of the home and bring dishonor to the family. Young 'Ntoni becomes a smuggler and is sent to prison for stabbing a customs officer. Lia becomes a woman of easy virtue. However, by the time death comes to old Padron 'Ntoni, Alessi and Mena have managed to pay off the debt and regain possession of the house.

Verga's veristic novels are packed with action, tension and drama. They are choral, spoken novels. The dialogue is terse, incisive, muscular and gripping. There is no description by the author of the various characters. They describe themselves or each other and reveal their innermost feelings through a few gestures and explosive phrases pregnant with meaning which stimulate the reader's intuition and imagination.

I MALAVOGLIA

Il ritorno di 'Ntoni

[In the concluding episode of *I Malavoglia*, we witness the brief homecoming of young 'Ntoni who has just emerged from prison. He, who had detested his village, his home, his life and work and who, to change his status, had broken violently with his family and dishonored their name, now that he knows what life can hold, takes one long, last look at the homestead and his village to which he realizes only too well he can never return.]

Una sera, tardi, il cane si mise ad abbaiare
dietro l'uscio del cortile, e lo stesso Alessi, che andò
ad aprire, non riconobbe 'Ntoni il quale tornava
colla sporta sotto il braccio, tanto era mutato,
5 coperto di polvere e colla barba lunga. Come fu
entrato e si fu messo a sedere in un cantuccio, non
osavano quasi fargli festa. Egli non sembrava più
quello, e andava guardando in giro le pareti, come
se non le avesse mai viste; perfino il cane gli
10 abbaiava, ché non l'aveva conosciuto mai. Gli
misero fra le gambe la scodella, perchè aveva fame
e sete, ed egli mangiò in silenzio la minestra che
gli diedero, come non avesse visto grazia di Dio da
otto giorni, col naso nel piatto; ma gli altri non
15 avevano fame, tanto avevano il cuore serrato. Poi
'Ntoni, quando si fu sfamato e riposato alquanto,
prese la sua sporta e si alzò per andarsene.

uscio	*gate*
lo stesso	*even*
sporta	*haversack*
Come	*When*
si fu messo a sedere	*had taken a seat*
cantuccio	*corner*
quello	*like himself at all*
andava	*kept*
scodella	*bowl*
minestra	*soup*
grazia di Dio	*food*
serrato	*gripped with emotion*
si fu sfamato	*had satisfied his hunger*

si sentì balzare il cuore dal petto *his heart leaped up in his breast*
smarrita *dismayed*
dacchè *since*
mi è andata *has turned*

da buscarmi il pane *a way to earn my daily bread*

stretto in una morsa *caught in a vise*

sulla porta *on the threshold*
non sapeva *could not*

nespolo *loquat tree* .

pezzetto *a little while*

inutilmente *in vain*

fece per sedersi *started to sit down*
si rizzò di botto *quickly stood upright*

fare un giro per *to look around*

gli era bastato l'animo *who had had the courage*
di dare una coltellata a *to stab*
di starsene nei guai *to be always in hot water*

stalla *stable*
vitello *calf*
lucente *sleek*
chioccia *setting hen*

Alessi non osava dirgli nulla, tanto suo fratello era mutato. Ma al vedergli riprendere la sporta, si sentì balzare il cuore dal petto, e Mena gli disse tutta smarrita: —Te ne vai? —Sì!— rispose 'Ntoni.

—E dove vai? —chiese Alessi.

—Non lo so. Venni per vedervi. Ma dacchè son qui la minestra mi è andata tutta in veleno. Dopo tutto qui non posso starci, perchè tutti mi conoscono, e perciò son venuto di sera. Andrò lontano, dove troverò da buscarmi il pane, e nessuno saprà chi sono.

Gli altri non osavano fiatare, perchè ci avevano il cuore stretto in una morsa, e capivano che egli faceva bene a dir così. 'Ntoni continuava a guardare dappertutto, e stava sulla porta, e non sapeva risolversi ad andarsene. —Ve lo farò sapere dove sarò;— disse infine, e come fu nel cortile, sotto il nespolo, che era scuro, disse anche:

—E il nonno?

Alessi non rispose; 'Ntoni tacque anche lui, e dopo un pezzetto:

—E la Lia, che non l'ho vista?

E siccome aspettava inutilmente la risposta, aggiunse colla voce tremante:

—È morta anche lei?

Alessi non rispose nemmeno; allora 'Ntoni che era sotto il nespolo, colla sporta in mano, fece per sedersi, poichè le gambe gli tremavano, ma si rizzò di botto, balbettando:

—Addio, addio! Lo vedete che devo andarmene?

Prima d'andarsene voleva fare un giro per la casa, per veder se ogni cosa fosse al suo posto come prima; ma adesso, a lui che gli era bastato l'animo di lasciarla e di dare una coltellata a don Michele, e di starsene nei guai, non gli bastava l'animo di passare da una camera all'altra, se non glielo dicevano. Alessi che gli vide negli occhi il desiderio, lo fece entrare nella stalla, col pretesto del vitello che aveva comprato la Nunziata, ed era grasso e lucente; e in un canto c'era pure la chioccia coi

pulcini; poi lo condusse in cucina, dove avevano
fatto il forno nuovo, e nella camera accanto, dove
vi dormiva la Mena coi bambini della Nunziata. . .
'Ntoni guardava ogni cosa, e approvava col capo,
5 e diceva: —Qui pure il nonno avrebbe voluto
metterci il vitello; qui c'erano le chiocce, e qui
dormivano le ragazze, quando c'era anche quel-
l'altra. . .— Ma allora non aggiunse altro e stette
zitto a guardare intorno, cogli occhi lustri . . .
10   Gli altri stettero zitti, e per tutto il paese era
un gran silenzio, soltanto si udiva sbattere ancora
qualche porta che si chiudeva; e Alessi si fece
coraggio per dirgli:
   —Se volessi, anche tu ci hai la tua casa. Di là
15 c'è apposta il letto per te.
   —No!— rispose 'Ntoni. —Io devo andarmene.
Là c'era il letto della mamma, che lei inzuppava
tutto di lagrime quando volevo andarmene. Ti
rammenti le belle chiacchierate che si facevano la
20 sera, mentre si salavano le acciughe? e la Nunziata
che spiegava gl'indovinelli? e la mamma, e la Lia,
tutti lì, al chiaro di luna, che si sentiva chiacchierare
per tutto il paese, come fossimo tutti una famiglia?
Anch'io allora non sapevo nulla, e qui non volevo
25 starci, ma ora che so ogni cosa devo andarmene.
   In quel momento parlava cogli occhi fissi a
terra, e il capo rannicchiato nelle spalle. Allora
Alessi gli buttò le braccia al collo.
   —Addio,— ripetè 'Ntoni. —Vedi che avevo
30 ragione d'andarmene! qui non posso starci. Addio,
perdonatemi tutti.
   E se ne andò colla sua sporta sotto il braccio;
poi, quando fu lontano, in mezzo alla piazza scura
e deserta, che tutti gli usci erano chiusi, si fermò ad
35 ascoltare se chiudessero la porta della casa del
nespolo, mentre il cane gli abbaiava dietro, e gli
diceva col suo abbaiare che era solo in mezzo al
paese. Soltanto il mare gli brontolava la solita
storia lì sotto, in mezzo ai faraglioni, perchè il mare
40 non ha paese nemmeno lui, ed è di tutti quelli che
lo stanno ad ascoltare, di qua e di là dove nasce e

pulcini *chicks*
forno *oven*

quell'altra (*Lia, who had run
 away from home*)

lustri *shining*

sbattere *the slamming*
si fece *plucked up*

ci *here*
Di là *in the next room*
apposta *just*

inzuppava *bathed*

acciughe *anchovies*
indovinelli *riddles*

rannicchiato *buried*

usci *doors*

solo *the only person*
brontolava *murmured*
storia *refrain*
nemmeno lui *either*

muore il sole, anzi ad Aci Trezza ha un modo tutto suo di brontolare, e si riconosce subito al gorgogliare che fa tra quegli scogli nei quali si rompe, e par la voce di un amico.

Allora 'Ntoni si fermò in mezzo alla strada a guardare il paese tutto nero, come non gli bastasse il cuore di staccarsene, adesso che sapeva ogni cosa, e sedette su un muricciuolo.

Così stette un gran pezzo pensando a tante cose, guardando il paese nero, e ascoltando il mare che gli brontolava di sotto. E ci stette fin quando cominciarono ad udirsi certi rumori ch'egli conosceva, e delle voci che si chiamavano dietro gli usci, e sbatter d'imposte, e dei passi per le strade buie. Sulla riva, in fondo alla piazza, cominciavano a formicolare dei lumi. Egli levò il capo a guardare i Tre Re che luccicavano, e la Puddara che annunziava l'alba, come l'aveva vista tante volte. Allora tornò a chinare il capo sul petto, a pensare a tutta la sua storia. A poco a poco il mare cominciò a farsi bianco, ed i Tre Re ad impallidire, e le case spuntavano ad una ad una nelle vie scure, cogli usci chiusi, che si conoscevano tutte. . . 'Ntoni tornò a guardare il mare, che s'era fatto amaranto, tutto seminato di barche che avevano cominciato la loro giornata anche loro, riprese la sua sporta, e disse:

—Ora è tempo d'andarmene, perchè fra poco comincerà a passar gente.

I Malavoglia. A. Mondadori, Milano, 1939.

al gorgogliare che fa *by its gurgling*

come non gli bastasse il cuore di *as if he could not find the heart to*

sbatter d'imposte *the banging of shutters*

formicolare *twinkle*

Tre Re *Orion*
luccicavano *glowed*
Puddara *Pleiades*
tornò a chinare *again dropped*
a pensare a *again recalled*

farsi bianco *grow white*
impallidire *grow pale*
spuntavano *became distinguishable*

s'era fatto amaranto *had grown purple*
seminato di *dotted with*
giornata *day's work*

298

IL NOVECENTO

Characteristics of the Century

The first decade of the 20th century was for Italy a period of growing prosperity, social progress and political evolution. The national aspirations of the country at that time fell roughly into two main currents: one democratic, the other nationalistic and imperialistic.

The first, inspired by humanistic and risorgimental traditions, was represented by the democratic parties, including a large sector of the socialists, who in varying degrees believed in a gradual transformation of Italian society through education, persuasion and social reforms conducted in a spirit of justice and tolerance, without revolutions or wars of conquest.

The second current, fired by memories of the Roman Empire, was represented intellectually by D'Annunzio and politically by the new nationalist movement, supported by banking, industrial and military interests. Both had been influenced by the irrationalistic doctrines of Friedrich Nietzsche (1844–1900) and Georges Sorel (1847–1922) and by envy of expanding British, French and German colonialism. After 1909, they were joined by the Futuristic movement. All extolled might, violence and the free expression of man's primitive instincts. They professed that the more man behaves like a brute, the more of a man he becomes. War was defined as "the sole hygiene of the world" because it ensures the survival of the fittest from whom will spring a generation of heroes and supermen. They also claimed to believe in the superiority of the Italian race and in the "infallible imperial destinies" of Rome.

Between these two currents stood the conservatives and the bulk of the nation which, though apolitical, shifted its weight now to one side now to the other.

The nationalists won their first success in 1911–1912 when the Italian government went to war against Turkey and conquered Libya in North Africa. From this date onwards the peaceful development and prosperity of Italy began to decline.

In 1914, World War I broke out and Italy, after one year of neutrality, entered the conflict on the side of the Allies against the Austro-Hungarian Empire. Her intervention had been demanded by the democrats and the nationalists and opposed by the socialists and Catholic politicians who spoke for the masses. The interventionism of the democrats was prompted by their desire to liberate the two Italian regions of Trento and Trieste still under Austrian rule, and to fulfill their moral duty by fighting side-by-side with the western democracies against the tide of German imperialism. The interventionism of the nationalists was motivated by their love of war for war's sake and by their imperialistic designs.

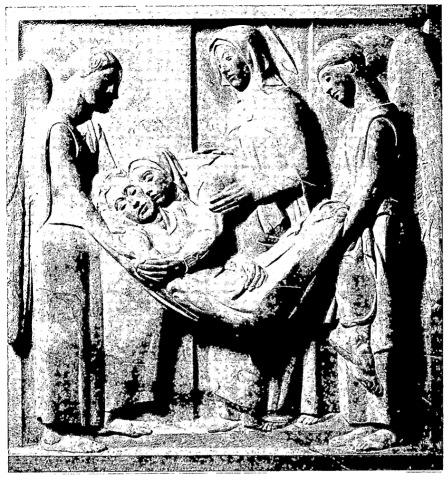

The war along the Italian-Austrian front was long and hard. For the first time, the nation, which had not yet recovered from the Libyan war, had to face one of Europe's most powerful and experienced armies, entrenched in strongly fortified positions in the Alps. However, notwithstanding strong passive opposition on the home front, inferior resources, untold sacrifices and a number of initial military setbacks, the Italian army succeeded in shattering the forces of that truculent Austrian Empire which Italy had considered through the centuries as her "eternal enemy".

At the close of World War I, Italy might have considered herself satisfied with and proud of her achievements. She had won a brilliant military victory, liberated Trento and Trieste, made secure her boundaries and could boast of

301

possessing three colonies (Eritrea, Somaliland, and Libya), all of which now made her a great nation. But there were powerful nuclei within the country that did not share this view. Italy was led astray by them. The humanistic and risorgimental tradition was broken once again.

To begin with, the immediate post-war years were marked in Italy, as everywhere else, by social and political unrest. The passage from a war to a peace economy hit all classes, especially the millions of workers who became unemployed when the war industries closed down. The number of idle was greatly increased by the hundreds of thousands of demobilized servicemen who, having won the war, found themselves without jobs. Yet, Italy, through a series of trials and errors, weathered the crisis successfully and by the end of 1921 was on the road to recovery.

However, the nationalistic forces, dissatisfied with Italy's territorial gains, had gravitated earlier towards the newly-founded Fascist movement which had exploited the unrest and had created, with the support of powerful interests and the acquiescence of government and army officers, its own military organization, the Fascist squads, which suppressed strikes and labor agitations. In 1922, after a series of cabinet crises, King Victor Emmanuel III (1869–1947) appointed Benito Mussolini (1883–1945), a former socialist and now leader of the Fascist party, head of the government. Within three years the Fascists instituted their own militia for the defense of the state, terrorized and suppressed all opposition parties and abolished freedom of speech, press and assembly. Italy thus ceased to be a democracy and was ruled by an iron-fisted dictatorship.

The split of the Italian soul and the spiritual disintegration of Italian culture that ensued were brilliantly described by G. A. Borgese (1882–1952) in *Goliath, the March of Fascism*, while the political collapse was masterfully documented by Gaetano Salvemini (1872–1957) in *The Fascist Dictatorship in Italy*. The symptoms of the disease which was to affect the whole Italian body politic can be clearly traced in certain sections of the literature of the period, especially among the writers who expressed moral, social, intellectual and political restlessness.

There were those who, like Giovanni Papini (1881–1956), author of *Un uomo finito* (Life and Myself), casting aside moderation and limitations, wished to emulate God and searched feverishly for "the new", for an absolute faith, truth or certainty and, failing to attain their goal, sank into dejection; while others turned to dogmatic orthodox systems or fell prey to new demagogies. From an opposite camp, Luigi Pirandello, in his first novels, sought to prove that there is nothing absolute in life. Truth, faith, justice, beauty and personality are ever changing; everything is relative and must be accepted as such. But this philosophy did not even touch the resolute seekers of "the

302

new" nor those politicians who, having placed their faith in nationalistic and chauvinistic theories, had meanwhile concluded that "the new" lay in the future.

The initiator of the new gospel was Filippo Tommaso Marinetti (1876–1944) who, with a small group of followers, published the first *Manifesto del Futurismo* in 1909. Their program expressed in brash and brutal terms their violent revolt against the morality, customs, traditions, history and art of the past. They advocated the destruction of libraries, museums and ancient cities. They had discovered a "new beauty" in speed, and claimed that "a roaring automobile, its engine adorned with great carburetor tubes similar to breath-exploding serpents, is more beautiful than the victory of Samothrace." They glorified "war, sole hygiene of the world, militarism, patriotism and scorn of women." In subsequent manifestos each expert laid down rules for the art of the future which "can be nothing if not violence, cruelty and injustice. It must unceasingly and tumultuously express contemporary life as it is, transformed into the triumph of science." Painting should express the sensations of color, noises and odors through the use of "shouting and screaming colors" such as "roooooosssissssimo" and "veeeeeerdiiiiiissssssimo". Music should give voice to the soul of crowds, factories, trains, battleships and

303

airplanes. For literature they demanded freedom of the word through the abolition of syntax, meter, rhythm and rhyme and the elimination of adjectives, adverbs and punctuation. Verbs could be used only in the infinitive. All these shackles were to be substituted with three new elements: noise, weight and odor so as to express, for instance "a landscape of odors as it is sensed by a dog", or "the conversation of motors". They left no stone unturned, no string unpulled.

In politics they wanted the word "Italia" to dominate over the word "Libertà"; they clamoured for a great naval fleet, a bigger army and the Italian citizen ever-ready for war. All this had to be accomplished through a cynical, shrewd, aggressive, expansionistic foreign policy for the promotion of pan-Italianism and the supremacy of Italy. They also proclaimed themselves anti-democratic, anti-socialistic and anti-clerical.

From its inception, Futurism manifested itself primarily as an artistic movement and as such slowly influenced all the arts which are nowadays qualified as modern. Politically, it appears today as the first symptom of the rising totalitarian ideologies and of those catastrophic wars which were to engulf not only Italy but Europe and the world during the first half of the twentieth century.

It would be a mistake, however, to believe that the new political and artistic doctrines were accepted by the Italian intelligentsia. They found their adherents among the new uprooted generation, semi-intellectual desperados and hackwriters. In actuality, the majority of the Italians either looked upon them with indifference or covered them with ridicule. The greater number of Italian writers remained immune to the new virus and continued in the

304

traditions of Manzoni, Verga and Carducci, or followed their own course. Two women novelists, Matilde Serao (1856–1927) and Grazia Deledda (1875–1936), applied veristic tenets to their works: the former in bringing to light the lower-depths of Naples; the latter, Nobel Prize winner of 1926, by explaining in modern terms her primitive Sardinia. Italo Svevo (1862–1928) was acclaimed as a forerunner of introspective fiction for his witty, human, psychological novels; Alfredo Panzini (1863–1939) poked fun, in a limpid, classical style, at the extravagances of the machine age; while Marino Moretti (1885–   ) described with nostalgia the poetic world of the humble, and Riccardo Bacchelli (1891–   ) began his series of remarkable historical novels. Two early recruits of the Futuristic school deserted it and worked out their own way: Massimo Bontempelli (1878-1960), a bizarre, imaginative realist and surrealist prose writer, and Aldo Palazzeschi (1885–   ) who, in small and large canvasses, depicted Florentine life at the turn of the century. Several new voices were heard in poetry. Most typical was that of Ada Negri (1870–1945) who was inspired by a sentimental form of socialism. Next to hers emerged those of the crepuscular poets led by Guido Gozzano (1883–1916), whose sweet and melancholy poetry solaced their short, consumptive lives. The richest and not least important vein was that of Umberto Saba (1883–1957), a master of semi-realistic and day-dreamed colloquial verse.

The figurative arts of the early *Novecento* carried over the main motifs of the preceding century. With the advent of Futurism architecture became rationalized, and the arch, column and decorative effects were abolished. Sculpture, less affected by Futurism, drew its inspiration from Etruscan and Roman models, translating them into symbolical or realistic forms. In painting, alongside the futuristic school three others developed: the metaphysical, an offshoot of cubism and surrealism, which aimed at a complete reform of painting techniques; the primitive, which advocated a return to the pure forms of the early Renaissance; and the neo-classic which attempted a compromise between the classic and the modern.

The most typical artists of this period include the sculptors Marino Marini (1901–   ), Giacomo Manzù (1908–   ), Mirko (1910–   ) and Afro (1912–   ); and the painters Amedeo Modigliani (1884–1920), Umberto Boccioni (1882–1916), Filippo de Pisis (1896–1956), Carlo Carrà (1881-1960) and Giorgio De Chirico (1888-   ).

During the Fascist rule the imperialistic spirit which had developed during the first twenty years of the century became official government policy. It grew by leaps and bounds with the invasions of Ethiopia and Albania, reaching its culmination on June 10, 1940, when the Fascist government, allied with Nazi Germany, dragged the Italian people into war against the Allies, and on December 11, 1941, when Mussolini declared war against the United States. This was a Fascist war, the Italian people and the armed forces did not have their hearts in it. In fact, when on July 9, 1943, the Anglo-American troops landed in Sicily and the Italians welcomed them as liberators, the King saw fit to depose Mussolini, the Italian Navy passed to the Allies, the Army disintegrated and the soldiers went home or fought side by side with the Allied troops. In the south, only the Germans continued to fight.

In central and northern Italy, still under Fascist and German control, men and women of all classes and professions, animated by the ideals of Mazzini and Garibaldi, organized the Italian Resistance Movement to help the Allied armies by sabotaging the activities of the Nazi and Fascist forces. Moreover, thousands of able-bodied men (partisans), organized guerilla bands and went into the mountains to harass the enemy day and night. They were men of great faith and courage. No one urged them to fight and die for the freedom of their country and the Allied cause. They knew that if caught they would be tortured and shot. But they obeyed the dictates of their conscience. The same spirit induced the humble peasants living on the mountains to risk their lives to help the partisans and to shelter in their homes thousands of Allied war prisoners who had escaped from Fascist camps. At times, the male population of an entire village would be ferreted out of their hideouts by Fascist and Nazi troops and shot en masse in reprisal. But this never deterred the Italian patriots from fulfilling what they believed was their duty as men towards other men. It has been reported that 200,000 men took part in Partisan warfare, 47,000 of whom were shot or hanged, and that 19,000 civilians of the resistance movement were killed by the enemy.

On April 28, 1945, Mussolini was caught by the partisans while trying to escape into Switzerland and was sentenced to death. A few days later, the Fascist and Nazi forces surrendered to the partisans or to the Allies, and Italy was once more free. As a result of the war she surrendered all conquered lands and lost all her colonies including the territory east of Trieste. In the referendum of 1946, the Italians voted against the monarchy and for the institution of a republic. Two years later, a new modern constitution was enacted in which Italy is described as "a democratic republic based on labor."

The dictatorship produced no Fascist writers or artists worthy of that name. Besides the writers who had made their name before the advent of Fascism and who continued to write without arousing the censors' suspicion, a few new ones—all anti-Fascist—were able to emerge. Among the most compelling were Corrado Alvaro (1895–1956) and Alberto Moravia (1907–), the latter now the best known Italian novelist abroad. At the age of twenty-one, Moravia published his first novel, *Gli Indifferenti* ("The Time of Indifference"), the story of a Roman family that symbolizes the boredom, moral disintegration, and absolute indifference to all real values into which the Italian upper middle class had fallen after seven years of government by supermen.

At the same time, there began to appear outside Italy the Italian literature of exile written by the intellectuals who, for political reasons, had found refuge abroad. There were about a hundred and they included the historians Gaetano Salvemini, Guglielmo Ferrero and the diplomat Count Carlo Sforza; the social scientist Don Luigi Sturzo; the critic and novelist G. A. Borgese, and the art critic Lionello Venturi. The novelist who gained world-wide reputation was Ignazio Silone (1900–), author of *Fontamara* and

Pane e Vino. In his first choral novel he describes the awakening of the moral conscience of the peasants and the dawning realization that their wretched conditions would never change under Fascism unless they were willing to unite, fight and, if need be, sacrifice their lives for their fellow-men. His second novel deals dramatically with the return of an anti-Fascist exile among the peasants and workers of both Abruzzi and Rome, who concludes, as he re-evaluates his religious and social beliefs, that only in the fusion of the best principles of both Christianity and socialism will humanity be able to live and prosper in a new spirit of brotherhood.

The first novel published in Italy which disclosed the spiritual plight of the Italians under the Fascist régime appeared in 1938–39, almost un-noticed, in serial form in an Italian magazine. It was *Conversazione in Sicilia* by Elio Vittorini (1908-1966). It is the story of a young Sicilian working in a north Italian city who, one day,—not long after the conquest of Ethiopia and the proclamation of the new Italian Empire, when Fascism had won its most resounding international victories—feeling apathetic, hopeless and anguished "over doomed mankind" ("per il genere umano perduto"), suddenly decides to take a train and return to his mother and to his primitive Sicilian home-town in an effort "to regain his lost childhood". The "conversation", part

realistic and part surrealistic, with biblical overtones, turns out to be a dialogue between man and himself, and the homecoming is none other than a spiritual pilgrimage of man to his origins, his real nature, his humanness; it is a return to his naked primitive state in an effort to find himself again and to rediscover his true inner self so that he may be inspired to become more human and less brutish.

D'Annunzio, Futurism and Fascism sought and extolled the animality in the Italian man and failed. Silone, Vittorini and Carlo Levi (1902–   ), in his now famous *Cristo si è fermato a Eboli* (Christ stopped at Eboli), representing the new trend in post-war literature, sought in him and rediscovered his innate goodness and his humanity and led him back to the humanistic tradition, a tradition which neither foreign nor domestic tyrants were ever able, through the centuries, to root out of the Italian soul. It was this very tradition which inspired the men and women of the Italian resistance, which made possible the physical rebirth of Italy after five years of devastation inflicted upon her by friend, foe and her own sons, and which today inspires the great revival of Italian arts, letters and industries.

XXXI

Luigi Pirandello

(*1867–1936*)

Pirandello was born in the ancient city of Agrigento (Sicily) at a time when the majesty of the surrounding Greek temples, testifying to the glory of the past, stood in shocking contrast with the squalor of the countryside and the misery of the population. His father was a sulphur mine operator, devoted to his family, but cursed with a volcanic temper which erupted frequently and terrorized family, friends and neighbors. It was not for nothing that the Pirandello mansion was called "The Chaos".

311

Pirandello pursued his studies at Palermo and at the University of Rome which he was forced to leave for insulting one of his professors. He completed them at Bonn in Germany where he obtained an assistantship in Italian literature. Soon after, he married and settled in Rome where, thanks to financial help from his father, he was able to do freelance writing. Everything went well until the birth of his third child when life became a long series of shattering catastrophes. His father and father-in-law lost their fortunes and Pirandello was thrown entirely on his own; moreover, his wife developed an incurable form of paranoiac jealousy. During the day Pirandello nursed her, took care of the children, taught at the Istituto Superiore di Magistero, gave private lessons and, at night, feverishly wrote short stories and serialized novels. During World War I, one of his sons was reported missing in action while the other lay seriously ill in a military hospital. One night, his wife tried to stab him while he slept. He accepted his misfortunes with stoicism and refused to have the unfortunate woman committed to an institution. For ten years he strove to appease her by forcing himself to be as she desired him, in order to convince her that it was he and not she who was mad. Nothing could alter the image of him that was fixed in her mind. It was not until 1919, when she drove her daughter to the brink of suicide, that he was induced by his friends to send her to a sanatorium.

It was inevitable that Pirandello's tragic conjugal experiences should color his artistic philosophy of being and seeming, of life and form, but they did not originate it, since he had already expressed the same views in the veristic short stories and philosophical novels which had brought him national recognition. His international fame as a dramatist came later. It began in 1910 when, in the midst of his trials, he was visited by a Sicilian actor who, in search of an author to round out his meager repertory, forced him to write two one-act plays (*La morsa* and *Lumie di Sicilia*) which were performed in Rome. Pirandello then realized that the narrative form provided too flimsy a frame for the full expression of his inspiration and began to devote himself seriously to the theater. But like Verga, he was ahead of his time and for several years met with bitter opposition on the part of critics and public who, though magnetized by his paradoxical representations of life, refused to recognize themselves in them. Since Pirandello's plays are thought-provoking and open to a number of interpretations they led the audience into bitter arguments which often ended in fist fights during and after the performance. In 1921, the Rome police had to intervene after the première of *Sei personaggi in cerca di autore*, to rescue the author from an angry crowd waiting for him at the exit of the Valle Theater. It was this play and this incident in particular which catapulted Pirandello and his theater into world-wide prominence.

Pirandello is to literature what Einstein was to be to physics. He introduced, first in his novels and later in the theater, the artistic philosophy of relativity by demonstrating that nothing is absolute and that human knowledge can be only relatively true or certain. Truth, justice, morality, beauty are relative since their interpretation, meaning and value change endlessly according to time, space and the individual concerned. What today is considered true, just, moral and beautiful, may tomorrow appear untrue, unjust, immoral and ugly.

He likewise atomized the human personality by demonstrating that we are not only what we think we are, but also what others think we are; we therefore have not one personality, but as many personalities as there are people who look at us and judge us. Yet man feels the urgent need to be one in order to know and distinguish himself from others. He consequently "constructs for himself" a social mask—a "personality" or "form"—which he wears over his natural face—"instinct" or "life"—in order that he may appear to others what he thinks he is. However, because life is fluid and subject to ceaseless changes, it causes us to change too in accordance with the different possibilities of being which lie within each of us. From this springs the tragic contrast and conflict between "life" and "form," i.e., between the ever-changing natural face and the fixed social mask.

Pirandello's philosophy has been defined as decadent, pessimistic and even nihilistic in the belief that it destroys all the eternal values and ideals which man cherishes and lives by. But Pirandello does not destroy these ideals. He merely warns us that they are not absolute but relative and does this to help us avoid future disillusionments. As a rule, he does not conclude his plays because he wants each one of us to draw his own conclusion. Nevertheless, if a message need be found in his art, it is not a nihilistic one. It is rather an appeal for mutual respect, reciprocal indulgence, and above all, for understanding and tolerance which alone can make it possible for man to live in peace and harmony with his fellow men. This message Pirandello clearly expressed in *Così è (se vi pare)* through his mouthpiece Laudisi, who supplies the following explanation to two disconcerted ladies in search of the truth:

Signora Sirelli: Ma secondo lei allora non si potrà mai sapere la verità?

Signora Cini: Se non dobbiamo più credere neppure a ciò che si vede e si tocca!

Laudisi: Ma sì, ci creda, signora! Però le dico: rispetti ciò che vedono e toccano gli altri, anche se sia il contrario di ciò che vede e tocca lei!

Pirandello wrote two volumes of poetry, a number of essays, seven novels, 246 short stories and forty-five plays. His works are lively, moving and haunting. His characters, whose conscious and subconscious he dissects and lays bare, are symbols of universal values that imbue his works with a cosmic and religious sense of life. Translated and performed in more than twenty-five languages, his plays have had world-wide influence and his innovations in theater technique were adopted widely, in the United States, notably by such playwrights as Thornton Wilder, Maxwell Anderson and Eugene O'Neill. In 1934, two years before his death, Pirandello was awarded the Nobel Prize for Literature.

SEI PERSONAGGI IN CERCA DI AUTORE

Commedia da fare

[*Sei personaggi in cerca di autore*, as stated in the subtitle, is "a comedy to be made". When the audience enters the theater the curtain is up and the stage is dark, empty, and without décor. This, when the lights go up, imparts at once the impression that no preparations have been made for the performance. At the set time, the actors, wearing street clothes, saunter casually on stage. After a while they begin rehearsing one of Pirandello's abstruse plays, *Il gioco delle parti* (Each in His Own Role), which neither actors nor director understand. The rehearsal is abruptly interrupted by the sudden arrival on stage of six persons in deep mourning who introduce themselves as real characters created by a playwright who, feeling himself inferior to his task, had rejected them, thus leaving them unfinished. But they are alive and burning with the passion of their own tragedy and are now in search of an author who will perpetuate them and allow them to enact it. Their tragedy, they maintain, does not need to be written or rehearsed because it is within them, they live it, their whole being is crystallized in it. The preposterous situation amuses the actors and enrages the director who orders the six characters thrown out. They insist, however, on being heard, explaining that they are born characters, as real as Sancho Panza, Don Abbondio or Hamlet, superior to actors since they live their own roles while professional actors act but do not live their parts. Moreover, their tragedy is real, while those on stage only pretend to be real.

Their arguments, and particularly one episode of their story, so intrigues the director that a compromise is reached: the six characters will be allowed to act out their story, a transcript will be made and they will show the professional actors how to re-enact it. But the play will not be concluded mainly because the real characters cannot see themselves in the personal and therefore inexact rendition that the professional actors will give of them.

In this play, of which only the beginning is given below, Pirandello has attempted to represent what for many years was the travail of his spirit, namely: the reciprocal and irreparable misunderstanding based on the empty abstraction of words; the multiform personality of each of us, and the tragic conflict dwelling in man between his movable life and his fixed form. Moreover, he shows the inability and impossibility of art to represent life as it really is, which gives rise to the collision between reality and art. In fact, if art were a perfect illusion of reality, it would no longer be reality: on the other hand, if it is a perfect reality, it is no longer art. In the particular case of "the Father", Pirandello maintains that if an individual, no matter how conventional his life has been, is caught for a single moment unconsciously committing an unconventional act, public opinion leaves him eternally fixed and nailed to that mold. He will never succeed in escaping from it, no matter how hard he may try. He thus becomes a real character. If he is lucky enough to find an artist, "a fecundating matrix, an imagination", who will raise and nourish him, then he will live forever.]

315

I personaggi della commedia da fare:

Il Padre
La Madre
La Figliastra
Il Figlio
Il Giovanetto
La Bambina

Gli attori della Compagnia:

Il Capocomico (Director)
Il Suggeritore (Prompter)
Il Direttore di scena (Stage Manager)
La Prima Attrice (Leading Lady)
Il Primo Attore (Leading Man)
L'Uscere (Stage hand)

palcoscenico *stage*

Su, su *come, now*
Manca *is . . . missing*

La segni, mi faccia il piacere
Make a note of it, please

prova *rehearsal*
fondo *rear*

per carità *for heaven's sake*

cagnolino *puppy*
scalette *stairs*

subito di scena *right away on stage*
per *by*

camerino *dressing room*
borbottando *grumbling*

Di giorno su un palcoscenico di teatro di prosa.

Il Capocomico: (battendo le mani) Su, su, cominciamo. (Al Direttore di scena) Manca qualcuno?

Il Direttore di scena: Manca la Prima Attrice.

Il Capocomico: Al solito! (Guarderà l'orologio). 5
Siamo già in ritardo di dieci minuti. La segni, mi faccia il piacere. Così imparerà a venire puntuale alla prova. (Non avrà finito di parlare che dal fondo della sala si udrà la voce della Prima Attrice). 10

La Prima Attrice: No, no, per carità! Eccomi! Eccomi! (È tutta vestita di bianco. Tiene un grazioso cagnolino tra le braccia. Salirà in gran fretta una delle scalette.)

Il Capocomico: Lei ha giurato di farsi sempre 15 aspettare.

La Prima Attrice: Mi scusi. Ho cercato tanto un'automobile per fare a tempo! Ma vedo che non avete cominciato ancora. E io non sono subito di scena. (Poi, chiamando per nome il Direttore di scena 20 e consegnandogli il cagnolino) Per piacere, me lo chiuda nel camerino.

Il Capocomico: (borbottando) Anche il cagnolino! Come se fossimo pochi i cani qua. (Batterà di

316

nuovo le mani e si rivolgerà al Suggeritore) Su, su, il secondo atto del *Gioco delle parti*. (Sedendo sulla poltrona) Attenzione, signori. Chi è di scena?

(Gli attori e le attrici sgombreranno il davanti del palcoscenico e andranno a sedere da un lato, tranne i tre che principieranno la prova e la Prima Attrice, che, senza badare alla domanda del Capocomico, si sarà messa a sedere davanti ad uno dei tavolini.)

Il Capocomico: (alla Prima Attrice) Lei dunque è di scena?

La Prima Attrice: Io? Nossignore.

Il Capocomico: (seccato) E allora si levi, Santo Dio!

(La Prima Attrice si alzerà e andrà a sedere accanto agli altri attori che si saranno già tratti in disparte.)

Il Capocomico: (al Suggeritore) Cominci, cominci.

Il Suggeritore: (leggendo nel copione) "In casa di Leone Gala. Una strana sala da pranzo e da studio".

Il Capocomico: (volgendosi al Direttore di scena) Metteremo la sala rossa.

Il Direttore di scena: (segnando su un foglio di carta) La rossa. Sta bene.

Il Suggeritore: (seguitando a leggere nel copione) "Tavola apparecchiata e scrivania con libri e carte. Scaffali di libri e vetrine con suppellettili da tavola. Uscio in fondo per cui si va nella camera da letto di Leone. Uscio laterale a sinistra per cui si va nella cucina. La comune è a destra."

Il Capocomico: (alzandosi e indicando) Dunque, stiano bene attenti; di là, la comune. Di qua, la cucina. (Rivolgendosi all'attore che farà la parte di Socrate) Lei entrerà e uscirà da questa parte. (Al Direttore di scena) Applicherà la bussola in fondo, e metterà le tendine. (Tornerà a sedere).

Il Direttore di Scena: (segnando) Sta bene.

"Gioco delle parti" "*Each in His Own Role*"

sgombreranno il davanti *will clear the front*

seccato *annoyed*
si levi *get out*

tratti in disparte *withdrawn to one side*

copione *script*

Scaffali *shelves*
vetrine con suppelletili da tavola *china closets with table-ware*
comune *main exit*

di là *over there*
farà *will play*
parte *side*
bussola *swing door*

317

Il *Suggeritore:* (leggendo c.s.) "Scena Prima. Leone
Gala, Guido Venanzi, Filippo detto Socrate".
(Al Capocomico) Debbo leggere anche la
didascalìa?

Il *Capocomico:* Ma sì! sì! Gliel'ho detto cento volte! 5

Il *Suggeritore:* (leggendo c.s.) "Al levarsi la tela,
Leone Gala, con berretto da cuoco e grembiule,
è intento a sbattere un uovo in una ciotola.
Filippo ne sbatte un altro, parato anche lui da
cuoco. Guido Venanzi ascolta seduto". 1*

Il *Primo Attore:* (al Capocomico) Ma scusi, mi devo
mettere proprio il berretto da cuoco in capo?

Il *Capocomico:* (urtato dall'osservazione) Mi pare!
Se sta scritto lì! (indicherà il copione).

Il *Primo Attore:* Ma è ridicolo, scusi! 1*

Il *Capocomico:* (balzando in piedi sulle furie) "Ridicolo, ridicolo!" Che vuole che le faccia io se
dalla Francia non ci viene più una buona commedia, e ci siamo ridotti a mettere in iscena
commedie di Pirandello, che chi l'intende è 2*
bravo, fatte apposta di maniera che nè attori nè
critici nè pubblico ne restino mai contenti? (Gli
attori rideranno. E allora egli, alzandosi e
venendo presso il Primo Attore, griderà:) Il
berretto da cuoco, sissignore! E sbatte le uova! 2*
Lei crede, con codeste uova che sbatte, di non
aver altro per le mani? Sta fresco! Ha da rappresentare il guscio delle uova che sbatte! (Gli attori
torneranno a ridere e si metteranno a far commenti tra loro ironicamente) Silenzio! E prestino 3*
ascolto quando spiego! (Rivolgendosi di nuovo
al Primo Attore) Sissignore, il guscio: vale a dire
la vuota forma della ragione, senza il pieno
dell'istinto che è cieco! Lei è la ragione, e sua
moglie l'istinto: in un giuoco di parti assegnate, 3*
per cui lei che rappresenta la sua parte è voluta-
mente il fantoccio di sè stesso. Ha capito?

Il *Primo Attore:* (Aprendo le braccia) Io, no!

Il *Capocomico:* (tornandosene al suo posto) E io
nemmeno! Andiamo avanti, che poi mi loderete 4(
là fine! (In tono confidenziale) Mi raccomando,

318

si metta di tre quarti, perchè se no, tra le astru-
serie del dialogo e lei che non si farà sentire dal
pubblico, addio ogni cosa! (Battendo di nuovo
le mani) Attenzione, attenzione! Attacchiamo!

5 *Il Suggeritore:* Scusi, signor Direttore, permette che
mi ripari col cupolino? Tira una cert'aria!

Il Capocomico: Ma sì, faccia, faccia!

(L'Uscere del Teatro sarà intanto entrato nella
sala. Si sarà appressato al palcoscenico per
10 annunziare al Direttore-capocomico l'arrivo dei
SEI PERSONAGGI, che, entrati anch'essi nella
sala, si saranno messi a seguirlo, a una certa
distanza, un po' smarriti e perplessi, guardandosi
attorno.)

15 *L'Uscere:* (col berretto in mano) Scusi, signor
Direttore.

Il Capocomico: (di scatto, sgarbato) Che altro c'è?

L'Uscere: (timidamente) Ci sono qua certi signori,
che chiedono di lei.

20 (Il Capocomico e gli attori si volteranno stupìti
a guardare dal palcoscenico giù nella sala.)

Il Capocomico: (di nuovo sulle furie) Ma io qua
provo! E sapete bene che durante la prova non
deve passar nessuno! (Rivolgendosi in fondo)
25 Chi sono lor signori? Che cosa vogliono?

Il Padre: (facendosi avanti, seguito dagli altri, fino
a una delle due scalette) Siamo qua in cerca di
un autore.

Il Capocomico: (fra stordito e irato) D'un autore?
30 Che autore?

Il Padre: D'uno qualunque, signore.

Il Capocomico: Ma qui non c'è nessun autore, perchè
non abbiamo in prova nessuna commedia nuova.

La Figliastra: (con gaia vivacità, salendo di furia la
35 scaletta) Tanto meglio, tanto meglio, allora,
signore! Potremmo esser noi la loro commedia
nuova.

Qualcuno degli Attori: (tra i vivaci commenti e le
risate degli altri) Oh, senti, senti!

Attacchiamo! *Let's begin!*

signor Direttore *Sir*

cupolino *prompter's box*

Tira una cert'aria! *There is an awful draft!*

certi signori *some people*

in *toward the*

lor signori *you*

fra *half*

in *under*

Tanto *So much the*

319

Il Padre: (seguendo sul palcoscenico la Figliastra) Già, ma se non c'è l'autore! (Al Capocomico) Tranne che non voglia esser lei . . .

Il Capocomico: Lor signori vogliono scherzare?

Il Padre: No, che dice mai, signore! Le portiamo al 5 contrario un dramma doloroso.

La Figliastra: E potremmo esser la sua fortuna!

Il Capocomico: Ma mi facciano il piacere d'andar via, che non abbiamo tempo da perdere coi pazzi! 10

Il Padre: (ferito e mellifluo) Oh, signore, lei sa bene che la vita è piena d'infinite assurdità, le quali sfacciatamente non han neppure bisogno di parer verosimili; perchè sono vere.

Il Capocomico: Ma che diavolo dice? 15

Il Padre: Dico che può stimarsi realmente una pazzia, sissignore, sforzarsi di fare il contrario: cioè, di crearne di verosimili, perchè paiano vere. Ma mi permetta di farle osservare, che se pazzia è, questa è pur l'unica ragione del loro mestiere. 20 (Gli attori si agiteranno, sdegnati).

Il Capocomico: (alzandosi e squadrandolo) Ah sì? Le sembra un mestiere da pazzi, il nostro?

Il Padre: Eh, far parer vero quello che non è; senza bisogno, signore; per giuoco. . . Non è loro 25 ufficio dar vita sulla scena a personaggi fantasticati? . . .

Il Capocomico: Ma che cosa vuol concludere con questo?

Il Padre: Niente, signore. Dimostrarle che si nasce 30 alla vita in tanti modi, in tante forme: albero o sasso, acqua o farfalla . . . o donna. E che si nasce anche personaggi!

Il Capocomico: (con finto ironico stupore) E lei, con codesti signori attorno, è nato personaggio? 35

Il Padre: Appunto, signore. E vivi, come ci vede. (Il Capocomico e gli attori scoppieranno a ridere.)

Il Padre: (ferito) Mi dispiace che ridano così, perchè portiamo in noi, ripeto, un dramma 40

doloroso, come lor signori possono desumere da
questa donna velata di nero . . .   questa donna   (*the mother*)

La Figliastra: (facendosi avanti al Capocomico,
sorridente, lusingatrice) Creda che siamo vera--   lusingatrice   *alluring*
5   mente sei personaggi, signore, interessantissimi!
Quantunque, sperduti.   Quantunque   *although*

Il Padre: (Scartandola) Sì, sperduti, va bene! (Al   Scartandola   *Pushing her aside*
Capocomico, subito) Nel senso, veda, che
l'autore che ci creò, vivi, non volle poi, o non
10   potè materialmente metterci al mondo dell'arte.
E fu un vero delitto, signore, perchè chi ha la
ventura di nascere personaggio vivo, può ridersi   ventura   *luck*
anche della morte. Non muore più! Morrà
l'uomo, lo scrittore, strumento della creazione;
15   la creatura non muore più! E per vivere eterna   la creatura   *the character he*
non ha neanche bisogno di straordinarie doti o   *has created*
di compiere prodigi. Chi era Sancho Panza? Chi   doti   *talents*
era don Abbondio? Eppure vivono eterni, perchè   prodigi   *wonders*
—vivi germi— ebbero la ventura di trovare una
20   matrice feconda, una fantasia che li seppe
allevare e nutrire; far vivere per l'eternità!

Il Capocomico: Tutto questo va benissimo! Ma che
cosa vogliono loro qua?

Il Padre: Vogliamo vivere, signore!

25   Il Capocomico: (ironico) Per l'eternità?

Il Padre: No, signore: almeno per un momento,
in loro.

Un Attore: Oh, guarda! guarda!

La Prima Attrice: Vogliono vivere in noi!

30   L'Attore Giovane: (indicando la Figliastra) Eh, per
me volentieri, se mi toccasse quella lì!   se mi toccasse   *if I were*
      assigned
Il Padre: Guardino, guardino: la commedia è da
fare; (al Capocomico) ma se lei vuole e i suoi
attori vogliono, la concerteremo subito tra noi!   la concerteremo   *we shall work*
      it out
35   Il Capocomico: (seccato) Ma che vuol concertare!
Qua non si fanno concerti! Qua si recitano   non si fanno concerti   *we do*
drammi e commedie!   *not indulge in work-outs*

Il Padre: E va bene! Siamo venuti appunto per
questo qua da lei!   da lei   *to you*

40   Il Capocomico: E dov'è il copione?

321

Il Padre: E' in noi, signore (Gli attori rideranno). Il dramma è in noi; siamo noi; e siamo impazienti di rappresentarlo, così come dentro ci urge la passione!

così come dentro ci urge la passione *just as our passions drive us from within*

From: L. Pirandello, *Sei personaggi in cerca di autore*, A. Mondadori, Milano, 1954.

322

XXXII

Guglielmo Marconi

(1874–1937)

Italian science did not die after Galileo. In spite of the difficulties it had to overcome, and although limited to certain fields, its contributions were impressive and its benefits world-wide.

In the field of anatomy, Marcello Malpighi (1628–1694) made invaluable observations on the structure of animal and plant life which enabled him to bring to completion the theory of the circulation of blood; Giovanni B. Morgagni (1682–1771), through painstaking research, founded the school of modern pathology; Francesco Redi (1626–1698) became a pioneer in experimental entomology. In mathematics, Bonaventura Cavalieri (1598–1647), a Jesuit priest, invented the method of indivisibles, foreshadowing integral calculus. Giovanni A. Borelli (1608–1679), physicist and astronomer, discovered the parabolic path of comets and set forth the theory of the mechanics of flight. Other important astronomical discoveries were made by Giovanni D. Cassini (1625–1712) who was invited by Louis XIV to become director of the new Paris Observatory.

The major conquests of Italian science, however, were achieved in the field of physics. Evangelista Torricelli (1608–1647), a student of Galileo, contributed the invention of the barometer and the microscope; Luigi Galvani (1737–1798), a physiologist and professor of comparative anatomy, made important discoveries on animal electricity and did research in electrotherapy and electric currents which enabled Alessandro Volta (1745–1827) to invent the Voltaic pile, the electrophorus, the electric condenser and the Voltaic cell. The discoveries and inventions of Galvani and Volta were so widely used that many electrical terms, such as "galvinism", "galvanize", "galvanograph", "galvanoscope", the "volt", a unit of electricity, and "voltage", are derived from the names of these two men.

No less important were the contributions of Galileo Ferraris (1847–1897), who discovered the rotary magnetic field from which he developed the alternating current motor; and those of Antonio Pacinotti (1841–1912), inventor of the dynamo.

However, two of the most extraordinary scientific feats were accomplished during the present century by Guglielmo Marconi, inventor of wireless telegraphy, and by Enrico Fermi (1901–1954), "architect of the atom bomb" and "father of the atomic age".

Enrico Fermi was one of the world's greatest physicists. He graduated from the University of Pisa, which Galileo had made famous. He began teaching and conducting experiments in 1926 at the University of Rome, his native city. His success in inducing artificial radioactivity by bombarding substances with slow neutrons richly deserved the Nobel Prize for Physics which he was awarded in 1938. On that occasion he left Rome, ostensibly to go to Sweden to receive the prize, but he did not return to Italy. Mussolini, in emulation of Hitler, had shortly before promulgated anti-semitic laws, and Fermi, whose wife was Jewish, decided to come with his family to the United States where he was offered a position in the Physics Department of Columbia University. Three years later he was called to the Institute of Nuclear Studies at the University of Chicago and there led that famous group of scientists, most of them exiles from their own countries, who accomplished the first self-perpetuating atomic chain reaction on December 2, 1942. The first news of the successful operation was immediately telephoned in a coded message to Dr. James B. Conant, then President of Harvard University and Director of the National Defense Research Committee. It said: "The Italian navigator arrived at the shores of the new world." Thus began the atomic age. Fermi died of cancer in Chicago on November 28, 1954. He was 53.

A few years after the unification of Italy, a young Irish Protestant mezzo-soprano named Annie Jameson came to Italy to study bel canto. During her travels she met and married an Italian Catholic country gentleman, Giuseppe Marconi, who lived in the Villa Pontecchi outside Bologna. From their union was born on April 25, 1874, a son, Guglielmo, who, twenty-five years later, was to unite England with the continent by wireless telegraphy, the New to the Old World in 1901, and the whole world by radiotelephony in 1924.

Marconi was never a model student. He had no interest in traditional classical and technical studies. At the age of twenty he was still without a school certificate or diploma, a flaw which caused his father great anxiety. His inclination was towards physics, electrology in particular, and little else. In this he was greatly helped by his mother who not only provided him with English and Italian technical magazines and treatises which he devoured, but also had him taught privately by eminent physicists. There was at that time at the University of Bologna a famous physicist, Prof. Augusto Righi, who had discovered and was demonstrating that hertzian waves are nothing more than light with a wave length longer than visible light. This is precisely what young Marconi had been thinking. He audited Professor Righi's course and at the same time conducted experiments with the most rudimentary instruments to create wireless telegraphy with electric waves.

In 1894, he succeeded in transmitting waves from one room to the other of his house. Encouraged by the first results, he transferred his "laboratory" out of doors. With the assistance of his brother, a farmer and a carpenter, all of whom knew nothing about electricity, he kept improving his home-made apparatus and began to increase the length of the waves. By the following year he had evolved and demonstrated his theory by transmitting long-wave signals from the front of his villa across a hill to a receiving station more than a mile away. That same year he went to London where his system was patented in 1896 and where he founded a wireless company for the commercial development of his discovery. He was then twenty-two years old. His spectacular career as a self-made physicist had just begun.

In 1899, he transmitted signals across the English Channel; in 1901, he received the first transatlantic signals in St. John's, Newfoundland, sent from his station at Poldhu in Cornwall; and in 1909, he was awarded the Nobel Prize for Physics.

During World War I, Marconi concentrated his research on short-wave signals and thereafter on microwaves. In 1916, in Genoa, he made his first experiments with short-wave transmission, and by 1923, succeeded in sending out the first short-wave messages from the Islands of Good Hope to England. In 1924, he inaugurated the short-wave communication service between England and Australia, almost at the antipodes.

Within a span of eighteen years, Guglielmo Marconi linked the world together through the air, and Enrico Fermi, through energy obtained from the nucleus of which the material universe is constituted, lighted the first atomic fire on earth. By so doing, both accomplished epoch-making feats whose consequences will be with humanity as long as our civilization endures.

SCRITTI

La congiunzione radiotelegrafica del Vecchio con il Nuovo Mondo

[The story of the experiments which led Marconi to the transmission of the first transatlantic signals was told by him in his address before the Royal Academy of Science of Stockholm on December 11, 1909, when he was awarded the Nobel Prize for Physics. The excerpt given below is taken from *Scritti di Guglielmo Marconi*, Reale Accademia d'Italia, Rome, 1941.]

eseguiti   *carried out*

Nel gennaio 1901 furono eseguiti con successo esperimenti fra due punti della costa meridionale dell'Inghilterra distanti 186 miglia l'uno dall'altro, fra Punta Santa Caterina, nell'isola di Wight, e il Lizard in Cornovaglia.   5

superare   *overcome*

L'altezza totale delle due stazioni non superava i 100 metri sul livello del mare, mentre per superare la curvatura della terra sarebbero stati necessari più di 1600 metri di altezza a ciascuno degli estremi.

primato   *record*

I risultati ottenuti con questi esperimenti, che 10 a quel tempo costituirono un primato di distanza, parvero indicare che le onde elettriche, prodotte col sistema da me adottato, avrebbero molto probabilmente potuto seguire, nel loro percorso, la curvatura della terra. Quindi anche per distanze 15 grandissime, come quelle che separano l'America dall'Europa, la curvatura della terra non avrebbe costituito una barriera insormontabile per l'estensione della telegrafia attraverso lo spazio.

arrestare   *interfere with*

Il convincimento che la curvatura della terra 20 non potesse arrestare la propagazione delle onde e

326

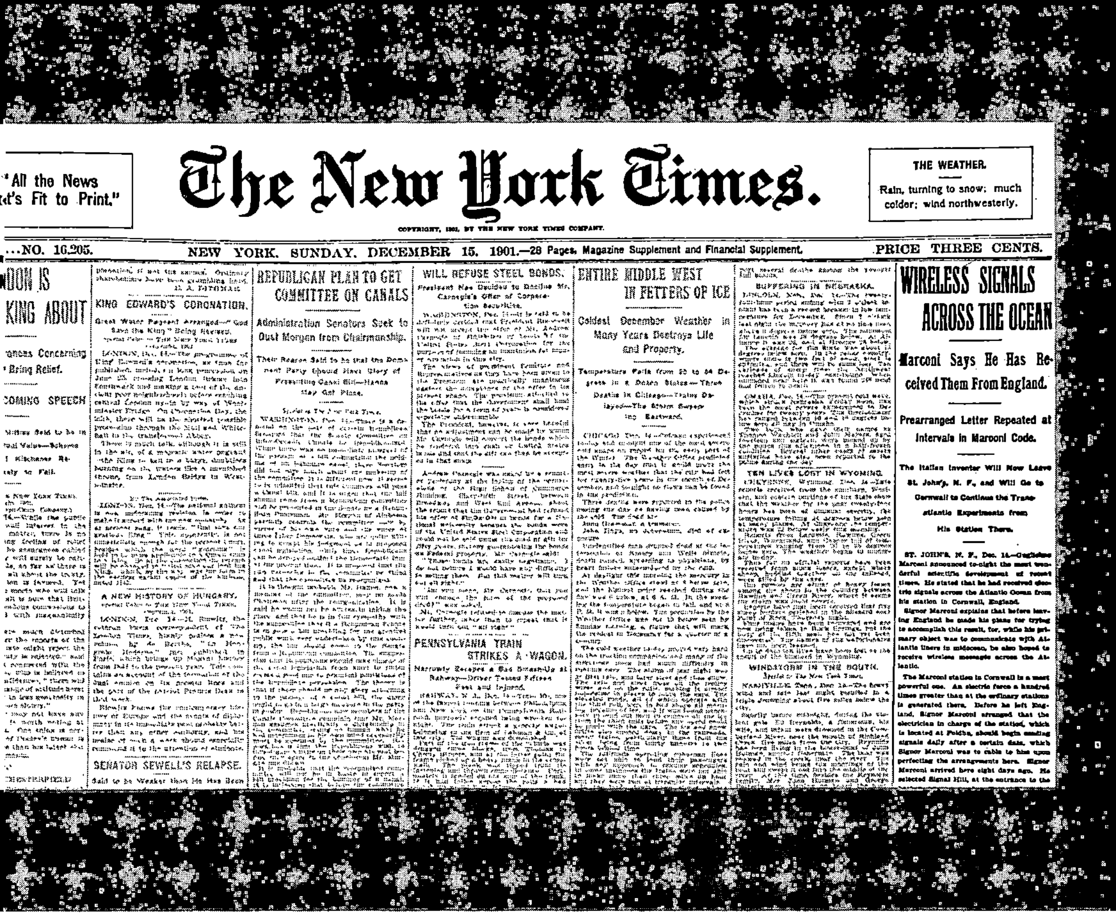

il successo ottenuto con i metodi di sintonizzazione
per prevenire la mutua interferenza, mi spinsero a
decidere, nel 1900, di intraprendere prove esperi-
mentali per determinare se fosse possibile ricevere
5 onde elettriche a distanza di circa 4000 chilometri.
Tali esperimenti, se favorevoli, avrebbero dato
immediatamente la prova della possibilità di
stabilire comunicazioni telegrafiche senza fili fra
l'Europa e l'America.
10   L'esperimento aveva, secondo me, grande
importanza dal punto di vista scientifico ed io ero
convinto che la scoperta della possibilità di trasmettere onde elettriche attraverso l'Oceano Atlantico e la conoscenza precisa delle reali condizioni

spinsero   *lead*

intraprendere   *undertake*
prove   *tests*

senza fili   *wireless*

327

nelle quali poteva funzionare la telegrafia senza fili su tali distanze, avrebbero certamente molto contribuito ad una più completa conoscenza dei fenomeni inerenti alle trasmissioni senza fili.

impiantato *erected*
realizzato *constructed*

impianto generatore di energia *power station*
potenza *capacity*

Il trasmettitore impiantato a Poldhu, sulla 5 costa della Cornovaglia, era realizzato in scala molto superiore a tutti quelli fino allora realizzati.

L'impianto generatore di energia aveva una potenza di circa kw. 25.

Numerose furono le difficoltà che si dovettero 10 risolvere per poter generare e controllare per la prima volta oscillazioni elettriche di tale potenza.

Nel corso dei miei precedenti esperimenti io avevo avuto la possibilità di convincermi che, per cercare di aumentare la distanza delle comuni- 15 cazioni, non fosse sufficiente limitarsi ad aumentare la potenza dell'energia elettrica del trasmettitore, ma occorresse anche aumentare la superficie o l'altezza delle antenne del trasmettitore e del ricevitore.   20

Poichè sarebbe stato troppo costoso adoperare conduttori verticali di grande altezza, io decisi di aumentarne il numero e la capacità, il che avrebbe probabilmente reso possibile la buona utilizzazione di considerevoli quantità di energia.   25

conduttori disposti a ventaglio
fan-shaped aerials

La sistemazione dell'antenna trasmittente a Poldhu consisteva in una serie di conduttori disposti

328

a ventaglio, sostenuti da una draglia isolata tesa fra due alberi alti solo 40 metri e distanti solo 60 metri l'uno dall'altro. Questi conduttori erano riuniti assieme alle loro estremità inferiori ed erano
5 connessi all'apparato trasmittente installato in un edificio.

A scopo di prova era stata eretta a Capo Cod, presso New York, una potente stazione, ma i lavori di finitura di essa furono ritardati da un uragano
10 che distrusse alberi e antenne.

Decisi, di conseguenza, di cercare di intraprendere gli esperimenti utilizzando una stazione ricevente installata provvisoriamente a San Giovanni nel Newfoundland, ove mi recai con due
15 assistenti verso la fine del novembre 1901.

Le prove ebbero inizio al principio del mese di dicembre dello stesso anno e il giorno 12 per la prima volta furono distintamente ricevuti a San Giovanni i segnali trasmessi dall'Inghilterra. Espe-
20 rimenti di controllo furono eseguiti nel febbraio 1902 fra Poldhu e una stazione ricevente installata sul piroscafo Philadelphia dell' ''American Line''. A bordo di questa nave furono ricevuti messaggi leggibili per mezzo di un apparato registratore fino
25 a una distanza di 1551 miglia, segnali di prova fino a una distanza di 2099 miglia da Poldhu.

Questi risultati, per quanto ottenuti con apparecchi imperfetti, furono sufficienti a convincere me e i miei collaboratori che, utilizzando
30 stazioni permanenti e di sufficiente potenza, sarebbe stato possibile trasmettere messaggi attraverso l'Oceano così com'era stato possibile trasmetterli su più piccole distanze . . .

Per quanto concerne l'utilità della radiotele-
35 grafia, è fuori dubbio che la sua utilizzazione è ormai diventata indispensabile per la sicurezza della navigazione. I grandi piroscafi e le navi da guerra ne sono ormai tutti muniti, e l'estensione di essa alle navi meno importanti è solo questione di
40 tempo, considerata l'importanza dell'aiuto fornito in caso di pericolo.

draglia isolata *insulated cable*
tesa *stretched*
alberi *masts*

Capo Cod (*Cape Cod, Mass.*)
i lavori di finitura di essa *its completion*
uragano *hurricane*

piroscafo *steamship*

leggibili *intelligible*
registratore *recording*
fino a *up to*
segnali di prova *test signals*

apparecchi *apparatus*

Per quanto concerne l'utilità *as regards the usefulness*
è fuori dubbio *there can be no doubt*

muniti *equipped*

considerata *in view of*

Per quanto grande *However great*

in modo speciale *especially*

Quali che *Whatever*

Per quanto grande possa essere l'importanza della telegrafia senza fili per le navi e la navigazione, io credo che essa sia destinata ad avere un'importanza per lo meno eguale come mezzo di comunicazione efficiente ed economico fra parti 5 distanti del mondo e in modo speciale tra i paesi d'Europa, le loro Colonie, e l'America.

Quali che possano essere i suoi attuali difetti e le sue deficienze, la telegrafia senza fili, sempre per grandi distanze, è destinata ad affermarsi, e 10 non soltanto ad affermarsi, ma a progredire e a svilupparsi . . .

XXXIII

Benedetto Croce

(1866–1952)

The most important Italian philosophers, beginning with Telesio, Bruno, Campanella, Vico, Pasquale Galluppi (1770–1846), Bertrando Spaventa (1817–1883), down to Giovanni Gentile (1875–1944) came from the south, which they have made into a living school of wisdom.

One of the deepest transformations to take place in the domain of philosophy and of philosophical and historical literature, at the beginning of the present century, was brought about by the intense and manifold activities of another southerner, Benedetto Croce, philosopher, historian, critic, twice minister, who became the exponent of neo-Idealism in revolt against the predominance of positivism. Croce was born in a small village of Abruzzi. He received his first education in a fashionable Catholic school. At the age of seventeen his parents and his only sister perished in an earthquake and he went to live in Rome with a relative, a retired statesman. There, he attended the university but without ever receiving any degree. Having fallen heir to the family estate, he settled in Naples where he dedicated himself entirely to studying and writing. He traveled throughout Europe and collected one of the richest private libraries in Europe. His early works dealt in the main with various historical periods and personalities of southern Italy. They revealed him an outstanding master of historical and philosophical research, an acute interpreter and evaluator of documentary material. In 1903, he began the publication of the internationally famous bi-monthly, *La Critica*, which he directed for over fifty years. From this period onward his intellectual activities were devoted to literary criticism, philosophy and historiography. He reinterpreted the major European poets and, in six volumes of essays, *Scrittori della nuova Italia*, presented one of the finest re-evaluations of contemporary Italian literature.

In his studies on literary criticism Croce introduced a new theory for the evaluation of a work of art, which he expounded in *Estetica come scienza dell'espressione e linguistica generale* (1902), one of the four volumes of studies which go under the general title of *Filosofia dello Spirito*. His theory is based on the fundamental principle that poetry and art are thoroughly intuitive and totally unaffected by logic, intellect or ethics, and must consequently be devoid of any philosophical, scientific or moral content. They

must represent the individual manifestation of intuitive knowledge as a primal revelation of truth and reality. Furthermore, since poetry and art are lyrical intuition and expression, form and content cannot be separated. Thus in evaluating poetry, the critic should judge only the work of art *in se* and *per se*, independently of the social and political life of the period to which it belongs, and of rules and grammar which belong to logic and not to aesthetics. With this theory, Croce affirmed the autonomous and endless original nature of art, which became for his many followers, (*i crociani*), a science of expression and a guiding discipline in the quest of truth. Thus Croce, without ever teaching formally, attained the stature of the national educator and became the most influential literary personality during the first half of the century.

However, his international fame is based most particularly on his philosophical system known as the "philosophy of the spirit". According to Croce, the spirit (or mind, in an abstract sense) is monistic and represents the only reality. Being omnipresent and active, it embodies and manifests itself in every moment and part of history and in the products of the human imagination which are its work. All reality is therefore idea and history perpetually in the making. We know nothing about it (reality) except in the form it takes in our sensations, thoughts and actions. Moreover, history becomes the manifestation of the universal mind, the always changing work and the only cognitive manifestation of the one and universal spirit, the only absolute reality without beginning and without end, self-created and self-explaining.

Croce's philosophy embraces the spiritual kinship of the world in the search for truth and in the assertion of human dignity and liberty. As such, it has exercised a profound influence on higher thought and its exponent is considered one of the greatest minds of contemporary Europe.

In 1925, when Fascism had established its dictatorship, Croce turned against it and the Fascists ransacked his library in an effort to intimidate him. International reaction to this act of political vandalism was so strong, however, that the régime never molested him again. He retired to private life and continued his intellectual activities, but his prestige was such that, though forced into silence, he became the moral leader of the anti-Fascist intelligentsia inside Italy. Intellectually he was a liberal, politically a monarchist and socially a conservative. When Fascism collapsed in 1943, and the reorganization of a new Italian state on modern political and social bases had become imperative, Croce's fervent intellectual followers saw the beginning of a new dawn and expected that the man who had led them through the dark and destructive vicissitudes of the past would again guide them in the spiritual, political and social reconstruction of their country. To their dismay they found out that, despite the international, political and social changes which had taken place between the two World Wars, Croce had remained a monarchist and a conservative, and there was neither political nor social content in the old-fashioned liberalism of the historian-philosopher. The great majority of them deserted him, some, out of despair, were driven into extreme doctrines, while others were left in a spiritual vacuum. However, though militating in opposite political camps, they never lost for him the respect, affection and gratitude that grown sons entertain for an old and venerable father.

When Croce died in Naples on November 20, 1952, he was still working in his vast library, which he endowed before his death and made into what is now a graduate institute of historical studies. His major works have been widely translated. His entire production consists of over sixty volumes and a formidable number of monographs and political pamphlets. They are the result of sixty years of painstaking speculative effort and represent the traditional universalism of Italian culture as well as the spiritual heritage of the humanist age.

IL POPOLO ITALIANO PRIMA E DOPO

LA SECONDA GUERRA MONDIALE

[Though Croce's political views were at times in disagreement with government policies, he was above all a sincere patriot. This is revealed in the moving appeal, which we reproduce below, that he sent out in 1945 to the press of the Allied countries on behalf of the Italian people when the Allies were preparing the United Nations Conference on International Organization to be held at San Francisco without inviting Italy to participate. Italy finally became a member of the United Nations on December 14, 1955.]

Leggo nei giornali che l'Italia non sarebbe invitata alla Conferenza di San Francisco, o che,

nel miglior caso   *at best*

nel miglior caso, come "cobelligerante", sarebbe invitata ad assisterci senza "parteciparvi".

Ma davvero si pensa di trattare   *But is it really possible that there are men who believe they can treat*

Ma davvero si pensa di trattare in questo 5 modo un popolo, il popolo italiano, che,—oltre ad aver inaugurato la moderna civiltà—lottò un secolo intero per la sua indipendenza e libertà, e

le conquistate   *their hard-won*

per sessant'anni amò e coltivò le conquistate

334

istituzioni liberali, alla pari con i più liberi popoli di Europa, progredendo in ogni forma della sua vita, e che nella prima grande guerra mondiale fu a fianco dell'Inghilterra e della Francia, della
5 Russia e degli Stati Uniti contro i tedeschi?

Un popolo che nell'indebolimento e smarrimento seguiti a quella guerra, soggiacque bensì per un ventennio all'insidia e alla violenza di una fazione impadronitasi dei poteri e dei mezzi dello
10 Stato, ma durante il quale l'opposizione dei migliori italiani non si lasciò mai domare e spegnere, e mantenne salda la sua antica fede, sostenendo carceri, confinamenti, esilii, privazioni e ogni sorta di danni e di minacce?

15 Un popolo che vide, allora, con dolore e con mortificazione, il suo oppressore esaltato da innumeri pubblicisti e giornalisti degli altri paesi, e ammirato e carezzato e visitato complimentosamente dai loro uomini di Stato, che non usavano
20 già tali omaggi ai suoi modesti governanti dell'età liberale, e applaudito nei parlamenti stranieri come conservatore dell'umana società e salvatore della pace europea; e tuttavia esso sentiva e sapeva che quel lodato e a noi invidiato regime, messo su da
25 una banda di avventurieri, non aveva radici nel passato e non aveva avvenire, e sarebbe finito, come simili regimi finiscono, in una provocata guerra disastrosa?

Un popolo che, essendo stata soppressa la sua
30 Camera dei deputati e la sua libera stampa, si trovò dall'arbitrio di un despota (che la comune opinione europea aveva reso possente) gettato d'un tratto in una guerra contro i suoi precedenti e naturali alleati e in sostegno della folle prepotenza
35 tedesca, e dovette augurarsi la sconfitta alle sue armi, perchè una vittoria dei tedeschi e coi tedeschi sarebbe stata per esso peggiore di ogni peggiore sconfitta, sottomettendolo a una disperata schiavitù in un'Europa tutta schiava?

40 E quando la lunga e crescente pressione del pubblico sentimento fece sì che il suo re, che quel

alla pari *on a par*

fu *stood*

smarrimento *bewilderment*
soggiacque *succumbed*
bensì *indeed*

impadronitasi dei poteri *which had seized the power*

mantenne salda *staunchly upheld*

oppressore (*Benito Mussolini*)

non usavano già *formerly did not use to pay*

esso (*the Italian people*)
quel lodato . . . regime *that régime (i.e., Fascist dictatorship) which they praised and envied us*

arbitrio *will*
despota (*Mussolini*)
possente *powerful*

armi *armed forces*

tutta schiava *wholly enslaved*
fece sì che *compelled*
re (*Victor Emmanuel III*)

335

despota aveva a sè asservito, si risolse finalmente a scacciare l'intruso, in pochi giorni esso spazzò via il fascismo, dileguatosi come un cattivo sogno al primo raggio di luce, e volle l'armistizio con le vincitrici potenze alleate. E poichè il fascismo ricevè 5 in una parte del territorio nazionale il vergognoso sussidio, di cui solo era degno, dell'occupazione tedesca, questo popolo dichiarò la guerra ai tedeschi, e per diciotto mesi ha combattuto contro tedeschi e superstiti fascisti con quelle divisioni del 10 suo esercito che gli è stato concesso di riarmare, con la sua flotta, e con gli eroici suoi partigiani, con il lavoro di centinaia di migliaia dei suoi soldati nelle retrovie, con tutto quanto ancora gli restava di mezzi utili alla guerra, accettando rassegnato, con 15 animo forte, la distruzione delle sue città, delle sue industrie, della sua agricoltura, e quella più straziante dei suoi monumenti di storia e di arte e dei suoi archivi e biblioteche.

E come si può dinanzi a tanta sventura, e a 20 tanta virtù che la redime, pensare a scomunicare il popolo italiano ed escluderlo dai consigli della pace da preparare all'Europa, esso che dell'Europa è figlio primogenito e devoto? E come si può, con animo tranquillo, assumere ora di giudicare e 25 condannare e punire questo popolo da coloro stessi, che discendendo nella propria coscienza, debbono pur confessare di aver concorso da lor parte a foggiare il mito dell'uomo geniale e irresistibile che lo guidava e, con la poco accorta loro politica, di 30 aver imbaldanzito costui e incoraggiatolo al peggio?

Ma io vorrei sottoporre ai lettori di questo giornale un'altra considerazione che va di là dal mio offeso sentimento d'italiano. Si dice—e ben credo che l'intenzione sia sincera,—che si vuol 35 ristabilire la pace nel mondo e il concorde lavoro dei popoli. Ma come si può far ciò se si aprono nell'animo di un popolo brucianti ferite, che non sono già salutari castighi rivolti a convertirlo, ma vendette che alimentano rancori e odi, perchè 40 sentite come ingiustizie, come duri atti di fratelli

---

Glossary (margin):

l'intruso (*Mussolini*)
dileguatosi *which vanished*

una parte del territorio nazionale (*northern and central Italy*)

concesso (*by the Allies*)

retrovie *rear lines*

animo forte *fortitude*

straziante *heart-rending*

scomunicare *ostracizing*

primogenito *eldest*
assumere *take the responsibility*

discendendo *delving*

geniale *of genius* (*Mussolini*)
la poco accorta loro *their short-sighted*
imbaldanzito *made bold*

di là dal *beyond*

già *indeed*
alimentano *foment*

verso un fratello, il quale non da un proposito (gli
italiani sono profondamente umani e non hanno
mai nella loro storia vagheggiato di opprimere altri
popoli), ma dall'intreccio delle cose è stato condotto
5 a follie ed errori transitori, terribilmente già
espiati?

Si studiino pure sapienti congegni di alleanze
e di sicurezza militare, ma non si dimentichi che
la storia è sempre feconda di casi impensati e, come
10 diceva il nostro Cavour, si compiace nell'improvvisare; e non è prudente lasciare esposto a seduzioni
pericolose un popolo, grande o piccolo che sia,
insanabilmente ferito nell'anima. Non si pretende
già con ciò distogliere dall'escogitare i mezzi
15 materiali, incerti e labili che siano, di allontanare
nuove guerre e distruzioni, ma soltanto si vuol
raccommandare di tener sempre bene in mente che
solo gli acquisti spirituali sono efficaci e durevoli, e
che se tanti imperi e tante egemonie politiche si
20 sono succeduti nella storia, il cristianesimo, fonte
perpetua di redenzione e di rinnovamento, non è
caduto e non cadrà, e il mondo moderno ha necessità sopratutto di un rifiammeggiante entusiasmo,
di una fede morale, di un risveglio di spirito
25 cristiano.

From: *Pensiero politico e politica attuale. Scritti e
Discorsi.* (1945) Laterza, Bari, 1946.

da un proposito *by design*

intreccio delle cose *concate-
nation of events*
terribilmente *at a terrifying
cost*
Si studiino pure sapienti
congegni *Go ahead and devise
judicious schemes*

pericolose *(communistic)*
grande . . . sia *whether it be
great or small*
distogliere dall' *to dissuade
(the Allies) from*
labili *unstable*

rifiammeggiante *rekindling*
risveglio *reawakening*

I: Giosuè Carducci

il levar del sole fu promess di vita nuova

TESTO: 1. Che fu il levar del sole, nel primo giorno dell'anno mille, per le generazioni uscenti dal secolo decimo? 2. Che aveva annunziato San Paolo ai primi cristiani? 3. Che aveva attinto Gregorio Magno dalle disperate rovine degli anni suoi? 4. Quali erano le caratteristiche del secolo decimo? 5. Che aspettavano, di ora in ora, i morituri? 6. Che era tutta la loro vita? 7. Dov'erano raccolte le turbe, quando la mattina dell'anno mille il sole si levò trionfante? 8. Che faceva, secondo Carducci, l'Italia dopo di aver disteso le sue membra? 9. Perchè guardava essa verso l'oriente? 10. Da dove, veramente, comincia la storia del popolo italiano?

II: San Francesco d'Assisi

1. What made St. Francis rebel against the society of his time? 2. What did he preach? 3. What was the purpose of his preaching? TESTO: 4. A chi rivolge San Francesco la sua laude? 5. Che illumina il Signore per noi durante il giorno? 6. Come sono state formate sora Luna e le Stelle? 7. Perchè San Francesco chiama l'acqua "umile"? 8. Com'è frate Fuoco? 9. Che produce sora nostra madre Terra? 10. Che chiede San Francesco a tutte le creature?

III: Jacopone da Todi

1. What are the main characteristics of the *Laude*, the *Laude spirituale* and the *Sacra rappresentazione?* 2. What did Jacopone do for the greater glory of God? 3. What literary significance may be attributed to *Il pianto della Madonna?* TESTO: 4. Perchè il Nunzio crede che la gente vuole uccidere Cristo? 5. Chi ha tradito Cristo e per quanto? 6. Che desidera mostrare la Madonna a Pilato? 7. Che grida la folla contro Cristo? 8. Perchè Cristo vuole che la Madonna rimanga in vita? 9. Perchè la Madonna non vuole abbandonare suo figlio? 10. A chi viene affidata la Madonna da Cristo?

IV: Marco Polo

1. Where were the centers of European learning during the 12th and 13th centuries and which is the oldest university of Europe? 2. What influence did Nicola Pisano exercise on sculpture and Cimabue on painting? 3. How were the communes or city-states established? 4. What role did

Genoa, Florence and Venice play in the expansion of commerce? 5. What was Marco Polo and what did he accomplish? Testi: 1. 6. Ci sono frutti e acqua nel deserto? 7. Che deve portare, chi desidera traversare il deserto? 2. 8. Che aveva fatto fare il Veglio tra due montagne? 9. Che sapevano fare i donzelli e le donzelle? 10. Che fine fece il Veglio della Montagna?

V: Dante Alighieri

1. What political camps and factions prevailed in Italy and in Florence during Dante's life time, and to which one did he belong? 2. Why was Dante banished from Florence? 3. What has he come to symbolize for the Italians? 4. What form of government did he advocate? 5. What schools of poetry flourished in Italy during the 13th century? 6. What was Guinizelli's concept of love and woman? 7. Who was Beatrice? Testi: 1. 8. Che pare Beatrice, quando si sente lodare? 2. 9. Che parve a Dante di vedere nel cielo, durante il suo "vano imaginare"? 3. 10. Che si propone Dante di dire su Beatrice, dopo la "mirabile visione"?
vedere angeli che tornarano in cielo con l'anima di Beatrice

VI: Dante Alighieri (Divina Commedia)

1. What did Dante try to accomplish through the example of his life and works? 2. What is the structure of the *Divina Commedia?* 3. Why has it universal appeal? Testi: 1. 4. Perchè Dante si trovò in una selva oscura? 2. 5. Come uscirono Paolo e Francesca dalla schiera ov'è Dido? 6. Dove *"siede"* la terra nella quale nacque Francesca? 7. Secondo il modo di esprimersi di Francesca, chi fu responsabile dell'innamorarsi e della tragica fine dei due amanti? 8. Perchè Francesca, narrando a Dante il principio del loro amore, dirà "come colui che piange e dice"? 9. Quale fu il punto della lettura che vinse i due amanti? 10. Perchè e come cadde Dante dopo di aver sentito le ultime parole di Francesca?

VII: Dante Alighieri (Divina Commedia)

Testo: 1. Che "ardore" ebbe Ulisse, quando si dipartì da Circe? 2. Per dove si mise? 3. Com'erano egli e i suoi compagni? 4. Che esperienza voleva egli fare? 5. Fummo noi fatti a viver come bruti? 6. Volta la poppa verso l'Est, che fecero dei remi Ulisse e i suoi compagni? 7. Quanti mesi avevano navigato, quando apparve loro una montagna? 8. Com'era la montagna? 9. Perchè la loro allegria tosto tornò in pianto? 10. Fino a quando il turbine percosse e fece girare il legno?

VIII: Francesco Petrarca

1. What were the most outstanding events of the 14th century?   2. How, according to Petrarch, could the regeneration of mankind be achieved? 3. What did he consider to be imperative for man?   4. From what sources did he draw his conclusions?   5. What was the impact of Petrarch's thought? TESTO: 6. Come chiama Petrarca il fiume Sorgue?   7. A chi chiede udienza il poeta?   8. Perchè, quando sarà morto, Petrarca desidera di essere seppellito in quel luogo?   9. Che aveva "così carco d'oblio" il poeta? 10. Quali sono le espressioni delle ultime due stanze che fanno pensare alla Beatrice di Dante?

IX: Giovanni Boccaccio

1. Was writing Boccaccio's only activity?   2. What are the characteristics of the *Decamerone* as compared to the *Divina Commedia?*   3. On what occasion, where and by whom were the stories of the *Decamerone* supposedly told?   4. What was Boccaccio's contribution to the development of Italian literature?   5. What influence did the *Decamerone* have outside Italy? TESTO: 6. Che mandò a dire Corrado al suo cuoco?   7. Che voleva Brunetta da Chichìbio?   8. Quando la gru fu servita, che domandò Corrado al suo cuoco?   9. Perchè, il mattino seguente, Corrado menò Chichìbio lungo la riva di un fiume?   10. Secondo Chichìbio, se Corrado avesse gridato Ho! Ho! che avrebbe fatto la gru cotta?

IL QUATTROCENTO

1. Why is the 15th century considered one of the most resplendent periods in the history of mankind?   2. What type of man was the ideal humanist?   3. What were the centers of humanistic activities?   4. What are the main characteristics of the architecture of the *Quattrocento?*   5. Who was the most prominent sculptor?   6. Who excelled in the art of glazed terra cotta?   7. What did the Tuscan painters try to bring closer together? 8. What realistic elements did they introduce into their religious paintings? 9. What were the two most famous *botteghe* of Florence?   10. Who were the poets who influenced Botticelli's art?

342

X: Leonardo da Vinci

TESTI: **1.** Perchè Leonardo considerava l'esperienza più importante dello studio delle lettere?   **2.** Che ha il pittore, prima nella mente e poi nelle mani?   **3.** In che modo possiamo veramente conoscere le forme delle cose?   **4.** Perchè l'uccello che si trova fra il vento, può sostenersi sopra di quello senza batter le ali?   **5.** Che tipo di aereo moderno corrisponde al "grande uccello" progettato da Leonardo?   **6.** Perchè Leonardo profetizzava con timore l'invenzione dell'aeroplano?   **7.** Come si chiama oggi quel "padiglione di pannolini intassato" concepito da Leonardo?   **8.** Che aveva egli ideato per proteggere le fanterie in guerra?   **9.** Che usiamo oggi per parlarci da remotissimi paesi?   **10.** Perchè Leonardo non descrive il suo "metodo di stare sotto l'acqua"?   **11.** Di che non s'avvede l'uomo il quale desidera sempre i nuovi mesi e i nuovi anni?   **12.** Perchè è cosa nefandissima il togliere la vita all'uomo?

[annotazione manoscritta: Cominci conoscere primo particoli e poi l'altra]

XI: Cristoforo Colombo

1. What did Toscanelli's chart describe?   2. What voyages had Columbus made before crossing the Atlantic?   3. How did he acquire his geographical knowledge?   TESTO: **4.** Che vide Colombo nell'isola della Giovanna?   **5.** Perduta un po' della loro paura, come si dimostravano le popolazioni della Spagnola?   **6.** Che religione professavano?   **7.** Come si intendeva Colombo con gli abitanti?   **8.** Che si prometteva di dare egli alle Loro Altezze?   **9.** Che differenza c'era tra Colombo e coloro che avevano parlato e scritto di quelle terre?   **10.** Che avrebbero trovato nelle nuove terre tutti i Cristiani?

XII: Amerigo Vespucci

1. What benefits did Vespucci derive from his classical studies?   2. What discoveries are attributed to him?   3. When, where, why and by whom was the name of "America" given to the new continent?   TESTO: **4.** Com'erano gli alberi della nuova terra descritti da Vespucci?   **5.** Come si chiamavano e in che direzione scorrevano i due fiumi che egli vide?   **6.** Perchè molte volte egli perdè il sonno?   **7.** In questa occasione, di quali versi si ricordò?   **8.** Scrivendo delle opinioni errate della maggior parte dei filosofi, che dice egli sottovoce?   **9.** Qual'era la natura degli abitanti dell'isola di Trinidad?   **10.** Quali erano le caratteristiche dei cannibali conosciuti da Vespucci?

XIII: Angelo Poliziano

1. Who was Lorenzo il Magnifico?   2. What are the characteristics of Poliziano's poetry?   3. Why is the *Orfeo* so important in the history of the drama?   4. When and where was it first performed?   5. What symbols may be seen in the character of Orfeo?   Testo: 6. In che condizioni si è ridotto Aristeo, dopo di essersi innamorato di Euridice?   7. Che dovrà dire la sua zampogna alla ninfa?   8. Su che avevano già esercitato il loro influsso il canto e la musica di Orfeo?   9. Chi aveva tolto a Orfeo la sua donna? 10. A che condizione Plutone gli rende la sua Euridice?

IL CINQUECENTO

1. What is meant by "Renaissance"?   2. How long did it last?   3. Who is considered the all-embracing genius of the age?   4. In what way did Italy fall short of the artistic achievements of the period?   5. What had been the policy of Lorenzo il Magnifico?   6. How did the discovery of America affect Italy?   7. What far-reaching events altered the course of Italian political life?   8. What were the effects of the Counter-Reformation?   9. What work of art symbolizes the tragedy of Italy?   10. Who was Torquato Tasso?

XIV: Niccolò Machiavelli

1. Of what field of studies may Machiavelli be considered the founder? 2. What was his diplomatic experience?   3. With what are his *Discorsi* concerned?   4. For what purpose did he advocate the application of the principle: the end justifies the means?   5. Would you ever apply such a principle? If so, under what circumstances?   Testi: 1.   6. Come dev' essere e parere un principe?   7. Come deve egli agire affinchè i mezzi siano giudicati onorevoli e lodati?   2.   8. Che forma di governo avrebbe dovuto introdurre in Italia un nuovo principe?   9. In che condizioni era ridotta l'Italia? 10. Che puzzava a ogni italiano?

XV: Ludovico Ariosto

1. How did his father's death affect Ariosto's career?   2. Who are Morgante and Margutte?   3. Why is the *Orlando Innamorato* important? 4. What are the characteristics of the *Orlando Furioso?*   Testi: 1.   5. Che si propone Ariosto di cantare, nella protasi del suo poema?   2.   6. Com'era Angelica, quando apparve a Medoro?   7. Rotto ogni freno di vergogna,

che fece Angelica? 8. Che v'era scritto fuori e in casa in mille modi?
3. 9. Qual'è il "duol che tutti gli altri passa"? **4.** 10. Che restò in
Orlando dopo che egli vide "l'ingiuria sua scritta nel monte"?

XVI: Michelangelo Buonarroti

1. Who are the men who influenced Michelangelo's life and art? 2. As
all the other artists of his time, on whom did Michelangelo depend for his
work? 3. Describe Michelangelo's character. 4. What conflict is expressed in his art? SONETTI: **1.** 5. Dov'è contenuta qualsiasi figura concepita da un ottimo scultore, e con che mezzo è solo possibile rivelarla?
2. 6. Ora che il corso della sua vita è giunto al comun porto, dove è rivolta
l'anima di Michelangelo? LETTERE: **1.** 7. Che aveva fatto Michelangelo
per aiutare la casa sua? **2.** 8. Che fece Papa Giulio una mattina che
Michelangelo era andato a parlargli? 9. All'ultimo, che disse la Signoria a
Michelangelo? **3.** 10. Perchè Michelangelo non credeva che fosse opportuno mandare a Roma il figlio di Urbino?

XVII: Baldassare Castiglione

1. What did the artists and writers of the Renaissance try to achieve?
2. What is the *Galateo?* 3. Who was Baldassare Castiglione? 4. What
other gatherings famous in Italian literature do those held at the court of
Urbino call to mind? 5. Compare the education and training of Castiglione's "perfect gentleman" with those imparted in our Liberal Arts colleges
today? TESTI: **1.** 6. In poche parole, quale dev'essere il fine del perfetto
Cortegiano? 7. In che si differenzia il fine proposto da Machiavelli al
Principe da quello proposto da Castiglione al perfetto Cortegiano? **2.** 8. In
che, sopratutto, la donna deve essere molto dissimile dall'uomo? 9. Quali
sono quelle condizioni che si convengono a tutte le donne? 10. Di che deve
aver conoscenza la donna?

XVIII: Luigi da Porto

1. What are the characteristics of the *novella?* 2. Who was inspired by
the plots of the *novellas?* 3. Who was Luigi da Porto? 4. What are the
sources of Shakespeare's "Romeo and Juliet"? TESTO: 5. Rinchiusa la
tomba e accesa la lanterna, che vide Romeo? 6. Desideroso di morire, che
ingoiò il giovane? 7. Che avrebbe dovuto sapere Romeo per mezzo delle
lettere di Giulietta? 8. Che aveva portato Pietro al suo padrone? 9. Che
fece Giulietta, dopo di aver emesso l'ultimo fiato? 10. Che fecero i due
padri, venuti in chiesa?

XIX: Giambattista Giraldi Cintio

1. What purpose, according to Giraldi, must horror have in a tragedy?
2. What is the *Ecatonmiti?* TESTO: 3. Che non curò lo sciagurato Alfiere, innamorandosi di Disdemona? 4. Perchè l'Alfiere pensò di sbarazzarsi del Caposquadra? 5. Perchè l'Alfiere non volle spiegare al Moro il motivo per cui, secondo lui, Disdemona vedeva volentieri il Caposquadra? 6. Vedendo che Disdemona portava un fazzoletto, che pensò l'Alfiere? 7. Perchè il Moro si fece alla finestra? 8. Che disse l'Alfiere al Moro, dopo di aver parlato con il Caposquadra? 9. Come divenne Disdemona, quando suo marito le chiese il fazzoletto? 10. Andatosene, che cominciò a pensare il Moro?

XX: Benvenuto Cellini

1. Through what media were the great men of the Renaissance immortalized? 2. What is the significance of Vasari's *Vite* for the art historian? 3. According to Cellini, should an artist like him be bound to anybody or anything? 4. What is Cellini's most celebrated work of art? 5. What is the importance of Cellini's *Vita?* TESTO: 6. Di che s'intendeva il nonno di Cellini? 7. Secondo Vitrurio, per essere un buon architetto di che altre cose bisogna aver conoscenza? 8. Da che fu causata la disputa tra il nonno di Cellini e Stefano Granacci? 9. In che notte nacque Cellini? 10. Perchè fu egli chiamato Benvenuto?

IL SEICENTO

1. What obstructed the free development of Italian thought in the 17th century? 2. What are the most striking differences between the Renaissance and baroque styles in architecture and sculpture? 3. Who are the two best known Italian representatives of the new style in art and literature? 4. What was the function of words in the poetry of the *marinisti?* 5. Where and how did secular music originate? 6. Where and when was the musical drama introduced? 7. Who were the most famous makers of violins and cellos? 8. Where was the first opera house built? 9. Name and locate the two leading music schools of the century. 10. What were Italy's most outstanding contributions to civilization during the *Seicento?*

XXI: Galileo Galilei

1. What branches of learning did Galileo pursue as a university student?
2. Through his observations in the Cathedral and his experiments from the Leaning Tower of Pisa, what did he discover? 3. What was the Copernican theory? 4. What enabled Galileo to prove that Copernicus was right? 5. On whose authority did Galileo's adversaries condemn his doctrine? Testi: 1. 6. Per giudicare un fatto reale, le attestazioni degli uomini sono preferibili a ciò che mostra l'esperimento? 7. In quali conclusioni e perchè Galileo stimerebbe meno l'attestazione di molti che quella dei pochi? 8. In che modo egli si renderebbe sconoscente e ingrato verso la Natura e Dio? 2. 9. A quale sonetto e a quale autore ci fa pensare la domanda che Galileo si rivolge, guardando una statua eccellente? 10. Con chi ci permette di parlare l'invenzione dell'alfabeto?

XXII: La Commedia dell'Arte

1. In what way does the *Commedia dell'Arte* differ from the literary play? 2. What did the masks tipify? 3. How did the *Commedia dell'Arte* reach its peak? 4. What influence did it exercise on the European theater? 5. What other dramatic forms supplanted the *Commedia dell'Arte* during the second part of the 18th century? Testi: 1. 6. Che deve spiegare il corago agli attori? 7. Che accadrebbe se l'attore uscisse troppo dal soggetto? 2. 8. Perchè Pantalone desidera che il Dottore gli presti mille scudi? 9. Di che parla il Dottore uscendo di casa? 10. Che deve dare Pantalone al Dottore e a Stoppino per farsi prestare i mille scudi?

IL SETTECENTO

1. Why were Italy's contributions to the Age of Reason and Enlightenment restricted to certain fields? 2. What is Vico's law of occurrences and recurrences? 3. Who initiated and what is the method of historical criticism? 4. How did the Arcadian poets try to counter *secentismo* and *marinismo?* 5. What were really the Italian "shepherds" and "shepherdesses" of the *Settecento?* 6. Who was Parini and what did he portray in *Il Giorno?* 7. How did Goldoni reform the Italian theater? 8. What are the distinctive traits of the plots and characters of Alfieri's tragedies? 9. Mention the best known works of the late Roman baroque and the name of a celebrated painter of the period? 10. How did Italy hold undisputed supremacy throughout Europe in the field of music during the *Settecento?*

XXIII: Pietro Metastasio

1. How did Metastasio become a dramatist? 2. Where did he work most of his life? 3. Of what does his reform of the melodrama consist? 4. What is the meaning of the mythical figure of Aeneas, in the history of Western civilization? Testo: 5. Da chi è chiamato Enea alle sponde d'Italia? 6. Perchè egli aveva celato il suo disegno a Didone? 7. Di chi aveva irritato lo sdegno Didone? 8. Perchè Didone crede di aver ragione di condannare Enea? 9. Non partendo, non restando, che prova Enea? 10. In quale episodio della *Divina Commedia* è menzionato Enea?

XXIV: Cesare Beccaria

1. What feelings did the works of the French Encyclopedists arouse in Beccaria? 2. What far-reaching principles was he the first to formulate? 3. Are you in favor or against capital punishment? State your reasons briefly. Testi: 1. 4. Perchè è inutile la tortura del reo nei casi in cui il delitto è certo o incerto? 5. Perchè l'uso della tortura è il mezzo sicuro di assolvere i robusti scellerati? 2. 6. Quando, secondo Beccaria, diventa necessaria la morte di qualche cittadino? 7. Che prova l'esperienza dei secoli della pena di morte? 8. Perchè la lunghezza della pena è il freno più forte contro i delitti? 9. Perchè le leggi non dovrebbero aumentare il feroce esempio dato dalle guerre? 10. Com'è la storia degli uomini?

L'OTTOCENTO

1. What is meant by *Risorgimento?* 2. Who were Mazzini, Garibaldi and Cavour? 3. Why is September 20 one of the most important dates in the history of Italy? 4. For how long had Italy not been a political unit? 5. Which of Foscolo's works inaugurated patriotic literature? 6. How did the novelists of that period elude censorship? 7. Why did the opera play a significant role during the struggle for the liberation of Italy? 8. What is the neoclassic style in architecture? 9. What was the main task of the Italian government after the unification of Italy? 10. What are the main differences between the poetry of Carducci and that of D'Annunzio?

XXV: Alessandro Manzoni

1. According to the tenets of the Italian romanticists, what should the writer interpret, where should he seek inspiration, and to whom should his works appeal? 2. What are Manzoni's *Inni Sacri?* 3. In which work does

he treat the ascension of man to God?　4. Who are Renzo, Lucia and don Rodrigo?　TESTO:　5. Chiuso il breviario, come proseguiva don Abbondio il suo cammino?　6. Dove stavano i due uomini?　7. Perchè don Abbondio mise l'indice e il medio della mano sinistra nel collare?　8. Che gli disse il bravo all'orecchio?　9. Come fu il nome di don Rodrigo nella mente di don Abbondio?　10. Allontanatisi i bravi, come rimase il curato?

XXVI: Giacomo Leopardi

1. What kind of life did Leopardi lead?　2. What had he accomplished before he was twenty years old?　3. In what did he refuse to believe? 4. What did he express in his *Canti?*　5. What can man do to combat the inimical forces of nature?　TESTI: 1.　6. Perchè l'Italia ha ragione di piangere?　7. Che esclama il poeta vedendo che nessuno combatte per lei? 2.　Perchè il sabato (la giovinezza) è il più gradito giorno, mentre il domani, al dì di festa (la virilità), tutto è tristezza e noia?　A che pensano la donzelletta, la vecchierella e lo zappatore?　3.　10. Perchè, secondo Leopardi, la vita mortale non si colora d'altra luce, quando la giovinezza è sparita?

XXVII: Giuseppe Mazzini

1. What is Mazzini's conception of the world and life?　2. In what does supreme virtue consist?　3. What did Mazzini advocate through *La Giovine Italia?*　4. What were the aims of the three political currents which emerged during the *Risorgimento?*　5. Where was Mazzini when his dream of a free and united Italy was realized?　TESTI: 1.　6. Che idea balenò a Mazzini, dopo l'incontro con il proscritto?　2.　7. Che accadde a Mazzini, dopo di aver fatto prestare il giuramento al Maggiore Cottin?　3.　8. Che è la patria, secondo Mazzini?　4.　9. Come sarà la vita interna e quella internazionale di ogni nazione, nell'Europa dei Popoli concepita da Mazzini? 5.　10. Da quali uomini e di quali paesi sarebbe formato il Consiglio Supremo dell'Associazione dei Popoli?

XXVIII: Giuseppe Garibaldi

1. Describe Garibaldi, the man and the warrior.　2. What is meant by the Garibaldi tradition?　3. What is considered his greatest undertaking? 4. By whom and for what reason was he invited to North America?　5. What did he advocate in the last years of his life?　TESTI: 1.　6. Perchè Garibaldi odiava la tirannide e la menzogna?　2.　7. Con chi e dove lavorò a Staten

Island?   8. A quali tempi riandava egli, quando gli fu rifiutato di imbarcarsi come marinaio?   9. Dove andava egli qualche volta cogli amici?   10. Che fortuna ebbe, quando giunse a Nizza?

XXIX: Giuseppe Verdi

1. By what school and for which position was Verdi turned down? 2. What events took place in his life between 1836 and 1840?   3. What is the name of the opera with which he re-established his reputation?   4. What does Verdi's music express?   TESTI: 1.   5. Dopo il primo fiasco, come e con quali spettatori fu accolta la *Traviata?*   2.   6. Secondo Barezzi, a che era nato e a che non era fatto Verdi?   3.   7. Che accadeva a Verdi se si decideva di andare a piedi, o se voleva andare in carrozza?   8. Che cosa è fare un Cavour alla romana?   9. Che ci vuole per fare una scarpa e per fare un'opera?   4.   10. Come si presentava Verdi al pubblico con le sue opere?

XXX: Giovanni Verga

1. What is the *verismo* of Verga?   2. What did he plan to describe in his cycle of five novels?   3. What is the difference between the style of Verga and that of D'Annunzio?   4. With what is *I Malavoglia* concerned?   5. How do the characters of the novel reveal their innermost feelings?   TESTO: 6. Perchè il cane e Alessi non riconobbero 'Ntoni?   7. Dato che Alessi non risponde alle domande di 'Ntoni, da che cosa questi capisce che il nonno è morto e la Lia è fuggita di casa?   8. Come capì Alessi che 'Ntoni voleva fare un giro per la casa?   9. Come guardava 'Ntoni il paese, quando si fermò in mezzo alla strada?   10. Quando il mare cominciò a farsi bianco, come spuntavano le case?

IL NOVECENTO

1. What inspired the democratic and the imperialistic currents and what did they advocate?   2. On whose side did Italy fight in World War I, and what was the outcome of the war on the Italian-Austrian front?   3. What caused the post-war social and political crisis, and how long did it last? 4. By what means was the Fascist dictatorship established?   5. What did the Futurists advocate and why?   6. Why is the war declared by the Fascist dictatorship against the Western Allies in 1940 considered as a Fascist, and not as an Italian, war?   7. What did the Partisans and the men and women of the Resistance do to liberate Italy and help the Allied armies?   8. What impelled them to fight and die?   9. How is Italy described in the new constitution?   10. What is the main concern of post-war Italian literature?

XXXI: Luigi Pirandello

1. Why did Pirandello's plays anger both critics and audiences?   2. Outline Pirandello's artistic philosophy of relativity.   3. Are we only what we think we are?   4. Is Pirandello a nihilist?   Testo: 5. Why is there a collision between art and reality?   6. Perchè borbotta il Capocomico, quando la Prima Attrice consegna il cagnolino al Direttore di scena?   7. Che commedie sono ridotti a mettere in iscena gli attori?   8. Secondo il Padre, che fanno parer vero gli attori, e qual'è il loro ufficio?   9. Perchè non muore più chi è creato personaggio?   10. Dov'è il copione del dramma che i *Sei Personaggi* vogliono recitare?

XXXII: Guglielmo Marconi

1. What were, and who made, the major Italian contributions to the field of physics during the 18th and 19th centuries?   2. Why is Enrico Fermi called "the architect of the atomic bomb"?   3. What did Marconi achieve with his experiments in 1894?   4. Why did he go to London when he was twenty-two years old?   5. What did Guglielmo Marconi and Enrico Fermi accomplish within a span of eighteen years?   Testo: 6. Che parvero indicare gli esperimenti eseguiti da Marconi in Inghilterra nel 1901?   7. In che consisteva la sistemazione dell'antenna trasmittente di Poldhu?   8. In che data e dove furono per la prima volta ricevuti i segnali trasmessi dall'Inghilterra?   9. Secondo Marconi, che importanza avrebbe avuto la radiotelegrafia?   10. Chi fu quell' "uomo senza lettere" che profetizzò la comunicazione per radiotelegrafia fra le varie parti del mondo?

XXXIII: Benedetto Croce

1. To what branch of learning has Southern Italy especially contributed?   2. According to Croce, how should a critic judge poetry?   3. What relation is there between the "Spirit" and history, in Croce's view?   4. What does his philosophy embrace?   5. What does his prodigious philosophical and literary production represent?   Testo: 6. Che ha fatto il popolo italiano, oltre ad aver inaugurato la moderna civiltà?   7. Come manifestarono i migliori italiani la loro opposizione alla dittatura durante il ventennio fascista?   8. Da chi fu esaltato, ammirato e applaudito, in quegli anni, l'oppressore del popolo italiano?   9. Perchè il popolo italiano dovette augurarsi la sconfitta delle sue armi?   10. Spazzato via il Fascismo, con che combattè esso per la vittoria degli Alleati, e che accettò rassegnato con animo forte?   11. Perchè gli Italiani nella loro storia non hanno mai vagheggiato di opprimere altri popoli?   12. Che bisogna tener sempre bene in mente?   13. Di che ha necessità sopratutto il mondo moderno?

List of Illustrations

352

VOCABULARY

VOCABULARY

This vocabulary includes all words that appear in the text with the following exceptions: words explained in the marginal notes and used only in those cases where they are defined; personal pronouns; definite articles; possessive adjectives; superlative forms of adjectives and adverbs in **-mente** when the basic adjectival form is given; and participial and gerundive adjectives derived from regular verbs whose infinitives are listed. Of the irregular verbs found in the text, the infinitive is given in all cases; finite forms are given, in the first person singular, in the case of the less common irregular verbs.

Since there is no one rule to cover all cases of stress in Italian, the following norms have been adopted for pronunciation:

1) Words bearing no accent are stressed on the penult, except if the stressed syllable contains an **e** or **o**; in which case the grave accent is used to designate open **è** or **ò**, the acute accent closed **é** or **ó**: e.g., **dare, fine, pure,** but **bèllo, néve, pòrto, cónte.**

2) Words stressed on the antepenult bear the grave accent on the vowel of that syllable if it is **à, ì, ù,** open **è** and open **ò,** the acute accent if it is close **é** and close **ó:** e.g., **ànima, fìngere, giùngere, prèndere, vòlgere,** but **créscere, rómpere.**

3) Words stressed on the last syllable are designated by the grave accent on **à, ì, ò, ù:** e.g., **pietà, altresì, andò, virtù;** but by the acute accent on **é,** which has the close sound in all examples given: e.g., **benché, né, perché, sé,** even though these forms are spelled **benchè, nè, perchè, sè** in the text proper.

Apocopation or the dropping of the final vowel of a word is frequent in both Italian prose and poetry in the following cases, particularly when the word that follows forms a unit with the first word and begins with a consonant that is not *impure s:*

1) the final **e** or **o** of masculine nouns when it follows a single l, **n** or **r** that is not preceded by another consonant: e.g., **il sol risplende, un pan tondo, il professor Solmi;**

2) the final **e** of verb forms when it follows a single l, **n** or **r** which is not preceded by another consonant: e.g., **che vuol dire?, parlan sempre, son debole, non par vero, aver bisogno;**

3) the final **o** of verb forms ending in **-mo:** e.g., **andiam ché si fa tardi, abbiam sete** (this is more common in poetry than in prose);

4) the final **e** or **o** of many adverbs and other indeclinable parts of speech when preceded by single **l**, **n** or **r**; e.g., **ben le par** in the text for **bene le pare; fin troppo** for **fino troppo; sol io** for **solo io; eppur si dice** for **eppure,** etc.

The apocopation of adjectives beyond that of **bello, buono, grande, quello, santo** and the pronominal adjectives in **-uno** (e.g., **nessun, ciascun**) is rare in prose, but somewhat more common in poetry (e.g., **il sol pensiero, non è ver, l'uman genere**).

Inversion. In literary and poetic style conjunctive pronouns are sometimes attached to a verb form instead of preceding it: e.g., **leggevasi, dicesi, vedoti** for **si leggeva, si dice, ti vedo** respectively. The first letter of the pronoun is doubled when the verb form ends in an accented vowel or is a monosyllable: e.g., **scolorocci** for **ci scolorò**, **amolla** for **la amò**, **fassi** for **si fa**, etc. At times, especially in poetry, the final **e** of the verb form is dropped after **l**, **n** or **r**: e.g., **vuolsi** for **si vuole**, **convienmi** for **mi conviene, non parle vero** for **non le pare vero.**

The following abbreviations are used in this vocabulary:

adj.	adjective	*f.*	feminine	*irr.*	irregular	*pron.*	pronoun
adv.	adverb	*fig.*	figuratively	*lit.*	literary	*prop. n.*	proper noun
apoc.	apocope	*foll.*	followed	*m.*	masculine	*refl.*	reflexive
arch.	archaic	*ger.*	gerund	*n.*	noun	*sing.*	singular
cap.	capitalized	*impf.*	imperfect	*p. abs.*	past absolute	*subj.*	subjunctive
cf.	compare (con-	*impers.*	impersonal	*past part.*	past participle	*v.*	verb
	jugated like)	*inf.*	infinitive	*pl.*	plural		
colloq.	colloquial	*interj.*	interjection as	*poet.*	poetical		
conj.	conjunction		in "ah"	*prep.*	preposition		
dim.	diminutive	*invar.*	invariable	*pres.*	present		

A

a to, at

abbaiare to bark; *n. m.* barking

abbandonare to abandon

abbastanza enough

abbisognare (di) to need

abbondanza abundance

abbracciare to embrace

abbreviare to shorten

abitante *m. & f.* inhabitant

abitare to inhabit, to live, to dwell

àbito clothes

abituale habitual

abitùdine *f.* habit

abusare (di) to abuse, to take advantage of

abuso abuse

accadèmico academician

accadére *irr.* to happen

accanto adjoining; -a beside, next to

accèndere *irr.* to light; to enrage; to inspire

accennare to mention

accertarsi di to ascertain

accettare to accept

acciàio steel

acclùdere *irr.* to enclose

accògliere *irr.* to receive; to rescue

accòlto *past part. of* accògliere

accompagnare to accompany

acconciare to settle

accòrdo agreement; d'- in agreement; mét-
 tersi d'- to make an agreement

accòrgersi *irr.* to notice; to realize

accòrre *syncope of* accògliere *irr.* to welcome

accòrto *past part. of* accòrgersi

accréscere *irr.* to increase; to aggrandize

accusare to accuse

accusato *n.* accused

acèrbo bitter

Achille Achilles (hero of Homer's Iliad)

Aci Trézza Sicilian village at the foot of
 Mount Etna

àcqua water

acquetare to calm down

acquistare to acquire, to gain, to earn, to buy

acquisto acquisition

ad *euphonic for* a

adattare to adapt

adatto suited

addìo goodbye, farewell

addormentare to put to sleep

adeguarsi to be equal to

adèsso now

adoperare to use

adorare to worship

adornare to adorn

adottare to adopt

Adriàtico Adriatic Sea

adultèrio adultery

adùltero adulterer

àere *m. poet. for* ària

aèreo *n.* aircraft

aeroplano airplane

affacciarsi to look out (of a door or window)

affermare to assert, to affirm

affettazióne *f.* affectation

affettuóso affectionate, impassioned

affidare to entrust

affinché in order that

afflitto (*past part. of* afflìggere) afflicted

affollarsi to crowd together

affrettarsi to hasten

affrònto affront

agghiacciato frozen

aggiùngere *irr.* to add

aggraziato graceful

agire to act

agitarsi to protest, to flounder

agnèllo *or* agnèlla lamb

agricoltura agriculture

ah *interj.* alas; Oh!

aiutare to help

aiuto help

ala (*pl.* le ali) wing

alba dawn

albèrgo hotel; *poet.* abode, dwelling (place)

àlbero tree; mast

albóre: primi albóri early dawning

alcuno *pron.* some; non ... - ... no one, none;
 adj. several; any

Alessandro Alexander the Great (356–323
 B.C.), King of Macedonia, who, in 331, at
 the battle of Gaugamela (Assyria), defeated
 Darius (?–330 B.C.), King of Persia

Alèssi Alexis

alfière *m.* ensign

alfine at last

aliante *m.* glider

alleanza alliance

alleato *n.* ally; *adj.* allied

allegrarsi *poet.* to rejoice, to be delighted

allegrézza joy

allevare to bring up

allòggio lodging

allontanare to keep away, to ward off; *refl.*
 to go away

allóra then; da - in pòi from that time on; fino - up to that time

alluminare *arch. for* illuminare

allungare to prolong

alméno at least

alpèstre alpine

Alpi *f. pl.* Alps

alquanto *adj.* several, some; *adv.* somewhat

altèro lofty, haughty

altézza height; -*cap.* Highness

altièro proud, haughty

alto high; haughty; a vòce alta in a loud voice

altrettanto as much; *pl.* as many

altriménti otherwise

altro *adj. & pron.* other; something *or* anything else; niènte - nothing else; non . . . - . . . nothing else; non . . . - che . . . nothing else but; non . . . - . . . che no other . . . but; che - what else

altróve elsewhere

altrùi *pron.* of others; others

alzare to raise; *refl.* to get up

alzato raised

amàbile charming

amante *m. & f.* lover, beloved

amare to love

amaro *adj.* bitter; *n.* bitterness

amato beloved

Amen! (*Hebrew*) So be it!

americano American

amicìzia friendship; fare - to make friends

amico friend

ammalato sick

ammazzare to kill

ammiràglio admiral

ammirato admired

ammiratóre *m.* admirer

ammirévole admirable

amóre *m.* love, Love; sake; benevolence; *cap.* Eros, god of love

amoróso *adj.* beloved; of love

ampólla phial

anarchìa anarchy

anche too, also, even

ancóra still, yet, again, more; non - not yet

andare *irr.* to go, to go about; -via to go away; andàrsene to go away, to betake oneself; va bène all right

Andrèa Andrew

angèlico angelic

àngelo angel

ànima soul

animale *m.* animal

ànimo mind; heart, courage

anno year; l'- scórso last year; l'- venturo next year

annunciare to announce

annunziare to announce

antenato ancestor

anténna antenna

antico ancient

Antònio Anthony

antro grotto

anzi rather, on the contrary; - tèmpo prematurely

apèrto (*past part. of* aprire) *adj.* open

Apocalissi *f.* Apocalypse

apparato apparatus

apparecchiato set

apparécchio apparatus

apparire *irr.* to appear; *n. m.* appearance

appartenére *irr.* to belong

appellarsi to appeal

appéna hardly, scarcely

Appennino Apennine mountains

applaudito applauded

applicare to set up

appoggiare to lean

appòsta purposely

apprèndere *irr.* to learn

appressarsi to approach

apprèsso later

appròdo landing

approvare to approve; - col capo to nod approvingly

appunto precisely

aprile *m.* April

aprire *irr.* to open, to open up

architettura architecture

archìvio archive

arco arch; bow

ardènte burning, ardent

àrdere *irr.* to burn

ardire to dare

ardóre *m.* ardor

argenterìa silverware

argènto silver

argoménto subject

àrie air

Aristèo Aristaeus

Aristòtile Aristotle (384–322 B.C.), Greek philosopher

arma (*pl.* le armi) weapon

armato armed

armistìzio armistice

armonìa harmony

aromàtico aromatic
arrabbiato angry
arrivare to arrive; to go; to happen
arrivo arrival
arrostire to roast
arte *f.* art
artìcolo article
artiglierìa artillery
artista *m. & f.* artist; **artista-mùsico** musical
   artist
ascètico ascetic
ascetismo asceticism
asciugare to dry
ascoltare to listen, to listen to
aspettare to wait, to wait for; to await; *refl.*
   to expect; **farsi** - to make people wait
aspètto *n.* aspect, appearance
assài very, quite, greatly, a great deal
assalire to assail; to seize
assassino murderer
assèdio siege
assegnare to assign
assegnato assigned, set
asservire to make subservient
asserzióne *f.* assertion
assième together; - a together with
Assisi a town in Ùmbria
assistènte *m. & f.* assistant
assìstere to be present
associare to associate
associazióne *f.* association
assòlto *past part. of* **assòlvere**
assoluto absolute
assòlvere *irr.* to acquit
assòrto absorbed
assurdità absurdity
astruserìa abstruseness
astuto astute, clever
astùzia astuteness
Atlàntico Atlantic
atrocità atrocity
attèndere *irr.* to await
attènto attentive; **stare** - to be careful
attenzióne *f.* attention; **fare** - to pay attention
attestazióne *f.* testimony, affirmation
attìngere *irr.* to draw
attinto *past part. of* **attìngere**
attitùdine *f.* aptitude
attivaménto promotion
attività activity
atto *n.* act, action; gesture; *adj.* apt, likely
attóre *m.* actor; **primo** - leading man
attórno around

attravèrso through
attribuirsi to arrogate unto oneself
attrice *f.* actress; **prima** - leading lady
attuale present
attuarsi to be realized
audace bold
augurare to wish
aumentare to increase
auròra aurora
auspìcio auspice
automòbile *f.* automobile
autóre *m.* author
autorità authority
avanti forward; **andare** - to go on; **farsi** - to
   come forward
avére *irr.* to have; to receive; - **a** to have to;
   - **bisógno di** to need; - **cura di** to take care;
   - **da** to have to; - **fame** to be hungry;
   - **inìzio** to begin; - **nóme** to be called;
   - **paura** to be afraid; - **piacére** to be pleased;
   - **ragióne** to be right; - **séte** to be thirsty
aviazióne *f.* aviation
avvedérsi *irr.* (*foll. by* **che** *or* **di**) to notice, to
   realize
avveniménto event
avvenire *irr.* to happen; - **di** to become of;
   n. m. future
avventurière *m.* adventurer
avviarsi to start walking
avvicinare to draw near; to go up to; *refl.* to
   draw near, to approach
avviso advice
avvòlgere *irr.* to wrap
avvòlto (*past part. of* **avvòlgere**) clothed
azióne *f.* action; share
azzurro blue

B

babilonése *m. & f.* Babylonian
Babilònia Babylonia (ancient city in the valley
   of the Euphrates)
bacchettóne *m.* bigot
baciare to kiss
bàcio kiss
badare to pay attention
bagnare to bathe
balbettare to stammer
ballare to dance
bambina little girl
bambino little boy, little child
banco bench
banda band
bandièra flag

banditóre *m.* advocate
barba beard
bàrbaro *n.* barbarian; *adj.* barbaric, barbarous
barbuto bearded
barca boat
baróne *m.* baron
barrièra barrier
basare to base
basìlica basilica (early oblong church building)
basso low, lowered
bastare to be enough; **Basta!** Enough!
bastiménto ship
battàglia battle
bàttere to beat; to clap
battésimo baptism
battezzarsi to be baptized
battuto beaten
beato blessed
bellézza beauty
bèllo beautiful, handsome; fine
bèn *apoc. of* **bène**
benché although
bène *n. m.* good, goodness; **il bèn fare** to do good; *pl.* estate; *adv.* well; indeed; very, quite; **volér -** to love; **sta -** all right; **va -** all right
benedétto *adj.* blessed; *n.* blessed one
benedire (*cf.* **dire**) *irr.* to bless
benedizióne *f.* benediction
benefattóre *m.* benefactor
benevolènza benevolence, good will
benigno benign
bére *irr.* to drink
berrétto cap; **- da cuòco** chef's cap
béstia beast, animal
bevuto *past part. of* **bére**
biancheggiare to whiten
bianco white
bibliotèca library
bióndo blond
bisognare to be obliged, to be necessary, to have need
bisógno need; *pl.* needs; **avér - di** to need
bócca mouth; lips
Bológna Bologna (city in northern Italy)
bòn *apoc. of* **buòno**
bontà goodness, goodheartedness
bórdo: a - di on board
bórsa purse; **- di stùdio** student loan
bòsco grove, forest, wood; *pl.* woods
bottéga shop, workshop
bràccio (*pl.* **le bràccia**) arm; **in -** in one's arms; **tra le bràccia** in one's arms

bravo *n.* bravo (a hired assassin); *adj.* fine; *interj.* Well done!
brève short; **in -** in short, in a short time
breviàrio breviary
brontolare to murmur
bruciante smarting
brulicare *n. m.* swarming, tingling
bruno dark
bruto brute
buffo comic
bugìa lie
bugiardo liar
bùio dark
buòno good, kind
buscarsi to earn
Busséto northern Italian town in the province of Parma
buttare to throw

C

cadére *irr.* to fall
Càdice Cadiz (city on the southwestern coast of Spain)
cagióne *f.* cause, motive
cagnolino puppy
Càiro (il) capital of Egypt
caldo warm, hot
calóre *m.* heat
calùnnia calumny
cambiare to change
càmbio *n.* exchange; **in - di** in exchange for
càmera room; **- da lètto** bedroom; *cap.* Chamber
camerata circle
cammino journey; path
campagna field, fields
Campidòglio Capitol
campo field
Canàrie *f. pl.* Canary Islands
cancellare to abolish
candéla candle
cane *m.* dog
cannìbale *m. & f.* cannibal
cannóne *m.* cannon
cantante *m. & f.* singer
cantare to sing
canto song; singing; canto (of a poem); corner
canzóne *f.* song; canzone (lyric poem)
càos *m.* chaos
capace able
capacità capacity
capéllo hair

capire to understand
capitano captain
capìtolo chapter
capo head; leader; **in -** on one's head; **a -** di at the head of; **approvare col -** to nod approvingly
capocòmico director
caposquadra *m. arch.* lieutenant
carabinière *m.* (Italian) policeman
caratterìstica characteristic
caravèlla caravel
carbonaro member of the Carbonerìa
Carbonerìa Italian secret political association of the early 19th century
càrcere *m.* imprisonment
carco *lit. for* càrico laden, burdened
carezzato flattered
caricare to load
Carlo Charles
carne *f.* flesh
caro dear
Carrara Tuscan city famous for its marble quarries
carrièra career
carro car
carròzza carriage
carta paper; **- da giuòco** playing card
casa house, home; family; **a -** at home; **in - di** in the house of
caso case; event, circumstance; **a -** by chance
casta caste
castagna chestnut
castèllo castle
castigo punishment
casto pure
Catài *m.* Cathay (China)
caténa chain; range
Caterina, Punta Santa St. Catherine's Point
cattivo wicked, bad
càusa cause; **a - di** because of
causare to cause
càuto cautious
cavalcare to ride (horseback)
cavalcióni: a - astride
cavalière *m.* knight
cavallo horse
Cavour, Camillo Bènso Cónte di (1810-1861) Italian statesman
celare to conceal
celebrare to celebrate
céna supper
centàuro centaur
centinàio (*pl.* **le centinàia**) hundred

centrale central
Cèrbero Cerberus (three-headed dog, guardian of Hades)
cérca: in - di in search of
cercare to seek, to look for; to try
cerimònia rite, ceremony; *pl.* kowtowing; **fare cerimònie** to bow and scrape, to kowtow
cèrto certain; **tenére per -** to hold for certain; *adv.* certainly
cervèllo mind, brain
cèrvia *lit. for* **il cèrvo** deer
cessare to cease; **far -** to quell
che *pron.* who, whom; that, which; what; *adj.* **- ?** what?; **- !** what! what a!; **quéllo -** what; *conj.* that, than; **non . . . - . . .** only; **più -** more than; *m.* **il -** which; **ché** in order that, so that, because, since
chéto quiet; **andar -** to go quietly
chi *pron.* who, whom; whoever; he who; someone who
chiacchierare to chat
chiacchierata chat; **fare una -** to have a chat
chiamare to call; *refl.* to be called; to call each other; **fare -** to send for; **mandare a -** to send for
chiarire to clarify; *n. m.* the brightening
chiaro *adj.* clear; **al - di luna** in the moonlight; *adv.* clearly
chiave *f.* key; **chiùdere a -** to lock
chièdere *irr.* to ask, to ask for; **- di** to ask for; **- perdóno** to beg pardon; **- scusa** to apologize
chièsa church
chièsto *past part. of* **chièdere**
chilòmetro kilometer (measure of length equal to one thousand meters, or to 3,280.8 feet)
chinare to lower
chiòccia setting-hen
chiòstro cloister
Chiróne Chiron (a centaur skilled in medicine)
chiùdere *irr.* to close; **- a chiave** to lock
chiunque *pron.* anyone
chiuso *past part. of* **chiùdere**
ci *pron.* us, to us; ourselves, each other; *adv.* here, there
ciascuno *pron.* each one, every one; *adj.* each, every
cibo food
Ciclòpe *m.* Cyclops
cièco blind
cièlo sky, heaven
cima tip; summit, peak, top; **in - a** to the top of
Cinquecènto 16th century

ciò *pron.* that; - che what, that which
cioè that is, that is to say
circa approximately, about
Circe Circe (legendary sorceress from Mt. Circèo, near Gaèta, who by magic turned her victims into beasts)
cìrcolo circle
circospètto circumspect
circostanza circumstance
citare to quote
città city
cittadino citizen
civiltà civilization
claque *f. (French)* paid applauders
Clarina *dim. of* Clara Clare
clima *m.* climate
cobelligerante cobelligerent
Cobinàn *m.* probably the present Kuhbanan in northeastern Iran
cocéssi *impf. subj. of* cuòcere
códa tail; - dell' òcchio corner of the eye
codardo cowardly
codésto that
cògliere *irr.* to catch
colà there
colazióne *f.* breakfast; fare - to have breakfast
collaboratóre *m.* collaborator
collare *m.* collar
còlle *m.* hill
collettivo collective
collettóre *m.* collector
collina hill
còllo neck
collocare to place
colómba dove
colònia colony
colónna column
colorare to color
colóre *m.* color
colóro *pron.* they; those, those men
cólpa fault
coltivare to cultivate
colùi *pron.* that man; - che he who, he whom; - il quale he who
comandare to command, to order
comando command
combàttere to fight; *n. m.* fighting
cóme like; how; as; as if; when; così - just as; - per as if to
cominciare to begin; in sul - at the beginning
commèdia play; comedy
commemorazióne *f.* commemoration
comménto comment

commèrcio trade, business
comméttere *irr.* to commit
commòsso *past part. of* commuòvere
commuòvere *irr.* to move
compagnìa company; fare - to keep company
compagno companion; follower
compagnóne *m.* boon companion
compassionévole moving
compiacérsi *irr.* to take delight
cómpiere to accomplish, to fulfill, to complete
compire to complete, to finish
compito *past part. of* compire
compiuto *past part. of* cómpiere
complèto complete
còmplice *m.* accomplice
compliménto compliment
complimentóso ceremonious
compósto composed
cómpra purchase
comprare to buy
comunanza: - d'orìgine common origin
comune *adj.* common, current; *n. m. cap.* Commune
comunicare to communicate
comunicazióne *f.* communication
con with
concèdere *irr.* to grant, to allow
concentraménto concentration
concentrare to concentrate
concepire to conceive
concèrnere to concern
concertare to direct; to work out
concèsso *past part. of* concèdere
concètto concept
concezióne *f.* conception
conclùdere *irr.* to conclude
conclusióne *f.* conclusion
concòrde harmonious
concórrere *irr.* to concur, to contribute
concórso *past part. of* concórrere
condannare to condemn
condensare to compress
condizióne *f.* condition, status, position
condótta behavior
condótto *past part. of* condurre
condurre *irr.* to lead, to drive; to take
condussi, conducésti *p. abs. of* condurre
conduttóre *m.* conductor
conferènza conference
conferire (a) to confer (upon)
confermare to confirm
confessare to confess
confessióne *f.* confession

confidare to entrust
confidenziale confidential
confinaménto internment
conflitto conflict
confluènte *m.* junction
confusióne *f.* confusion
confuso confused; confounded; **in -** confusedly
congedarsi to take leave
congiùngere *irr.* to join
congiunto *past part. of* congiùngere
congiuntura: **per -** without evidence; casually
congiunzióne *f.* linking
connèsso connected
conoscènte *m. & f.* acquaintance
conoscènza knowledge
conóscere *irr.* to know; *n. m.* knowing
conquista conquest
conquistare to conquer
conquistatóre *m.* conqueror
consegnare to hand
conseguènza consequence; **per -** , **di -** consequently
conservatóre *m.* custodian
conservatòrio conservatory
considerare to consider
considerazióne *f.* consideration
considerévole considerable
consìglio counsel; council
consìstere to consist
consolante consoling
consòrte *m.* husband
consultare to consult
consumarsi to be consumed
contare to tell
cónte *m.* (*title*) count
contemplare to contemplate
contenére *irr.* to contain
contènto happy, satisfied
contenuto content
continuare to continue
contìnuo continuous
contrada province, region
contraddire *irr.* to contradict
contraddizióne *f.* contradiction
contràrio contrary, opposite; **al -** on the contrary
contribuènte *m. & f.* contributor
contribuire to contribute
cóntro against
controllare to control
contròllo control
conveniènte convenient, suitable

convenire *irr.* to be fitting; to be expedient; to be suitable; **convenirsi a** to become (be suitable to)
conversare to converse
conversazióne *f.* conversation
conversióne *f.* conversion
convertire to convert, to change
convìncere *irr.* to convince
convinciménto conviction
convinto *past part. of* convìncere
copèrto covered; **- di** covered with
copialèttere *m. sing.* letterpress
copióne *m.* script
coprire *irr.* to cover
còr *poet. for* cuòre
coràggio courage
coraggióso courageous
còre *poet. for* cuòre
cornice *f.* frame
Cornovàglia Cornwall
coronare to crown
còrpo body
corporale corporal
Corrado Conrad
córrere *irr.* to run, to speed; to spread
corrispondènza correspondence
corrispóndere *irr.* to respond
corruzióne *f.* corruption
córso course
córte *f.* court
cortegiano courtier
cortése courtly; gracious
cortesìa courtesy, gallantry
cortile *m.* courtyard
córto brief
còsa thing, affair, matter; *pl.* affairs; **una - qualùnque** any old thing
còscia drumstick
cosciènza conscience; consciousness
così so, thus; likewise; **- cóme** just as; **- . . . cóme . . . . . .** as well as . . .
cosicché so that
còsta coast
costà over there
costanza constancy
costituire to constitute
còsto: **ad ógni -** at any price
costóso expensive
costrétto *past part. of* costrìngere
costrìngere *irr.* to compel
costruire to build
costùi *pron.* he, this man
costume *m.* custom; *pl.* manners

cotésto this
cotóne *m.* cotton
còtto *past part. of* cuòcere
creare to create
creatura creature; baby
creazióne *f.* creation
crébbe *p. abs. of* créscere
credènte *m. & f.* believer
crédere to believe
créscere *irr.* to grow
cristianésimo Christianity
cristianità Christianity
cristiano Christian
Cristo Christ
crìtico critic
cróce *f.* cross
crònaca chronicle
crucifige! Crucify Him!
crudèle cruel
crudeltà cruelty
crudo *poet. for* crudèle
c.s. (cóme sópra) as above
cucina kitchen
cucinare to cook
cui whom; which; il, i, la, le - whose, of which
culto cult
cuòcere *irr.* to cook
cuòco cook; berrétto da - chef's cap
cuòr *apoc. of* cuòre
cuòre *m.* heart
cùpola cupola, dome
cura care; avér - di to take care of
curare to heed; curarsi di to care for, to be
    concerned about
curato parish priest; Signór - Reverend Father
curióso curious
curvatura curve

D

da *prep.* by, from, to; for; since; at the house,
    office of; - quando ever since
dacché since
danno harm; damage; injury
danzare to dance
dappertutto everywhere
dare *irr.* to give; to grant; to inflict; to trans-
    mit; - un'occhiata to glance; *refl.* - a to
    take to; - la mòrte to commit suicide
Dàrio *see* Alessandro
data date
davanti before, in front of
débole *n. m.* the weak
dècade *f.* ten days

decìdere *irr.* to decide
dècimo tenth
decisivo decisive
deciso *past part. of* decìdere; *adj.* decisive
dedicare to devote
deficiènza shortcoming
defunto deceased
degnarsi to deign
dégno worthy
deh! *interj.* I pray you!
Dèi (gli) (*pl. of* dio) the gods
deliberare to resolve
delicato delicate
delitto crime
della Scala, Bartolomèo (?–1304) Lord´ of
    Veróna
democràtico democratic
democrazìa democracy
denaro money
denominare to name
dènso dense
déntro in, into, inside; - di within; là - in
    there; qui - in here
deploràbile deplorable
depórre *irr.* to place (down)
deputato deputy
derisióne *f.* derision
derivare to derive
descritto *past part. of* descrìvere
descrìvere *irr.* to describe
desèrto *n. m.* desert; *adj.* deserted
desiderare to desire; to want; da - desirable
desiderato *adj.* desired
desidèrio desire
designare to designate
dèspota *m.* despot
destare to wake; *refl.* to wake up
destinare to destine
destino destiny, fate
dèstra: a - on the right
destraménte adroitly
dèstro right
desùmere *irr.* to infer
determinare to determine
determinato determined, definite; specified
dettatura dictation
détto *past part. of* dire
devòto devoted
di *prep.* of, with, about
dì *m.* day
diàlogo dialogue
diamante *m.* diamond
Diana Diana (goddess of the woods)

diàvolo devil
dicèmbre *m.* December
dichiarare to declare
Didóne Dido (Queen of Carthage)
diè *lit. for* diède (*p. abs. of* dare)
diètro behind, after; - a behind
difèndere *irr.* to defend
difètto defect
differènte different
differènza difference
differire to postpone
diffìcile difficult
difficoltà difficulty
dignitosaménte with dignity
dilémma *m.* dilemma
dilettare to delight; dilettarsi in *or* di to
    delight in, to take pleasure in
dilètto pleasure; *adj.* beloved
diligènza diligence
dimane (diman) *poet. for* domani
dimenticare to forget
dimorare to dwell, to live
dimostrare to demonstrate, to reveal
dinanzi before; straight ahead; - a before
dinastìa dynasty
Dio God; Santo - ! By Jove!
dipèndere (da) *irr.* to depend (on)
dire *irr.* to say, to speak, to tell; - male to
    speak ill of; - nell' (*or* all') orécchio to
    whisper; a - vero in truth; per - così so to
    speak; sentir - to hear people say; volér -
    to mean
dirètto *past part. of* dirìgere
direttóre *m.* director; - di scèna stage director
dirìgere *irr.* to direct
dirimpètto opposite
diritto *n.* right; *adj.* straight
disastróso disastrous
discéndere *irr.* to descend
disciòlto (*past part. of* disciògliere) unbound,
    let loose
disciplina discipline
discòrdia discord
discórso discourse
discréto discreet
discussióne *f.* discussion
disdégno *liter. for* sdégno
Disdèmona Desdemona
disegnatóre *m.* draftsman
diségno drawing; plan
disertare to ravage
disgràzia misfortune
disgusto disgust

disìo *poet. for* desidèrio
disonorévole dishonorable
disórdine *m.* disorder
disperato *adj.* despairing, desperate
disperazióne *f.* despair
dispèrso scattered
dispiacére *m.* displeasure, affliction; dar - to
    cause sorrow, affliction; *v. irr.* to displease;
    mi dispiace I am sorry
dispórre *irr.* to dispose
disposizióne *f.* disposition; disposal
dispósto (*past part. of* dispórre) disposed,
    willing
dìsputa argument
dissuadére *irr.* to dissuade
distante distant, away
distanza distance; grande - long distance
distèndere *irr.* to stretch
distìnguere *irr.* to distinguish
distìnto distinct
distribuire to distribute
distribuzióne *f.* assignment, arrangement
distrùggere *irr.* to destroy
distrussi *p. abs. of* distrùggere
distruzióne *f.* destruction
dito (*pl.* le dita) finger
divenire *irr.* to become
diventare to become
divenuto *past part. of* divenire
diversità variety
divèrso different, various, several, scattered
divertènte amusing
divìdere *irr.* to divide
divino divine
divisióne *f.* division
divulgare to divulge
dólce sweet; gentle, beloved
dolcézza sweetness
dolènte sorrowful, sorry
dolór *apoc. of* dolóre
dolóre *m.* sorrow, grief; pain
doloróso painful, grievous; harrowing
domanda question, request; fare una - to ask
    a question
domandare to ask
domani tomorrow
domare to subdue
doménica Sunday
domèstico manservant
domìnio rule
dòn Don, title equivalent to: Sir for a noble-
    man, Mr. for a commoner, Reverend for a
    priest

donare to give, to bestow
dónde whence
dònna woman; wife; lady; - di Corte Court
 Lady
dóno gift; dare in - to give as a gift
donzèlla damsel
dópo after
dopodomani the day after tomorrow
dóppio double
dormire to sleep; *n. m.* sleep
dòsso back
dòte *f.* dowry
dottòre *m.* doctor
dottrina learning
dóve where; fin - as far as
dovére *irr.* to have to, must; to owe; *n. m.* duty
drago dragon
dramma *m.* drama
drammàtico dramatic
dùbbio *n.* doubt; *adj.* doubtful
dubitare to doubt
duca *m.* duke
ducato ducat
Duecènto 13th century
dùnque therefore
duòl *lit. for* dolóre
duòmo duomo (an Italian cathedral)
duràbile lasting
durante during
durare to last
durévole lasting
durézza harshness
duro hard; harsh; difficult

E

e and
ecc. (eccètera) etc.
eccellènte excellent
eccellènza excellence
eccètto except
ècco behold; èccomi here I am
econòmico economical
ed *euphonic for* e
edifìcio building
edifìzio building
educare to educate, to bring up
effètto effect
efficace effective
efficiènte efficient
egemonìa hegemony
Egitto Egypt
egrègio remarkable, great; - Signór . . . Dear
 Mr. . . .

eguaglianza equality
eguale equal
Eh *interj.* Eh!
eleménto element
elèttrico electric
elevato elevated
Elisabétta Elizabeth
élla *lit. for* éssa
élmo helmet
emanare to give off
Emanuèle Emmanuel
eméttere *irr.* to send out, to let out
emisfèro hemisphere
empièndo (*ger. of* empire [émpiere]) filling
empire to fill
Enèa Aeneas (Prince of Troy)
energìa energy, power
enèrgico energetic
entrare to enter
entrata entrance
entusiasmo enthusiasm
entusiasta enthusiastic
època epoch
eppure and yet
Èquatóre *m.* Equator
èra era
èrba grass
Ercole Hercules
erède *m. & f.* heir
erètto *past part. of* erìgere
erìgere *irr.* to erect
eròico heroic
errante wandering; shifty
errare to wander; to err
errato wrong
erróre *m.* error; - di lìngua slip of the tongue;
 - di memòria slip of the memory
esagerare to exaggerate
esaltaménto exaltation
esaltare to exalt
esame *m.* examination
esaminare to examine
esclamare to exclaim
esclùdere *irr.* to exclude
escogitare to devise
esecutóre *m.* performer
esecuzióne *f.* rendition
eseguire to carry out
esèmpio example; per - for instance; sénza -
 unparalleled
esercitare to exercise
esèrcito army
esercìzio exercise

esìlio exile
esistènza existence
esìstere to exist
èsito outcome, result
esortazióne f. exhortation
esperiènza experience; experimentation; experiment
esperimentale experimental
esperiménto experiment; - di contròllo control test; fare - to experience
espèrto experienced
espiato expiated
espórre irr. to expose, to express; to relate
espósto past part. of espórre
esprìmere irr. to express
èssere irr. to be; - di to belong to; - per . . . to be on the point of; v'è there is
ésso pron. it; he (rare)
Est m. East
ésta poet. for quésta
estate f. summer
estensióne f. extension
estìnguere irr. to extinguish
estràneo stranger
estremità end
estrèmo adj. extreme; n. m. extremity
èsule m. & f. exile
età age; era; l' - più bèlla youth
etèreo ethereal; - padiglión poet. for firmament
eternità eternity
etèrno. eternal
etrusco Etruscan
Euridice Eurydice (wife of Orpheus)
Euròpa Europe
europèo European
evidènte evident
evitare to avoid

F

fa ago
fàccia face
fàcile easy
facilità ease
facilitare to facilitate
falcóne m. falcon
fallàcia fallacy
fama fame
fame f. hunger; avér - to be hungry
famìglia family
famóso famous
fanciulla girl
fanciullésco childish
fanciullo boy

fango mud
fantasìa phantasy, imagination
fanterìa infantry
faraglióne m. faraglione (strange cliff-like rocks rising out of the sea)
fare irr. to do, to make; refl. to make oneself; to be done, to be made, to become; to be celebrated; da - to be made; far - to make someone do. Other uses of fare will be found under each complementary verb, noun, adverb, etc. Example: for sapér fare, look under sapére.
farina flour
fascismo Fascism
fascista n. & adj., m. & f. Fascist
fatica labor, work; effort
faticóso fatiguing
fato fate
fatto n. occurrence; pl. affairs; (past part. of fare)
fàvola fable
favóre m. favor
favorévole favorable, successful
favorire to favor
fazióne f. faction
fazolétto handkerchief
fé f. poet. for féde
fe' poet. for féce
febbràio February
fèbbre f. fever
fecóndo fertile; - di rich in
féde f. faith; dar - a to put one's faith in
fedéle faithful
fedeltà fidelity
federazióne f. federation
Felice Felix
felice adj. happy
fémmina female; girl
femminile feminine
fenòmeno phenomenon
ferire to wound
ferita wound
ferito wounded, hurt
fermare to stop
férmo firm, still; per - assuredly
feróce ferocious
fèrro iron
fèrtile fertile
fèsta feast, holiday, joy; far - a to welcome
feudale feudal
fia poet. for sarà
fiaba fable
fiamma flame; a - in flames
fie (rarer than fia) poet. for sarà

fianco: a - di side by side with; di - to one side
fiasco fiasco (failure); far - to be a failure
fiatare to breathe
fiato breath
fidarsi (di) to rely on
fidato trusted
fìglio son; *pl.* children
fìglia daughter
figliastra step-daughter
figliuòla daughter
figliuòlo son, child
figura figure
Filippo Philip
filo: sènza - wireless
filosòfico philosophical
filòsofo philosopher
fin *apoc. of* fine, *m. & f.* and fino *prep.*
finale final, last
finché while, as long as, until
fine *m.* aim, goal, purpose; al - at the end
fine *f.* end; alla - in the end
finèstra window
fìngere *irr.* to feign, to pretend
finire to finish, to end; *n. m.* close
fino *prep.* till, until, since; - a as far as; - allóra up to that time; - che till, as long as; - da since; - dove as far as; - quando until
finsi *p. abs. of* fìngere
finto *past part. of* fìngere
fiónda sling
fióre *m.* flower; in - in blossom
fiorentino Florentine
Firènze Florence
fischiare to whistle
fissare to stare
fisso *adj.* staring; guardare - to stare
fiume *m.* river
flàuto flute
flòtta fleet
flùido fluid
fóce *f.* mouth (of a river)
foggiare to fashion
fòglia leaf
fogliame *m.* foliage
fòglio sheet
folgorare to glitter
fólla crowd, mob
fòlle mad
follìa folly, madness
fóndo bottom, rear (of a theater); in - at the farther end of; *pl.* funds
fónte *f.* source, spring
forestièro stranger

fórma form, shape; phase; a - di in the shape of
formare to form; to create
formidàbile formidable
fòrmula formula, set form
fornito furnished
Fòro Forum
fórse perhaps
fòrte *adj.* strong, hard; fortified; *adv.* overwhelmingly; bitterly; nel - di in the thick of
fortézza fortress
fortificazióne *f.* fortification
fortuna fortune, luck; - che luckily
fòrza force, strength; power
fòssa grave
fra between, among, in the midst of, in; - me e me within myself
fràgile frail
Francésca Frances
Francésco Francis; San - St. Francis
francése French
Frància France
franco franc (once equivalent to $0.20)
frate *m.* brother, friar
fratèllo brother
frattanto meanwhile
fréccia arrow
fréddo cold
fréno bit
freschézza coolness
frésco fresh, cool
frétta haste; in - hastily
fròde *f.* trick
frónte *f.* forehead, brow; a - in front
frutto fruit
fuggire to flee (from); to avoid
funèsto dire, tragic
funzionare to function
funzióne *f.* function
fuòco fire; a - afire
fuòri *prep.* out; - di outside; *adv.* outside; di - outward; - di sé stésso beside one self
fùria fury; di - hastily; sulle fùrie in a temper
furóre *m.* fury
fuso melted

G

gàio gay
galantuòmo gentleman
Gallo Gaul
gamba leg
gelosìa jealousy
gelóso jealous

generale general
generare to generate, to create
generazióne *f.* generation
gènere *m.* kind; - umano mankind
generosità generosity
generóso generous
genitóre *m.* father; *pl.* parents
gennàio January
Gènova Genoa (city in northwestern Italy)
gènte *f.* people
gentile gentle, gracious
gentilézza civility, kindness, nobility
gentiluòmo gentleman
gèrme *m.* germ
gèsto gesture
Gesù Jesus
gettare to throw
ghiottóne *m.* glutton
già already; once; indeed
giacché since
giacére *irr.* to lie
giacque *p. abs. of* giacére
giallo yellow
giammài never; non . . . - never
giardino garden
Gibiltèrra Gibraltar
gìglio lily
ginnàsio classical high school
ginòcchio (*pl.* le ginòcchia *or* i ginòcchi) knee
giocare to play
giocóndo gay, smiling
giòia joy
Giórgio George
giornale *m.* newspaper; - di bórdo logbook
giornalista *m. & f.* journalist
giornata day, day's work
giórno day; di - daytime; di - in - from day
   to day
Giòsafat Jehosaphat
Giovàn *apoc. of* Giovanni
gióvane *m.* young man; *f.* young woman; *adj.*
   young
giovanile youthful
Giovanni John
giovare to pay off
Giòve Zeus
gióvine *m. or f. for* gióvane; *adj.* young
giovinézza youth
girare to turn, to whirl
giro: in - around
gittare *lit. for* gettare
giù down
Giuda Judas

giudicare to judge
giùdice *m.* judge
giudìzio judgment
giugno June
Giuliètta Juliet
Giùlio Julius
giùngere *irr.* to reach; to arrive
giunto *past part. of* giùngere
giuòco game; fun; carte da - playing cards
giuraménto oath
giurare to swear
Giusèppe Joseph
giustìzia justice
giusto just, right
glòria glory
glorióso glorious
godére to enjoy
gónna skirt
governante *m.* head of government
governare to manage; to feed
govèrno government
gradito pleasant
grado degree, step; rank
grande great, big, large, tall; magnificent
grandézza size
grano wheat
grasso fat
gratis free of charge
gràzia grace, favor; dar gràzie to thank
grazióso gracious; (*colloq.*) cute
gridare to shout
grido shout, call
grigiastro greyish
gru *f.* crane
gruppo group
guadagnare to earn, to gain
guadagno profit, profits
guai (a) *interj.* woe (unto)
guardare to look; - fisso to stare; *refl.* to look
   at each other
guàrdia guard
guarire to heal
guèrra war; nave da - warship
guerrièro warrior
guida guide
guidare to guide, to lead
Guido Guy
gùscio shell

H

Ho! *interj.* Oh!

I

Iddìo God
idèa idea
ideare to conceive the idea
idèntico identical
identificare to identify
idolatrìa idolatry
ìdolo idol
ièri yesterday; **- nòtte** last night; **- séra** last evening, last night; **l'altro -** a few days ago
ignorante ignorant
ignòto unknown; *n.* stranger
illuminare to illuminate, to light
illustre illustrious
imàgine *f. lit. for* **immàgine**
imaginare *lit. for* **immaginare**
imbarcare to embark; *refl.* to sail
imbiancare to grow white
immaginare to imagine; *refl.* to imagine
immaginàrio imaginary
immaginazióne *f.* imagination
immàgine *f.* image
immane vast
immediato immediate
immènso immense
imminènte imminent
immortale immortal
immòto motionless
imparare to learn
impaziènte impatient, anxious
impediménto obstacle
impensato unforeseen, inconceivable
imperatóre emperor
imperdonàbile inexcusable
imperfètto imperfect
impèro empire
impórre *irr.* to impose, to command
importante important
importanza importance
impósi, imponésti *p. abs. of* **impórre**
impossìbile impossible
impósto *past part. of* **impórre**
impostura deceit
imprésa enterprise, undertaking; adventure
impressióne *f.* impression
imprigionaménto imprisonment
improvvisaménte unexpectedly
improvvisare to improvise
in in, to, on
inargentare to sprinkle with silver
inaspettato unexpected
inaugurare to inaugurate

incantato bewitched
incertézza uncertainty
incèrto uncertain
inchinarsi to bow, to submit
inclinare to incline
incominciare to begin
incomprensìbile incomprehensible
incònscio unconscious
incontrare to encounter
incóntro meeting; **- a** toward; **- là** facing
incoraggiato encouraged
incoronare to crown
incredìbile incredible
incrociato crossed
indagare to inquire into
indeboliménto weakening
indégno *n.* unworthy one
indescrivìbile indescribable
indiano Indian
indicare to indicate, to point out
ìndice *m.* index
Índie *f. pl.* Indies
indiètro back; **all' -** backwards
indipendènte independent
indipendènza independence
indispensàbile indispensable
individuale individual
indivìduo *n.* individual
indótto *past part. of* **indurre**
indugiare to delay
indùgio delay
indurre *irr.* to induce
indùstria industry
ineffàbile inexpressible
inerènte (a) inherent (in)
inesoràbile inexorable
inètto inept
inevitàbile unavoidable
infallìbile infallible
infàmia infamy
infatti in fact; indeed
infelice *n. m.* unhappy one; *adj.* unhappy, unfortunate
inferióre *n.* inferior; *adj.* lower, inferior
infiammato: - di aflame with
infido faithless
infine in short, finally
infinità: un' - di numberless
infinito *adj.* numberless
infino: - che until
inflitto (*past part. of* **inflìggere**) inflicted
influènza influence
influsso influence

informazióne *f.* information
infuocarsi to ignite
ingannare to deceive
inganno deception
ingégno mind; wit
Inghiltèrra England
inginocchiarsi to kneel, to get on one's knees
inginocchiato kneeling
ingiùria insult, affront; *pl.* injuries, damage
ingiustìzia injustice
inglése English
ingoiare to swallow
ingrato *adj.* ungrateful; *n. m.* ungrateful one
inimicìzia enmity
iniziare to begin, to start
iniziazióne *f.* initiation
inìzio: avére - to begin
innamorarsi (di) to fall in love (with)
innamorato *n. m.* lover, beloved; *adj.* enamored; **èssere -** to be in love
innanzi before; **da óra -** from now on; **più -** further on
innegàbile undeniable
innocènte innocent
innocénza innocence
innùmero innumerable
inóltre besides, moreover
inondare to flood
insanàbile incurable
insano insane
insegnare to teach
inseguire to pursue
insìdia insidiousness, deceit
insième together, at the same time
insistènza insistence
insìstere to insist
insolènza insolence
insormontàbile insurmountable
inspirare *lit. for* **ispirare**
installato installed
insurrezióne *f.* insurrection
intanto meanwhile
integrità integrity
intellètto intellect
intelligènte intelligent
intelligènza intelligence
intèndere *irr.* to intend; to understand; to hear, to give heed
intenerirsi to be moved
intensità intensity, density
intènto *n.* purpose; *adj.* **- a** intent on
intenzióne *f.* intention
interessante interesting

interèsse *n. m.* interest
interferènza interference
intermèdio intermediate
internazionale international
intèrno interior
intéro entire, whole
interrómpere *irr.* to interrupt
interrótto *past part. of* **interrómpere**
interruppi *p. abs. of* **interrómpere**
intervallo interval
intéso *past part. of* **intèndere**
ìntimo intimate
intórno around; **- a** concerning, about; **all' -** around
intraprèndere *irr.* to undertake
intréccio plot
introdurre *irr.* to introduce
intruso intruder
inùtile useless
invano in vain
invasióne *f.* invasion
invecchiato aged
invéce instead
inventare to invent
invenzióne *f.* invention
invèrno winter
inviare to send
invìdia envy
invidiato envied
invidióso envious
invitare to invite
invito invitation; **fare un -** to extend an invitation
invocare to request
involontariaménte involuntarily
iperbòlico hyperbolic
ira wrath, anger
iracóndo angered
irascìbile hot-tempered
irato irate
irònico ironic
irradiare to irradiate, to illuminate
irresistìbile irresistible
irritare to arouse
iscèna (*euphonic for* **scèna**): **méttere in -** to stage
iscritto (*euphonic for* **scritto**): **in -** in writing
ìsola island
Ispagna *euphonic for* **Spagna**
ispiare *euphonic for* **spiare**
ispirare to inspire
Israèle Israel
istante *m.* instant

istinto instinct
istituire to organize
istituzióne *f.* institution
Itàlia Italy
italiano Italian
itàlico Italian

L

là there; **di** - over there
labbro *poet. for* **le labbra** *f. pl.* lips
làcrima tear
lacrimare to weep
lacrimóso tear-stained
ladro thief
ladróne *m.* thief
lagnarsi to complain, to mourn
làgrima tear
lagrimare to weep
lamentare to lament; *refl.* to moan
laménto lament
lampo flash of lightning
Lancialòtto Lancelot (*Knight of the Round Table, and lover of Guinevere*)
lànguido languid
languire to languish
lantèrna lantern
larghézza width
largo large; wide
lasciare to leave; to leave aside; to let, to allow
laterale lateral, side
latino Latin
lato side; **da un** - on one side
laudare *poet. for* **lodare**
làude *f.* canticle, praise
làuro laurel
lavorante *m. & f.* worker
lavorare to work
lavóro work, labor; activity
lazzo joke
lealtà loyalty
lécito admissible
léga league
legale legal
legare to bind, to chain; - **insième** to intertwine
légge *f.* law
lèggere *irr.* to read
leggèro light
leggiadro comely, graceful
leggìo reading-stand
légno wood; ship
leóne *m.* lion; *prop. n.* Leo

letìzia joy
lèttera letter; *pl.* literature; **sénza** - without literary knowledge
letteratura literature
lètto bed; **càmera da** - bedroom
lettóre *m.* reader
lettura reading
levare to raise; to remove; *refl.* to rise
li *poet. for* **gli**
lì there
Lia *for* **Rosalìa** Rosalie
liberale liberal; generous
liberalità generosity
liberare to liberate
lìbero free
libertà freedom; - **privata** personal freedom
libro book
licenziare to dismiss
lido seashore; *lit.* port
lièto happy
limitarsi (a) to limit oneself (to)
lìngua tongue; language; **erróre di** - slip of the tongue
liquefare (*Cf.* **fare**) *irr.* to liquefy
liquefatto *past part. of* **liquefare**
lira lira (the monetary unit of Italy, once equivalent to $0.20); lyre (*Music*)
lista list
livèllo level
lo *poet. for* **il**
lòco *lit. for* **luógo**
lodare to praise
lodévole praiseworthy
Lodovico Ludwig
Lombardìa Lombardy (region of northern Italy)
Lóndra London
lontano far off, far, remote; **più** - farther away, farther
lór *apoc. of* **lóro**
Lorènzo Lawrence; - **il Magnìfico** Lorenzo the Magnificent (1448–1492)
lòtta fight
lottare to fight
luce *f.* light
Lucìa Lucy
lùcido bright
Ludovico Ludwig
lùglio July
lume *m.* lamp, light
luna moon; **al chiaro di** - in the moonlight
lunghézza length
lungo *adj.* long; *prep.* along

luògo place; dare - to give way; tenére - to take the place
lupo wolf
lusso luxury
lutto mourning

M

ma but
macchiare to soil
màcchina machine
Maddalèna Magdalen
Madònna Our Lady
madre *f.* mother
maestà majesty
maèstra mistress; teacher
maèstro teacher; maestro
màggio May
maggióre *adj.* greater; il maggiór . . . the greatest . . . ; la maggiór parte the majority; *n. m.* Major
magnanimità magnanimity
Magnificènza Excellency; Vóstra - Your Excellency
magnífico munificent, magnificent
magno great
mai never, ever; - più never again
malaménte badly, shabbily
maldicènte *m.* slanderer
male *m.* harm; evil; *adj.* bad, badly; dire - di to speak ill of; far - a to harm, to do wrong to; far del - a to harm; fare il - to do wrong
malignità maliciousness
malinconìa melancholia
malincònico sad
mallevadóre *m.* guarantor
malo evil
mamma mother
man *apoc. of* mano
mancanza lack
mancare to be lacking; to be missing
mància tip
mandare to send; - a chiamare to send for; - fuòri to put out
mangiare to eat
mànica sleeve
manièra manner; di (*or* in) - che in such a way that
manifestazióne *f.* manifestation
manifèsto obvious
mano *f.* hand; a - dèstra to the right
mansuèto meek, subdued
mantenére *irr.* to keep, to support
manto mantle

Maométto Mahomet
mare *m.* sea; - Ocèano the Atlantic Ocean
Marìa Mary; the Virgin Mary
marinàio seaman
Màrio Marius
maritare to marry (off)
marito husband
marmo marble; *pl.* blocks of marble
Maròcco Morocco
màrtire *m. & f.* martyr
marzo March
màschio male
matemàtico mathematician
materiale material
matrice *f.* matrix, womb
matrimònio marriage; fare un - to perform a marriage
mattina morning
mattino (early) morning
matto crazy
mattutino *adj.* morning
mausolèo mausoleum
mazzolino little bunch
medésimo self, same
mèdico physician
mèdio middle finger
meditato thoughtful
mèglio better; - che better than; stare - to feel better
mellìfluo mellifluous
mèmbro member (*pl.* i mèmbri); limb (*pl.* le mèmbra)
memòria memory; dégno di - worth remembering; erróre di - slip of memory; sapére a - to know by heart; *pl.* memoirs
Mèna *for* Filomèna Philomena
menare to lead; to bring
mendace deceitful
mendicare to beg
méno less; a - che unless; per lo - at least
mentalménte mentally
ménte *f.* mind
mentire to lie
ménto chin
méntre while; - che while
menzionare to mention
menzógna falsehood
meravìglia wonder
meravigliare to marvel; *refl.* to wonder
meraviglióso marvelous, extraordinary
meridionale southern
meridióne *m.* South
meritare to deserve

mèrito merit
mescolare to mix
mése *m.* month
messàggio message
messère *m.* Sir; Lord, my Lord; Mister
mésso *past part. of* méttere
mestière *m.* trade, profession
metallo metal
mètodo method
mètro meter (a measure of length equal to 39.37 inches)
méttere *irr.* to put, to place; - in to set up; far - to have placed; - in perìcolo to endanger; *refl.* - a to begin to; - a sedére to take a seat; - d'accòrdo to make an agreement
mèzzo *n.* midst; means; *adj.* half; in - a in the middle of; per - by means; per - di through
mezzogiórno high noon
Michèle Michael
mièle *m.* honey
migliàio (*pl.* le migliàia) thousand
mìglio (*pl.* le mìglia) mile
miglióre better; rèndere - to improve
Milano Milan (capital of Lombardy)
milióne *m.* million
militare military
milìzia militia
mille thousand; l'anno - the year one thousand
millènnio millennium
minàccia threat
minacciare to threaten
minaccióso threatening
minèstra soup
minièra mine
mìnimo least, minimal
ministro executor
minóre smaller, less; minor
minuto *n.* minute; *adj.* tiny
miràbile wondrous, wonderful
miràcolo miracle
miracolóso miraculous
mirare to look upon; to gaze upon
misèria misfortune
mìsero wretched; poor; *n.* wretched one
missióne *f.* mission
mito myth
mòbile moving
modèllo image
moderare to moderate
modèrno modern
modèstia modesty
modèsto modest

mòdo manner, way; di - che so that; in - che in such a way that; in - da in such a way as; fare in - che to see to it that
móglie *f.* wife
mòlle soft
moltiplicare to multiply
moltitùdine *f.* multitude
mólto *adj.* much; *pl.* many; i mólti the many, the majority; *adv.* very, much, greatly, a great deal
momentàneo momentary
moménto moment
monarca *m.* sovereign
monarchìa empire
mondiale *adj.* world
móndo world
monéta coin
Monsignóre Monsignor
montagna mountain
montare to mount, to climb
mónte *m.* mountain, peak, mount
Montevidèo capital of Uruguay
monuménto monument
morale moral
morire *irr.* to die; *n. m.* death
mormorare to murmur
mormorìo murmur
Mòro Moor
mòrso bite
mortale mortal, deadly
mòrte *f.* death; darsi la - to commit suicide; pèna di - death penalty
mortificato mortified
mortificazióne *f.* mortification
mòrto *n. & adj.* dead
Mosè Moses (great Hebrew prophet and lawgiver)
mòsso *past part. of* muòvere
mostrare to show, to reveal; to prove; - di (*plus inf.*) to appear to
mostruóso monstrous
mòto motion
mòtto witticism; non far - not to say a word
movévano *impf. of* muòvere
moviménto movement
Mulehet a region in northern Iran
muòvere to move, to arouse; *refl.* to move (oneself)
muricciòlo low wall
muro wall; *irr. pl.* le mura city walls
mùscolo muscle
mùsica music; fare della - to write music
musicale musical

mutare to change
muto speechless, silent
mùtuo mutual

N

napoletano Neapolitan
Nàpoli Naples
narrare to narrate
nàscere *irr.* to be born, to arise
nàscita birth
nascóndere *irr.* to hide
nascósto *past part. of* **nascóndere**
naso nose
natìo native
nato *past part. of* **nàscere**
natura nature
naturale natural
nave *f.* ship; - **da cabotàggio** tramp ship;
  - **da guèrra** warship
navigare to navigate
navigazióne *f.* navigation
nazionale national
nazióne *f.* nation
né *conj.* nor; **non . . . -** neither . . . nor;
  - . . . - . . . neither . . . nor; **- . . . più** nor . . .
  any longer
neanche: non . . . - not even . . .
necessàrio necessary
necessità necessity, need
nefando evil, wicked
negare to deny
negativo negative
neglètto forgotten
nemico *n.* enemy; *adj.* inimical
nemméno not even
neppure: non . . . - . . . not even
néro black, dark
nèspolo loquat tree
nessuno *adj.* no; **non . . . -** not . . . any; *pron.*
  nobody; **non . . . - . . .** no one
néve *f.* snow
Niccolò Nicholas
nido nest
niènte nothing; - **altro** nothing else; **non . . .**
  più - not . . . anything else; **servire a -** to
  serve no purpose
ninfa nymph
nipóte *m.* nephew
Nizza Nice (Italian city ceded to France in
  1860)
no *poet. for* **non** no
nòbile noble

nobilitare to ennoble
nòdo knot
nòia boredom
nóme *m.* name; **avér -** to be named; **per**
  ricordare il - di in memory of
nominare to name
non no, not; **- . . . che . . .** only; **- . . . né**
  neither . . . nor; **- . . . più** no longer . . . ;
  - . . . più . . . never again; **se -** except
nondiméno nevertheless
nònno grandfather; *pl.* grandparents
Nòrd *m.* North
normale normal
nossignóre no, sir
notare to notice
notìzia news
nòto known
notorietà notoriety
nòtte *f.* night; **di -** at night; **ièri -** last night;
  la - at night; **tutta la -** all night long; **si**
  fa - night is falling
Novecènto 20th century
novèlla story, short story; *lit. for* **notìzia**
novellière *m.* short story writer
novèmbre *m.* November
novità innovation
nòvo *lit. for* **nuòvo**
nòzze *f. pl.* nuptials; wedding
'Ntòni *for* **Antònio**
nube *f.* cloud
nudo naked, bare
nulla nothing; **sénza . . . -** without . . . anything
nullo *adj. lit. for* **nessuno**
nume *m.* god
nùmero number
numeróso numerous
Nunziata *for* **Annunziata** (a girl's name to
  honor the Annunciation to the Virgin Mary)
nùnzio messenger
nuócere *irr.* to harm
nuotare to swim, to float
nuovaménte once again
nuòvo new; **di -** again
nutrire to nourish
nùvolo *or* **nùvola** cloud

O

o or; **o . . . o** either . . . or; **O!** *interj.* O!
obbediènza obedience
obbligare to oblige
òbbligo obligation

oblìo oblivion
occasióne *f.* occasion, opportunity, chance
occhiata: dare un' - to glance
òcchio eye; códa dell' - corner of the eye
occidènte *m.* West
occórrere *irr.* to be necessary
occulto obscure, hidden
occupare to overcome; *refl.* to keep busy
occupato busy
occupazióne *f.* occupation
Ocèano Ocean
od *euphonic for* o
odiatóre *m.* foe
òdio hatred
odóre *m.* odor, perfume
offèndere *irr.* to offend
offensòre *m.* offender
offèrta offer
offésa offense; fare - a to offend
offéso *past part. of* offèndere
offrire *irr.* to offer
oggètto object
òggi today
ógni every, each
ognuno *pron.* everyone, each, each one
òh! oh!
oimè! Alas!
óltre: - a besides
oltremòdo unusually
omàggio homage
ómbra shade; shadow; all' - in the shade
ombróso shady
òmo *poet. for* uòmo
ónda wave; *poet.* sea
ónde therefore
onèsto honest, decent, respectable
onnipotènte almighty
onóre *m.* honor
onorévole honorable
òpera work; deed; opera
operare to operate
operaziòne *f.* action
opinióne *f.* opinion
òppio opium
oppórre *irr.* to oppose; oppórsi a *refl.* to oppose
opportuno opportune
opposizióne *f.* opposition
oppósto (*past part. of* oppórre) *adj.* opposite
oppressóre *m.* oppressor
opprìmere *irr.* to oppress
oppure or
ór *apoc. of* óra *conj.*

óra *n.* hour; time; alle óre tre at three
o'clock; a quest' - by this time; di - in -
from one moment to the next; *conj.* now;
da - innanzi from now on
oratóre *m.* speaker
orazióne *f.* speech; prayer
ordinaménto organization
ordinare to order
órdine *m.* order
orécchio *or* orécchia ear; dire nell' (*or* all') -
to whisper
Orfèo Orpheus (Thracian poet and musician)
organizzato organized
organizzazióne *f.* organization
oriènte *m.* East
orìgine *f.* origin, source
orizzónte *m.* horizon
ormài henceforth; now
ornare to adorn
òro gold
orològio watch
orrèndo horrendous, horrible
orrìbile hòrrible
osanna *m.* hosanna
osare to dare
oscillazióne *f.* oscillation
oscurare to obscure
oscuro dark
ospitalità hospitality
òspite *m. & f.* guest; host
osservanza observance
osservare to observe; to keep
osservazióne *f.* remark
òsso (*pl.* le òssa) bone
ostàcolo obstacle
ostile hostile
ottenére *irr.* to obtain, to get
ottenuto obtained
òttimo excellent
ottóbre *m.* October
Òttocènto 19th century
óve where
Ovest *m.* West
ovùnque everywhere
oziosaménte in a leisurely manner

P

pace *f.* peace
pacificarsi to make peace
padiglióne *m.* pavilion; etèreo - *poet. for*
firmament
padre *m.* father
padróne *m.* master

paése *m.* town; city; country
pagare to pay
pàia *pres. subj. sing. of* **parére**
pàio couple
palafrenière *m.* guard
palazzo palace
palcoscènico stage
palla ball
pàllido pale
palma palm tree; palm (of the hand)
pane *m.* bread
panière *m.* hand basket
panno cloth; *pl.* clothes
Pantalóne *m.* Pantaloon
Panza, Sàncio Sancho Panza (the squire of Don Quixote, in the novel by Miguel Cervantes)
Pàolo Paul
papa *m.* pope
paracadute *m.* parachute
paradiso paradise
paragóne *m.* comparison
parécchio (*in the pl.*) several
parére *irr.* to seem; - (a) to think (to have an opinion)
paréte *f.* wall (of a room)
pari *adj. invar.* even, equal, like
parlaménto parliament
parlare to speak
Parma city in Emìlia
paròla word
parte *f.* part; share; place; direction; (*theater*) role; da una - on one side; la maggiór - the majority
partecipare to participate
partènza departure
particolare *m.* detail; *adj.* particular, special, private
partigiano Partisan
partire to leave
partito *n.* party
parto confinement
passare to pass, to surpass; to go, to go over; to spend
passato *n.* past; *adj.* passed
passeggèro *adj.* passing
passeggiare to take a walk; to walk
passeggiata stroll
passióne *f.* passion
passo passage; step; plight
pasto meal
pastóre *m.* shepherd
patire to suffer

pàtria fatherland, country
pàtrio *adj.* of the fatherland
patrìzio patrician
patto pact
paùra fear; avér - to be afraid
pauróso *n.* timid
pazzìa madness
pazzo mad; . . . da pazzi . . . for mad men
peccare to sin
peccato sin
peccatóre *m.* sinner
pèggio *adv.* worse; *n.* worst
peggióre *adj.* worse, worst
pégno pawn, pledge; in - as collateral
pellegrino pilgrim
péna sorrow; punishment; - di mòrte death penalty
pendènte hanging
penóso painful
pensare to think
pensatóre *m.* thinker
pensièro thought, idea
pentirsi to repent; to change one's mind
pentito repentant
per for, through; in; on; in order to; in behalf of; on account of; because of
perché because, why; in order that; - ? why?; il - the reason why
perciò therefore
percórso *n.* course
percòsso *past part. of* **percuòtere**
percuòtere *irr.* to strike; to knock at
pèrdere *irr.* to lose
pèrdita loss
perdonàbile excusable
perdonare to pardon
perdóno pardon; chièder - to beg pardon
peregrino nomad
perfètto perfect
pèrfido *n.* faithless one
perfino even
perìcolo danger; méttere in - to endanger
pericolóso dangerous
pèrla pearl
permanènte permanent
perméttere *irr.* to allow
però however, but; *arch.* therefore
perpètuo perpetual
perplèsso perplexed
persìstere to persist
persóna person

personàggio character
persuadére *irr.* to persuade
persuasióne *f.* conviction
pervenire (a) *irr.* to reach, to arrive; - in cima to reach the top
pesante heavy
pésce *m.* fish
pètto chest, breast; bosom
pèzzo piece; (un) gran - a long time
piacènte lovable
piacére *m.* pleasure; favor; avér - to be pleased; fare il - di to do (one) the pleasure of; far - to please; per - please
piacére *irr.* to please; to like; to appeal
piacévole pleasant
piacevolézza charm
piaga wound
piàngere *irr.* to weep; to mourn; *n. m.* mourning
piano *adj.* flat, plain
pianta plant
piantare *fig.* to rivet
pianto *n.* weeping; lament; *past part. of* piàngere
pianura plain
piatto plate
piazza square
piazzuòla small square
picchiare to knock; to hit
pìccolo small
piède *m.* foot; leg; a pièdi on foot; in pièdi standing
pièga fold
piegare to bend
piemontése Piedmontese
pièno full; - di filled with
pietà pity, compassion
pietate *f. poet. for* pietà
pietóso pitiful; merciful
piètra stone
Piètro Peter
pigliare to take
Pilato Pilate
pìngere *irr.* to paint
pino pine tree
pio pious, good
piòggia rain
piómbo lead
piròscafo steamship
pittóre *m.* painter
pittura painting

più more; i - the majority; il - the most; mai - never again; quanto - as much as; - che more than; - . . . . che more . . . than; - di more than; né . . . - nor . . . any longer; non . . . - . . . no longer; non . . . di - not . . . any more
Plutóne Pluto (the god of the lower world)
Pò: il Pò the Po river
pò' *apoc. of* pòco
pòco little; a - a - gradually; fra - before long; un - a little; *pl.* few, a few
poèma *m.* poem (of great length)
poèta *m.* poet
pòi later, then; moreover; da allóra in - from that time on; - che after, since
poiché since
polare polar
polìtica policy
polìtico *n.* political figure; *adj.* political
polizìa police
pòlo pole
poltróna armchair
pólvere *f.* dust, powder
pómpa pomp
pontificato pontificate
popolano common man
popolato populated
popolazióne *f.* population
pòpolo people; nation
pórre *irr.* to place, to put; to give
pòrta door
portaménto bearing
portare to bring, to carry, to take along; to bear; to wear; to lead; - il lutto to wear mourning; - via to carry off; far - to have (someone) carried
pòrto port, harbor
porzióne *f.* portion
pòsa pose
posare to rest; *refl.* to come to rest (fall)
positivo positive
possedére *irr.* to own
possènte powerful
possèsso possession
possìbile possible
possibilità possibility
pósto *n.* place; (*past part. of* pórre)
potènte powerful
potènza power; capacity
potére *irr.* to be able, can, may
pòvero poor
povertà poverty

pranzo dinner; **sala da - e stùdio** combination dining-room and study
pràtica practice; experience
praticàbile accessible
pràtico experienced
prato meadow
precedènte preceding, former
precètto precept
preciso precise
prefazióne *f.* preface
preferire to prefer
pregare to pray, to beg, to urge
preghièra prayer
prèmio reward; **in -** as a reward
prèndere *irr.* to take; to seize; to possess; to pick up; to take prisoner; **far -** to have (someone) taken
preparare to prepare; to organize
preparativo preparation
prepotènza truculence
presentare to present, to introduce
presènte *m.* present; **al -** at present; *adj.* present; **la -** this letter
presenteménte at the moment
presentiménto presentiment, premonition
presènza presence; mien
presieduto presided
préso *past part. of* **prèndere**
pressióne *f.* pressure
prèsso *adv.* near
prestare to lend
prèstito loan
prèsto soon; **bèn -** very soon
presuntuóso *n.* presumptuous man
pretèndere *irr.* to claim
pretèsto pretext
prevenire *irr.* to prevent
prezióso precious
prèzzo worth
prima *adv.* first, before, beforehand; **- di** before; **- che** before; *adj.* first
primato record
primavèra spring
primieraménte primarily
primo first
principale *m.* employer; *adj.* principal
principalménte mainly
prìncipe *m.* prince
principiare to begin
princìpio principle; beginning
privare to deprive
privato private; **libertà -** personal liberty
privazióne *f.* privation

privo deprived, devoid
prò: a - in favor
probàbile probable
problèma *m.* problem
procurare to endeavor
pròdigo generous
prodótto *past part. of* **produrre**
produrre *irr.* to produce
proferire to utter
professare to profess
professóre *m.* professor
profèta *m.* prophet
profetizzare to prophesy
profezìa prophecy
profóndo profound, deep
progettare to plan
progètto project, plan
progredire to progress
progressivo progressive
proibire to forbid
prolisso prolix
pròlogo prologue
prolungare to prolong
promréssa promise
prométtere *irr.* to promise
prónto *adj.* quick, ready
propagazióne *f.* diffusion
propìzio propitious
propórre *irr.* to propose, to resolve
proporzionato well balanced
proporzióne *f.* proportion; **in - di** in proportion to
pròprio *adj.* own, proper; *adv.* exactly, just; merely
pròsa prose; **teatro di -** playhouse
proscritto banished, exiled
proseguire to continue
Prosèrpina Proserpina (wife of Pluto and queen of the lower world)
pròspero prosperous
pròssimo approaching, imminent
pròtasi *f.* protasis, opening (of a poem)
protèggere *irr.* to protect
protezióne *f.* protection
pròva proof; rehearsal; test
provare to try, to prove, to demonstrate; to experience; to rehearse
provenire *irr.* to come
provìncia province, region
provocato provoked
provvedére *irr.* to provide
provvisòrio temporary
provvisto *past part. of* **provvedére**

prudènte prudent
prudènza prudence
pubblicare to publish, to make public
pubblicista *m. & f.* publicist
pubblicità publicity, advertising
pùbblico *n.* audience; *adj.* public
pulire to clean
punire to punish
punto *n.* point; passage; *adv.* **non . . . -** not . . . at all
puntuale punctually
pur *apoc. of* **pure**
purché provided that
pure even, also; nevertheless
Purgatòrio Purgatory
puro pure
purtròppo alas
putto child

Q

qua here; **di -** here, over here; **di - e di là** both here and there, on both sides
qualche (*sing. only*) some
qualcheduno someone
qualcuno someone, one
quale *pron.* who, which, whom; **- . . . -** some . . . others; *adj.* which, what, what a
qualità quality, kind
qualsìasi any
qualùnque any, whatever; **una cosa -** any old thing; **uno -** any one
quando when; **da -** ever since; **fin -** until
quantità quantity
quanto how much, how many; as much, as much as; whatever; what; **in - a** as for, as regards; **per -** as far as, although; **- più** as much as; **tanto . . . - as . . . as; tanto . . . - . . .** as much . . . as . . . ; **tutto -** all that
quantùnque although
quarto *adj.* fourth; *n.* quarter
quasi almost, hardly
Quattrocènto 15th century
quèllo *adj. & pron.* that; **- che** that which, the one who, he who; **- cui** that which
quésti *m. pron.* the latter
questióne *f.* question
quésto *adj.* this; *pron.* this, this one
qui here; **di -** from here
quindi thence, from there; afterwards, then; therefore
quintessènza quintessence
quinto fifth

R

ràbbia rage
raccògliere *irr.* to gather, to collect
raccòlto *past part. of* **raccògliere**
raccomandare to recommend
raccontare to tell
radiante radiant
radice *f.* root
radiotelegrafìa radiotelegraphy
radiotelegràfico radiotelegraphic
Raffaèllo Raphael (1483–1520), Italian painter
raffreddarsi to become cold
ragazza girl
ràggio ray
raggiùngere *irr.* to overtake; to achieve, to attain
ragionaménto reasoning
ragionare to reason; **- di** to discuss
ragióne *f.* reason; **avér -** to be right
ragionévole reasonable
rallegrarsi to rejoice
rammentare to remember
ramo branch
rancóre *m.* rancor
ràpido rapid
rapire to snatch, to abduct, to carry off
rappacificare to reconcile
rapportare to report
rappresentare to represent, to perform
rassegnato resigned
rassicurare to reassure
razza race
ré *m.* king
reale real
realizzare to construct
reame *m.* kingdom
recare to carry, to bring; to go; *refl.* to go
rècita performance
recitare to recite, to act, to perform
réclame *f.* (French) advertising, advertisement
redentóre *m.* savior, Redeemer
redenzióne *f.* redemption
redìmere *irr.* to redeem
regalare to give as a present
rège *lit. for* **ré**
regime *m.* regime
regina queen
regióne *f.* region
regnare to reign, to rule
regnatóre *m.* ruler
régno kingdom; realm

règola rule
relazióne *f.* connection, relationship
religióne *f.* religion
religióso religious
remare to row
remòto remote
rèndere *irr.* to give back, to give again; to
    make, to render; to become; – miglióre to
    improve
Rénzo *for* Lorènzo
rèo *n.* accused; *adj.* guilty
replicare to reply
repubblicano republican
reputare to deem
reputazióne *f.* reputation
resìstere to resist
réso *past part. of* rèndere
responsàbile responsible
restare to remain; to be left
restituire to give back
rèsto rest
rètro *arch.:* di – behind
reumàtico rheumatic
reumatismo rheumatism
riarmare to rearm
ribalderìa fraudulent act
ricco rich
ricevènte receiving
ricèvere to receive
ricevitóre *m.* receiver
richiamare to recall
richièdere *irr.* to require
richiùdere *irr.* to close again
ricompensare to compensate
riconfortare to cheer
riconóscere *irr.* to recognize, to acknowledge
ricordare to recall; *refl.* to remember; per – il
    nóme di in memory of
ricostituire to reconstitute
ricuperare to recover
ricusare to refuse
rìdere *irr.* to laugh; *refl.* – di to laugh at
ridìcolo ridiculous
ridótto *past part. of* ridurre
ridurre *irr.* to reduce
ridussi, riducésti *p. abs. of* ridurre
riempire to fill
rièsco *pres. of* riuscire
rifare *irr.* to do over
riferire to refer, to report
rifiutare to refuse
rifiuto derelict
riflèttere *irr.* to reflect, to ponder

riga line
riguardare to look around; to concern
rima rhyme
rimanére *irr.* to remain, to be left
rimasto *past part. of* rimanére
rimembrare *lit. for* ricordare
rimpatriare to repatriate
rimpàtrio repatriation
rinchiùdere *irr.* to close, to enclose
rinchiuso *past part. of* rinchiùdere
ringraziare to thank
rinnovaménto regeneration
rinnovare to renew
rinovare *lit. for* rinnovare
rinnovellarsi to return, to be renewed
rinvenire *irr.* to come to, to regain conscious-
    ness
rinvenuto *past part. of* rinvenire
rinvigorito invigorated
ripararsi to protect oneself
ripètere to repeat; to rehearse
riposare to rest
ripòso rest
riprèndere *irr.* to take up again, to pick up
    again, to continue
risata laugh, burst of laughter
riso laughter; smile
risòlsi *p. abs. of* risòlvere
risoluzióne *f.* decision
risòlvere *irr.* to solve; *refl.* to resolve, to make
    up one's mind
Risorgiménto Risorgimento (to indicate the
    political resurgence of Italy between 1821
    and 1870)
rispettare to respect
rispètto *n.* respect; *adv.* – a compared to
rispóndere *irr.* to answer; – a to measure
    up to
rispósta answer
ristabilire to re-establish
ristorare to restore to health
ristrìngersi *irr.* to heal
risultato result
risvéglio reawakening
ritardare to delay
ritardo delay; èssere in – to be late
ritornare to return
ritórno return; fare – to return
ritrovare to find
riunito joined
riuscire *irr.* to succeed
riva bank, shore
rivedére *irr.* to see again

rivòlgere *irr.* to turn; *refl.* to address; to turn oneself
rivòlsi (mi) *p. abs. of* rivòlgersi
rivòlto (*past part. of* rivòlgere) turning, aimed
rivoluzióne *f.* revolution
ròba possessions
robusto strong
ròccia rock, cliff
ródere *irr.* to gnaw, to corrode
Róma Rome
romano Roman
rómpere *irr.* to break
ròsa *n.* rose; *adj. invar.* pink
rósso red
rotarsi to revolve
rótto *past part. of* rómpere
rovina calamity; ruin
rovinare to ruin
rùdere *m.* ruin
rumóre *m.* noise
ruòta wheel

S

sàbato Saturday
sacchéggio plunder
sacco bag
sacrifìcio sacrifice
sacro sacred
sàggio *n.* wise man; *adj.* wise
sala room, hall; (theater) house; set; - da pranzo e stùdio combination dining-room and study
salare to salt
sale *m.* salt
salire *irr.* to rise, to go up, to ascend
salmo psalm
saltare to jump; - a tèrra to jump ashore
salutare to greet; *adj.* salutary
salute *f.* health
salvatóre *m.* savior
salvézza salvation; safety
salvo *prep.* except
San *apoc. of* Santo
sanare to heal; *refl.* to be cured
sàngue *m.* blood
sanguigno: di - with blood
sano sane; star - to keep well
Santità Holiness
santo *n.* Saint; *adj.* saintly, holy, blessed
sapére *irr.* to know, to learn; (*plus inf.*) to know how; far - to let people know
sapiènte learned
saracèno Saracen

sardo Sardinian
sasso stone
Sàtana *m.* Satan
Savòia Savoy (Italian region ceded to France in 1860)
sbagliare to blunder about
sbarcare to put ashore
sbàttere to beat
scacciare to oust
scala stair; scale; in - on a scale
scampare to escape
scaricare to unload
scarpa shoe
scatto: di - abruptly
scégliere *irr.* to choose
scellerato *n.* criminal; *adj.* iniquitous
scélta choice
scèna scene; stage; **direttóre di** - stage manager; **di** - on stage; **in** - on the stage
scenàrio scenario
scéndere *irr.* to descend
scéso *past part. of* scéndere
scèttro scepter
scherzare to joke
schiava slave
schiavitù slavery
schiavo slave
schièna back
sciagura misfortune
scientìfico scientific
scintillante sparkling
scòglio rock
scolàstico traditionalist
scolorare to blanch, to render pale
scolpire to sculpture; to engrave
scompigliare to upset
sconfitta defeat
sconsolato disconsolate
scontènto dissatisfied
scopèrta discovery
scòpo purpose; a - di pròva for testing purposes
scoppiare to burst forth
scoprire to discover; to uncover; to pull off
scòrgere *irr.* to perceive, to see
scórrere *irr.* to run, to flow
scòrsi *p. abs. of* scòrgere
scórso last
scòrto *past part. of* scòrgere
scòsso (*past part. of* scuòtere) shaken
scritta: fare la - to draw up a deed
scritto *n.* writing; **per iscritto** in writing; *past part. of* scrìvere

scrittóre *m.* writer
scrittura writing
scrivanìa desk
scrìvere *irr.* to write
scudo shield; crown (gold coin)
scuòtere *irr.* to shake off
scuro dark
scusa excuse; **chièdere -** to apologize
scusare to excuse; *refl.* to apologize
sdegnato indignant
sdégno indignation; scorn; wrath
se *conj.* if, whether; **- non** except
sé *pron.* him, himself; her, herself; it, itself
sebbène although
seccato annoyed
sécco *adj.* dry
séco *pron.* with him, with her; with himself,
with herself; with them, with themselves
sècolo century
secónda: **a - di** according to
secóndo *adj.* second; *adv.* according, according
to
sedére *irr.* to seat; to sit; to lie; *refl.* to sit down
seduto seated
seduzióne *f.* seduction
segnale *m.* signal
segnare to make a note
ségno sign; omen; **per -** as a marker
segretàrio secretary
segréto secret; **in -** secretly
seguènte following
seguire to follow, to pursue
seguitare to continue, to follow
Seicènto 17th century
sélva forest
sembianza countenance
sembrare to seem
sémplice simple
sèmpre always; **per -** forever; **- più** ever more
senato Senate
sénno: **fuòr del -** out of one's senses
sensibilità sensibility, sensitivity
sènso sense, common sense
sentènza sentence
sentiménto sentiment, feeling; **uscir del -** to
lose one's senses
sentire to hear, to listen; to smell; *refl.* to feel;
- dire to hear people say; **farsi -** to make
oneself heard
sénza *prep.* without; **- che** *conj.* without
separare to separate
sepólcro tomb
sepólto buried

sepoltura burial; grave; sepulcher, mausoleum
seppellire to bury
séra evening, night; **di -** in the evening; **ièri -**
last evening, last night; **la -** in the evening
serbare to reserve, to keep; *refl.* to remain
seréno *n.* sunshine; *adj.* serene
sèrie *f.* series
sèrio serious
sérpe *f.* snake
serpènte *m.* snake
servire to serve; **non - a niènte** to serve no
purpose; **a che sèrve?** to what purpose?
refl. **- di** to make use of
servitóre *m.* servant
servìzio service
sèrvo servant
séte *f.* thirst; **avér -** to be thirsty
sètta sect, religion
Settecènto 18th century
settentrionale northern
settentrióne *m.* North
severò severe
sezióne *f.* section
sfortunato unfortunate
sfòrzo effort
sfruttamènto exploitation
sgarbato rude
sgombrare to clear; **- il davanti** to clear the
front
sgridare to scold
sguardo glance
si *impers. pron.* one
sì *(affirmation)* yes
sì *adv. apoc. of* così so, thus; just; such a;
far - che to act in such a way that, to show
that; **- che** in such a way that
sicché therefore, and so
siccità drought
siccóme since
sicurèzza security, safety
sicuro sure, certain; safe
significato meaning
Signóra Madam; **la - . . .** Mrs. . . .
signóre *m.* gentleman; **Signóre** *m.* Lord;
Milord; Sir; master; mister; gentleman; **il
Signór . . .** Mr. . . . ; **Signór Curato** Reverend Father; *pl.* ladies and gentlemen
signorile noble
silènzio silence
silenzióso silent
sìmile like, similar
similitùdine *f.* likeness
Simóne Simon

sin *apoc. of* sino
sincèro sincere
singhiozzante sobbing
sinistra: a - on the left
sinistro left
sino: - a until, as far as; - da since, from
sintètico synthetical
sintonizzazióne *f.* syntonization
sire *m.* sire, father, lord
sissignóre Yes, sir
sistèma *m.* system
sistemazióne *f.* set-up
sito place
Sivìglia Seville (city in southern Spain)
smarrire to lose
smarrito bewildered
snèllo slender
soave gentle, delicate, pleasant
società society
Sòcrate Socrates (B.C. 469–399) Greek phi-
    losopher
soddisfare to satisfy
soffrire *irr.* to suffer
soggètto subject; impromptu play
soggiórno sojourn, abode
soggiùngere *irr.* to add
sógno dream
soldato soldier
sóle *m.* sun; al - in the sun
solènne solemn
solére *irr.* to be wont, to be accustomed
sòlito accustomed; usual; al - ! Same old story!
sollevare to raise
sollièvo respite
sólo *adj.* single, alone, only; *adv.* only
soltanto only; but, except
sòlvere *irr.* to solve
sómma sum; in - in short
sommergìbile *m.* submarine
sonétto sonnet
sónno sleep
sopportare to suffer
sopprèsso *past part. of* sopprìmere
sopprìmere *irr.* to suppress
sópra on, over, upon, above; al di - di above;
    di - above
sopradétto above-mentioned
soprascritto above-mentioned
sopratutto above all
sopravvenire *irr.* to arrive
sòra *poet. for* suòra sister, nun
sórdo deaf
sorèlla sister

sórgere *irr.* to arise
sorridènte smiling
sorriso smile
sòrta kind; di - of any kind
sòrte *f.* fate
sórto *past part. of* sórgere
sospètto suspicion
sospirare to sigh
sospiro sigh; fare un - to draw a breath
sostégno support
sostenére *irr.* to sustain, to bear, to support,
    to withstand
sostenuto supported
sottile fine; subtle
sótto under; below, beneath; - a, - di below;
    tornare - to set (again)
sottométtere *irr.* to submit
sottopórre *irr.* to submit
sovranità sovereignty
Spagna Spain
spalancato wide open
spalla shoulder
sparire to vanish
sparso (*past part. of* spàrgere) scattered, strewn
spaventare to frighten, to terrify
spavènto wonder
spàzio space
spazzare: - via to sweep out
speciale special
spècie *f.* species
spègnere *irr.* to extinguish
spème *f. poet. for* speranza
spèndere *irr.* to spend
spènsi *p. abs. of* spègnere
spènto *past part. of* spègnere
speranza hope
sperare to hope
sperduto lost
spergiuro perjurer
spéso *past part. of* spèndere
spésso *adj.* thick; *adv.* often
spettàcolo spectacle
spettare to concern; - a to rest with
spettatóre *m.* spectator; *pl.* audience
spiacére *irr.* to displease
spiàggia shore
spiegare to explain
spina thorn
spìngere *irr.* to push, to urge, to induce; - lo
    sguardo to look
spinsi *p. abs. of* spìngere
spinto *past part. of* spìngere
spìrito spirit, soul

spirituale spiritual
splendóre *m.* splendor
spogliare to disrobe, to strip
spòrta haversack
sposare to marry
spòso husband
sputare to spit
stabilire to establish
staccarsi to tear oneself away
stagióne *f.* season; time of life
stamani this morning
stampa press
stanco tired
stare *irr.* to stay; to be; to stand; to remain;
- attènto to be careful; - mèglio to feel
better; - per to be about to; - sano to keep
well; sta bène all right; stàrsene to be, to
stay, to remain
stato state; Stati Uniti United States of
America; uòmo di - statesman
stàtua statue
statura stature
stazióne *f.* station
Stéfano Stephen
stélla star
stèndere *irr.* to spread
sterminatóre *m.* exterminator
stésso same, self
stile *m.* style; stiletto
stimare to esteem, to value; to estimate
stordito stunned
stòria history; story; di - historical
stòrico *n.* historian; *adj.* historical
strada street, road
stradétta small road
stranièro foreign
strano strange
straordinàrio extraordinary
strétto (*past part. of* strìngere) close, held
close, pressed
strìngere *irr.* to press, to hold close, to con-
strict
strinsi *past part. of* strìngere
strùggersi *irr.* to be consumed
strumentale instrumental
struménto instrument, device
studènte *m.* student
studiare to study
stùdio study; bórsa di - student loan
studióso studious
stupèndo stupendous
stùpido stupid
stupìto dumbfounded

stupóre *m.* astonishment
su *prep.* on, over; in - up
sùbito suddenly, at once, soon
succèdersi *irr.* to follow one another
succèsso success
Sud *m.* South
sudóre *m.* sweat
sufficiènte sufficient; large enough
suggerire to suggest
suggeritóre *m.* prompter
suicidarsi to commit suicide
suócero father-in-law
suonare to play (an instrument)
suòno sound
superare to exceed; to overcome
supèrbia pride
supèrbo haughty
superfìcie *f.* surface
superióre superior
superlativo superlative
supèrstite remaining
supino on one's back
suprèmo supreme, final, last
sur *lit. for* su
sussìdio help
svanire to vanish
svegliare to awaken; far - to have (someone)
awakened
sventura misfortune
sventurato unfortunate
sviluppare to develop
sviluppo development
svolgiménto development

T

tacére *irr.* to be silent
tacqui *p. abs. of* tacére
tagliare to hack
tale such, so; likewise
talménte in such a way
talvòlta from time to time
Tàngeri Tangier (city in Morocco)
tanto so, such; so much; so many; so long;
- . . . quanto as . . . as; - . . . quanto . . .
as much . . . as . . .
tappéto carpet
tardi *adv.* late; più - later
tardo *adj.* late
tàrtaro Tartar
tàvola table
tavolino (small) table
teatro theater; - di pròsa playhouse
téco with you

tedésco German

telegrafìa telegraphy; - sénza fili wireless telegraphy

telegràfico telegraphic

temére to fear

temperaménto temperament

temperato temperate; mild

tempèsta storm

tempestóso stormy

tèmpo time; weather; da mólto - a long time ago; fare a - to be on time

temporale m. storm

tendènza tendency, inclination

tèndere irr. to tend; to stretch out

tendina curtain

tenére irr. to hold; to keep; - luògo to take place; - per cèrto to hold for certain

tenerézza gentleness

tènero tender; young

tentare to tempt; to try

teorìa theory

terminare to end

tèrmine m. end

tèrra earth, land, ground, soil; a - on the ground; in - on the ground; saltare a - to jump ashore

terrìbile terrifying

territòrio territory

terróre m. terror

tèrzo third

tèsta head

testimòne m. & f. witness

testimònio testimony

tétto roof; fig. house

tigre m. lit. for la tigre tiger

tìmido adj. timid, apprehensive; n. timid person

timóre m. fear

tìngere irr. to stain, to tinge; tìngersi di to become tinted with

tirànnide f. tyranny

tirare to pull; to draw; to shoot

Tirrèno Tyrrhenian Sea

Tiziano Titian (1477–1576), Venetian painter

toccare to touch; - a to be up to

Tòdi town in Ùmbria

tògliere irr. to take, to take away; to deprive; refl. to remove

tòlto past part. of tògliere

tómba tomb

tòno tone

Tonocaìn probably the present Damgham, in Northern Iran

tòrcere irr. to twist

tormentare to torture

tormentato damned

torménto torment, torture

tornare to return; to turn; - a . . . again . . .

tórpido sluggish

tórre f. tower

torrènte m. torrent

tòrrido torrid

tortura torture

Toscana Tuscany

tòsto soon

totale adj. total

tra among, between

tradiménto betrayal

tradire. to betray, to fail

traditóre m. traitor

tradizióne f. tradition

tràgico tragic

traggo pres. of trarre

tramontana north

tramónto waning

tranne except; - che unless

tranquillo peaceful; serene, undisturbed

transitòrio transitory

trarre irr. to drag; to draw

trascórrere irr. to pass, to elapse

trascórso past part. of trascórrere

trasmésso past part. of trasméttere

trasméttere irr. to transmit

trasmettitóre m. transmitter

trasmissióne f. transmission

trasmitténte transmitting

trasportare to carry

trassi, traésti p. abs. of trarre

trattare to treat; to deal; to deal with; - di to write about; refl. - di to be a question of

tratto: ad un - suddenly, all of a sudden

trattorìa small restaurant

traversare to cross

traversata crossing

travòlto troubled

tréccia tress

Trecènto 14th century

tremare to tremble

tremolare to tremble, to quiver

tribolazióne f. tribulation

tribunale m. tribunal

tributo tribute

Trinità Trinity

trionfante triumphant

triste sad

tristézza sadness

tristo evil, sad

Tròia Troy (ancient city in northwestern Asia Minor destroyed by the Greeks)

trómba trumpet

trónco trunk

tròno throne

tròppo *adj.* too much; *adv.* too

trovare to find; to discover

tumulto tumult

tumultuante tumultuous

tuòno thunder

turba multitude

turbaménto flurry

turbato angered

tuttavìa still

tutto *adj.* all, every; - il . . . the whole . . . ; *pron. sing.* everything; *pl.* everybody; fare del - to do one's utmost; tutti e due, tutt'e due both

U

ubbidiènza obedience

ubbidire to obey

uccèllo bird

uccìdere *irr.* to kill; fare - to have (someone) killed; *refl.* to commit suicide

ucciso *past part. of* uccìdere

udiènza audience

udire *irr.* to hear, to listen

uffìcio function

uguale equal

Ulisse Ulysses

ùltimo last

umanésimo humanism

umanità humanity; mankind

umano human; humane; gènere - mankind

ùmile humble

umiliazióne *f.* humiliation

umiltà humility

umiltade *poet. for* umiltà

undècimo eleventh

ùnico only

unità unity, unit

unito united

università university

univèrso universe

uno *adj. & pron.* one; ad - ad - one by one; l' - e l'altro both; - qualùnque anyone

uòmo (*pl.* uòmini) man; - di stato statesman

uòvo (*pl.* le uòva) egg

urna urn; *fig.* tomb

usare to use, to make use of

usato *adj.* usual

uscènte emerging

uscère *m.* stage hand

ùscio door

uscire *irr.* to go out; to come out; to emerge; to leave; - del sentiménto to lose one's senses

uso use, custom; d' - customary

usura usury

ùtile *adj.* useful; *n. m.* usefulness

utilità usefulness

utilizzare to utilize

utilizzazióne *f.* utilization

V

vagheggiare to yearn

valènte gifted

valére *irr.* to be worth; *refl.* to avail oneself; vale a dire that is to say

valle *f.* valley

valóre *m.* value; valor, worth, bravery

valoróso valiant

vano vain

vantarsi to boast

vaporare to give forth

variare to vary

vàrio various

vasto vast

vecchierèlla little old woman

vècchio *adj.* old, aged; ancient; *n.* old man

vecchióne *m.* venerable old man

vedére to behold, to see; far - to show

védova widow

véglio old man

véla sail

velato veiled

veléno poison

velenóso poisonous; àcqua velenósa poisonous liquid

vélo veil

velóce swift

velocità velocity

véna vein

véndere to sell

vendétta vengeance

vendicare to avenge

vendicativo vindictive person

venerando revered

Venèzia Venice

veneziano Venetian

venire *irr.* to come; (*as auxiliary instead of* èssere) to be

ventènnio twenty years

vènto wind

vèntre *m.* abdomen
ventura luck, good fortune
venturo next
venuta *n.* coming
vérde green
vergógna shame
vergognóso shameful
verità truth
véro *n.* truth; **in -** in truth; *adj.* true, real,
  really
versétto verse
vèrso *n.* line, verse; *prep.* toward
verticale vertical
véscovo bishop
vèste *f.* dress
vestire to dress; to wear; **- di** to dress in
vestito *adj.* dressed
vi *adv.* there; it, to it
via *n.* street, road, path; way; **per la -** by way;
  adv. away; **per -** by means; **via!** Come now!
viàggio voyage, trip; **fare un -** to take a trip;
  fare buòn - to have a nice trip
vicinanza vicinity; proximity
vicino near, nearby; approaching; *n.* neighbor
vile mean, base, worthless
villàggio village
vìncere *irr.* to win; to subdue, to overcome
vincitóre *n. & adj. m.* victorious
vincitrice *adj. f.* victorious
vino wine
vinto *adj.* spent; overcome; *past part. of* vìncere
viòla violet; (musical instrument) viola
violare to violate
violènto violent
violènza violence
Virgìlio Virgil (B.C. 70–19), Roman poet
virtù *f.* virtue; ability, power; properties;
  - dell'ànimo faculties of the mind
visìbile visible
visiòne *f.* vision
vìsita visit
visitare to visit

viso face
vista sight; view
visto *past part. of* vedére
vita life; affairs; **in - sua** during his lifetime
vitèllo calf
vitto board
vittòria victory
vivace lively
vivacità vivacity
vivènte living
vìvere *irr.* to live
vivo *m.* the living; *adj.* live, alive
vìzio vice
vizióso evil
vocale vocal
vocazióne *f.* vocation
vóce *f.* voice; rumor; **a - alta** aloud, in a loud
  voice; **sótto -** in a whisper
vòglia desire; longing
volentièri willingly
volére *irr.* to want; to expect; **- bène** to love;
  - dire to mean; **volérci** to take, to require;
  n. m. will power, desire
vòlgere *irr.* to turn; *refl.* to turn
vólo flight
volontà will
vólpe *f.* fox
vòlsi *p. abs. of* vòlgere
vòlta time; . . . **alla -** . . . at the same time;
  ógni - any time; **una -** once
voltare to turn; *refl.* to turn
vólto *n.* face; *past part. of* vòlgere
volutaménte by choice
voluto desired
vóto wish
vuòto empty

Z

zitto silent; **stare -** to be (to remain) silent,
  quiet; **- !** Hush!
zòna zone

ITALIA
(Carta Física)

© C.S. HAMMOND & CO., N.Y.

SCALA DI CHILOMETRI
0   50   100   150

SCALA DI MIGLIA
0   50   100   150

Trieste

Venezia

Adige

Lago di Garda

Lago di Como

Lago Maggiore

Milano

Po

Genova

Appennini

Firenze

Arno

Tevere

Mare Adriatico

Mare Ligure

Corsica (Francia)